THE WINTER ARMY

THE
WINTER ARMY

The World War II Odyssey
of the 10th Mountain Division,
America's Elite Alpine Warriors

MAURICE ISSERMAN

Houghton Mifflin Harcourt
Boston   New York
2019

1-20

For information about permission to reproduce selections from this book, write to trade.permissions@hmhco.com or to Permissions, Houghton Mifflin Harcourt Publishing Company, 3 Park Avenue, 19th Floor, New York, New York 10016.

hmhco.com

Library of Congress Cataloging-in-Publication Data
Names: Isserman, Maurice, author.
Title: The winter army : the World War II odyssey of the 10th Mountain Division, America's elite alpine warriors / Maurice Isserman.
Other titles: World War II odyssey of the 10th Mountain Division, America's elite alpine warriors
Description: Boston : Houghton Mifflin Harcourt, 2019. | Includes bibliographical references and index.
Identifiers: LCCN 2019009836 (print) | LCCN 2019012409 (ebook) | ISBN 9781328871190 (ebook) | ISBN 9781328871435 (hardcover)
Subjects: LCSH: United States. Army. Mountain Division, 10th — History. | World War, 1939–1945 — Regimental histories — United States. | Mountain troops — United States — Training of. | Skis and skiing — United States — History. | World War, 1939–1945 — Campaigns — Italy. | World War, 1939–1945 — Mountain warfare. | Mountain warfare — History — 20th century.
Classification: LCC D769.3 10th (ebook) | LCC D769.3 10th .187 2019 (print) | DDC 940.54/1273 — dc23
LC record available at https://lccn.loc.gov/2019009836

Book design by Emily Snyder

Printed in the United States of America
DOC 10 9 8 7 6 5 4 3 2 1

This book is dedicated to the memory of my parents, Flora and Jack Isserman, who would have laughed at being described as part of any "greatest generation" but certainly were to me.

Also to two other personal heroes of my acquaintance, Donald B. Potter, H Company, 85th Mountain Infantry Regiment, 10th Mountain Division, my colleague for many years on the faculty at Hamilton College, and Harris Dusenbery, HQ Company, 1st Battalion, 86th Mountain Infantry Regiment, 10th Mountain Division, fellow Reed College alumnus, in his case Class of 1936.

In the late summer of that year we lived in a house in a village that looked across the river and the plain to the mountains. In the bed of the river there were pebbles and boulders, dry and white in the sun, and the water was clear and swiftly moving and blue in the channels. Troops went by the house and down the road and the dust they raised powdered the leaves of the trees. The trunks of the trees too were dusty and leaves fell early that year and we saw the troops marching along the road and the dust rising and leaves, stirred by the breeze, falling and the soldiers marching and afterward the road bare and white except for the leaves.

The plain was rich with crops; there were many orchards of fruit trees and beyond the plain the mountains were brown and bare. There was fighting in the mountains and at night we could see flashes from the artillery. In the dark it was like summer lightning, but the nights were cool and there was not the feeling of a storm coming.

— Ernest Hemingway,
A Farewell to Arms, *1929*

Thanks to the failure of the press, and to the stupidity of Hollywood, the Home Front has no real conception of war, and only by [soldiers'] letters home can the truth be made known.

— Sergeant Denis Nunan, C Company, 87th
Mountain Infantry Regiment, 10th Mountain
Division, to his mother from Castel
d'Aiano, Italy, March 23, 1945

Contents

Introduction: "Always Forward"

ON FEBRUARY 16, 1945, MAJOR GENERAL GEORGE PRICE HAYS, COMmander of the US Army's 10th Mountain Division, spoke to men from the unit's 85th Regiment. In three days they would lead the attack on dug-in German defenders holding the high ground of Mount Belvedere in Italy's northern Apennines. Although new to combat, the 10th Division soldiers were uniquely qualified for the audacious mission they were being assigned.

General Hays was a seasoned soldier. As a young officer in 1918 he had been awarded a Medal of Honor in France, and in the current war had commanded artillery units in fighting in both Italy and France before taking command of the 10th the previous autumn. Hays was wiry, weather-beaten, and plainspoken, and reminded one of the young soldiers gathered to hear him on a mountain hillside near Belvedere of a tough old cowhand.

The men he addressed were well trained, fit, and eager to join the fight against the Nazi war machine. But unlike their commander, they were unseasoned. Their division, some of whose members had been training for combat for three full years, was the next to last the US Army would send to fight in Europe, arriving in Naples in late December 1944 and early January 1945. Their first weeks as frontline soldiers had been relatively uneventful, with little real fighting and few casualties. And yet the general, who was not given to flattery or flowery words, told them they were "the finest troops I've ever been associated with." He counted on their rigorous training and their exceptional esprit de corps to see them through the coming days of fighting. And because of that, he was going to do something he had never done before as a senior combat commander: personally discuss the details of an upcoming attack with the enlisted men, NCOs, and junior officers who would risk their lives to carry out the assignment ahead of them. Hays's own son was serving as a platoon leader in another regiment in the 10th Mountain Division, the 87th, and was scheduled to take part in the attack — a fact he decided not to share with those he addressed now.

Standing before them in a large natural outdoor amphitheater, Hays described the plans for the next few days. As he spoke, he pointed out enemy positions on a large map, his voice and leather-gloved hand cutting through the cold mountain air.

Mount Belvedere and adjoining peaks were the key to the German defensive line in the North Apennines, and their capture was essential to the success of the Allied offensive in Italy in the fighting to come in the spring. Twice before, other divisions had attempted to secure the position and failed. Now it was the 10th's turn. Hays gave the men some stern advice on what to expect and how to conduct themselves. Most important, he stressed the need for speed and audacity: "You must continue to move forward. Never stop. If your buddy is wounded, don't stop to help him. Continue to move forward, always forward, always forward."

Dan Kennerly, a twenty-two-year-old private from rural Georgia, serving in D Company of the 85th Mountain Infantry Regiment, recorded the gist of Hayes's words in the diary he kept in Italy. Before enlisting, he had spent a season playing football for the University of Georgia. Now he was moved to comment on the eve of his first battle, "The General would make a hell of a football coach."

Private Jack R. Smolenske, from Denver, Colorado, twenty years old and serving in Headquarters Company, 3rd Battalion of the 85th, gave a briefer account of the general's talk in an entry the following day in his own diary: "Saturday, February 17, 1945: Gen. Hays gave us the dope for the attack on *Mt. Belvedere*. We move up after dark. No one fires but special men. Must be on top at dawn no matter what. It looks bad."

Smolenske was right. It would be bad — much worse, in terms of death and maiming and horror, than Smolenske and his comrades could then imagine. Other Allied divisions had tried and failed to gain those heights before without success. But the men of the 10th made it to the summit of Belvedere on February 20, moving on to adjacent peaks, and holding the heights against ferocious German counterattacks over the next five days.

The February gains opened the way for future advances on the Apennine front—and beyond. In early March, the mountain troopers would return to the offensive, gaining more hilltops. And beginning in mid-April, they spearheaded the final Allied offensive in Italy, the first soldiers to break out of the northern Apennines and reach the broad open plains of the Po Valley. From there they raced northward to the Alps to cut off the only route that retreating German forces could use to escape to Austria. In the epic battles of the late winter and spring of 1945, these newcomers to combat won the respect of their tough veteran opponents. General Fridolin von Senger, commander of the IV Panzer Corps, personally surrendered his command to General Hays in May 1945 and later noted in his memoir, "His [Hays's] division had been my most dangerous opponent."

The costs were high for the division as well. In less than four months at the front, from mid-January through April, the 10th suffered the highest casualty rate—in terms of the percentage killed per day in combat —of any US division in the Italian campaign.

After General Hays's speech, "Always Forward," or in Italian, *Sempre Avanti,* became the informal motto of the 85th Mountain Infantry Regiment. In two words, it also sums up the entire 10th Mountain Division's experience in the last months of fighting in the long, bitter campaign to defeat the Germans in Italy. They were almost always in front, sometimes far in front, of the rest of the Allied advance. They never retreated, or turned back short of capturing their objective. Always forward.

In the eyes of both General Hays and General von Senger, the US Army's 10th Mountain Division was a remarkable unit. Remarkable for what its members accomplished on the battlefield. Remarkable too for their training in mountain warfare, with a special emphasis on learning to ski while carrying a rifle and a ninety-pound rucksack. No American troops had ever undergone a similar course of instruction, and few had ever undergone so physically rigorous a preparation for battle. In the end, as it turned out, they did very little fighting on skis. But their identity as ski troops proved vital to their wartime achievements.

At least from a historian's perspective, the men of the 10th also were remarkable for the richness of the stories they left behind. Scores of diaries and between fifteen and twenty thousand letters donated by veterans of the division to the 10th Mountain Division Resource Center of the Denver Public Library provide an unmatched level of detail in the account that follows.

The collection donated by one young enlisted man, Marty L. Daneman, who served with HQ Company, 2nd Battalion of the 85th Regiment, evinces the passion he and many of his comrades shared for setting down in carefully observed and often vividly described detail a chronicle of their wartime experiences. His particular collection, running to several hundred letters written between April 1943 and May 1945, were mostly to his fiancée, and later wife, Lois Miller. In one such letter composed in early March 1945, after taking part in the capture of Mount Belvedere, Corporal Daneman described to Lois what it was like to be on the receiving end of an artillery barrage:

> Was I afraid? *Yes,* but in a peculiar way. At 1st you wonder if you'll be shot & you're scared of not your own skin, but of the people that will get hurt if you are hit. All I could think about was keeping you & the folks from being affected by some 88 shell. I don't seem to worry about myself because I knew if I did get it, I'd never know it. After a while I didn't wonder *if* I get hit — I'd wonder *when.* Every time a shell came I'd ask myself "Is this the one?" In the 3rd phase I was sure I'd get it & began to ½ hope that the next one would do it & end the goddam suspense.

Writing with passion and candor, soldiers in the 10th were determined to accomplish the nearly impossible task of giving civilians safe at home a clear idea of what it was like to endure, day after day, the hardship and horror of battle. Their collective account of their wartime experiences amounts to the first, and in some ways the finest, history of the 10th Mountain Division. In tracing the mountain troopers' odyssey from 1941 to 1945, whenever possible this book describes their ordeal in their own words.

The 10th played a vital role in the concluding months of the long and bloody Italian campaign. The US Army disbanded the division soon after the war, but it was reactivated in 1985 as the 10th Mountain Division (Light Infantry). In the last years of the twentieth century and the first decades of the twenty-first, this division of mountain fighters has been frequently deployed overseas, including repeated assignments in Afghanistan and Iraq. The warriors of the new 10th Mountain Division are acutely aware of their predecessors' contribution to final victory in the Second World War. "Climb to Glory" is now the division's motto, which is also a good short description of the story that is to follow.

THE WINTER ARMY

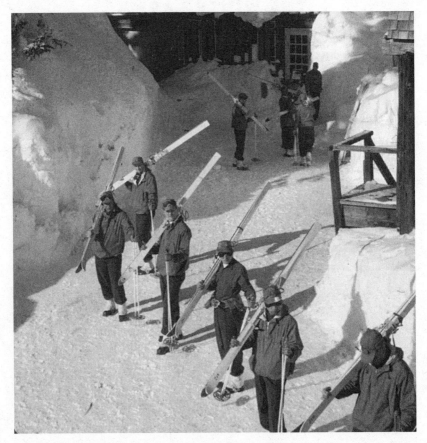

87th Mountain Infantry troopers in front of Tatoosh Lodge, 1942.
THE DENVER PUBLIC LIBRARY (TMD937)

1

Origins, 1940–41

"Soldiers Out of Skiers"

It is more reasonable to make soldiers out of skiers than skiers out of soldiers.

— Charles Minot Dole to President Franklin
Delano Roosevelt, July 18, 1940

ON A BLUSTERY EVENING IN FEBRUARY 1940, FOUR SKIERS TOOK refuge inside the Orvis Inn in Manchester, Vermont. Like many other weekend visitors to nearby Bromley Mountain, they had enjoyed a crisp day on the slopes. But their leisure had been cut short by a gathering storm and the descending darkness, which settled over the town shortly after 5 p.m.

The inn did good business, and the four friends were lucky to find seats before the roaring fire. There, in line with New England tradition, they sipped hot rum, tired but satisfied after a good day's skiing, talking casually.

The men were royalty among the American skiing community: Roger Langley, athletic director of a Massachusetts prep school and president of the National Ski Association of America, was there, along with Robert Livermore, a member of the US Olympic ski team in 1936, and Alex Bright, another veteran of the 1936 team and founder of the exclusive Ski Club Hochgebirge of Boston. The fourth member of the group, destined to become the most important civilian figure in the history of the 10th Mountain Division, was Charles Minot "Minnie" Dole, the forty-year-old founder and director of the National Ski Patrol System.

The conversation that evening eventually turned from the storm outside to the storm in Europe, that is, the war that had begun six months earlier with the German invasion of Poland on September 1, 1939, and a separate conflict in Finland, invaded by the Soviet Union's Red Army on November 30, 1939.

With a tense quiet prevailing for the time being on the western front separating the German Wehrmacht from its French and British opponents, the only active European battlefront that winter was in Finland. The Finns, despite being vastly outnumbered by their Soviet foes, put up a doughty defense of the Karelian Isthmus in what was dubbed the "Winter War," winning international admiration — although, ultimately, not the war. In March 1940 Finland was finally forced to capitulate, making territorial concessions to the Soviet Union.

In February, however, the Finns were still resisting the invaders. "Finns Beat Back a Quarter of Million Russians in Biggest Offensive of War" was the lead story on the front page of the *Burlington Free Press,* Vermont's best-known newspaper, on February 9, 1940. Dole and his companions, possibly the very next evening, were particularly impressed by the performance of white-camouflage-clad Finnish ski troops, who, in a signature tactic, launched devastating hit-and-run attacks on lumbering columns of Soviet soldiers and vehicles before swiftly and silently disappearing into the snowy vastness of the surrounding forests. In Dole's recollection, the four skiers agreed that this was "a perfect example of men fighting in an environment with which they were entirely at home and for which they were trained."

The Finns, the four skiers agreed, were obviously well prepared to fight a winter war. They wondered, however, what might happen if the United States were engaged in a similar conflict — if, hypothetically, Germany, having defeated Great Britain, then invaded Canada, followed up that conquest by sweeping down from the north into New England or other regions of the United States that were under snow a good portion of the year. How well would American soldiers fare if they had to face a determined enemy in conditions similar to the storm blowing outside that night in the snow-clad Vermont hills? From the

Italian Corpo Alpini to the French Chasseurs Alpins and the Austro-Hungarian Gebirgsbrigaden, European armies had long maintained specially trained alpine units for mountain and cold weather fighting. Such soldiers had proved their valor and their worth in the World War of 1914–1918, when fighting between Italians and Austrians in the Alps cost tens of thousands of lives. Geography dictated that Europeans needed to take alpine fighting seriously, since so many borders ran along the crests of mountains. In continental European armies, accordingly, service in mountain units could be a springboard to distinguished military careers. Erwin Rommel, the "Desert Fox" of the North African campaign in the Second World War, commanded a battalion of German mountain troops in the First World War, taking part in the 1917 offensive that broke through the Italian front at Caporetto — an epic defeat immortalized, for American readers, in Ernest Hemingway's 1929 novel *A Farewell to Arms*.

Bob Livermore and Alex Bright had gotten a close-up view of German prowess in winter sports at the 1936 Winter Olympics in Bavaria. The Germans took home three gold medals, while the United States claimed one. In 1939–40 it was Germany (by then, through annexation by Hitler in 1938, including formerly independent Austria) that in Dole's judgment possessed "the finest trained and equipped specialized Winter and mountain troops of any army in the world," consisting of three full mountain divisions (*Gebirgs-Divisionen*), a force that grew to ten divisions over the course of the war. German mountain soldiers, *Gebirgsjäger* (literally "mountain hunters"), were an elite light infantry, distinguishable from ordinary soldiers by the edelweiss insignia on their uniform sleeves and caps. They trained to fight in rough terrain and freezing cold conditions, and, contrary to the legend of the inflexibly disciplined and unthinking Teutonic soldiery, to exercise individual initiative in battle.

The US Army, in contrast, was strictly a flatland operation. It had never in its entire history fought a major engagement on truly mountainous terrain (unless one counts the relatively gentle slopes of 2,389-foot Lookout Mountain in Chattanooga, seized from its Confederate defenders in the Civil War), and certainly not with specially trained troops. For most of its existence the army had functioned as a frontier constabulary, and on the eve of the Second World War its elite units were still cavalry.

(As of February 1940, there were two cavalry divisions in the army, but no specialized armored or airborne divisions, never mind mountain divisions.) And since the end of the nineteenth century, most soldiers in peacetime were stationed in distinctly un-alpine locations: Texas, Louisiana, Georgia, Hawaii, the Philippines, Panama, and the Caribbean. How would this "tropical army" (to use Dole's phrase) stand up to an attack by well-trained mountain troops?

The friends sheltering that night in the Vermont inn agreed that the United States needed to prepare to fight a mountain war — although, given the current isolationist mood of the country, they imagined that conflict solely in terms of a defensive struggle on North American soil. Langley volunteered to write a letter to the War Department in Washington urging the creation of mountain units in the US Army and offering the services of National Ski Association members as advisers and trainers — and even as battlefield scouts in the event of an actual German invasion. But when the sun came up the next morning, the threat must have receded in his mind; in any case, it was several months before he did so. And down in Washington, where temperatures rarely dropped below freezing, apocalyptic snowy scenarios were not a major concern. Secretary of War Harry Woodring replied to Langley's letter on a warm spring day in June 1940 with a polite dismissal.

That might have been the end of it. But Minnie Dole, in an expression of the sense of inherited duty mingled with entitlement characteristic of the kind of well-educated, old-family New England stock from which he came, decided he would continue to pursue the matter. Dole was raised in comfortable circumstances in Andover, Massachusetts, the son of a paper company executive. On turning eighteen in the First World War, and acting against his parents' wishes, he dropped out of school to enlist in the US Army. But as it turned out, he began military training on the very day in November 1918 when an armistice ended the war. Following his brief military experience (notable chiefly for his acquisition of the diminutive nickname "Minnie," bestowed on the beardless recruit by a gruff sergeant), he finished up his prep school education at Phillips Andover Academy. From there he went on to Yale (where he joined the famed and highly selective Whiffenpoofs a cappella singing group), graduating in 1923. Over the next decade he married, and became a successful insurance executive, with a home in Greenwich, Connecticut, and an office in New York City. Dole could well have lived out the remainder of his life in patrician ease, his stint with the Whiffenpoofs (of which he remained quite proud throughout his life) his most notable achievement.

But something in him craved more; perhaps he was still searching for the kind of adventure that he had missed by enlisting too late for the World War. In 1932, Lake Placid, New York, hosted the Winter Olympics, only the third such ever held, an event that would contribute to the growing popularity of skiing in the United States in the later 1930s. Prior to the Olympics, most Americans, outside of college and university ski clubs and a few regional ski centers, had thought of the sport as a distinctly European one, something they might read about in Hemingway short stories like "Cross Country Snow" but were no more likely to try themselves than they were to attend a bullfight. The appearance of the first rope tows on ski slopes in North America, starting in the Canadian Laurentians in 1933, followed by Woodstock, Vermont, in 1934, and soon to be ubiquitous on skiable slopes across the country, also helped popularize the sport, eliminating the need to trudge up the hill after every ski run, allowing skiers to make many more runs on a day's outing, which contributed to the ability of novices to improve their mastery of the sport in a much shorter time.

———

Perhaps inspired by the Olympics, Dole traveled to Lake Placid the following winter of 1933. On the slopes surrounding the picturesque Adirondack village, the thirty-three-year-old strapped on a pair of skis for the first time since childhood. He fell in love with the sport that day, finding in it not only a hearty, convivial pastime but also, evidently, a renewed sense of purpose and identity. (When he sat down to write the story of his life three decades later, he titled it *Adventures in Skiing*.) The next winter, he vacationed at Peckett's ski resort on Sugar Hill, near Franconia Notch in New Hampshire's White Mountains. Tourists had been staying at Peckett's since the nineteenth century, but the establishment began to attract a new clientele in 1929 when it launched the first resort-based ski school in the United States teaching alpine skiing techniques. Austrian ski instructor Sig Buchmayr became the school's director in 1932 and, through the men he trained to ski, had an outsized impact on the future of skiing in the United States. Wealthy celebrities like businessman W. Averell Harriman and radio broadcaster Lowell Thomas were among the pupils who were instructed in the "Arlberg technique" by Buchmayr. (Harriman went on to launch and develop the glamorous new ski resort known as Sun Valley in the Sawtooth Mountains near Ketchum, Idaho, in the later 1930s, featuring both the first ski chairlift in the United States and a steady stream of Hollywood visitors, while Thomas vigorously promoted skiing and ski resorts in radio travelogues.)

For novice skiers like Minnie Dole, the Arlberg technique proved an ideal way to master the seemingly impossible task of navigating a downhill run on skis on a steep slippery slope without inevitably winding up with either face or backside planted deep in the snow. The technique had been developed by ski instructor Hannes Schneider in the resort town of St. Anton am Arlberg in Austria's Tyrolean Alps. Schneider, whom some would call "the father of modern skiing," began a career as a guide in 1907, then went off to war to train ski troops as a member of the Austro-Hungarian Gebirgbrigaden. He returned to St. Anton following the Armistice in 1918. Schneider's ski school in St. Anton was the largest in the world in the interwar years, and he became mentor to a generation of European ski instructors, the "Arlbergers," as well as wealthy European and American skiers. (Hemingway was one of Schneider's pupils in the 1920s.) He achieved international celebrity status in his own right, turning skiing into a performance art. In 1931 he starred in a popular movie with actress Leni Riefenstahl (in her pre-Nazi days), *Der Weisse Rausch*, or "The White Ecstasy," shot on location in St. Anton. Five years later, Schneider and protégés Otto Lang and Benno Rybizka were among the stars of the 1936 International Ski Meet and Winter Sports Show in Madison Square Garden in New York City, where they put on a thrilling performance of downhill ski turns on an artificial snow slope 152 feet long. The show played to sold-out audiences three nights in a row. "The balance and poise which these experts displayed," the *New York Times* reported of Schneider and his fellow Arlbergers, "was not lost on attentive spectators." The

Arlberg franchise subsequently proved a valuable commodity in the United States. Otto Lang opened an Arlberg school on Mount Rainier in Washington State, and Benno Rybizka did the same in Jackson, New Hampshire.

Schneider's technique consisted of a series of maneuvers of increasing difficulty that could be learned in succession in groups of similar skill level, and that, once mastered, permitted skiers to exercise a new level of controlled descent in downhill skiing and racing. These included the snowplow, snowplow turn, stem turn, stem christiania (or christie), and parallel turn. The technique also had the great advantage of permitting a single instructor to instruct multiple novices simultaneously.

Some would-be skiers soon tired of their Arlberg training and preferred the comforts of a hot drink before a roaring fire in the ski lodge. They would be scorned by skiing enthusiasts as "lodge skiers." For those who stuck it out, the physical mastery of this sequence of turns proved enormously gratifying — sometimes even transformative. The ten days Minnie Dole spent learning the Arlberg technique at Peckett's in 1934 changed him from a clumsy beginner into a serious and graceful skier. "The day that I performed the full-stop Christie" (a parallel skidded turn), and Buchmayr commented, "*Gut, Gut,* Mr. Dole," was a memorable one for the Greenwich insurance executive; his Austrian mentor, he recalled, "might just as well have been hanging an Olympic medal around my neck, my pleasure was so great."

But skiing offered pains as well as pleasures. The American ski industry lagged behind its longer-established European counterparts in looking out for the safety and well-being of those who now began to flock to the slopes in New England and elsewhere. Minnie Dole found this out firsthand just a few years after mastering the Arlberg technique. On a New Year's holiday at the end of 1936, Dole broke his right ankle while skiing on the Toll Road on Mount Mansfield in Stowe, Vermont. He was left shivering in the snow for several hours before four men, one of them his good friend and Greenwich neighbor Franklin Edson, dragged him down the mountain on an old sheet of roofing tin that happened to be close at hand. Later that winter, Edson fell and smashed into a tree while racing in Pittsfield, Massachusetts, with horrendous results. He broke both legs and punctured a lung. Although aid came relatively quickly, his rescuers were not trained to care for someone so grievously injured. Edson died shortly after he reached the hospital.

Dole's response to his friend's death is evidence of the crusading zeal and organizational acumen central to his character. Over the next several years, in cooperation with the National Ski Association's Roger Langley and others, he pulled together a nationwide network of volunteer skiers, trained in mountain rescue techniques and committed to patrolling the slopes of major ski areas. His efforts drew on the experience of local patrols already in place (Mount Mansfield in Vermont, Mount Hood in Oregon) as well as the example set by the highly professional system of ski rescue in Davos, Switzerland. The resulting organization, by 1940 dubbed the National Ski Patrol System (NSPS), went on to provide expert aid and comfort to tens of thousands of injured or otherwise incapacitated skiers in coming decades, saving scores of lives. Later on, many of the techniques used by ski patrollers for caring for civilian skiers on peaceful slopes would prove adaptable to the care of wounded soldiers on mountainous battlefields.

With his thinning hair and wire-rim glasses, wardrobe choices that favored ascots, and pipe in hand, Dole at first glance bore a closer resemblance to a classroom philosopher in an Ivy League college, but he proved himself a shrewd operator who knew how to wield influence, at least in the elite circles in which he traveled. Boston skiers were notoriously tough-minded about the dangers of their sport and initially inclined to reject the call for a ski patrol as unnecessary or even unmanly. Dole called upon Boston skier Robert Livermore, whom he had met in the early stages of his campaign for a national ski patrol, for help. A half-dozen years earlier, in 1931, Livermore had become famous in New England ski circles as part of a small band of Harvard students who were the first to ski from the summit of New Hampshire's Mount Washington down over the formidable headwall of Tuckerman Ravine, a glacial cirque on the mountain's southeastern flank. Five years later he was a member of the US team that competed in the fourth Winter Olympics in Garmisch-Partenkirchen in the Bavarian Alps in Germany. Livermore had local sway, which he used to get Dole a hearing. Once Dole had a conversational foot in the door, he was tenacious and convincing. He was at once down-to-earth, full of practical suggestions, but also evangelical in his organizational enthusiasms. "It was Minnie's persuasiveness that kept most of us going," Livermore recalled. "He was a great salesman, he wouldn't take no for an answer, and his faith in the Ski Patrol was contagious. Once he talked to you, you couldn't *not* share his belief."

Likewise, Hal Burton, who before becoming a ski trooper wrote the ski news column for the *New York Daily News,* and knew Dole well, described him as "an imperious man accustomed to getting what he wanted, not easily discouraged by an official brushoff." Those qualities would serve him well in the months to come. In the summer of 1940, after surveying the opinion of NSPS members and finding them overwhelmingly in favor of using the resources of the organization to encourage the creation of mountain-trained units in the US Army, Dole launched his campaign. His first step was to send a note to the nearest available general, Hugh Drum, commander of the US First Army, headquartered on Governors Island in New York Harbor. Drum didn't respond directly, but his aide-de-camp, Captain Christian Clarke, wrote back with good and bad news. The good news, he said, was that General Irving I. Phillipson, chief of staff under General Drum, "is enthusiastic in his support of your proposal." The bad news was that "the American Army will probably be concentrated in the South for training next winter."

Dole decided to ignore the bad news and act on the good. He and NSPS treasurer John Morgan (notable in skiing history for helping lay out the first ski trails at Sun Valley) met General Phillipson on Governors Island on July 7, and a sympathetic Phillipson suggested that they contact the War Department directly. Within days, Dole and Morgan took the train to Washington, where on a hot July day they received a decidedly cool response from military officials. Bored with fielding crackpot proposals from enthusiastic amateurs, one officer sniffed as he told Dole: "Hell, we have a hundred guys a day like you. They even want to show us how to shoot guns around corners."

But the catastrophic war news from Europe in the spring of 1940, with Norway and Denmark invaded by the Nazis in April, followed by Belgium and the Netherlands in May, heightened Dole's sense of the urgency of his mission. Worse was to come. In late May and early June, the British Expeditionary Force was evacuated from Dunkirk. And on June 22, France was forced to sign an armistice leaving Germany in control of half the country. Would Britain be the next to fall to Nazi aggression? And if that happened, would the Nazis cross the ocean to attack America's northern neighbor? And then?

The hypothetical but far-fetched threat to North American security that Dole and his friends discussed the previous February now seemed a lot more possible, even imminent. Given the urgency of the situation, Dole shifted his appeals to the highest level of authority. In a letter to President Franklin Delano Roosevelt dated July 18, 1940, a little over a month after the Nazis entered Paris, Dole offered the services of the NSPS to the army to help train mountain soldiers. He added that the army should look to the nation's ski slopes for potential recruits. "In this country there are 2,000,000 skiers, equipped, intelligent and able," he wrote, the logical source for a mountain fighting force, because "it is more reasonable to make soldiers out of skiers than skiers out of soldiers." Dole signed off with guarded optimism: "With the knowledge that unusual and untried ideas are too often pigeon-holed, I bring this to your attention."

In the midst of a third presidential election campaign, and preoccupied with the unfolding disaster in Europe, President Roosevelt might have ignored or dismissed Dole's suggestion out of hand. Crippled by polio since his late thirties, the president was not a skier. But something about Dole's proposal appealed to him. Roosevelt had been physically active as a young man, hiking and sailing, and despite his disability retained a keen interest in promoting outdoor recreation as a public good. As governor of New York State he had opened the 1932 Winter Olympic Games at Lake Placid, and as president he had authorized funding through New Deal work relief projects for the creation of new ski trails in New England. And on the south side of Oregon's Mount Hood, the New Deal's Works Progress Administration had built a spectacularly beautiful publicly owned ski facility, Timberline Lodge, with a mile-long chairlift. At the lodge's dedication ceremony in 1937, the president hailed the "new opportunities for play in every season" that it would provide in years to come. Even though he likely never strapped on a pair of skis, Roosevelt certainly left his mark on the sport. He may also have recognized in Dole a kindred spirit, another public-minded member in good standing of the northeastern gentry.

In any case, a White House aide informed Dole that his letter was being forwarded to the War Department for consideration. That referral came at a politically opportune moment, for the War Department had a new leader, the veteran internationalist statesman Henry Stimson, replacing the isolationist Woodring. Stimson, an honorary member of the American Alpine Club who had climbed in the Alps in younger days, was at the same time in a separate effort being lobbied by fellow mountaineers to do something about training mountain fighters. Making use of well-placed Yale alumni connections, Dole contacted the War Department and asked for a meeting. In early September, he met with two of Stimson's top aides in the department's overcrowded headquarters in the "Munitions Building" on B Street (now Constitution Avenue) adjoining the Lincoln Memorial. Dole again raised the specter of well-trained German mountain troops pouring down the St. Lawrence River and the Champlain Valley. Who would stop them? Only equally well-trained American mountain troops, perhaps aided by NSPS volunteers acting as guides and scouts. Impressed with Dole's "sound premise," Stimson's aides promised to bring the matter to the secretary of war's attention, and to do what they could to secure a meeting for Dole in the near future with the army chief of staff, General George C. Marshall, whose office was in the same building.

On September 9, Dole received a cable from Stimson's office proposing a meeting with General Marshall the very next morning. Elated, he and John Morgan rushed to a Brooks Brothers store in New York, bought clean shirts, and got tickets on the night train to Washington, DC. Back at the Munitions Building for a 10 a.m. meeting, they had to wait an hour, fidgeting nervously outside and rehearsing their argument, before they were ushered into Marshall's office.

Hardworking, disciplined, unvarying in his daily personal routine (he almost certainly would have been out earlier in the day for the regular half-dozen-mile horseback ride he took before showing up at his office precisely at 7:45 a.m.), Marshall did not have the time or inclination to suffer fools. Dole somehow had gotten the impression that Marshall was "a gentle sort of person," but he had a temper, and only a couple of months earlier he had snapped at no less a personage than Franklin Delano Roosevelt at a White House meeting when he felt the president was not taking the problems of military mobilization seriously enough. So it is likely he had already decided that there was good reason to give fifteen minutes of his crowded day to these two civilians.

Six days after Dole and Morgan's meeting with General Marshall, Congress passed the nation's first peacetime draft bill, the Burke-Wadsworth Act. Spurred by the Nazi victories in Europe, the United States began to prepare seriously for war. Under the bill's authority, and Marshall's leadership, the US Army expanded from under 200,000 soldiers in 1939 (when it ranked seventeenth in the world in overall size, behind the army of Romania) to over 8 million by 1944. By then Army Ground Forces (there were also separately organized Army Service Forces and Army Air Forces) included ninety combat divisions, most of them regular infantry, but also counting sixteen armored divisions and five airborne divisions. (Of two cavalry divisions in existence in 1940, one was disbanded in 1942, and the other switched to mechanized transportation.) Was there also room in Marshall's vast new army for a mountain division? Much hinged on the chief of staff's response to what two civilian skiers had to say that September morning in 1940.

Marshall listened carefully to Dole and Morgan. Carefully but briefly. Fifteen minutes after they stepped into the office, they were on the way out, leaving the general with a three-page paper titled "Winter Training" summarizing their case. "You have raised an interesting question, gentlemen," were Marshall's parting if noncommittal words. He did promise a quick response, and was as good as his word, within days forwarding their paper, along with a supportive memorandum of his own, to the assistant chief of staff in charge of army operations and training (in military nomenclature, G-3).

Less than two weeks later, Dole would be having lunch in the luxuriously appointed Yale Club on Vanderbilt Avenue in midtown Manhattan with two lieutenant colonels from G-3. Thanks to his meeting with Marshall, the army changed its mind and agreed to do some training in the North that winter after all. A pilot program was ordered for ski training, starting as soon as there was enough snow. The soldiers undergoing training would not be mountain troops, on the model of the German

Gebirgsjäger, for they remained part of regular army divisions. But in a promising sign, the NSPS was invited to be an integral part of the program, consulted on questions of training and equipment. As a token of its new status as an official partner in the military's preparation for war, the NSPS soon received a check from the army for $2,500, with more to come, allowing it to move from its cubbyhole of an office on John Street in lower Manhattan to the prestigious and architecturally distinguished Art Deco premises of the Graybar Building, rising in midtown above Grand Central Terminal on Lexington Avenue.

By late November, soldiers from the army's 41st Infantry Division (a newly federalized National Guard division, drawn from the Pacific Northwest states) were skiing on the slopes of Washington State's Mount Rainier. Other soldiers, drawn from five other infantry divisions (the 1st, 3rd, 5th, 6th, and 44th), trained in locations ranging from New York's Adirondacks to Minnesota, Wisconsin, and Wyoming. The press took notice, and *Life* magazine, which made its way every week into more American homes than any other publication during the Second World War, featured a photograph of a dashing "Ski Trooper" on the cover of a January 1941 issue. Although the accompanying article made clear that this was a limited training experiment, with uncertain practical or long-term application ("The Army has no intention of creating an army on skis"), the notion of soldiers on skis suddenly had a wider audience within both the military and the general public than just Minnie Dole's skiing buddies.

An army on skis was still a long way off. But there were some patrols on skis that winter that experimented with the kind of training that ski troops would require to be effective. On Mount Rainier and in the nearby Olympic Mountains, men of the 41st Division were learning to survive outdoors in cold and snow for days at a time, living out of the gear they carried in rucksacks as they skied ever deeper into wilderness. A patrol under the command of Lieutenant John Woodward, formerly captain of the ski team at the University of Washington, where he was a slalom ace, made a four-day crossing of the Olympics, through twelve-foot drifts of snow, followed by another two-week-long set of maneuvers in the mountains. A separate patrol, under the supervision of Captain Paul R. Lafferty, formerly ski coach at the University of Oregon, spent a week making a circumference of Mount Rainier, crossing many of its glaciers en route.

Elsewhere, and for most of the soldiers involved, the winter exercises were not nearly as strenuous — more of a pleasant holiday from army routine. Many had previous ski experience as civilians, and their skis, snowshoes, and other specialized equipment were procured by army quartermasters on the civilian market. The 26th Infantry Regiment of the 1st Division sent a thousand soldiers in batches to Lake Placid over the course of the winter of 1940–41 for weeklong training sessions in cross-country skiing. The regiment's commander, Colonel James T. Muir, reported himself pleased with the results: "I believe that ski training is an asset; like the Texans' six-shooter, you may not need it, but if you ever do, you will need it in a hurry, 'awful bad.'"

But if the country ever did need mountain soldiers "awful bad," a week's instruction in cross-country skiing was not going to provide a sufficient or reliable supply. Although a few junior officers, like Woodward and Lafferty, based at Fort Lewis in Tacoma, Washington, were experienced skiers and outdoorsmen, the chief lesson to be learned that winter was the army's primitive state of knowledge about the requirements of mountain warfare. The Quartermaster Corps' guidebook on equipping soldiers for service in Alaska, one of the few snowy places where the army maintained a significant presence, had last been revised in 1914. In any case, the army's experiment with mountain training ended when the snows melted in the spring of 1941, and the soldiers went back to their regular round of flatland duties and training. Although Minnie Dole had secured President Roosevelt's interest and General Marshall's patronage, key figures in the military establishment continued to regard the whole idea of mountain soldiers as a frivolous distraction from the serious business of building an army capable of fighting the real war to come in Europe and the Pacific.

In mid-February 1941, as Dole brooded about the still uncertain prospects of American ski troops, he received a letter from a young friend, David Bradley, reminding him of the importance of his mission. Bradley, a Dartmouth alumnus and former captain of the college's ski team, had been the 1938 US national champion in the Nordic combined competition (cross-country skiing and ski jumping). Bradley was one of nine Dartmouth alumni who won a slot on the US ski team scheduled to compete at Sapporo, Japan, at the 1940 Winter Olympics, but the war intervened and the games were canceled. Instead, he traveled to Europe as a war correspondent, covering the Finnish-Soviet war for midwestern newspapers. Back in the United States, he wrote to Dole to share some thoughts about that war, drawing on his experience as both reporter and skier. From what he had witnessed, he told Dole, "the strength of the ski troop is not so much in its concentrated organization, but rather in the unpredictable initiative of each member. The Finnish skiers were their own armies, their own general staffs." Accordingly, if the US Army ever organized its own mountain troops, their training should focus on instilling in the soldiers "initiative and self-reliance," plus a range of outdoor skills. In addition to learning skiing and climbing technique, every ski trooper should be able to find his way through rough terrain with a map and compass, handle an ax, pack a mule, light a fire in the rain, "and know the very special techniques of survival in winter conditions." He provided details (with hand-drawn illustrations) of Finnish ski bindings, winter boots, tents, and other gear. And he concluded that the army should "call in the thousands of experienced skiers, send them to a good training place in Colorado, and from them build the nucleus of an expanding winter defense force."

"Initiative and self-reliance," the qualities displayed by the Finnish ski troops, were highly regarded personal values for Minnie Dole. Seeing the need, and acting largely on his own, the only resources at his disposal a typewriter and an iron will, Dole had in a single year pulled together a national network of some four thousand volunteers grouped into nearly two hundred patrols, a total membership greater by a thousand than an army regiment. But what did Dole have to show thus far for his efforts in the campaign for mountain troops? Not a regiment, not a battalion, not a company, not so much as a platoon. Dole dropped his publicly optimistic tone as he complained to Bradley of what he regarded as the lethargy and bureaucratic narrow-mindedness of the military authorities with whom he had been dealing: "So many of the conclusions that you have drawn are so pertinent and logical that it is hard to understand how the Army can overlook them. I originally made a number of suggestions and their only reply was that 'This was a start this year and it had to be fitted into the organization as it then existed.' I am extremely hopeful that in another year we may be able to convince them that a lot of the things that they are doing are wrong."

Dole understood that mountain troops were never going to be taken seriously by the army as long as they were viewed as exotic auxiliaries, "fitted in" but subordinate to existing flatland units. They had to have their own distinctive and separate organization, like the army's newly organized 1st Armored Division, activated in the summer of 1940, preferably with their own separate mountain training camp (perhaps in Colorado, as Bradley had suggested). Dole circulated Bradley's letter to sympathetic officers, and it may have had an effect on prevailing opinion within at least some quarters of the military establishment.

Two months after Dole received and began circulating the Bradley letter, Colonel (soon to be promoted to general) Harry L. Twaddle, acting assistant chief of staff in G-3, proposed the construction of a new army base in mountainous terrain suitable for training mountain troops. There was some pushback from other military planners, who argued that existing camps, like Fort Lewis, were within driving distance of mountains and would be sufficient for that purpose. But their objection to mountain troops went deeper than the question of where to base them; the very concept of specialized units offended the sensibilities of military conservatives because such units were going to have unique organizational requirements. The "table of organization" (which in military terminology is a prescription for organizing, manning, and equipping a unit) would need to be altered for a unit specially trained to fight in rough cold weather terrain. For one thing, a mountain division was going to need pack animals, not trucks, to transport supplies and weapons. For another, such a division would have to be equipped with lighter weapons, since heavy artillery and machine guns would be difficult to move and deploy in mountain settings. The size of command and support units would have to be reduced as well to facilitate mobility in and over the mountains. It all seemed . . . irregular.

Twaddle met that argument head-on in July in a memorandum to General Leslie McNair, the chief of staff at Army General Headquarters (in which position he oversaw organization, equipment, and training of army ground forces): "G-3 believes that there is a definite need that our Table of Organization also include a mountain division. This is a distinct type that cannot be readily improvised by attachment but must be specifically organized and trained." While mountain troops could always be deployed on lowland terrain as needed, the opposite, he argued, was not the case. But McNair disagreed, echoing the argument of conservative skeptics: rather than "organize a special division," he favored a plan to "adapt an infantry division . . . to operations in difficult terrain." Innovation and novelty were not highly regarded by the military establishment.

The war of memorandums, in which other senior planners fired their own broadsides that summer, might have continued in this indeterminate stalemate for months or years to come. The real war, however, kept providing new evidence of the virtues of specially trained mountain troops, first in Finland, then in Norway, and finally in the Balkans. In the fall of 1940, Italian Fascist leader Benito Mussolini, having joined the war after the fall of France in the hope of sharing the booty of Axis victory, sent the Italian army to invade Greece through Albania. But Greek troops beat them back into the mountains, with fearsome losses. Despite having well-trained mountain troops from their Corpo Alpini, the Italian invasion force largely consisted of regular army troops, ill-equipped for the terrain and the winter conditions they encountered. It was only Germany's intervention on behalf of its hapless Italian allies that brought Greek defeat in the spring of 1941. In what proved an influential analysis, Lieutenant Colonel Leonard S. Gerow drew on observations from the US military attaché in Rome, noting that in the fighting in the Balkans, Italian divisions "were not organized, clothed, equipped, trained for either winter or mountain fighting," resulting in heavy losses, as much from weather as from combat. Gerow concluded that "an army which may have to fight anywhere in the world must have an important part of its major units especially organized, trained, and equipped for fighting in the mountains and winter."

The lessons from Europe that Gerow emphasized finally swung the argument Dole's way. On October 22, 1941, he received a letter from General George C. Marshall informing him that as of November 15, the US Army would include in its ranks a unit designated the 1st Battalion (Reinforced), 87th Infantry Mountain Regiment. (That word order proved a little too confusing even by the standards of the army's usual opaque nomenclature; by the following spring the designation would be changed to 87th Mountain Infantry Regiment.) No separate base as yet—the 87th would train for the time being at Fort Lewis in Tacoma. But the army was already scouting out possible new locations. Secretary of War Henry Stimson wrote Dole a few days later, saying that while the decision had been Marshall's, not his, the creation of the 87th was "most gratifying to us whose interest in this form of training is keen."

That might have been the end of Dole's involvement with mountain warfare. But then something truly extraordinary happened. While Dole's campaign may not have been the decisive factor in the decision to organize a battalion of mountain soldiers, he had made an impression on military leaders as a capable and creative thinker and administrator. With this in mind, the army requested that the National Ski Patrol not only continue to advise on training and equipment but also recruit and vet candidates for the mountain troops—an unprecedented official role for a civilian organization. The NSPS would be, in effect, the admissions office for the 87th, and candidates had to fill out and submit a three-page questionnaire about their outdoor qualifications, along with three letters of recommendation from what Dole referred to as "qualified people —athletic coaches, headmasters, etc."

Young male skiers around the country, many of whom had been tutored in the Arlberg technique on elite college ski teams, soon took note of the NSPS's recruiting campaign. Charles B. McLane of Manchester, New Hampshire, former captain of the Dartmouth College ski team (and son of a trustee of the college), set out in mid-November to prove the Dole thesis that it would be easier to turn skiers into soldiers than the reverse. So enthusiastic was he to join up that, instead of enlisting locally, he took a bus cross-country to present himself in person at Fort Lewis. McLane looked the personification of the rah-rah college boy of the era as he stepped off the bus on a quiet Sunday morning, decked out in a green team sweater bearing a big white *D* for Dartmouth. He had even brought his own skis. He was at Fort Lewis to report to the mountain troops, he informed the bemused officer who met him at the camp entrance. "Lad," the major is said to have replied, "you *are* the mountain troops."

Not entirely true — in November a dozen officers and a single enlisted man already in service had been officially activated as mountain troops. But McLane was the first US Army *recruit* to sign up with the 87th with the specific intent of becoming a mountain soldier. Thousands more, including 118 former Dartmouth students (more than from any other single college or university), joined him over the next several years.

There was not much for McLane to do in his first weeks at Fort Lewis — so he went skiing. Captain Paul Lafferty, now assigned to the 87th, drove McLane and a few other newly arrived enlisted men up to Mount Rainier for ski outings. In fact, they were returning from a good day's skiing on Sunday, December 7, when Lafferty's wife, Jean, who was in the car with them, absentmindedly switched on the radio, and they learned that the United States had been at war with Japan for the last few hours. As rumors swirled in the aftermath of Pearl Harbor of coming Japanese attacks on the West Coast, by air or sabotage, troops were hustled off base from Fort Lewis to guard bridges, dams, and other vulnerable facilities all over the Pacific Northwest. Every night there was a blackout. The mountain troops, by then consisting of a dozen officers, a couple of dozen NCOs, and a handful of privates, were left largely to their own devices. Dodging heavily laden army trucks rolling by after dark, or lying in the barracks with the only light coming from the tips of burning cigarettes, McLane recalled, "we guessed at the odds of the Regiment surviving that first week."

Back east at the National Ski Patrol's New York office those first weeks in December, there was a mere trickle of applications — two or three a day. But a battalion of infantry needed nearly nine hundred men, and there were already plans being developed in Washington to expand the single authorized battalion to the three that, with support units, would make up a full regiment — and beyond that, to create two additional regiments, which, joining the 87th, would constitute a division. Dole mobilized NSPS members across the country to identify likely recruits. He sent out a stream of press releases, and letters to college ski teams and to other outdoor organizations, publicizing the opportunity to join the new unit. Soon hundreds of applications were arriving weekly at the office in the Graybar Building.

One particularly well-qualified candidate sent his application to the NSPS office in March 1942. It was submitted by a 1936 Dartmouth graduate named Larry Jump. Under "Remarks" at the end of the three-page questionnaire, he wrote, "Much of my life has been out-of-doors, camping, canoeing, hiking and skiing." That included ten years of downhill skiing in his native New England, as well as in France, Switzerland, and Austria, plus mountain climbing in the Pacific Northwest, the Canadian Rockies, and the Chamonix region of the French Alps. He spoke and read French and German. He had also served for six months as a volunteer ambulance driver with the French army. Not surprisingly, he was among those approved by the NSPS and went on to serve with the 87th Regiment.

By the time the NSPS ceased recruiting ski troopers in February 1944, it had received and reviewed over twelve thousand applications and sent somewhere between seven thousand and eight thousand recruits to what became the 10th Mountain Division, making up roughly half or a little more of the fourteen thousand who would go off to fight in 1945. Not all of them were Larry Jumps; some had never strapped on a pair of skis before they put on an army uniform. But what united the thousands of men who joined the 10th via the NSPS application was their status as volunteers. They *wanted* to be mountain troops.

The *New Yorker* magazine, which since its founding in the mid-1920s had become a sort of clubby house organ for sophisticated and comfortably situated New Yorkers and New Englanders, made its own contribution to spreading the news about the recruiting drive for mountain soldiers while also reinforcing the ski troops' image as a socially elite outfit. A front-of-the-magazine feature titled "Minnie's Ski Troops" ran in the issue dated February 21, 1942, two and a half months after Pearl Harbor and roughly two years since the day when Dole and his friends first hatched the idea of American mountain troops. "A New York insurance broker named Charles Minot Dole — Minnie to his friends," the piece began, with the affectionate irony typical of such entries, "is in large part responsible for this country's first alpine military force, now in training on skis on the slopes of Mt. Rainier." Dole professed distaste for the article, its tone, and especially its title. But he probably appreciated its practical impact on the recruiting effort.

———

In addition to the mountain soldiers arriving daily at Fort Lewis in those first months of war, the army was also shipping in Missouri mules, penned together in newly constructed corrals on the base. Colonel Onslow S. "Pinkie" Rolfe, the 87th's first commander, a 1917 graduate of West Point and highly decorated veteran of the First World War, and, at best, a wobbly amateur skier, may have owed his appointment to his birthplace, New Hampshire. The closest he had come to a mountain assignment was during the three years he served in Hawaii in the 1920s, where he used to go horseback riding on the slopes of volcanoes. But if he didn't know much about skiing, or mountains in general, as an old cavalry officer he knew quite a lot about mules. And that was one subject the otherwise tough-as-nails officer liked to joke about. Near the gate that led to the corrals, watering troughs, blacksmith shops, and harness shops that constituted "mule-land" at Fort Lewis, Rolfe had a sign hung declaring, "Through these portals pass the most beautiful mules in the world" (a satiric reference to a well-known sign hanging in the 1920s and 1930s over the stage door of a Broadway theater that proclaimed, "Through these portals pass the most beautiful girls in the world").

Sometime in the late winter of 1942, Minnie Dole traveled to Washington State to visit the 87th. By then three companies of the new unit had moved to the enticingly named Paradise Valley, a location some sixty-odd miles away, and five thousand feet higher than Fort Lewis, on the south side of Mount Rainier. Designated a national park in 1899, and home to Otto Lang's Arlberg technique school, the great white volcano was an ideal place for ski soldiers to practice their snowplows, stem turns, and christies. And more than ideal in terms of the luxury accommodations they occupied — the National Park Service–licensed hotels Paradise and Tatoosh Lodges. (The mules and the regiment's mule skinners remained at Fort Lewis.)

As he recounted in *Adventures in Skiing,* Dole was welcomed to the regiment's new quarters by Colonel Rolfe, who, he wrote, "led me by the arm to a large bulletin board. Plastered in the middle of it was my

Minnie Dole with namesake, Camp Hale, 1943.
NEW ENGLAND SKI MUSEUM

bête noire — the *New Yorker* article about 'Minnie's Ski Troops.'" Dole wasn't sure what to make of the colonel's gesture: "I don't think Pinkie was very impressed with it, or me." That night, however, after a few drinks, Pinkie asked Minnie to address the troops, which he did, he recalled, describing some of the "battles . . . I had been through in Washington, and how the whole idea of American mountain troops had been born in Manchester, Vermont."

Pinkie followed with a speech of his own. He made it clear he hated the term "ski troops," regarding it as effete and elitist. You aren't "ski troops," he growled, as he had on previous occasions, "you're mountain troops." But then, abandoning the scolding tone, he indulged in a little mule humor, or, perhaps more accurately, a mule parable, this time for Minnie's benefit. "Anyone who knows anything about the mountains knows that we have to have mules to carry equipment and mountain artillery. And mules won't go anywhere without a little bell mare to lead them. We will have a little bell mare any day now and I propose we name her 'Minnie.'"

Two years had passed since four skiers shared a drink and hatched a wild idea on a cold winter's eve on the other side of the country. Minnie Dole's determination, contacts, and organizational skills had turned that midwinter night's scheme into a going concern. As Colonel Rolfe promised, the bell mare, the leader of the regimental pack train, was subsequently known as "Minnie" in honor of Charles Minot Dole.

The musical 87th: left to right, Charles Bradley, Glenn Stanley, Charles B. McLane, and Ralph Bromaghin playing guitar.
THE DENVER PUBLIC LIBRARY (TMD358)

2

Training, 1942

"Ninety Pounds of Rucksack"

The moral of this story, as you can plainly see,
Is never trust a skier an inch above your knee.
For I trusted one and now look at me;
I've got a bastard in the Mountain Infantry.

> — *Privates Ralph Bromaghin and Charles B.*
> *McLane, "Ninety Pounds of Rucksack,"*
> *10th Mountain drinking song, 1942*

IN JANUARY 1941, WHEN *LIFE* FIRST FEATURED A US ARMY "SKI Trooper" on its cover, there was as yet no such thing; ski troops were an experiment, nothing more. By the time a photograph of a "Mountain Trooper" (Sergeant Walter Prager of the 87th Mountain Infantry, formerly coach of the Dartmouth ski team) appeared in that space on November 9, 1942, the hypothetical had become accomplished fact. The mountain regiment founded at Fort Lewis the previous year now amounted to a massive military enterprise, involving thousands of recruits, ten thousand civilian workers, and tens of millions of dollars in federal expenditures. The question was no longer whether the United States Army would have mountain troops. It was instead where and when they would join the fight.

The months between the two *Life* covers witnessed another series of military setbacks for the Allied cause in the Second World War comparable to the disasters of 1940. Adolf Hitler unleashed the Wehrmacht on the Soviet Union in June 1941, and German forces nearly reached Moscow before the Red Army's stiffening resistance and the Russian winter combined to halt its drive (the latter factor in the German setback another reminder to American military planners of the value of cold weather training and clothing). The Japanese bombed Pearl Harbor in December 1941 and in the next few months conquered the Philippines, the Dutch East Indies, the Solomon Islands, and Singapore — and in June 1942 even the Aleutian islands of Attu and Kiska in the Bering Strait, which were American territory. While German U-boats sank a record 1,660 Allied ships in the Atlantic in 1942, German armies returned to the offensive in North Africa and the Soviet Union. The only good news for the Allies that year was the US Navy's victory over the Japanese fleet at Midway Island in the Pacific in June, the Nazi failure to capture Stalingrad in the fall, and the Anglo-American landings in North Africa in early November. In the long run, and taken together, those Allied victories proved the turning point of the war. But it did not seem that way in 1942. The outcome of the war remained very much in doubt throughout the first year of the existence of the 87th Mountain Infantry Regiment.

In the midst of bad news from overseas, the mountain troops led an itinerant life. Starting in mid-February 1942, they shuttled sixty miles from Fort Lewis to Mount Rainier for ski training. And it was on Rainier's slopes that the unique character of the 10th Mountain Division began to take shape.

It was not uncommon for recruits to the mountain regiments to find themselves serving together with prewar classmates, friends, skiing partners, or relatives, which probably made the transition to military life less jarring — but also complicated the adjustment to differences in rank and authority. Hal Burton, an experienced skier and climber from the Adirondacks who joined the 87th Mountain Infantry Regiment early on (and was also one of the ski troops' earliest chroniclers), described the spirit of the Paradise Valley training days on Mount Rainier in exaggerated but illuminating terms as "more like a college reunion than a military encampment." Private Ralph Townsend and Lieutenant Paul Townsend, both veterans of the University of New Hampshire ski team, as well as brothers, served in the same regiment; Sergeant Walter Prager served in a company commanded by Lieutenant John Litchfield — whom the sergeant used to address as "Litch" when the lieutenant was a Dartmouth skier on the team that Prager coached.

The lodges at Paradise Valley reverted to civilian control and clientele at the end of May, and the remaining troopers in residence dispersed to Fort Lewis and temporary bases, or to maneuvers in California and Colorado. In the last months of the year, the mountain troops arrived at the location in the United States most closely associated with the history of what would become the 10th Mountain Division: newly constructed Camp Hale high in the Colorado Rockies.

Nineteen forty-two was a year of growth as well as movement for the mountain troops. The single battalion (authorized strength of 860) based at Fort Lewis at the start of the war grew over the course of the following spring to three battalions, with the second battalion activated on May 1 and the third battalion on June 1. In the army's triangular organizational structure, three squads of riflemen made up a platoon (normally squads were twelve men each, but initially in the mountain troops they were nine men strong), three rifle platoons plus a heavy weapons platoon and various other personnel made a company (roughly two hundred men), and three companies plus a heavy weapons company and other personnel made a battalion. Companies were labeled alphabetically. The first battalion consisted of three infantry companies, A, B, and C, plus a heavy weapons company D. The second battalion was made up of infantry companies E, F, and G and the heavy weapons company, H. And the third battalion comprised infantry companies I, K, and L (skipping J, just to complicate things), plus the heavy weapons company, M. Those three battalions made a full regiment (authorized strength of 2,872, including an additional headquarters company, and units supporting the infantry, smaller than the standard 3,118-man infantry regiment). And as the 87th arrived at a new base in Colorado at the end of the year, a second mountain infantry regiment, the 86th, also began to take form, with its first battalion activated on November 26, 1942. Three such regiments, plus supporting units, would add up to a division.

Despite Colonel Pinkie Rolfe's insistence that they stop thinking of themselves as ski troops, or their commander's declaration upon first meeting the men at Camp Lewis a few days after Pearl Harbor that "we are mountain troops and skiing will only play a small part," the mountain infantry forged a distinctive unit identity based on their shared experience of training as skiers.

Approximately one hundred men of the 87th Mountain Infantry Battalion (Reinforced) in white camouflage suits in the middle of a snow-covered field in front of Paradise Lodge, Mount Rainier, Washington.
THE DENVER PUBLIC LIBRARY (TMD357)

Minnie Dole was untroubled by the term "ski troops," but he maintained, perhaps a little defensively, that it carried no implication of special status. As he wrote in September 1942 to his National Ski Patrol associate Bob Livermore (by then a private in the US Army, undergoing basic training at Camp Wolters in Texas): "It will interest you to know that I have received a letter from Major [Paul R.] Lafferty, which came unsolicited, and which states in no uncertain terms that by far the best material going to the mountain troops is coming through our [NSPS] office. He states that the old line Army men and sergeants were originally skeptical, thinking that we might send them a bunch of lodge skiers, but that they have now all retracted their statements and said that they wished we could get all of the material for them." As Dole saw it, there were no snooty, lazy "lodge skiers" signing up with the 87th in expectation of an easy time or unearned privileges—just a bunch of good American soldiers, eager to do their bit.

The men of the regiment *were* eager, as they proved that first winter and spring on Mount Rainier. The training was physically demanding. Apart from regulars on the ski jump circuit, or Olympic competitors, few American skiers had ever before trained as intensively as the men of the 87th. And for that matter, few American soldiers outside of airborne troops and Rangers would undergo such rigorous training. They were on the slopes six days a week, six hours a day, for eight straight weeks, all under the expert eye of some of the country's leading ski instructors, among them Captain (later Major) Lafferty, commander of A Company of the 87th, and their Swiss-born NCOs, Walter Prager and Peter Gabriel. The instructors taught the new recruits the Arlberg technique, the phased progression from snowplow to stem christies, but with new utilitarian modifications. Soldiers on skis carrying heavy packs and rifles had to sacrifice speed and style for stability and endurance. In particular, the exaggerated shoulder rotation that was a feature of the Arlberg technique had to be abandoned, since it would throw a soldier wearing a heavy pack off balance.

In their winter war against the Russians in 1939-40, the Finns were fighting not in mountains but on snowy flatland terrain, and simple cross-country skills were all they needed. What the American ski troopers learned was a combination of Austrian alpine and Scandinavian cross-country skiing. In addition to the classic turning sequence, they did a lot more cross-country traversing and uphill climbing than would have been the case with civilians learning to ski on a college team or at a resort like Peckett's in New Hampshire or Sun Valley in Idaho. They learned to use skins attached to the bottom of their skis to give them traction going uphill, and to slow themselves on descent. And, of course, they faced hazards unknown to civilian skiers. Falling down with the burden of a ninety-pound pack made getting back up a struggle, especially for some young ski troopers who weighed barely more than their packs. And falling down with a nearly ten-pound shoulder-slung M1

Garand rifle entailed the risk of getting whacked in the head by one's own weapon.

Unlike the experimental training the winter before, when soldier-skiers were equipped more or less at random with a variety of civilian-market equipment, the soldiers in the 87th were issued newly standardized army ski gear. Depending on his height, a soldier received a pair of hickory skis ranging in length between six feet nine inches and seven feet three inches long. The skis had a long parallel groove running along the bottom from just below the tip to near the end of the ski, along with metal edges, both designed for better control. They were painted white for camouflage. Later on, the solid hickory skis were replaced by laminated skis, which were better at turning. Bindings varied at first, but the army eventually decided on the "Kandahar" cable and toe bindings, constructed of aluminum and steel, which also improved control. Ski poles came with bamboo or metal shafts and leather grips. Blunt square-toed boots, grooved around the heel to accommodate the bindings, did double duty as ski and climbing footwear. They were made with leather uppers, and, at the start of the war in 1941–42, with smooth rigid leather soles and heels. The bottom of the boot could be studded with nails to grip ice and rock. The troopers were issued a size larger than with normal army boots so they could wear two pairs of thick woolen socks.

Clothing was developed to meet the special needs of mountain warfare. The olive drab (or in army lingo "OD") "Class A" uniforms worn by the men in the 87th were standard GI issue, as were their denim fatigues, but their field uniforms were unlike anything worn before by an American soldier. The traditional bulky greatcoats the army issued for cold weather were useless for skiing. (In a brief training experiment in 1942, paratroopers were sent to the Alta ski area in Utah to learn to ski; their wool olive drab overcoats soaked up several pounds of water each day, which did not improve their shaky skiing technique.) One alternative tried out in 1941 was a one-piece hooded jumpsuit (or "penguin suit" as it was dubbed), rejected for a variety of reasons, including the obstacle it presented to the performance outdoors of some basic bodily functions. Instead, ski troopers at Rainier were issued "over-whites," reversible thigh-length windproof cotton parkas, with a white side to blend in with snowy backgrounds and an olive drab side for snowless terrain, along with white or OD pants, available in wool gabardine or poplin. White leather mittens cut for a trigger finger and thumb allowed for maximum hand warmth while providing the flexibility needed for firing a weapon. White or OD canvas gaiters worn over mountain boots completed the troopers' outerwear. (Gaiters of a different design were also worn by regular troops, but they were more useful to the ski troops, since they kept snow from sifting down their ankles and into their boots.) Underneath the cotton over-whites, everything else the soldiers wore— OD sweaters, shirts, long underwear, and socks—was made of wool, a fabric that, unlike cotton, allowed sweat to evaporate easily. On warmer or colder days, soldiers could easily shed or add a layer of clothing as needed. Finally, in what proved one of the most distinctive and popular items provided the ski troops, they wore a cotton ski cap, flannel-lined, with a visor and ear flaps that could be pulled down for cold days.

In November 1941, the same month when the 87th Regiment was activated, the army established a Mountain and Winter Warfare Board to oversee the training and equipping of mountain troops. Nominally under the command of Colonel Rolfe, thirty-three-year-old Captain Albert H. Jackman, a 1931 Princeton University graduate and one of the few highly skilled mountaineers in the prewar Army Reserve, was the most important officer associated with the board, and it was Jackman who coordinated its testing program. (In 1944, by then a lieutenant colonel, Jackman would join the 10th Mountain Division as executive officer of the 604th Field Artillery Battalion.) Jackman sought and relied heavily on the expertise and advice of civilian skiers and mountaineers. The National Ski Association had already established a quasi-official advisory group, known as the Equipment Committee, in November 1940. It was chaired by Bestor Robinson, an active member of the Sierra Club in northern California, who had been a pioneer of big wall climbing in Yosemite Valley in the 1930s. "Committee," conjuring an image of men sitting around a table shuffling papers and making motions, fails to do justice to the full contributions of Robinson and his colleagues. Along with Captain Paul Lafferty, Robinson led a twenty-strong party of soldiers and civilians (among the latter David Brower, another Sierra Club rock climber of distinction, and future member of the 10th Mountain) on a ski tour of the High Sierra in April 1941 to test equipment in deep snow and blizzard conditions. Robinson later joined the Army Quartermaster Corps.

Adams Carter was another leading climber who played an important role in equipping the mountain troops. In 1934, Carter and fellow Harvard student Brad Washburn made a first ascent of 12,324-foot Mount Crillon in Alaska, and in 1936 he was part of an Anglo-American expedition that reached the summit of Nanda Devi in the Indian Garhwal range, at 25,643 feet the highest first ascent achieved until after the Second World War. In 1939, a few months before the start of the war, Carter was on a climbing holiday in Switzerland. He noticed that his partner, local climbing guide Hermann Ogi, was wearing a strange new kind of boot unlike anything he had ever seen before, with rubber-cleated soles. Ogi was testing out the boots for their inventor, Italian climber Vitale Bramani. Carter was inclined to scoff at the innovation until Ogi let him try them on. It was a revelation. Unlike the traditional nail-studded leather soles on climbing boots, "Vibram" soles (named for their inventor) gripped far better on slippery surfaces, and did not conduct cold via metal nails from ice and snow to the wearer's foot inside. Back in the States, Carter tracked down a pair of boots with the new-style soles belonging to a New Hampshire climber, and by 1943 knock-off copies were being issued to the mountain troops, replacing the smooth-leather-soled boots. After the war, Vibram soles, fondly known to a generation of young climbers as "waffle-stompers," became standard for climbing boots, an indirect legacy of the US Army's experiment with mountain warfare.

Bob Bates had also been on that 1939 Swiss mountain trip along with his friend and fellow Harvard graduate Carter. And he too had an impressive climbing résumé. In 1937, with Brad Washburn, Bates made a first ascent of 17,192-foot Mount Lucania, Canada's third-highest mountain, and in 1938 was part of the first American expedition to attempt K2 in the Karakoram Range in present-day Pakistan, the world's second-highest mountain after Everest. Bates enlisted in the army after Pearl Harbor and was assigned to the Quartermaster Corps. In the summer of 1942 he, Washburn, Albert Jackman, and a dozen or so other climbers spent a month on an Army Quartermaster–sponsored expedition to Denali (then known as Mount McKinley), at 20,156 feet the highest mountain in North America, where they tested everything from lip balm to sleeping bags at their base camp, eighteen thousand feet up on the mountain's Harper Glacier. They were supplied by parachute drops from army planes. And on a couple of days off from testing, Bates, Washburn, and two others climbed to the summit of the mountain, in what was only its third ascent; a fourth ascent came the following day, by a party including Jackman. Back in his Washington, DC, office, Bates took delivery of one of the new nylon climbing ropes soon issued to the mountain troops (a vast improvement over the old hemp ropes, since nylon, being stronger and more flexible, and having more stretch, was less likely to break a climber's ribs in the event of a fall). Bates decided to test the new rope on the spot, tying it off, wrapping it between his legs and over his shoulder, climbing out through the upper-story window of his office, and, much to the horrified surprise of secretaries on lower floors, bouncing down the side of the building on rappel. He was satisfied, and the new ropes, a regulation olive drab, seven sixteenths of an inch in diameter and 120 feet in length, were soon on their way to the mountain troops. Later in the war Bates was dispatched to Italy, to advise troops from flatland divisions fighting in the mountains on cold weather survival technique.

An M29 "Weasel" cargo carrier, Camp Hale.
THE DENVER PUBLIC LIBRARY (TMD613)

Among their other duties on Mount Rainier in the spring of 1942, the men of the 87th served as guinea pigs in evaluating the merits of many kinds of mountaineering gear, clothing, and food. They experimented with a motorized toboggan that, like the regular child's version, was difficult to steer and even more prone to flip over. (At Colonel Rolfe's insistence, Minnie Dole gave it a try when he visited the 87th and wound up being flung through the air when it rolled over on a steep snowbank. Dole, never quite certain about Rolfe's feelings toward him, wondered if the 87th's commander was trying to kill him off.) It wasn't until the following summer that separate trials in the Columbia Icefields of the Canadian Rockies proved the usefulness of a squat Studebaker-manufactured cargo-carrying snow vehicle with wide rubber and metal tracks (technically a "fully tracked" vehicle, like a tank). It was dubbed the "Weasel" after the mountain predator, more officially known in a prototype version as the T-15, and in a later improved version as the M29 cargo carrier. Along with mules, the Weasel cargo carriers became standard transport for the mountain regiments, although they were not without problems, having a tendency to throw off their tracks, and were prone to bogging down in deep powder snow. They also saw combat use by the army in France and by the marines on Iwo Jima and Okinawa. They were the precursors of better-designed postwar civilian over-snow vehicles, including snowcats and snowmobiles.

Physical exertion in cold weather required soldiers to consume extra calories to preserve energy and body weight, and the food they ate in the field had to be transported in their rucksacks. Finding the right combination of high calories and low weight was a challenge. On maneuvers, high on the mountain slopes, the troopers sampled pemmican (a loaf of dried meat, fat, and fruit, which enjoyed a brief vogue among Himalayan mountaineers in the late 1930s, and which they detested) and K-rations (lightweight nonperishable packaged food, heavy on canned luncheon meat and the like, which got the official nod). Shelter was another key to survival in a cold and hostile environment. The soldiers tried out the standard-issue waterproof nylon tents and found them completely unsatisfactory for cold weather conditions. Their breath condensed on the interior wall while they slept, causing mini-blizzards when brushed against in the morning, with the subsequent puddles on the floor soaking into their sleeping bags. Unfortunately, despite the negative reviews, the army went ahead and ordered forty thousand more of the nylon tents, and the ski troopers would be stuck with them for the next two years. In time they came to rely on a low-tech alternative, digging snow caves and igloos, finding that they slept better and kept warmer and drier that way. Much of their education in outdoor survival skills that spring was self-taught, through trial and error. Thus, they learned to sleep with their boots tucked against their bodies in their sleeping bags — not the most comfortable arrangement, but preferable to pulling on frozen footwear in the morning.

The most dramatic and thoroughly documented test of food and equipment on Rainier was conducted in early May by eight of the most expert skiers and mountaineers in the regiment. Officially led by Captain Jackman — although, as he would acknowledge, Corporal Peter Gabriel, formerly of the Franconia Ski School, "really led the party" — they set off to climb the mountain on skis, something that had been accomplished only once before. They took twelve days for their expedition, establishing two intermediate camps, the highest at 12,300 feet, where they tested gas stoves, tents, skis, and food (among their recommendations, more cocoa powder in the field rations) and relaxed in the sun on a rare string of cloudless days. Lieutenant John Jay, descendant of the first chief justice of the US Supreme Court, a former star of the Williams College ski team, and a pioneering ski documentarian, filmed the climb to use in future promotional and instructional films for the mountain troops.

The Jackman-Gabriel party made their bid for the summit on May 16, substituting crampons for skis, which would have been useless on the final icy stretch. Reaching the top of the highest peak in the Cascade Range at 14,410 feet, more than nine thousand feet above Paradise Valley, was exciting, especially for a University of Wisconsin graduate like Private Charles Bradley. Although a veteran skier, he had not grown up surrounded by big mountains, and he was thrilled at the vista unfolding before him, including the stately procession of glaciated volcanoes stretching away to the south — Washington's Mount St. Helens, and Oregon's Mount Hood and Mount Jefferson. And capping it off, he recalled, there was "a great ski run back to camp."

The gear improved and the men improved. They became lean and resilient, confident in their skiing abilities. "Our faces grew dark and tough as leather," Charles McLane reflected a year after the Rainier training, "our muscles grew hard, our reactions quickened." Colonel Rolfe, who turned forty-seven that winter, was one of those out there on the slopes of Paradise Valley, being instructed by men far younger and junior to him in the basics of the Arlberg technique, and became a fair skier himself. Two months into training at Paradise Valley, he reported to Major General Mark Clark, then serving in Washington as chief of staff for Army Ground Forces, after observing recent maneuvers by the troopers at altitudes up to 9,500 feet on Mount Rainier, "I do not believe I have ever seen a better group of physically trained men in my life."

When not out skiing, the soldiers in the 87th practiced some of the basics of military life, learning to salute, to stand at attention, to peel a potato when assigned KP. But six hours of skiing took a big chunk out of each training day. And in terms of what was seemingly the most basic purpose of the infantryman, firing a weapon at the enemy, there was no instruction at all, at least until they got back to Fort Lewis. The discharge of firearms on national park land was forbidden. The rifles they carried strapped to their rucksacks while skiing were just so much extra dead weight to be lugged around. There was much in the experience of the mountain troops in those early and formative months that was decidedly not in accordance with traditional military expectations.

Army basic training for the flatland divisions consisted in large measure of doing things that, unlike skiing, no civilian would likely consider recreational — close order drill, long marches, group calisthenics, obstacle courses, and the like. And all the while living in crowded, hastily thrown-up barracks, usually on some dusty base in what felt like the middle of nowhere. In contrast, the soldiers of the 87th were transferred soon after their arrival at Fort Lewis to one of two well-appointed ski lodges (where some lucky ones were assigned single rooms), with inspiring vistas, snowdrifts twenty to thirty feet deep, and that huge glaciated mountain looming behind them. When Rudy Konieczny, a former champion downhill ski racer from Adams, Massachusetts, joined up with the 87th in the spring of 1942, he differed from most of his fellow recruits by having already served eighteen months in the regular army. Arriving at Paradise Valley, he couldn't believe his amazing good fortune: "I'm in snow up to my head, and getting paid for it!" And not just snow, but deep powder snow, permitting a swifter, flashier style of skiing than the icy crusts that develop on the damper thaw-and-freeze-prone northeastern slopes, the conditions that contributed to Minnie Dole's breaking his ankle back in 1936. The ski lodges on Rainier were located just above the timberline, which gave the option of skiing on open slopes or descending below timberline, maneuvering between trees.

Six months before Charles McLane enlisted in 1941, he gave some thought to what the coming war meant for him and his Dartmouth classmates in a commencement address in June. Although the United States was still technically at peace, most of the young men graduating that day expected to be in the military within months. "There will be very little that is natural in this war," McLane warned his classmates. "It will not be natural to wear a uniform and march, nor to take orders without question from men whom in peacetime we would not obey, nor to feel like cogs in a wheel turned by people we never see, nor to kill men we might like for friends." As McLane could not have imagined when giving this speech, it was in the unlikely location of the slopes of Mount Rainier where he would be called upon to make his individual adjustment to the unnaturalness of military life.

Army recruits often felt overwhelmed in their early days of training. Young men living away from home or school for the first time and still basically civilians at heart found themselves under the authority of tough NCOs and aloof officers. They had to accustom themselves to a new and strange way of collective life, always in a group whether eating, sleeping, or training. To develop as good soldiers, the army believed, the young men in its charge had to surrender their civilian-bred sense of individuality. "Success in combat demands the subordination of the individual to the accomplishment of the group mission," the army's 1941 field manual *Military Training* observed. "A feeling of unity must be achieved if the group of individuals is to function as a unit."

That is why in those initial weeks of basic training, soldiers spent so much time in close order drill. "The purposes of drill," the army's 1939 field manual *Infantry Drill Regulations* explained, were various, from providing an orderly way of moving troops from one place to another to "giving interesting spectacles to the public." Most important, in the training of recruits, constant drill aided "disciplinary training by instilling habits of precision and response to the leader's orders." In close order drill, no one in formation was supposed to stand out. The whole point of the exercise was to turn individuals into a unit.

For typical recruits, early instruction focused on learning military courtesy, discipline, sanitation, first aid, map reading, and individual tactics, as well as drill. Only afterwards were new recruits given specialized training. In contrast, recruits in the 87th started their specialized training, skiing, within days of joining the army. And while skiing certainly requires precision, it does not lend itself to instilling habits of either obedience or uniformity. Synchronized skiing, the closest thing to skiing in formation, is a stunt, not easily learned or adaptable to military ends. Terrain, slope, and snow conditions, not a leader's orders, determined the ski soldier's path on a downhill run. Skiing necessarily has less to do with unit cohesion than with demonstrations of individual judgment and mastery. "The better a person skis, and the more expert he becomes," New Hampshire ski instructor Benno Rybizka wrote in his widely read 1938 how-to book *The Hannes Schneider Ski Technique,* "the more his own individuality and temperament come to be expressed by his body position when racing or skiing in general." There are formal rules for performing good ski turns in descent, like bending the knees and maintaining balance, edge control, strong ankle pressure. But ultimately each skier works out the mechanics of grace on the slopes for himself or herself. Skiing, even military skiing, reinforced rather than undercut feelings of autonomy and individualism. Charles McLane wrote an article for the 1943 issue of the *American Ski Annual* reflecting on his military experience thus far, and suggested that on maneuvers in the mountains, "a good squad was not necessarily one that was tactically correct, but rather one that skied well." Whether that would prove the case in actual combat remained to be seen. That McLane *believed* it to be true in his first year in the 87th, during which he rose from the rank of private to lieutenant, says much about the emerging self-identity of the ski troopers.

Ironically, one of those skeptical about the value of placing skiing at the center of a training program for mountain warfare was none other than Hannes Schneider, father of the Arlberg technique, whose son Herbert would soon join the mountain troops. When Germany took over Austria in 1938, Schneider incurred the wrath of the new rulers for his anti-Nazi views and, according to some accounts, for publicly defending the Jewish secretary of the Austrian Ski Federation. He was one of sixty thousand Austrians imprisoned in the immediate aftermath of the Anschluss. Schneider's freedom was secured by American admirers who provided refuge in the United States. He moved to North Conway, New Hampshire, in February 1939, taking over direction of the Eastern Slope Ski School from his protégé Benno Rybizka. (According to legend, on arriving in the shadow of New Hampshire's Mount Washington, at 6,223 feet the highest peak in the northeastern United States, Schneider looked up and asked innocently, "But where are the mountains?")

———

"I had a very interesting talk with Hannes Schneider this week," Adams Carter reported to a climbing friend in February 1942. "His main point was that you should no more have 'ski troops' than you should have 'crampon troops' or 'ice-ax troops.' He wonders if the ski is not being put a little too much onto a pedestal and if the fact that it is really a means to an end and not the end in itself is not being ignored." The soldiers on Mount Rainier were receiving instruction in the use of crampons and ice axes, as well as snowshoes (which they heartily despised). "We Climb to Conquer" became the unit's motto. But the other things they did while out on mountain maneuvers, like climbing, could not dilute the glamour and excitement of the ski trooper identity. Skiing was much more than a means to an end for them.

True to the pattern of college and university sociability in those years, the Paradise Valley encampment soon acquired its own version of the Whiffenpoofs, the 87th Regimental Glee Club, founded by Charles McLane and Ralph Bromaghin. The latter, in addition to being a talented amateur musician, was a former Sun Valley, and before that Mount Rainier, ski instructor. A revolving cast of characters joined them to fill out a quartet. Charles Bradley, younger brother of the David Bradley who had written to Minnie Dole about the Finnish-Soviet war, was invited to join in a musical gathering on the very night he first arrived

at Rainier; he called the mountain troops "one of the singingest outfits to ever shoulder an army pack." The Glee Club performed spirited
parodies of popular and traditional songs in the evening for their comrades after a long day's skiing and before civilian audiences on the weekends. The most enduring of their creations, with lyrics co-authored by
McLane and Bromaghin, proved to be "Ninety Pounds of Rucksack"
(a reference to the weight that the troopers sometimes carried on their
backs while skiing), sung to the tune of a bawdy old Royal Navy favorite, "Bell Bottom Trousers." Like the original, the song celebrated male
physical and sexual prowess, along with freedom from domestic responsibility. "I was a barmaid in a mountain inn," it began:

> There I learned the wages and miseries of sin;
> Along came a skier fresh from off the slopes;
> He's the one that ruined me and shattered all my hopes.

Singing:
[Chorus:]

> Ninety pounds of rucksack
> A pound of grub or two
> He'll schuss the mountain. Like his daddy used to do.

And so on for several more stanzas, with the chorus sung with greater
gusto each time it came round until the sadder but wiser barmaid winds
up the mother of a "bastard in the Mountain Infantry." A schussing bastard. Not a cramponing bastard. And certainly not a snowshoeing bastard. (The glee club had not one but two songs devoted to mocking their
snowshoe training.)

If the son in question was in the mountain infantry, then he was probably also a pretty well-educated bastard — another stark contrast with
the army as a whole. Little over a tenth of American soldiers during
the Second World War had spent as much as a semester attending college or university before their service, and only a quarter had graduated
from high school, numbers that reflected high school and college enroll-
ment for the country as a whole. Educated soldiers were siphoned off

to the Army Air Corps, or military intelligence, or a host of other specialized assignments, in an army with an increasingly long logistical tail. At its peak strength in 1944-45, there were over 8 million soldiers in the army; fewer than 700,000 of those were in the infantry. In general, infantry regiments became the dumping ground for the least-educated recruits. There was heroism and endurance but little romance in being a rifleman. In the First World War, British soldiers on the western front took to referring to themselves as "PBI," or "Poor Bloody Infantry." In the Second World War, some army cynics decided that "GI" stood for "Goddamned Infantry."

In contrast, the 87th was an infantry unit that highly educated recruits were vying to join. In 1942, roughly half the soldiers in the regiment had at least some college education (and that understates the overall educational level, because many recruits coming directly from high school were college-bound before enlisting). With the National Ski Patrol System as the primary recruiting agent, and with the three-letters-of-recommendation requirement, the colleges and universities they came from usually had ski teams or outdoor clubs, which eliminated most schools from the South as well as those on the lower rungs of the higher education system. (The southerners who did join the 87th that first year were recruited for their familiarity with mules rather than skis.) While there are no hard numbers available, the anecdotal evidence suggests that a disproportionate number of those in the mountain infantry with college and university backgrounds came from elite institutions, Ivy League universities and private liberal arts colleges in the Northeast such as Harvard and Dartmouth, premier state universities in the West like the University of Washington and the University of California at Berkeley, as well as some top-ranked universities from non-mountainous but colder regions of the Midwest like the University of Chicago and the University of Michigan.

Beginning in 1941, every new recruit took the Army General Classification Test, a multiple-choice exam designed to measure general learning ability and suitability for specialized training programs. It provided a route out of the ranks and, for some, away from the front line. The highest score was 160. Anyone scoring 110 or above was rated "Superior" and considered eligible to attend Officer Candidate School (OCS). Two thirds of recruits to the mountain infantry, twice the average for other divisions, scored 110 or higher on the test. In the 86th Regiment, formed at the end of 1942, better than one in ten scored above 130, or "Very Superior." And yet relatively few availed themselves of the opportunity to go on to OCS unless guaranteed that on receiving their commission, they could return to the mountain troops. And there were only so many positions open for second lieutenants in any given regiment. As a result, in the fighting to come, regiments like the 87th would have a lot of overqualified corporals and sergeants.

It would be another year before Chicago high school student Martin (Marty) Daneman would enlist in the mountain troops. (He volunteered on his eighteenth birthday in the spring of 1943.) When he began basic training, he was dazzled by the company he was keeping. As he wrote to his girlfriend Lois:

> Maybe it would interest you to know about the sort of people I have for buddies. They are all oldern than I am, and most of them are far better educated than me. If nothing else, I'll be intellectual when I get out and start to live a normal happy life with you . . . There is every type of person — authors galore . . . There are quite a few German refugees, also well educated people. The rest are mostly from New England and N.Y. The N.E. [New England] boys all speak quite queerly — cah, cahnt, rahlly, pahzitivally, etc.

Daneman was Jewish and Brooklyn-born, a background that would have earned him a place in an infantry platoon in the standard Hollywood war movie of the era, typically portrayed as a melting pot of American ethnic and regional backgrounds (excluding African Americans, of course, who were forced to serve in segregated units). The 1945 film *A Walk in the Sun,* depicting the experience of a platoon sent on a dangerous mission to destroy a bridge in the Italian countryside, featured characters from Brooklyn and Texas, and included an Italian and a Mexican. Italians and Mexicans, Native Americans and Jews were found in the ranks of the mountain regiments, and even a few Americans of Chinese descent. But on the whole, the unit skewed sharply WASP. There were three Shapiros who served in the 10th Mountain Division in the Second

World War, three Chavezes, four Rossis, six O'Malleys, and one Chew. And 103 troopers whose last name was Davis.

As Daneman noted, a number of foreign-born recruits also served in the mountain infantry, perhaps five hundred all told. In addition to the Germans, there were Austrians, Norwegians, Swedes, and Swiss among them. The skiers were the best known of the foreign-born troopers, but their numbers included some serious mountaineers as well, like German-born Joe Stettner and his younger brother Paul. The two of them made a daring ascent of the formidable east face of Longs Peak in Colorado in 1927, a year after emigrating from Munich to Chicago, and were among the first climbers in the United States to place pitons for protection in rock climbing. Joe referred to his foreign-born compatriots in the mountain troops as the "international brigade," a reference to the pro-Loyalist foreign volunteers in the Spanish Civil War of the 1930s. Some had previous experience in mountain warfare, including First Sergeant Philipp Winter, who had served as an officer in the Austrian army, fighting in the Dolomites in the First World War, and Private Roy Pakkala, a Finnish immigrant and veteran of the Winter War against the Red Army. Many of the foreign-born soldiers chose to become naturalized citizens during the war.

All in all, soldiers in the mountain regiments tended to be not just better educated but also from more affluent, or at least more cosmopolitan, backgrounds than the average World War II American soldier. And those differences also distinguished them from their NCOs, who, especially in the early days, were career soldiers transferred from established divisions to the mountain infantry as what the army called "cadre"—veterans around whom a new unit could be formed. There was no "three-letter requirement" for them, nor any expectation that they had previous cold weather or mountain experience. Which meant when they were all out on the slopes together, it was the privates who knew what they were doing and the sergeants who were floundering, something that did little to embellish their authority. In most military units, new recruits were not invited and not likely to share their opinions on the training they received. Not so in the 87th. "What was encouraging," Charles McLane wrote in 1943 of the Mount Rainier days, "was the spirit in which maneuvering was carried out. Not only noncoms and officers were interested in the solutions and the mistakes, but privates were anxious to get in a word. *Critiques* cut deep into meal time, and in long evenings the day's problems were worked and reworked."

On the one hand, the mountain troopers' training and esprit de corps bore some resemblance to that of another recent addition to the army's table of organization, the airborne divisions. Like the men of the 87th Regiment, paratroopers were volunteers. They underwent their own form of especially rigorous training, and wore distinctive uniform items that made them instantly recognizable as part of an elite unit (silver wings, jump boots that they wore bloused, cargo pants). There were differences. Paratroopers received extra "jump pay" for hazardous duty ($50 a month for privates, $100 a month for officers, a not inconsiderable sum given that base monthly pay for a private in a regular unit was $50). Mountain troopers received no extra pay (and, later on, some sought to transfer to airborne units for precisely that reason). In terms of elite status, that might have given airborne an edge.

On the other hand, paratrooper memoirs are not filled with instances of privates offering *critiques* of their training maneuvers. Unlike mountain troops, who often had previous experience as skiers, the overwhelming majority of men who volunteered to be paratroopers had never jumped out of an airplane prior to joining the army. There were civilian parachutists before the war, but they were few in number and obscure; there were no parachutist celebrities, and no civilian sport of parachuting. The act of jumping out of an airplane required courage and a mastery of technique, but it did not involve the individual athleticism of, say, a well-executed stem christie. Airborne divisions, like the mountain division, were an elite, but traditional military values of uniformity and hierarchy were more securely rooted among paratroopers than among mountain troopers.

On April 10, 1942, as training started to wind down for the men of the 87th Regiment on Mount Rainier, construction began on a new home base for them, and for the planned expansion of the single mountain regiment into a full division. A year earlier, in April 1941, US Army Chief of Staff George C. Marshall ordered that a site be found somewhere in the West for the construction of a home base for what was, at that moment, the still hypothetical ski troop unit. Specifications for the site included a mountain location with a lot of winter snow, accessible by rail and automobile, and with sufficient space to accommodate the housing and training of up to fifteen thousand soldiers. The base would allow for mountain troopers to undergo both basic training and specialized mountain training in the same place, in the correct sequence, on a year-round basis, and at a high altitude. Various options were considered, including sites in West Yellowstone, Montana, and Bend, Oregon. But the choice in the end was an isolated alpine location called Eagle Valley on the edge of the Sawatch Range of the Colorado Rockies. The Sawatch, stretching ninety miles, has been called the "backbone of the continent," and forms the Continental Divide from Tennessee Pass in the north to Marshall Pass in the south. The range contains fifteen peaks over fourteen thousand feet in elevation, including the three highest peaks in the Rockies.

Below Tennessee Pass, seven miles farther north, lay Eagle Valley, uninhabited save for a small rail depot at its northern end known as Pando. Apart from mountains, the region was best known for its mineral wealth, with Leadville, eighteen miles to the southwest of Eagle Valley, the center of the Colorado silver boom of the 1880s and early 1890s, when it was known as the "Magic City." Farther to the west of Leadville, across twelve-thousand-foot Independence Pass, was another once booming but similarly faded mining town called Aspen. The town was dominated by a 10,705-foot peak called Aspen Mountain, which was just beginning to attract skiers.

A tortuous road through the mountains, and a roundabout railroad route on the tracks of the Denver and Rio Grande Western Railway, connected Eagle Valley to Denver, 120 rail miles away to the northeast, a nine-hour train ride, or a four-hour drive by car or bus. While under construction, the encampment was officially named Camp Hale, after the late Brigadier General Irving Hale, a Denver-raised West Point graduate who had served with distinction in the Philippines during the Spanish-American War. Located at an altitude of 9,250 feet, Camp Hale was the highest military establishment in the United States, a distinction it would never lose.

Eagle Valley was about a half mile wide and two miles long. The Eagle River flowed through the valley toward its confluence to the north with the Colorado River. Snowfall began to cover the floor of the valley in October and persisted into June, and in the depths of winter would accumulate to twelve feet deep. On surrounding mountain peaks, some over fourteen thousand feet in elevation, there was year-round snow. In the winter, temperatures dropped to thirty degrees below zero. The camp's planners thought that, despite the altitude and the cold, the sheltering walls of the valley would lessen winter's discomfort by blocking icy winds. The valley itself was surrounded by open national forest land, which provided room for maneuvers without the firearms restrictions prevailing in Rainier National Park. Any and all weapons, from rifles to machine guns to artillery, could be fired.

Camp Hale's construction, starting from scratch in such a remote location, and requiring the efforts of ten thousand imported civilian workers, proceeded remarkably smoothly. The construction workers were housed in prefabricated temporary barracks, a trailer park, and every available room in Leadville, doubling the population and restoring prosperity to that once booming mining center for the first time in decades. (It also led to a mass influx of prostitutes, with the result that when the soldiers arrived months later, Leadville was declared off-limits by army authorities.)

A massive earth-moving project tamed the meandering Eagle River, confining it to a single channel running through the center of the valley, and draining the swampy marshland surrounding it. Acres of willows, spruce, and sagebrush were cleared. Landfill dug from surrounding mountainsides firmed up and leveled the valley floor. An existing road, Highway 24, descending into the valley from Tennessee Pass on the Continental Divide, was shortened and straightened. Once the ground was prepared in April and May, construction of barracks, mess halls, warehouses, training facilities, office buildings, stables, theaters, chapels, a field house, firing ranges, and two hospitals (one with beds for soldiers, the other with stalls for mules and horses) proceeded rapidly through the summer and early fall. The barracks had sharply pitched roofs to shed snow and were designed to house sixty-three men each, plus their skis. More than a thousand buildings painted a uniform white went up in neat rows along a grid consisting of four avenues (named "A" through "D") intersected by twenty-one numbered streets. The barracks were concentrated to the west of the Eagle River, the mule stables to the east. The hospital was at the northern end of the valley, near the train depot, while the rifle and pistol ranges and areas set aside for bayonet and gas mask drill were at the southern end. Also on the southern end was a beginner's ski slope with a rope tow, known as "B Slope." The workers were racing against the changing seasons, because all the foundations for the buildings and underground utilities had to be completed before the ground was covered with snow. Construction also took place at a site seven miles to the south of the main camp and a thousand feet higher, on Cooper Hill, which rose above Tennessee Pass on the Continental Divide. There, workers laid out beginning, intermediate, and advanced ski slopes, serviced by a state-of-the-art six-thousand-foot T-bar ski lift, which rose another thousand vertical feet above the pass. From the summit of Cooper Hill, 14,440-foot Mount Elbert and 14,428-foot Mount Massive, the two highest peaks in the Rockies, and the second- and third-highest peaks in the lower forty-eight states, stood out on the horizon.

The civilian workers were paid well, especially by the Depression standards of the recent past, and additionally motivated by the belief that they were contributing to the war effort, but there were delays and labor disputes. Workers complained about the altitude, and also about a thick pall of coal smoke that was beginning to gather over the little valley from the increase in railroad traffic and, as it got colder in the fall, the coal-burning stoves installed to heat the new buildings.

While the camp was under construction, the army authorized creation of a Mountain Training Center (similar to other centers devoted to desert and amphibious warfare) to oversee the training of the mountain troop regiments. The MTC served as the functional equivalent of a divisional staff in the days before there were enough regiments to formally constitute a division. Colonel Rolfe, soon to be promoted to brigadier general, assumed command. As of early September, the center's official base was Camp Carson in Colorado, but on November 16 it moved to Camp Hale. It was followed the next day by the 601st Field Artillery Battalion (Pack); a second field artillery battalion, the 602nd; the 126th Engineer Mountain Battalion; and the 3rd Battalion of the 87th Mountain Infantry. There was also, of all things, a cavalry unit, the 10th Cavalry Reconnaissance Troop, or 10th Recon. Horses proving impractical in deep snow, the 10th Recon was converted to another purpose, with the cavalrymen transferred out and mountaineers and skiers transferred in. The 10th Recon became an instructional unit training soldiers in outdoor skills, although efforts to drop the "Cavalry" from its title proved unavailing, and confusion reigned at higher headquarters about its real function. (At one point its officers were ordered to Fort Riley in Kansas for advanced training at Cavalry School, although in the end they were spared that journey.) Another unique unit, which trained at Hale but had no tie to the mountain troops, also arrived late in 1942 — the 99th Infantry Battalion (Special). What made the 99th "special" was that it consisted entirely of first- and second-generation Norwegian-speaking immigrants. Originally intended for special operations inside Nazi-occupied Norway, the 99th was instead thrown into the fighting in France in June 1944.

The ski troops were, as always, magnets for publicity, and as their new home in the Rockies took shape, it became one of the better-known army camps in the United States. The ski correspondent for the *New York Times*, Frank Elkins, had been an enthusiastic publicist for the ski troops from the beginning, and in mid-October he filed a glowing and imaginative travelogue about what awaited them when they arrived at Camp Hale — although he doesn't seem to have actually visited the construction site himself: "Rocky Elk trails lead to passes and ridges that call for skilled rope climbing in Summer and equally skilled crampon and ice piton work in Winter. On several sides of the camp are long open slopes and forest trails where skiers will learn to 'schuss' and 'Christy' with full military equipment. Hundreds of instructors will bark their familiar, 'Bend the Knees!' to classes all over the slopes." It was a spectacular site for an army camp, in its own way as impressive as Mount Rainier or other well-known ski resorts, certainly to ski-minded soldiers — at least the first time they saw it. "Camp Hale is in a beautiful valley surrounded by rolling mountain tops similar to Sun Valley's best," Lieutenant Bill Dunkerly, a ski instructor, wrote of his own first impressions on arrival in December 1942 in a note published in the Sierra Club's monthly bulletin.

Construction was scheduled to finish on November 15, 1942, and advance elements of the mountain troops began moving into newly finished barracks in October. The main body arrived in December, under the command of just-promoted Brigadier General Rolfe. In those first months, Hale still felt more like a construction site than a neatly laid-out army camp. Piles of construction debris lay on all sides, and discarded nails proved a particular problem, puncturing the tires of army vehicles. Construction costs came to just over $31 million, about $2 million above the original estimate, and more expensive than the typical camp with all the modifications that had to be made to standard barracks and other buildings on account of the cold weather. Still, for all the problems and delays, to put together a small city capable of housing, feeding, training, and providing other necessary services to fifteen thousand soldiers (plus thousands of animals) in eight months was a remarkable achievement.

Camp Hale took on some of the glamour of the prewar ski resorts, complete with celebrity skiers. "Nation's Skiing Stars Prepare for Mountaineer Troop Service," Frank Elkins reported in the *New York Times* in mid-December 1942, relying on an official press release for his information. Chief among the "stars" arriving at Camp Hale was newcomer Torger Tokle, a twenty-two-year-old Norwegian immigrant, who was a bona fide celebrity at a time when ski jumping was a highly popular spectator sport in the United States; even his enlistment in the army in October merited a story in the *New York Times*. Since his arrival in the United States in January 1939, Tokle had won forty-two out of forty-eight ski jumping events in which he competed, smashing twenty-four records in the process, and setting a world distance record of 289 feet in a jump at Iron Mountain, Michigan, the previous March.

Other notables mentioned in the press release were Walter Prager and Peter Gabriel, plus Cornell University ski coach Ernst Engel, Dartmouth ski team captain Percy Rideout, Olaf Rodegaard of the Mount Hood Ski School, and Florian Haemmerle, instructor at the Sun Valley Ski School — a veritable League of Nations of American, Swiss, Norwegian, and Bavarian skiers. Whatever doubts persisted among higher-ups about the military utility of ski troops, they were certainly proving themselves a gift to army public relations.

Bob Livermore, newly commissioned as a second lieutenant upon graduating from Officer Candidate School at Fort Benning, arrived at Camp Hale in mid-April 1943, assigned to Company F in the 87th Mountain Infantry Regiment. It had been just over three years since that stormy night when he, Alex Bright, Roger Langley, and Minnie Dole had sat sipping their hot grog in the Orvis Inn in Manchester, Vermont,

Sergeant Torger Tokle.
THE DENVER PUBLIC LIBRARY (TMD452)

having the conversation that launched the ski troops. Shortly after his arrival in Colorado, Livermore wrote to "Cap" (Minnie, who seemed to accumulate nicknames, was known to ski friends as "Cap'n Dole of the Ski Patrol"), offering some first impressions of the fulfillment of their mutual dream. The camp, he confessed, was not quite what he expected. He was surprised "at the appearance of the men slopping around in every conceivable kind of uniform or lack of it, with skis, snowshoes, weasels and 'god knows' what at every corner." Still, given who he was and to whom he was writing, perhaps he wasn't all that surprised, and may even have taken a little pleasure in the distinctly irregular qualities of the scene before him. "I could feel the polish oozing right out of my Benning-trained system," he concluded, "even my shoes!"

A lack of polish, even a touch of "god knows what" whimsy, did not make much difference in the sheltering confines of Eagle Valley. To the extent that the ski troopers "bastard in the Mountain Infantry" identity contributed to a sense of unit cohesion, it probably made them better able to withstand the rigors of training on the slopes of Mount Rainier and the Colorado Rockies. Still to be determined was how an outfit as unorthodox as the mountain troops would perform in the storm of war still to come.

PFC John Parker Compton.

3

Camp Hale, 1943

"Heaven and Hell"

Well, here I am at Camp Hale, and let me tell you it's really
something! . . . you either like it immensely or dislike it immensely.
I belong to the former group.

— *Private John Parker "Eagle" Compton to his*
parents, October 5, 1943

"DEAREST PUNKIN," EIGHTEEN-YEAR-OLD PRIVATE MARTIN L. DANE-
man wrote to his seventeen-year-old girlfriend Lois Miller on arrival at
Camp Hale on April 29, 1943. He was assigned to Headquarters Company of what was to become the 3rd Battalion of the 86th Mountain Infantry Regiment, and had been in the army for a week. "Here I am at last
a ski trooper who doesn't yet know how to ski."

Daneman had taken the overnight passenger express train known as
the Rocky Mountain Rocket from Chicago's LaSalle Street Station to
Denver's Union Station, which completed the thousand-mile run between the two cities in under twenty hours. On arrival at the Denver ter-
minus in the morning, he transferred to a bus for the four-hour ride to
Camp Hale and his new life with the ski troopers. The last stretch of the
trip proved the hardest. It was another six months before regular bus
service became available to ferry soldiers around the camp. In April,
new arrivals could sometimes hitch a jeep ride into camp, but Daneman

wasn't in luck that day. Instead, from the Pando bus stop at Hale's northern end, he had to drag his heavy barracks bag through the camp gates to a headquarters building a half mile away, becoming aware for the first time just how thin the air was going to seem at 9,200 feet, while at the same time coming to regret his two-pack-a-day cigarette habit. After reporting in, he was directed to a two-story barracks building assigned to his company, another long, breathless hike away. There he found a vacant upper berth among the steel double-decker bunks. Finally he could write to his girlfriend, something he went on to do virtually every day he spent in the army until departing for Italy a year and a half later.

Lois, whom Daneman had met in high school in Chicago, had recently moved to San Francisco to live with her divorced mother. Marty, as everyone called him, a city boy who grew up in Brooklyn and Newark before his family settled in Chicago, had never been so far west or so high up before. Everything was new and marvelous: "This morning at 11 we caught a bus in here & came thru the most gorgeous plus country I've ever seen . . . We're right in the heart of a valley, 10000 ft up in the Rockies."

They came by the thousands to Camp Hale that year, some older but many of them boys just out of high school, like Daneman. Born after, or at least with no direct memory of, what was still being called the World War or the Great War, they had only a hazy notion of what their own war would be like, and where they might be called upon to fight and die. They were a post-Hemingway generation, and thus not inclined to romanticize war in chivalric or Victorian language, but still young and naïve enough to think of it as something of an adventure. There were many three-letter men in their ranks, arriving with the endorsement of the National Ski Patrol, but the proportion of experienced skiers and climbers was declining. Some, like Daneman, had no prior outdoors experience. (He cited his background as a high school runner and weightlifter as qualifications on his application to the mountain troops, by then sufficient to win approval from the NSPS.)

Albert N. Brockman was another eighteen-year-old ski trooper who had yet to learn how to ski when he passed through the gates of Camp Hale. He enlisted in Pennsylvania on February 1, 1943, and three weeks later reached the camp, initially assigned to A Company of the 86th Regiment. For those arriving that first winter, when the snow still lay deep on the ground, their basic and specialized training were jumbled together, as had been the case on Rainier a year earlier. Brockman wrote to his sister Betty on February 22: "Our skis will be issued soon and I will start training. Now we are having our basic and we drill for hours." Two weeks into basic training, Brockman wrote Betty to let her know that his company had just gotten their skis and other outdoor gear: "We are going to start skiing as soon as we finish on the rifle range . . . Yesterday I used Dick's camera and had one of the fellows take pictures of me in my camouflaged uniform with skis, rifle, pack and all. They will look pretty good if they turn out." A letter to Betty later that month reported on Brockman's first day on the slopes: "I have been skiing all day. We were practicing the stem turn today which is almost like the snow plow turn . . . During the morning I was on the tow with a dumb cluck who fell off and he pulled me off too. I got a slight charley horse in my leg from all the pulling and struggling trying to get back on."

By the end of March, with freshly honed skiing skills, Brockman's company was sent into the surrounding mountains for five days of maneuvers. On the final day, he reported to Betty, they climbed a thirteen-thousand-foot mountain on skis, attacking a "make believe enemy." At day's end, they were back in the snow caves they had dug for shelter when unexpected orders came to pack up and make the fourteen-mile ski back to camp, a four-hour slog without food or rest, arriving close to midnight. "I was one tired soldier," he concluded.

Unlike Brockman, who completed elementary ski training and spent nearly a week at high altitude on ski maneuvers within a month of his initial arrival at Camp Hale, Daneman, arriving at the end of April, when the snow had melted in the camp and the lower slopes surrounding it, would not don a pair of skis until the following October.

The variations in Brockman's and Daneman's experience, in the lack of any fixed, defining pattern of training, illustrate one of the many ways in which Camp Hale in 1943 differed from tried-and-true army practices. At flatland camps, large groups of recruits, all equally green, arrived at the same time and went through a lockstep instructional process as set down by Army Ground Forces directives; at Hale, in contrast, the Mountain Training Center instructors were constantly improvising, depending on the season and the supply of qualified volunteers, which ebbed and flowed. Some days three new recruits might show up at the camp, on other days a hundred, with previous time in service ranging from a week to years. As the official history of the MTC recounted: "Time after time General Rolfe begged Army Ground Forces not to send him raw recruits, but there was no satisfactory way to stop them, and the men kept coming direct from induction centers. This meant postponing their mountain training three months or else combining it with their basic training, neither of which was a good solution. Furthermore, the basic training had to be conducted in echelons, as the men trickled in."

Because Daneman arrived in warm weather, his time in basic bore a greater resemblance to the traditional version. He described the training with amused detachment some decades later; it had, he recalled, consisted largely of the systematic destruction "by means of tyrannical discipline of any remaining sense of individuality we had. Our total subjugation to the whims of authority was made crystal clear." A speck of dust found on a rifle during inspection on a dusty field (there hadn't been time to sow grass seed when the camp was constructed the year before) earned a demerit, which could mean the difference between receiving or being denied a weekend pass. Once, in the absence of visible dust on his rifle, having taken extra care preparing for inspection, Daneman still wound up receiving a demerit from the inspecting officer — for the dust on the bottom of his boots.

In letters to Lois, he chose to emphasize the positive side of the experience: "At last we've started basic & now I'm beginning to feel that I'm learning something." This was May 10, a dozen days after his arrival at camp. Newly arrived recruits were usually, although not always, assigned a week or two of light duty to help them adjust to the altitude. "We had some exercises to start off with & then an hour of drill," Daneman continued. "Back to class for more lectures, this time about guard duty. Then came chow & mail call."

Robert B. Ellis, also eighteen when he made his way to Camp Hale in the spring of 1943, came from a very different background than Daneman and Brockman. His parents had been American medical missionaries in Iran, where he was born in 1924, and he did not live in the United States until he was a teenager, his time abroad including a year in school in Switzerland. In the spring of 1943 he volunteered for the mountain troops, arriving at Camp Hale in mid-April, assigned to L Company of the 86th Regiment. His cohort of recruits for some reason had the ill luck to begin basic training at once, without the usual acclimatization. On his second or third day in camp, after drilling for four hours in wet driving snow, he wrote to his mother: "It certainly is going to be a tough three months of training I must say. The altitude is about 10,000 ft, and you certainly feel it. My nose bled today and everyone here has a cough, some sore throats, etc. The sergeant says you'll probably have a sore throat the whole time you're here." Their training days began with reveille at 5:30 a.m., and sometimes they did not get to bed until 11 at night. He liked the men in his platoon, almost all of whom he described as "college men," very competitive, and "certainly the hardest and toughest I have ever seen." Hard and tough they may have been. Still, as Ellis noted in a postscript to the letter, the day before "10 out of 50 men collapsed because of the altitude and exhaustion."

Around the time Private Ellis began basic, the newsprint edition of the official camp newspaper, the *Camp Hale Ski-Zette,* appeared for the first time. (It had a previous life as a mimeographed sheet.) Four pages long, published weekly for the next fourteen months, it offered a summary of war news, plus local reporting on the doings of what amounted to a small city — sports, entertainment, even wedding announcements. The tone was relentlessly upbeat and, given the mountain troopers' fondness for bawdy drinking songs, surprisingly wholesome. The *Ski-Zette,* for example, ran "pin-up" pictures of mountains instead of the usual girlie photos. In an aside in the first issue, the *Ski-Zette* noted that the camp commander, Colonel L. D. Brogan, was fond of calling Hale the "camp nearest Heaven."

There was disagreement among the men at Hale as to how accurately that described the camp's immediate neighborhood. Earlier that year, someone forwarded Minnie Dole a letter from an anonymous trooper in the 87th about the defining feature of life at Camp Hale: "The fellows are beginning to dub it Camp Hell . . . for the simple reason that almost every one of us was in excellent physical condition when we arrived from California," where the regiment had been on maneuvers in the fall of 1942, "and in almost no time at all we began to develop this 'Pando Hack' or 'Pando Plague.'"

Camp Hale was probably the most scenic military establishment in the continental United States, surrounded as it was by high and pristine mountaintops, but aesthetics aside, its construction in the Eagle Valley proved a colossal blunder. The valley walls helped to shelter the camp's inhabitants from the winter winds — but in the absence of cleansing breezes, the smoke produced by coal-burning locomotives (three to a train to get them up and over the steep grade leading to camp), plus that added by hundreds of coal-burning stoves in barracks and other buildings, pooled overhead in a dense brown cloud. It turned the accumulated snow below a sooty black and wreaked havoc on the respiratory system of camp inhabitants. The naturally dry alpine air only made things worse. Robert Ellis's lips split soon after he arrived and would not heal for weeks. At night it became standard practice to dump a bucket of water on the barracks floors to try to keep a little humidity in the air as the men slept. It didn't seem to help.

Within a day or so of arrival in camp, newcomers began to experience the symptoms of the infamous "Pando Hack" (also known as "Pandomonia"): first, a dry feeling in the nose and throat, followed by a slight cough, and two or three days later a painful sore throat and a brutal cough. Some men were so ill they could eat nothing solid; some could speak only in whispers. Sick call lists along with lines and wait times in the infirmary expanded, but medics had nothing to prescribe but aspirin and gargling, neither of which had much effect. The only cure was to get out of the smoggy valley, and some troopers began to look forward to maneuvers in the surrounding mountains for just that reason. Nineteen-year-old John Parker Compton, nicknamed "Eagle," arrived at Hale in September 1943 and was assigned to G Company, 86th Regiment. He had grown up in Westchester, New York, and was the grandson of the chairman of the board of the Ralston Purina Company, learning to ski on family vacations in the Canadian Laurentians, and at boarding school in Switzerland. (In an early letter to his grandparents he wrote that Camp Hale "sort of reminds me of when I was in Switzerland.") Notwithstanding this privileged background, at least to judge from Compton's letters home, the life of an army private was a source of genuine satisfaction to him. None of which made him immune to the common ailments of the camp. "My Pando Hack got better on bivouac — of all places," he wrote his parents some time later. "It's funny, I never get a sore throat, just a tickle as soon as I do any climbing." And Compton counted himself one of Camp Hale's fans.

Health problems were exacerbated by the difference between "mile-high" Denver and nearly two-mile-high Pando, separated by only a few hours' travel but by four thousand feet in elevation. Camp Hale's altitude was only a few hundred feet lower than that at which military pilots were required to strap on their oxygen masks. Charlie Houston, a noted Himalayan mountaineer (leader of the 1938 K2 expedition), was a navy physician during the war who studied the effects of high altitude on pilots. In a postwar study, he described the effects of "Acute Mountain Sickness," which occurs at an altitude above seven thousand to eight thousand feet after rapid ascent (which he defined as "a day or less"), including debilitating if usually temporary symptoms of "headache, nausea sometimes with vomiting, shortness of breath, disturbed sleep, difficulty with thinking."

Altitude sickness was only poorly understood in the 1940s even by experienced mountaineers, and certainly was an unfamiliar ailment to the average army doctor or medic. Many recruits began their time as mountain troopers feeling miserable from the effects of altitude, even before their Pando Hack developed; some wound up hospitalized for weeks at a stretch (and it didn't seem to occur to medical staff that a simple cure would be to move patients to a lower elevation). Training standards had to be modified so that for every thousand feet in elevation gain, an hour was added to expected marching time. By the fall of 1943, an Altitude Board at Camp Hale composed of medical officers met periodically to review cases of soldiers who could not acclimatize. "A large percentage of men can't take it up at this elevation," Private Harris Dusenbery, assigned to C Company of the 86th Regiment, wrote to his wife, Evelyn, in Portland, Oregon, in October 1943, shortly after his arrival, "but the only way to find out is to try the men out and to transfer to other camps those who can't staff the gaff. I am told that sixty men have transferred from our company to other camps in the last few months."

All of this might have been justified if the acclimatization the mountain regiments gained during training could have been expected to provide an edge in the coming fight. No one knew in 1943 where they would eventually be shipped overseas, although Norway, Italy, and Burma were the possibilities most often raised in barracks conversations. There was no battlefield where they might plausibly be deployed that would require them to fight at altitudes of nine thousand feet (where they presently lived), let alone thirteen thousand feet (where they climbed for maneuvers). Even if they were sent to the Alps, it wasn't summits but passes that would be their objective, and those were thousands of feet lower. (The Brenner Pass, the principal route through the Alps from Italy to Austria, was only 4,495 feet, lower than the Paradise Valley buildings that housed the 87th on Mount Rainier.) And in any case, whatever level of acclimatization the mountain troops acquired to altitude while training would have worn off long before they could travel by train across the continent and by troopship over the ocean to reach their ultimate frontline destination. Overall, the advantages Camp Hale offered in terms of proximity to snow slopes and other mountain training grounds were outweighed by its toll on the health and morale of the mountain troopers.

The camp's deficiencies were compounded by deficiencies in the mountain regiments' leadership, displayed early in 1943 during maneuvers on Homestake Peak. The 13,209-foot mountain is located on the northern end of the Colorado Rockies' Sawatch Range, part of the Continental Divide, about twelve miles to the southwest of the camp. Army Ground Forces had decided it was time for the mountain troops to put a sizeable force into the field to test the effectiveness of their training. A battalion of infantry from the 87th Regiment, along with the 99th Field Artillery battalion, received orders to set out from Tennessee Pass to Homestake Peak on February 4 for eight days of maneuvers. Their assignment was to establish a defensive line just below the summit of the mountain, repelling raids by designated "enemy" units. The ski troopers' main camp was located at about two thousand feet below the summit, on the shores of Homestake Lake.

Civilians Minnie Dole and John Morgan of the National Ski Patrol were invited by the War Department not only to observe but also to join the maneuvers. They flew to Denver with Major Walter Wood, an experienced mountaineer who, as a civilian adviser in 1941, had helped test cold weather gear for the army in Alaska and the Yukon, currently assigned to G4 (Logistics), and Captain Jack Tappin, a champion skier in civilian life, commissioned in 1942 and serving with G3 (Operations and Training) at Army Ground Forces headquarters. From Denver, they drove to Camp Hale via Tennessee Pass. The last time Dole had visited the mountain troops had been on Mount Rainier, about as glorious and pristine a setting imaginable. Whatever he was expecting this time, Dole's first view of the new camp brought up images of dark satanic mills, not some idyllic ski resort. It reminded him "of a large industrial development. It had a huge pall of smoke hanging over it." That night, reunited with old friends John Jay and Paul Townsend, Dole listened to their "succession of gripes" about everything from the Pando Hack to the lack of weekend leave. Major Wood reminded the ski troopers that, after all, there was a war on, and they should be happy not to be training in some godforsaken Louisiana swamp. But Jay and Townsend made clear to Dole in language "that blistered the walls" that Hale was no paradise (or Paradise Valley).

On the second day of maneuvers, Dole, Morgan, and others on the inspection team set off on skis from Tennessee Pass up Homestake Peak, burdened with heavy packs, but grateful that, unlike the soldiers they accompanied, they weren't carrying M1 rifles (an extra nine and a half pounds), and that a path through the deep powder snow had been broken by the men who went before. As they were soon to learn, from the first moments of the exercise, inexperienced officers bungled the operation. They had required the soldiers to stand around for two hours before beginning to climb, during which the men were thoroughly chilled, and then set out at an unreasonable pace in light of the burdens they carried. Some men hadn't been properly instructed in how to wax their skis for ascending slopes, and exhausted themselves as they floundered upward. The mules in the accompanying pack trains also balked when the snow came up to their bellies. Supplies had to be reloaded onto sleds and hauled up by soldiers acting as beasts of burden, attached to the loads by harnesses. Some soldiers got lost; others gave up and fell out of line; a few actually deserted. Fully half the soldiers on the maneuvers had never been snow camping before. On the way up the mountain, Dole and his companions encountered an exhausted, ice-encrusted soldier who confessed in a southern accent that he was heading back to camp without permission, explaining, "I just cain't take this stuff." Before turning in that night at the Homestake Lake encampment, as the temperature dropped to thirty degrees below zero, Dole took a walk with a sergeant around the tents. They were astounded to come upon two soldiers standing barefoot in the snow. Dole recorded the ensuing exchange:

> "What do you guys think you're doing?" the sergeant exploded.
>
> "We figured that if we froze them up a bit, we'd get evacuated out of this hellhole."
>
> The sergeant must have been hanging around the mule skinners because what he said next would have blistered even a mule's ear.

In what was likely the highest casualty rate in the history of army maneuvers until then, some 260 soldiers, roughly a quarter of a battalion, developed frostbite or other ailments in the first twenty-four hours of the exercise, perhaps self-induced in a few cases, but mostly involuntarily. In actual combat, a 25 percent casualty rate in a single day would have been considered catastrophic. It could have been worse; there were no deaths, although that was partly through sheer luck. Major Wood intervened when a group of soldiers were ordered to retrieve airdropped supplies off an avalanche-prone hillside on the east face of Homestake Peak. Two days later, Colonel David Ruffner, commanding the pack artillery, a Virginia Military Institute graduate and veteran of the First World War regarded as highly competent but lacking in mountain experience, had several artillery rounds fired on Homestake's east face from the 75 mm howitzers the mules and men under his command had hauled up from Tennessee Pass. He wanted to see if his guns could trigger an avalanche — a technique that, hypothetically, might be used in combat to sweep aside an oncoming enemy force. It worked, all right, and tons of snow and ice cascaded spectacularly down the mountainside. But Ruffner miscalculated just how far the avalanche would travel, and it reached all the way to Homestake Lake, threatening though thankfully not engulfing soldiers camping on the far shore.

In the midst of this accumulation of mishaps, the planned tactical exercise was canceled. The troopers remained on the mountain practicing high-altitude and deep snow travel and survival skills. As a stream of injured and demoralized men were evacuated from Homestake over successive days, those who knew their winter warfare history began to call the whole misadventure "the retreat from Moscow."

In his postwar memoir, Dole wrote that he came away from his visit to Hale "enthralled that the camp was in existence and in capable hands." But he didn't sound so enthralled at the time. The Homestake maneuvers, he wrote in a report for the War Department, were yet another example of the army ignoring the advice of the real experts, the men he and the NSPS had recruited to the mountain troops, few of whom had yet risen to officer rank. The solution to the mountain troops' problems was for the army to stop being so "rank happy, with rank at the top and brains at the bottom." Major Wood and other observers filed their own critical reports.

Back in New York two months later, Dole received a letter from another recent visitor to Camp Hale, Frank Howard of the California Ski Association, offering additional insight into the mountain troopers' winter of discontent. On the basis of conversations with men he knew well from civilian life, Howard wrote, "I think that the main thing the boys feel is that they are not getting competent leadership ... The statement I heard over and over from everyone from the junior officers who ski to the privates was 'If this outfit should go into combat we'd be slaughtered.' Whether this statement is true or not the feeling that it is has a serious effect on the men's morale. There was dissatisfaction, too, with the borrowed officers from 'HQ only knows where,' the officers who get lost where a boy scout could find his way home."

It might seem unlikely that Dole or any other civilian could persuade the army that the wisdom of enlisted men should count more than the authority of rank. But surprisingly, Army Ground Forces chief General Leslie James McNair, who had opposed the creation of the ski troops back in 1941, and who was never entirely convinced that they were a good idea, nonetheless found Dole's argument in this case persuasive. In a critical letter to General Rolfe (which amounted to a reprimand in all but name), McNair pointed out the failures in leadership revealed by the Homestake maneuvers and declared: "The large proportion of experienced woodsmen, mountaineers, guides and trappers in the enlisted and lower commissioned grades provides an excellent source of technical knowledge. This source should be used to the utmost in the development of instructional training technique which is founded on time-tested mountain and winter procedures."

Two things happened in response to McNair's letter. One is that

Rolfe saw to it that nearly two hundred enlisted men and NCOs from the mountain regiments were dispatched to Officer Candidate School at Fort Benning, with the promise that upon being commissioned second lieutenants, they would return to serve with one of the mountain regiments. And in midsummer, Rolfe himself was sacked as commander of the mountain troops, replaced by Major General Lloyd Jones. The Missouri-born Jones, fifty-four years old with no previous skiing or mountaineering experience, and suffering from a chronic case of bronchitis, was not an obvious choice as Rolfe's successor. But he was reputed to know something about cold weather fighting, having commanded the force of soldiers and sailors that occupied Amchitka in the Aleutian Islands in January 1943 in preparation for a future assault on Japanese-occupied islands in the chain. As for Pinkie Rolfe, he was reassigned to the post of deputy commander of the 71st Infantry Division and subsequently took part in the invasion of Germany in 1945.

At the same time as the shift in command, the mountain infantry regiments finally acquired divisional status in July 1943. Although the original 87th Mountain Infantry Regiment had by this time been dispatched for duty elsewhere, there were now three infantry regiments at Hale: the 86th Regiment, activated on December 12, 1942; the 85th Regiment, activated on July 15, 1943; and, on what turned out to be temporary assignment, the 90th Regiment, also activated in mid-July, and drawing heavily on men who had previously trained with the 86th. The new division included a number of auxiliary units (including three battalions of field artillery, a medical battalion, a mountain engineer battalion, an anti-tank battalion, and a signal company). With the completion of the three-infantry regiment triangle, the 10th Light Division (Pack, Alpine) came into official existence — the "Light" in its name meaning both that at an authorized strength of roughly thirteen thousand men, it was smaller by about a thousand men than a regular army division, and that its heaviest artillery pieces, 75 mm howitzers, were of lesser caliber than the standard 105 mm and 155 mm weapons. The men of the division were authorized to wear a distinctive patch on their uniforms, two red bayonets crossed against a blue powder keg–shaped background, forming the Roman numeral ten. The following year, mountain troopers were authorized to wear their ski boots and ski caps off-base, another morale-builder.

With the creation of the 10th, the Mountain Training Center was now officially dissolved. A hundred-strong Mountain Training Group remained as its legacy. Although some of the Mountain Training Group's personnel stayed on at Hale, others were dispatched to Seneca Rock, West Virginia, to instruct flatland troops in rock climbing and other outdoor skills. Soldiers from other units, meeting instructors from the 10th Mountain Division, were amazed at the low-key, non-military quality of the instruction. Sergeant James Goodwin of the Mountain Training Group, who came to Seneca Rock in 1943, recalled listening to another instructor, an Austrian refugee, gently encouraging some reluctant trainees to tackle a steep rock pitch. "Men, climbing rocks iss like making luff to vimen. It takes courage, but it's lots uff fun!" The young men thought about that for a moment, and then all turned eagerly to the challenge.

Despite the fact that its authorized numbers were fewer than that of a regular division, the 10th remained understrength. The army had suspended the NSPS's role in recruiting mountain troops in the summer of 1942, with the result that many qualified skiers and mountaineers joined other units. At the army's request, the Ski Patrol resumed its recruiting efforts at the start of 1943, with the goal of gaining two thousand recruits in the space of ninety days to fill the ranks of the new 86th Regiment. Civilian skiers and mountaineers, along with rangers, trappers, timber cruisers, and other men with outdoor backgrounds, still headed to Camp Hale, but the NSPS was finding it necessary to dilute its standards to meet the quota. Minnie Dole, in an interview with a New York journalist in January 1943 about the recruiting effort, told him that the NSPS was "eager to contact husky schoolboys and collegians who have a burning desire to serve with mountain troops . . . Almost any Eagle scout has the makings of a mountain trooper." It was under this loosened mandate that recruits like Marty Daneman came to serve in the 86th.

Recruitment efforts were aided by the mountain regiments' skillful courtship of the press and public favor, overseen by public relations officer and filmmaker Captain John Jay. Jay's documentary film about the training on Mount Rainier in 1942, *They Climb to Conquer,* and a 1943 follow-up, *The Ski Patrol,* wowed civilian audiences and were popular among the soldiers at Camp Hale, who enjoyed seeing themselves and their friends on the screen. At Jay's behest, an attractive young skier named Debbie Bankart, one of the few female ski instructors before the war, took a print of *The Ski Patrol* on a national tour of schools and ski clubs, distributing application forms after each showing. She proved one of the 10th's best recruiters.

Newspaper and magazine reporters were frequently invited to watch demonstrations of the skiing and climbing abilities of the troopers in the field. One early feature story that ran in the *Denver Post* in mid-January 1943 proclaimed in its headline, "Troops Training at Camp Hale Are Tough Triple-Threat Men; Must Be Able to Ski, Ride Mules and Use Mountain Motorized Equipment; None But Real He-Men Need Apply." The *Saturday Evening Post,* a weekly magazine second only to *Life* in popularity and influence in the 1940s, devoted its cover for March 27, 1943, to an illustration of a kneeling ski trooper in white camouflage outerwear. The model for the cover was Horace Quick, a former Park Service ranger and member of the 87th Regiment. Purists noted that the stiff-soled mountain boots worn by troopers could not possibly bend in the middle as illustrated. But the image delighted Minnie Dole, who bought a thousand copies of the issue, and the cover was used as a poster to drum up interest in the mountain troops.

———

Hollywood also helped, with a couple of films that celebrated the cinematically screen-pleasing maneuvers of the ski troops on their home territory. A 1943 Warner Bros. documentary short, the twenty-minute-long *Mountain Fighters,* filmed at Hale, featured a fictional lead character named "Sven Torger," based on the real Torger Tokle, and included thrilling scenes of ski troopers schussing the slopes. It was followed in 1944 by Paramount's *I Love a Soldier,* starring Paulette Goddard, a soppy feature film about a wartime courtship, mildly redeemed by still more thrilling downhill racing performed by some of the best skiers at Camp Hale. The official postwar *History of the Mountain Training Center* noted drily that as a result of the avalanche of favorable publicity cascading out of Camp Hale, "the average American citizen seemed more interested in the 'ski troops' . . . than was the War Department."

Manufacturers also liked to link their corporate image to the mountain troops. The Goodyear rubber company ran a full-page advertisement in the weekly magazine *Collier's* in the spring of 1944, depicting ice-ax-wielding troopers on high mountain ridges, taking the "'High' Way to Berlin," with Bramani rubber soles on their combat boots, while Winchester firearms ran a similar advertisement in the *Saturday Evening Post,* depicting a skiing trooper with an M1 Garand rifle strapped to his back, describing such men as "the finest of our fighters . . . superb physical specimens."

For all the glamour that clung to the ski troopers like a dusting of powder snow, the mountain regiments still faced a deficit of qualified recruits in the summer of 1943. Accordingly, over the next few months the army transferred several thousand non-volunteers to the ranks of the 10th, many of them assigned to the 90th. A large proportion of the newcomers were, in the mysterious logic of military decision making, drawn from southern units, along with a group of NCOs from Hawaii. Few of the transfers were happy to find themselves at Camp Hale or in the ski troops, and they radiated gloom. They were given the mocking nickname "Pineapple Boys" by more experienced mountaineers. Glen Dawson, a leading Sierra Club climber and skier assigned to the Mountain Training Group on joining the 10th, noted in his journal in November 1943: "At first most of the men here asked to come, but to fill up the division a large number were shanghaied and they hate it here. It seems like they are spoiling whatever morale the volunteers had."

The youngest, rawest recruits often developed in a few months' training an expertise in coping with mountainous terrain that many of their NCOs and officers failed to match. Marty Daneman, who less than eight months earlier had arrived at Hale with no outdoor experience at all, in December 1943 wrote to his girlfriend describing one officer's backcountry incompetence. On the second day of an overnight training exercise, his company was heading down a ridgeline back to Camp Hale when "the Major noticed that our artillery liaison officer was missing" and someone would need to climb back up the mountain to find him. "I was elected — so I climbed all the way up again, found the Lt., pondering over a map, & led him down. He was very much ashamed & I don't blame him," Daneman observed, before adding charitably, "tho it is easy to get lost up there."

Among the wave of unwilling and incompetent additions to their ranks, the mountain troops also gained a few particularly well-suited recruits in 1943. One of their number was Paul Petzoldt, a Wyoming climber who, on the 1938 American K2 expedition, reached an elevation of over 26,000 feet on the world's second-highest mountain before having to turn back. When Petzoldt arrived as a thirty-five-year-old private at Camp Hale, he was put to work scrubbing floors. A medical officer recognized his name and came up with a better assignment. He arranged for Petzoldt to be promoted to sergeant and put in charge of a squad to experiment with toboggans, zip lines, and other techniques for quick evacuation of the wounded from mountainous terrain. On maneuvers, where cases of frostbite were common, as well as the occasional broken leg, and in one case acute appendicitis, Petzoldt supervised evacuations.

Another celebrity figure in mountain sports arrived at Camp Hale in late May 1943. "Friedl Pfeifer, One-Time Head of Sun Valley, Joins Skiers," the *Ski-Zette* trumpeted in a headline in the July 16, 1943, issue. The thirty-two-year-old Pfeifer had been first assistant ski instructor at Hannes Schneider's Austrian resort at St. Anton for more than a decade when the Nazi Anschluss and Schneider's arrest prompted him to flee to the United States. There he was hired by Averell Harriman to oversee the Sun Valley ski school, where he coached a string of Hollywood celebrities in the Arlberg technique, including the actress Claudette Colbert and actor Gary Cooper. For three years running, Pfeifer won the United States national slalom ski championship. He also fell in love with a Salt Lake City girl (daughter of a bank president, no less), whom he married in 1940. It was a seemingly idyllic life for a wartime refugee until, on an early morning two days after Pearl Harbor, federal agents pounded on his door, informed him he was being arrested as an enemy alien, put him in handcuffs, and hustled him away from his wife and newborn son. It was several weeks before his family secured his release from a North Dakota detention center. As a non-citizen with a wife and baby he could have sat out the war, but he chose instead to join the mountain troops, where he was among the most highly qualified of the 10th's ski instructors, along with other St. Anton alumni like Luggi Foeger, Toni Matt, and Herbert Schneider. On an early training exercise in June, Pfeifer was part of a detachment that made a twenty-mile march across the mountains, ending up in the down-at-the-heels mining town of Aspen. Camping at the base of Aspen Mountain, he was reminded by the view of the mountains surrounding St. Anton am Arlberg in the Austrian Alps and, as he later put it, "felt at that moment an overwhelming sense of my future before me."

Other newcomers to Camp Hale that spring and summer included a contingent of several hundred women from the Women's Army Auxiliary Corps (WAAC), soon renamed the Women's Army Corps (or "WACs"). They served in positions from the mess halls to the hospital to the motor pool, freeing up male soldiers for other roles. They were a welcome addition, as far as the men of the 10th were concerned.

Not so another group who arrived toward the end of the summer — several hundred German prisoners of war. Robert Ellis, now serving with F Company of the 85th, reported to his family: "About 300 German prisoners were brought here the other day, and we see them being taken here and there in trucks, closely guarded of course. They look quite healthy and wear the hats of Rommel's Africa Corps." In addition to good health, the German prisoners seem to have retained high morale, marching smartly to and from labor assignments, singing as they did so. They did not behave like defeated men, and the Americans in the camp took their behavior as deliberately insolent. Some fantasized about turning their rifles from the targets on the firing range onto the passing columns of prisoners. Harris Dusenbery wasn't among them, but wrote mildly to his wife in October, "The boys say that those prisoners fare a lot better than the soldiers do here." Fraternization between the two groups was officially forbidden, but as far as the men of the 10th were concerned, the rule was unnecessary; they weren't looking to make friends with the enemy.

In the winters of 1942–43 and 1943–44, there was no better place in the world to learn to ski than Camp Hale. Soon after it opened, *New York Times* reporter Frank Elkins wrote yet another column about his favorite wartime topic, the ski troopers. "These soldiers," he noted in late January 1943, "receive the finest ski instruction in the world and get paid for it." Army publicists probably had mixed feelings about the characterization; it would be attractive to recruits, but it reinforced a Camp-

Hale-as-Sun-Valley theme they were not eager to promote. As a simple observation, though, it happened to be true.

Most new recruits began their ski training on B Slope, which rose from 9,300 feet at the south end of the camp to the top of scenic Taylor Hill, nearly twelve thousand feet high, which visually marked the end of the camp's vista when seen from the valley floor. There were four skiing slopes located around the camp, each with its own five-hundred-foot rope tow, but B Slope, which faced north, had the best snowpack and was the most used. On B Slope, recruits learned cross-country skiing, climbing (sidestepping, kick turns, herringbone), and the basics of downhill technique. Twenty-year-old Brooklyn-born Arnold C. Holeywell arrived at Hale at the end of February 1943, assigned to E Company of the 86th. In early April he wrote to his mother, clearly thrilled with the training he was receiving: "Well, this starts 5th week here at Camp Hale! And this morning for the first time I went skiing. It was great! The sun these days is bright and hot. It sure adds to the pleasure of skiing. You don't know the enjoyment of being able to ski in a place like this . . . We would ski for about 50 feet then stop in the shade of a pine and then start off again. What fun. I'm really enjoying this army life."

After gaining familiarity with the basics on B Slope, the trainees that first winter at Hale moved up to Cooper Hill, above Tennessee Pass. (Later on, all instruction, including beginning skiing, would be offered on Cooper Hill.) Several dozen ski instructors, housed in barracks thrown up before the war for a Civilian Conservation Corps (CCC) camp, awaited the students. For an enlisted man, being designated a ski instructor was the best assignment in the mountain regiments. Dick Nebeker, just out of high school, arrived at Camp Hale in January 1943 to join C Company of the 86th Regiment, and without spending any time in basic, was immediately dispatched to Cooper Hill because of his previous experience as a ski instructor at the Alta ski area in Utah. "This was really living!" he recalled after the war. "I had a white tape armband to identify myself as a ski instructor. I could instruct and order lieutenants and captains, and was only 18." The instructors had their own cook, handpicked by Walter Prager. As Nebeker remembered fondly, "We had good chow and slept in a warm barracks in our eider down sleeping bags."

Dick Nebeker (left) with two other soldiers, Cooper Hill training area, 1943.
THE DENVER PUBLIC LIBRARY (TMD351-2017-455)

Donald B. Potter was on the Williams College ski team, completing his third semester at the college in early 1943, when, like a lot of other Williams skiers, he decided to drop out and enlist in the mountain troops, initially assigned to B Company of the 86th. Within a few weeks of his arrival in March, he too was taken out of basic training to join the ski instructors on Cooper Hill. After his first day on the slopes, he wrote to his sister back in the Adirondacks, where he had learned to ski as a child, that being a ski instructor "is swell for one's own skiing" and that he had already learned a "powerful lot." He went on: "G.I. skiing is regular snow plow, stem & stem christies—it's no different from any other controlled method (under such names as Arlberg, etc.) I have an advanced class, and it looks like I'll have a chance to really make something out of them."

Fresh from Fort Benning, Second Lieutenant Frederick C. Miller arrived at Hale in February 1943, initially assigned to B Company of the 87th Regiment. He had skied before the war so went directly to Cooper Hill. "This skiing we do each day is not exactly like the civilian skiing I used to do," he wrote to his mother during his first month at Hale:

10th Mountain Division ski instructors, Cooper Hill.
THE DENVER PUBLIC LIBRARY (TMD351-2017-1958)

We have steep slopes, good tows and equipment and all, but it's all done with 35-lb packs, so we may become used to them . . . I'm in an advanced class — the highest — and the instruction is given by men who last year were receiving $5 an hour [a very good wage in 1942] for the same job. My instructor is especially good — he comes from Hannes Schneider's School at North Conway — Arthur Doucette . . . I never felt so well on skis before. As a matter of fact, I expect to be picked for special instruction and made an Officer Supervisor of enlisted instructors. Hope I can climb mountains half as well as I can ski down them.

For the recruits dispatched to Cooper Hill, getting there on foot was part of the training. On Monday mornings, troopers set out on a seven-mile march up Highway 24 wearing eighty- to ninety-pound packs, their skis attached to their knapsacks, and rifles slung over their shoulders. Once atop the pass, they would bivouac for the week in their two-man nylon tents. Every day for five days, they were out on the slopes eight hours a day, sometimes longer, taking the T-bar ride to the summit of Cooper Hill, making the mile-plus run to the base as their Austrian instructors bellowed, "Bend zee knees!," and then lining up to do it again.

10th Mountain troopers with skis attached to rucksacks.
THE DENVER PUBLIC LIBRARY (TMD479)

Sometimes on clear nights they'd keep skiing in the moonlight until 8 or 9 p.m. On Fridays, they marched back down to camp. They would repeat the same routine the following week (and if they failed to master the basics, they might be back for a third week). At the end of ski training they took a proficiency test, which, given the quality of instruction, most of them passed. Marty Daneman, the self-described "ski trooper who didn't know how to ski" when he arrived at Hale, felt that by the time he was done with B Slope and Cooper Hill, and passed the proficiency test, he "could ski with the best of them. Well almost."

In warmer weather, outdoor training shifted from the slopes to the cliffs east of camp, and another set of cliffs about three miles north of camp along Homestake Creek. There troopers learned the basics of rock climbing, including rope craft, five kinds of knots (overhand, square, butterfly, bowline on a bite, and bowline), belaying, rappelling, and the Tyrolean traverse. They had excellent equipment, better than that available to prewar civilian climbers. Harris Dusenbery wrote to his wife after attending rock climbing school in praise of the new nylon climbing ropes, which he described as "wonderful so soft and pliable . . . Also they have 10% stretch in them. This comes in very handy in breaking falls." And the troopers had the benefit of instruction from some of the country's leading climbers, although there were never quite enough of them.

Among the best-known climbers in the mountain troops was David Brower. In 1939 he and three other Bay Area climbers garnered national attention for the first ascent of Shiprock, a lofty isolated peak on New Mexico's high desert plains, an achievement he chronicled in an article in the pages of the *Saturday Evening Post.* Brower first arrived at Hale in late 1942 as a thirty-year-old private, departing in January for Officer Candidate School at Fort Benning, and returning in May as a second lieutenant to an assignment as instructor with the 86th Regiment. Brower's *Manual of Ski Mountaineering,* published by the University of California Press in 1942, was already a basic text for instructors throughout the 10th Mountain Division, and he contributed to writing the army's own field manual for mountain fighting.

Most of the 10th's rock climbing and mountaineering instructors had been active before the war in regional outdoor organizations like Brower's Sierra Club in California, the New England–based Appalachian Mountain Club, and the Seattle-based Mountaineers. The outdoor clubs proudly publicized the military service of their members during the war. The December 1943 issue of the journal of the Mountaineers, for example, listed several hundred members then in uniform, mostly in the army (including twenty-year-old Seattle native Fred Beckey, a private with the medics in the 85th Mountain Infantry Regiment who arrived at Camp Hale in July, and who in a long postwar climbing career would be credited with over a thousand first ascents). The same issue of *The Mountaineer* included an article by another member serving in the military, Lieutenant John W. James, also of the 85th, who called Camp Hale "the ski school and mountaineering school of the world." Climbing, unlike skiing, remained a fairly exotic pursuit in the United States in the 1930s, counting its enthusiasts in the thousands rather than the millions. And its leading figures never quite gained the celebrity of the star skiers of the prewar era — in part because climbing didn't lend itself to dramatic film portrayals in the way skiing did. But the war would boost the popularity of mountaineering as well as skiing. In his article, Lieutenant James predicted that when peace came, many veterans of the 10th would continue to climb mountains "for their own enjoyment and exercise," and that as a result, the "future of mountaineering is most surely in good hands."

———

One other skill the mountain troops were expected to learn was how to care for, pack, and lead mules. While trucks and jeeps delivered supplies to soldiers on the front lines in flatland units, mules were better suited for the rough, roadless terrain that the mountain troops would encounter. Each regiment had attached to it a quartermaster company of full-time mule skinners, many of them former cowboys and including a couple of rodeo stars, along with several hundred mules. The pack artillery battalions attached to the division (the 604th, 605th, and 616th) drew their cadre from prewar artillery units in which artillerymen had long familiarity with mules and used them to transport their 75 mm pack howitzers, which broke down for transportation into six parts. The mule skinners of the quartermaster and artillery units were under strict orders not to mistreat the mules, and having spent enough time in their company, they knew how to get the most effort out of them. Individual artillerymen were assigned a single mule to care for, including grooming and feeding. There was never much love between men and mules, but as Sergeant Charles Webb of the 616th recalled, "Once a soldier and his animal became acquainted and accustomed to each other, it was better that the assignment did not change."

The army thought it would be a good idea if regular mountain troopers also had some familiarity with mule packing. No one seems to have written home after time devoted to such training with much enthusiasm about the experience. Marty Daneman reported to girlfriend Lois in December 1943 at the start of his week of mule duty: "By the end of the week I should not only be a first rate mule skinner, but I should smell like 1 as well—There is nothing which smells as 'sweet' as a mule." Harry Robert (Bob) Krear, twenty-one years old, a former member of the Pennsylvania State University ski team who joined L Company, 86th Regiment, in the fall of 1943, felt aggrieved after he was kicked in the stomach "by a mule that did not even know me, and I had not even uttered a bad word in its direction." Earl E. Clark, a second lieutenant who had joined the 87th soon after its formation, was put in temporary charge of the mule pack trains bringing supplies up to the mountains during maneuvers in June 1943, a new experience for the young officer. It "introduced several thousand new cuss words into my vocabulary," he noted in a letter home. First, the mule he was given as a riding mount tossed him into a very cold mountain creek. Then, during the first night out, all of the mules stampeded, many of them shedding their loads as they ran free, so that Clark and his men spent the hours until dawn gathering up the strays and reloading them with boxes of rations and ammunition that weighed between 80 and 110 pounds each. "What an animal!" he concluded, not affectionately.

In addition to their training in outdoor skills, the men of the 10th were also, of course, being trained to kill. Here too, Camp Hale's location and climate turned out to be not entirely advantageous. Private John Parker Compton wrote to his brother Jim, a marine lieutenant, in late October 1943, a few weeks into basic, to report on his training on the firing range. His platoon had spent the week putting in thirteen-hour days, every day, practicing marksmanship with their newly issued M1 rifles: "Through rain, snow, and sleet 54 recruits in their third week trudged the two miles to the range—complete with knapsacks, rifles, and lunches. When we got there the sun was still behind the mountains, but there was light enough to start firing by seven-thirty. We all practiced till Thursday from 200, 300, and 500 yards . . . We fired kneeling and off hand from 200 yards, prone from 500, and prone, sitting, and rapid fire from 300. I forgot to mention rapid fire from the sitting position at 200 too." On Friday they were tested ("record fire"), and Compton got the highest score in the platoon, qualifying as an expert at 189 out of 210, "only 6 points from the all-time camp record." The M1, he concluded, "is a beautiful rifle. I clean it every night for an hour."

Sometimes it was so cold the men could barely squeeze the trigger of their rifle, and sometimes the fog and blowing snow were so thick that the targets on the firing range disappeared from sight. Then weapons training shifted to fifty-foot indoor ranges built into concrete-walled training halls. Inside, soldiers could fire only .22-caliber rifles; missed shots from the heavier .30-caliber M1s would have soon chewed the wall behind the target to bits.

Camp Hale was a noisy place most days. When they weren't on one of the base's firing ranges (there were separate ranges for practicing with pistols and machine guns), the troopers might be found practicing tossing hand grenades. They assaulted pillboxes with flamethrowers, bazookas, and dynamite. They blew up barbed wire entanglements with Bangalore torpedoes. Trainees were also required to take what was called an "infiltration course," which reminded Private Albert Brockman of "one of the scenes you see in the movies of the western front in the last war." Except it was a lot more realistic than a movie, because while they were advancing on an entrenched "enemy" position, live machine gun bullets were being fired over the soldiers' heads, and real dynamite charges were exploding to their left and right. Brockman offered a graphic description of the experience in a letter to his father:

> When you first climb over the trench after hearing the machine gun bullets going over you would be surprised how low you can get to the ground. The bullets sound just like someone snapping their finger real loud when you are in a trench. You crawl forward about 5 feet and see two holes that have dynamite in them. There's no way to go around so you go between them and about that time they go off, dirt showers down on you and you can't hear anything. Then you come to a barbed wire fence and after you get through that you come to a trench filled with water. You climb through that and then the dynamite really start to go off and dirt comes down in torrents . . . Once a rock from one of the explosions hit my helmet and I thought it was a bullet. I ground my face in the dirt and left it there for the rest of the course . . . I was never so dirty in my life as when I finished that.

The reward for all the arduous training during the week, dependent on good behavior and passing inspection, was a weekend pass, available every other week, allowing soldiers thirty-six hours' freedom off-base, from noon on Saturday to midnight on Sunday. Denver, the nearest big city, was a four-hour drive over mountain roads that were a questionable proposition in wintertime. The few soldiers with private automobiles could subsidize their own trips to the city by charging passengers from the camp a stiff one-way fare of between $1.50 and $3.50. Denver had restaurants and bars and movie houses and, at least compared to Hale, clean air and low altitude. The Brown Palace Hotel on 17th Street in downtown Denver, built in 1892 and famous for housing the "Unsinkable Molly Brown" after she survived the sinking of the *Titanic,* was a favorite if expensive place to stay. The men of the 10th did not endear themselves to the hotel's management the night a group of them, equipped with the green army climbing ropes, famously demonstrated rappelling technique from a perch on a high balcony to the floor of the hotel's atrium.

Colorado Springs to the southeast, and, like Denver, several thousand feet lower in elevation, was another favorite location for a weekend pass. Robert Ellis got his first weekend leave after two months of training and reported to his family that it was "absolutely wonderful to get away from camp and its interminable routine for a few days." With three friends from his company, he'd "had the grandest time just laughing and talking and walking in the parks and avenues. It's a beautiful resort town and would be a great place to spend a real vacation."

Leadville was much closer, forty-five minutes away by bus, but because of its reputation for prostitution and illegal gambling was off-limits to soldiers until February 1943, when, supposedly, the worst illicit attractions had been contained. The authorities made a show of closing down the most notorious commercial offenders against public order and morality, and wholesome alternatives were promoted, like the shows and dances for the soldiers sponsored by the local USO club. For the most part, though, the main attractions remained bars and brothels.

College and fraternity affiliations provided some soldiers with opportunities for off-base relaxation with those from similar backgrounds. "Nine of us from Williams went to Glenwood [Springs] this weekend," nineteen-year-old Private Donald Potter wrote his mother a few months after arriving at Hale. "We stayed at the Summers' ranch. George Summers is a fraternity brother so they are glad to have any Williams men and especially Sigs. They have an amazing place—a peeled log summer mansion with every gadget imaginable. We did some riding, lots of singing and plenty of relaxing on a nice green lawn."

Some soldiers got off the beaten track and had genuine adventures in doing so. Among them was Private Arnold Holeywell of Brooklyn. On a Saturday in early September, he set off shortly after noon with a buddy, hitchhiking to Grand Junction, nearly two hundred miles away at the confluence (hence "junction") of the Colorado and Gunnison Rivers in western Colorado. It took the two troopers seven hitches and eight hours to reach the town, and after checking in to a hotel they made their way to the Cone Inn, a local dancehall. Denver and Leadville streets were crowded with men in uniform, but for at least this one weekend, not so Grand Junction. That proved advantageous. Holeywell wrote home to his mother: "I must say it was really great because we were the only GI's in the town and we had the pick of any of the girls. After looking the situation over we saw two very attractive girls. We invited them over to our table and struck up a good conversation." Several hours of talking, drinking, and dancing ensued, before they escorted the young ladies home to their respective parents' houses, with another date set for the next morning. "You know you have to work fast on a 36 hour pass," twenty-year-old Holeywell confided. "You can't waste any time and we didn't." Which wasn't quite as racy an observation as it sounded in what was, after all, a letter to his mother. The next day they took their new female acquaintances out on Grand Lake in a speedboat lent to them by the father of one of the girls, and after the weather turned bad, the novice sailors accepted a tow from another boat back to the yacht club. "What fun," Holeywell concluded. "We were the talk of the town." All that, and the two happy troopers still managed to get back to Camp Hale before the midnight deadline on Sunday.

With limited opportunities for relaxation off-base, the morale of Camp Hale's soldiers depended to a large extent on what went on in camp and the immediate vicinity. The camp had an enlisted men's club, NCO club, and officers' club. There were three movie theaters, each of which offered two shows nightly. There was a recreation center with bowling alleys, pool tables, and a soda fountain. In the course of 1943, USO tours brought Hollywood actresses like Jinx Falkenburg and Jane Wyman to camp to entertain the troops. World heavyweight boxing champion Joe Louis, an army sergeant, fought an exhibition match in October (and, in the rigidly segregated US Army, may have been the only black soldier to visit Camp Hale during the war).

Some of the speakers who came to Hale to give public lectures reflected the special interests of the camp's residents. German-born Fritz Wiessner, a naturalized US citizen since 1935, and probably the best overall climber in the United States throughout the preceding decade (and also the exclusive manufacturer of the wax the troopers applied to their skis), gave an illustrated talk about the expedition he had led to K2 in 1939. "The Himalayas sure are terrific looking mountains," Donald

Potter wrote enthusiastically to his mother after hearing Wiessner's talk. "This man came within 100' of reaching the summit . . . The pictures were marvelous and he was awful interesting."

Then there were those who made their own entertainment, like eighteen-year-old Stuart Abbott, a former Boy Scout and avid amateur naturalist (he volunteered at the Field Museum of Natural History as a high school student in Chicago), who arrived at Hale as a member of L Company, 86th Regiment, in December 1943. Within days he wrote home to a seventeen-year-old Chicago friend, urging him to enlist in the mountain troops on his next birthday. Camp Hale, he admitted, "is a long way from no place & that doesn't help those who feel they have to see the bright lights." But Abbott found living in "more or less of a wilderness" enchanting, marveling at the deer tracks that came right to the edge of camp, and the mountain lakes, now frozen over, that he was sure would teem with trout come spring. The state of Colorado awarded soldiers the same hunting privileges as state residents, and on an army base there was no shortage of weapons. Abbott intended to take full advantage: "Here is the chance to put to practice all your dreams of the past about camping hunting etc. Of course your time is limited but I am determined to make the most of the weekends. You can hunt all you please . . . One of the boys that came in with me has gone out after snow-shoe rabbits this afternoon with a borrowed carbine & stolen ammo. Nobody cares, it is a common enough practice with little risk attached."

And in addition, there was skiing and climbing; the very things that the men trained hard at during the week were also available for weekend diversions. Stan and Jean Cummings took full advantage. Stan Cummings was one of the lucky few who had a spouse accompany him to Camp Hale. Both he and his wife, Jean, were 1940 college graduates, he from Brown University, she from Pembroke College. Marrying the summer following graduation, they moved to Chicago, where Stan went to law school and Jean pursued a master's degree in science. He arrived at Camp Hale in the summer of 1943, age twenty-five, assigned to A Company in the 85th, and was soon promoted to staff sergeant. Jean followed him soon after, finding a civil service job on the base, first as a clerk-typist and then as a lab technician in the hospital. They spent almost every weekend on one outdoor adventure or another, which Jean chronicled in letters to Stan's parents. In late September her husband took her rock climbing for the first time, on the same one-hundred-foot-high cliffs to the northeast of camp where he had learned the basics only a few weeks earlier. "I went up and down places with no trouble at all that Stan said some of the fellows got scared over and wouldn't even try," she wrote proudly. "As you can see we lead kind of a strenuous life out here — I'm sore from something after nearly every week-end." Three months later, just after the New Year, they spent a day on Cooper Hill: "We went up in a truck with a bunch of other fellows and there was a terrific crowd there the whole afternoon. I have never seen really good skiers before, but on that hill were the champion skiers of the world. I was always afraid they would bump into me but as Stan said, they have such perfect control that they can stop on a dime. Of course, there were also some of the worst skiers in the world, which includes me."

Ski troopers outside the Jerome Hotel in Aspen, Colorado.
THE DENVER PUBLIC LIBRARY (TMD739)

Others went farther afield on weekends to ski at Steamboat Springs in Colorado or even Alta, an eight- to ten-hour drive away in Utah. Charlie McLane, back from Officer Candidate School, brought a station wagon with him to camp, and he, Percy Rideout, and three or four others would somehow make the round trip in a weekend, putting in a full day's skiing in the deep powder, and still be back in time for 6 a.m. reveille Monday morning. Aspen, which had so enchanted Friedl Pfeifer on first view, soon became a favorite of Camp Hale's best skiers, although it was an eighty-two-mile drive on a roundabout route through the intervening mountains. The Jerome Hotel provided cheap lodging, and a lethal concoction called the "Aspen Crud," combining a milkshake with bourbon, proved a favorite after-ski drink. And the skiing was glorious. Pfeifer was not alone among the mountain troopers in thinking that Aspen would figure in their postwar lives. He and Percy Rideout dropped by a meeting of the Aspen Town Council and hatched plans for a postwar ski resort that they thought had the potential to rival Sun Valley in elite appeal.

But before anybody's postwar dreams could be realized, there was a war to be won. And it wouldn't be won in Aspen. It did not escape the attention of the men of the 10th in 1943 that while they were out skiing, others wearing the same uniform were fighting and dying. Denis Nunan, a thirty-two-year-old private from New York, had served with C Company of the 87th since Fort Lewis days. In January 1943, a year after his enlistment, he was excited by rumors that the mountain troops would soon depart for an invasion of Norway, but those proved false. At that moment the only ground fighting in the European theater was in North Africa, where American and British troops had landed the previous November. The US Army ran into trouble as it pushed eastward into Tunisia, and was bloodied by the veteran soldiers of Erwin Rommel's Afrika Korps. In February, watching Camp Hale troops in camouflage whites serving as extras for the filming of the Warner Bros. pseudo-documentary *The Mountain Fighters,* Nunan wrote to his mother and wondered about the propriety of "us parading up and down in front of a camera, while the boys in Africa are being pushed all over the map!"

In fact, a feeling of sitting uselessly on the sidelines began to grip the mountain troopers as the months passed at Camp Hale and contributed to declining morale. It was one of the reasons why increasing numbers of 10th Division men sought to transfer to other units. "Everyone here seems to be trying for a transfer to the air corps," John Parker Compton wrote his parents in November 1943. "2 more fellas went to the paratroops," Marty Daneman wrote to girlfriend Lois in December 1943. "I may go too." According to one informed estimate, of the nearly eighteen thousand men who trained as mountain troopers at one point or another at Camp Hale between December 1942 and June 1944, almost ten thousand were gone for one reason or another (from Pando Hack to voluntary transfer) before the division was shipped overseas in December 1944, a 54.8 percent attrition rate.

Historians have long debated what motivated the soldiers who fought in the Second World War. Was it essentially a matter of loyalty to the men with whom they served — "primary group" or "small unit" cohesion? Or was there a broader sense of agreement and association with a greater cause — patriotism, anti-fascism, the "Four Freedoms" — that underlay their willingness to risk their lives? For a long time the consensus lay with the former; in more recent scholarship the pendulum seems to have swung back toward the latter. In letters from Camp Hale, mountain troopers rarely spoke about war aims as such. But occasionally they did. Some ski troopers were well aware of the stakes involved in the life-and-death struggle overseas to determine the fate of the world, as can be seen in their reaction to the "Why We Fight" documentaries produced by Frank Capra during the war.

Oscar-winning Hollywood director Capra (*It Happened One Night,* 1934; *Mr. Smith Goes to Washington,* 1939) enlisted in the army in December 1941. Assigned to the Army Signal Corps, he was given an assignment directly from General George C. Marshall to produce a series of films illuminating American war aims, to be shown to soldiers as part of their basic training. Capra conceived of the series as a "counterattack" on Nazi propaganda films, especially Leni Riefenstahl's celebration of the Nazi Party's annual Nuremberg rally in her 1935 documentary *Triumph of the Will.* The first in Capra's series, *Prelude to War,* came out in 1942; the last, *War Comes to America,* was finished in 1945. In between were several films focused on specific theaters of war: Britain, China, and Russia. The last, titled *The Battle of Russia* and released in 1943, featured graphic footage of the fighting in Leningrad and Stalingrad, as well as Nazi atrocities against Russian civilians. It was shown to Marty Daneman's company at Camp Hale in December 1943. Afterwards, Daneman wrote to Lois, sharing his reaction: "This morning we saw a picture on the battle of Russia . . . Did you ever feel hate — I mean real hate & the desire to kill people. That's the way this picture makes you feel about the Germans & you can't help it. Not when you see pictures of the 10–11 year old girls they've raped & the frozen bodies of murdered civilians. It's really horrible darling & I'm glad that scenes like those won't ever take place in America." Daneman's response may have been atypical; many soldiers probably welcomed training films on any subject, chiefly as an opportunity to sit in a warm, dark theater and make up a little for lost sleep. That Daneman was Jewish, making him a distinct minority within the mountain troops, may also have inclined him to greater sensitivity to the horror of Nazi atrocities, even if in 1943 the full extent of the Holocaust remained obscure outside occupied Europe.

Of course, the mountain troops also drew an unusually high proportion of foreign-born soldiers whose homelands had been conquered or annexed by Germany, men like Norwegian Torger Tokle and Austrians Herbert Schneider, Ernst Engel, and brothers Rupert and Werner von Trapp, whose family's flight from the Nazis would later be celebrated, and considerably romanticized, in *The Sound of Music.* Earlier in 1943, the *Ski-Zette* featured a four-part series by an Austrian Jewish refugee serving as an NCO in the 10th, chronicling the persecution of Jews in Vienna after the Anschluss in 1938. He wrote anonymously, in an effort to protect relatives still at risk in his homeland. Drawing on personal experience, he described the confiscation of his apartment by a Nazi official, and his subsequent imprisonment. Such firsthand accounts, from men they knew, were probably more believable to skeptical 10th Mountain soldiers than official propaganda.

Harris Dusenbery, newly recruited to the 86th, may have seen the same screening of Capra's *Battle of Russia* as Daneman; in any case, he too wrote home that December to his wife, Evelyn, to share his thoughts on the larger question of "Why We Fight." A Reed College graduate, twenty-nine years old when he enlisted, married and with a child born before Pearl Harbor, he could have stayed at home in Portland, Oregon, with a draft exemption. But for his own reasons, including the fact that he had two brothers in the service, he volunteered for the mountain troops. He hoped for a combat infantryman assignment in the belief that he "could expect a greater measure of freedom in the ski troops as a simple rifleman" than in other military occupations. At Camp Hale, Dusenbery was reading the *Meditations* of the Roman Stoic philosopher-emperor Marcus Aurelius, which he must have packed in his bag when he left home because it was unlikely to be found in the post library. He was much taken with the ideals of Stoicism, especially the belief that although human beings have little control over what happens to them, they have much control over how they respond to what happens to them. "The best way of avenging thyself," Marcus Aurelius argued, "is not to become like the wrong-doer" — a good philosophy for a soldier.

Like Daneman, Dusenbery believed the Allied cause was just and worth fighting for, but he had qualms about the way the argument over war aims was presented in films like the "Why We Fight" series. As he explained to Evelyn in a letter written the week before Christmas 1943:

> The army tries to teach us to hate our enemies. But as far as I'm concerned . . . these attempts at indoctrination of emotion have completely failed. I can get roused up about and hate Fascism with a great good will and also the leaders of those governments arouse similar feelings. But to hate the German people or the Japanese people or even the German soldier or Japanese soldier, I seem to be utterly incapable of doing that. I can imagine a family in Berlin just like my own worshipping the same Christ we do and attempting to celebrate Christmas under the most trying circumstances, waiting in fear for the sirens, indicating that the RAF is again coming over . . . To be asked to hate a people is foolish and primitive. The same applies to the people in Japan.

Dusenbery's efforts to sort out the ethics of warfare in terms of both Christian theology and Hellenistic philosophy may seem a little eccentric, even by the unusual intellectual standards of the 10th — but then the 10th was an outfit where eccentrics like Dusenbery could feel reasonably at home.

Dusenbery may have had another reason for rereading Marcus Aurelius in the winter of 1943. If the mountain troops were ever going to fight anywhere, the homeland of Marcus Aurelius increasingly seemed the likeliest bet. From July 1943 through the first week of June 1944, the big news from the European theater of war, at least in terms of ground combat, was the Italian campaign, first in the invasion and conquest of Sicily in July and August. That thirty-eight-day campaign proved a harbinger of hard fighting to come. Though badly outnumbered, the Germans forced their adversaries to pay a heavy price (over twenty thousand casualties) for victory, making skillful use of the island's mountainous terrain to delay the Allied advance. The invasion sparked Benito Mussolini's overthrow, but it also brought German troops pouring southward through the Brenner Pass to occupy their former ally.

The next step in the Allied campaign to bring the war to what British prime minister Winston Churchill optimistically described as the "soft underbelly" of Hitler's empire came when the British 8th Army crossed the Straits of Messina from Sicily to the toe of the Italian boot on September 3, followed by the American 5th Army landing at Salerno just south of Naples on September 9. Men from the 10th followed the war news from Italy closely. "General Clark Leads American British Troops at Landing at Naples; Nazi Resistance Stiff," read the headline in the *Camp Hale Ski-Zette* two days after the Salerno landings.

A few days after the Allied landings in Italy, and a simultaneous Red Army offensive to capture and cross the Dnieper River, Private Robert Ellis of L Company, 86th Regiment, wrote home: "The war seems to be going pretty well, and we're counting on the Russians to break through. The view here is pretty optimistic with most people — officers included, thinking it will be over by this time next year."

Allied intelligence analysts expected to meet little Italian resistance in the invasion of the mainland, about which they were correct. On September 8 it was announced that the Italian regime had signed an armistice officially taking Italy out of the war. By the beginning of October, the 8th Army captured the port of Bari and the airfields at Foggia in the east, and the 5th Army captured the port of Naples in the west. The Allies expected a rapid German withdrawal to ensue, and to be in Rome before the end of October at the latest. In that they proved sadly mistaken.

The Italian boot proved anything but a soft underbelly. Instead of withdrawing, the Germans, commanded by Field Marshal Albert Kesselring, dug in along a defensive line, dubbed the Gustav Line, stretching from the Tyrrhenian Sea along the western coast to the Adriatic Sea in the east, with the area around Monte Cassino in the southern Apennines the most strongly held. What had been envisioned as a war of maneuver and mobility now turned into a bloody slugging match that soon came to be compared to trench warfare on the western front in the First World War. Except there were no mountains on the western front to contend with. A famous Bill Mauldin cartoon that ran in the army newspaper *Stars and Stripes* in December 1943 showed his dog-faced GI protagonists, Willie and Joe, looking distinctly confused as they cling for dear life to a sheer rock face and their sergeant gives the order to "Hit th' dirt, boys!" Hanson Baldwin, the *New York Times'* chief military cor-

"Hit th' dirt, boys!"

Cartoon by Bill Mauldin, Stars and Stripes, *December 16, 1943.* © 1943 BY BILL MAULDIN. COURTESY OF BILL MAULDIN ESTATE LLC.

respondent, a journalist not given to Mauldin's biting irony, would comment in a year-end summary of war news that "it is a great shame there are so many mountains in Italy."

If there was one thing that the men of the 10th understood, it was mountains and the challenges they presented. Already in mid-November 1943, John Parker Compton, G Company, 86th Regiment, was writing to his parents: "I'm beginning to think there's much too much over-optimism about the war . . . If things keep going very slow in Italy, I may find myself in the Austrian Alps next summer." As a prediction of the 10th Mountain Division's future, he was off by about a year.

As 1943 drew to a close, some familiar but long-absent mountain troopers returned to Camp Hale, the men of the 87th Regiment. They had been deployed six months earlier to fight in one of the strangest and most obscure campaigns of the Second World War. The story they had to tell of where they had been and what they had experienced over the past half year was not a happy one.

Lieutenant Earl E. Clark, Camp Hale.
THE DENVER PUBLIC LIBRARY (TMD431)

4

Kiska, 1943

"This Little Expedition"

What has done more than anything else to drag down the old morale is the fact that this little expedition cost me something that I can never replace — the life of my closest friend. Yes, poor old Funk, my roommate for this last year and buddy that I wrote so much about was killed shortly after the landing operation. He died a hero.

— Lieutenant Earl E. Clark to his mother,
August 29, 1943

IN EARLY JUNE 1943, SECOND LIEUTENANT EARL E. CLARK, AN OFFI-cer in the Service Company of the 87th Regiment (the company responsible for carrying ammunition and other supplies forward to line companies), returned to Camp Hale from three days of maneuvers in the high country. It had been a miserable experience for men and officers alike, conducted in nonstop sleet. And Lieutenant Clark was nursing grievances beyond the bad weather (and some recalcitrant mules that were in his charge). He liked neither his current assignment nor his superior officer, whom he regarded as a martinet. "I would prefer anything to taking what I have these last few days," he wrote home to his family on June 3.

Clark was superbly qualified for the mountain troops, a former Eagle Scout and one of the original three-letter men in the 87th. As a teenager he had climbed with Paul Petzoldt in Wyoming's Teton mountains and was a founding member of the Chicago Mountaineers climbing club, which, despite its flat midwestern hometown, included a number of America's leading climbers (like the Stettner brothers, both of whom also served in the 10th). Clark had come to Camp Hale as one of the 87th's new junior officers following his completion of OCS at Fort Benning. But after a year and a half of military service, he felt the army was ignoring his greatest strength, his outdoors experience. As he complained on another occasion, "My mountain knowledge does not mean a thing" to senior officers "because it interferes with the fact that they do not know a damn thing about it and refuse to accept the knowledge of a lesser rank." Such feelings were not uncommon among the 10th's best skiers and mountaineers. Clark was so disgruntled he decided to apply for transfer to the Air Corps — where, of course, his "mountain knowledge" would count for even less. But those plans were put on hold, for on June 11 he and the bulk of the 87th Regiment boarded a train at Pando station to begin a journey that delivered them three days later to Fort Ord on California's Monterey Bay. Six weeks after that they were once again on the move, heading toward their first combat assignment.

Back in 1940, when Minnie Dole proposed the creation of mountain troops, he stressed their importance to the defense of the continental United States from foreign invasion. As it turned out, the 87th's baptism by fire did take place on American soil — although about as far as one could get from the Champlain Valley, where Dole imagined US Army ski troopers swooping down from the ridgelines of Vermont's Green Mountains to attack columns of German *Gebirgsjäger*. Instead the soldiers of the 87th were dispatched to evict Japanese soldiers from the island of Kiska in the distant Aleutians, part of the sole campaign in the Second World War fought on US territory.

Still later that fall of 1943, in the early morning hours of November 20, US Marines readied themselves to climb down from navy transports into landing craft off the coast of the Japanese-held atoll of Tarawa in the Gilbert Islands, the first American amphibious landing in the central Pacific. One marine was overheard complaining to a buddy that the Japanese "had done a Kiska on us," that is, abandoned the island before the invasion force showed up. Wishful thinking, perhaps, or more likely a dark joke — about to get a lot darker, for in the course of the next three days, nearly a thousand marines died in a battle in which the 4,500-man Japanese garrison fiercely resisted the landings, fighting virtually to the last man.

The young marine's comment suggests how the tale of the Allied invasion of Kiska had become a byword in the Pacific theater and beyond for a pointless and even absurd military operation. The landings on Kiska by American and Canadian troops, the largest amphibious operation to date in the Pacific, did not go as planned. A journalistic wag from *Time* magazine described the operation, with a tip of the hat to the military cynic's favorite acronym, SNAFU, or "situation normal, all fouled up" — except with another word usually substituting for "fouled" — as an example of JANFU, "joint army-navy foul-up." And positioned at the sharp end of the army's contribution to the Kiska foul-up was the 87th Mountain Infantry Regiment.

The Aleutian archipelago, whose inner islands are geologically part of the North American continent, had been US territory since being acquired from the Russian Empire in the Alaska Purchase of 1867. The archipelago's 120 islands stretch more than a thousand miles from the Alaska Peninsula into the North Pacific, skirting the southern edge of the Bering Sea, and pointing westward toward Siberia's Kamchatka Peninsula. Japan's Kuril Islands similarly lead to Kamchatka from the main Japanese islands to the south. Viewed on a map, the two island chains seem to create a series of steppingstones between northern Japan and the American Pacific Northwest. The distance between Attu, the westernmost of the Aleutian Islands, and Paramushiro, site of the Japanese naval base on the northernmost Kuril island, is only 650 miles, well within range of American B-17 bombers.

As early as 1911, Alfred Thayer Mahan, the leading American naval strategist before the First World War, advocated developing Kiska's natural deep-water harbor, protected by an island (Little Kiska) across its mouth, as a base for striking Japan and its Pacific possessions in some future conflict. But as naval vessels grew in size, Kiska's relatively small harbor shrank in potential utility. A quarter century later, army air power enthusiast Brigadier General Billy Mitchell declared that the Aleutians were an ideal "jumping off place to smash Japan" with American bombers.

Neither Mahan's nor Mitchell's advice led to any significant buildup of American forces in the Aleutians until 1941, when a base was established at Dutch Harbor on the island of Unalaska. In early June 1942, as part of the same naval offensive that led to the Battle of Midway in the central Pacific, the Japanese dispatched two small aircraft carriers, the *Junvo* and the *Ryuio,* and other vessels into the North Pacific, hoping to lure part of the US Navy's Pacific Fleet after them. Their gambit didn't work; thanks to the ability of US naval intelligence to read coded Japanese radio traffic, Admiral Chester W. Nimitz, commander of the Pacific Fleet, knew that the main attack was coming on Midway Island in the central Pacific. The American carriers headed for Midway, where they would soon sink four of their Japanese counterparts. Although the diversion failed, the Japanese fleet in the North Pacific did launch several air attacks on the American base at Dutch Harbor, damaging a fuel depot and other facilities and killing several scores of Americans. The Japanese also landed troops unopposed on the western Aleutian islands of Kiska and Attu on June 7. In the months that followed, they turned the islands into fortresses, with caves and tunnels sheltering the garrisons from air attack and naval bombardment.

Japanese strategy in the Aleutians thereafter was strictly defensive. American fears to the contrary, this proved the furthest extent of Japanese ambitions in the region, and not the prelude to an attack on Alaska or the Pacific Northwest. Perpetually locked into some of the worst weather in the world, the Aleutians would not be the launch pad for a grand offensive by either side in the Pacific war. Of course, American military planners had to assume the worst. And American public sentiment was aroused by the notion that invaders were actually occupying American soil — even if few Americans before June 1942 would have been able to find the Aleutians on a map. In the end, tens of thousands of men would be sent to fight and die on the chain's freezing, desolate, and fogbound shores.

The US military occupied Adak Island, 250 miles east of Kiska, in August 1942 and Amchitka Island, ninety miles east of Kiska, in January 1943, building bases on both to use for air assault against and eventual landings on Kiska and Attu. Regular bombing attacks were made on Kiska Harbor beginning in September 1942.

Although Attu, the westernmost of the Aleutians, was farther from the American bases than Kiska, its invasion came first, since it was held by a smaller garrison. US soldiers landed on Attu on May 11, 1943, and military planners expected them to rout the 2,500 defenders in three days. But it was always a mistake to underestimate Japanese tenacity in a fight-to-the-death battle, and three days turned into three weeks. Wisely on their part, the Japanese did not contest the beaches where the landings took place but instead withdrew into strong defensive positions in the mountainous interior of the island.

There, weather and terrain favored them. The US Army's 7th Infantry Division, which spearheaded the fight, had been trained for desert not arctic warfare. From caves and well-camouflaged bunkers on the high ground, the Japanese poured a withering fire on Americans advancing across the open frozen tundra and icy rocky slopes. Before the last Japanese soldiers were killed or committed suicide (many dying in a final banzai attack), 549 Americans died and over a thousand were wounded. Attu was second only to Iwo Jima in the Pacific campaign in the cost in American lives, not in absolute numbers but as a percentage of the force sent to capture the island. Many more were disabled by cold and exposure, suffering frostbite and trench foot due to inexperience with cold weather operations, thin field jackets, and leather boots that did little to keep out the cold and damp.

Meanwhile, back at Camp Hale, soldiers who did know how to fight in arctic conditions, and had the proper clothing and equipment to do so, wondered if they would ever stop training and get into the war. Later, General George C. Marshall conceded in conversation with Minnie Dole, "I should have sent alpine troops to Attu." So it was that a month to the day after the initial landings on Attu, the 87th Regiment boarded the train in Pando, bound for Fort Ord and six weeks of amphibious training. Where they were headed after that they did not yet know, other than that it would be in the Pacific. While the 87th practiced scrambling down the sides of ships on cargo nets into landing craft, Allied forces were making landings in New Guinea in the South Pacific, and that might have seemed their logical destination. On

July 27, nearly four thousand men from the regiment, now officially designated the 87th Mountain Infantry Regimental Combat Team (some support and headquarters companies were left behind), boarded a rusty old troopship, the USS *Grant,* in San Francisco Bay. Instead of sailing southwest, they headed northwest. New Guinea was not to be their final destination.

Somewhere in the Pacific, Earl E. Clark, newly promoted to first lieutenant and still assigned to Regimental S-4 (logistics), wrote a letter to his mother, Lillian, saying: "Just a line tonight to let you know all is well even though this may not reach you for many many days. We are at sea as I write this and, at the moment, tossing around in a very rough sea . . . You will not hear very much from me, now, mom, dear, for quite some time. However do not worry. Be patient and know that I will be safe."

While the men of the 87th were training at Fort Ord, the six thousand Japanese on Kiska had been subjected to hundreds of air raids from bombers based on Amchitka. They expected, with reason, invasion to follow at any time. But instead of fighting to the last man, as they had on Attu, Japanese commanders decided they had a better use for Kiska's garrison elsewhere in the Pacific and began evacuating their troops by submarine. With American landings looming, however, the small-scale submarine withdrawal was taking too long. In a daring operation on July 28, on the day after the 87th boarded ship in San Francisco Bay, taking advantage of heavy fog and American inattention, a small Japanese fleet daringly slipped through the US Navy blockade and sailed into Kiska Harbor. In less than an hour, 5,183 soldiers were loaded onto the ships and sailed to the safety of the Japanese base at Paramushiro. A rearguard unit, left behind to destroy equipment and plant booby traps, was taken off the island a few days later by submarine. A stray dog was the only living nonnative holdout from the Japanese Kiska garrison.

Despite the sudden silencing of Japanese radio traffic, and the absence of antiaircraft fire directed at American planes passing over the island, Rear Admiral Thomas C. Kinkaid, commanding the American-Canadian invasion force preparing to attack Kiska, refused to believe it had been evacuated. The Japanese were just lying low in some kind of trick. Kinkaid vetoed proposals from intelligence staff to send a small scouting party ashore prior to the invasion to determine whether the island was still being held by the enemy. Operation Cottage, as the landings were officially designated, consisting of an invasion force of 34,426 combat troops, roughly a tenth of whom were from the 87th Infantry, would go ahead as scheduled in mid-August.

After over a week at sea, the 87th arrived at the US base on Adak Island on August 5. There they spent another week getting their land legs back, as best they could on the spongy tundra. Denis Nunan of C Company wrote home several months later about the experience: "We bivouacked on a part of the island the Navy and Air Corps had no use for, so we were always wet and muddy." It was a relief to get back on board ship, where at least they were momentarily dry and well fed, even though they were debarking for Kiska on the inauspicious date of Friday, August 13. The invasion armada consisted of nearly one hundred ships, including three battleships, a heavy cruiser, nineteen destroyers, and transports carrying a force that, in addition to the 87th, included the US 7th Division, veterans of Attu, the 13th Royal Canadian Infantry Brigade, and the US-Canadian 1st Special Service Force (famed later in the war as the "Devil's Brigade" for their exploits in Italy and France).

By the evening of August 14, the American-Canadian invasion flotilla was in position off Kiska. The battleships *Pennsylvania* and *Tennessee* bombarded the island to prepare the way for the landings the next morning. Apart from some Rangers who landed during the night, the 87th would be the first unit sent into the fight at dawn on August 15. The island was twenty-two miles long and between three and four miles wide. The three battalions' landing zones were spread out along Kiska's western coast, thought by US intelligence to be less heavily defended since Kiska's harbor, along with a Japanese-constructed submarine base and seaplane base, lay on the other side of the island. From the beaches, the mountain troopers would climb to the high ridgeline dominating the interior. Regular infantry battalions, landed on D-Day plus two, would follow their lead.

It seemed almost a certainty that an uphill battle on rough terrain against an entrenched enemy was going to be costly. Judging from the fighting on Attu, military planners expected a 20 percent American casualty rate overall during the invasion of Kiska, which would obviously be much higher for the first men to hit the beaches, perhaps as high as 80 percent. Denis Nunan, older at age thirty-three than most of his fellow troopers, was scheduled to go in with the first wave and was fatalistic about the chances for survival. Six months earlier he had written to his mother complaining that his regiment was sitting safely at Camp Hale while other GIs fought and died in North Africa. Now approaching his own initiation in combat, and after taking communion from the Catholic chaplain of C Company, he wrote another letter to his mother. Instead of posting it, he tucked it into a pocket of his shirt, with a message on the envelope asking anyone who found it on his body to send it on to the intended recipient. "From now on it's up to God," he wrote. "Don't worry about receiving this—remember that I went without fear, even though I wanted terribly much to get another chance to enjoy life."

On board the transport ship *Harris,* former Olympic skier Bob Livermore, an officer with F Company, was also scheduled to land with the first wave. In a diary entry written soon after the landings, he recorded his feelings on the eve of battle:

> Turned in about 7 the night before, just as in preparation for a big ski race, everyone a mixture of unnatural calmness, nervous laughter, and still unfinished business bustle. Reveille at midnight with sandwiches and coffee, final packing of the battle packs (poncho, Sterno and socks) stowing away 136 rounds of [ammo], four grenades and a K ration. First wave into the boats at 3 a.m. with Kiska about five miles off the starboard bow as we headed north.
>
> It looked very quiet, very steep, very, very ominous. The sea was calm, clouds about a hundred feet above us, and the moon shining through breaks like sun on the plains when there are thunderstorms scattered about. I remember praying that the moon would stay off our boats, that the offshore breeze would keep the sound of engines away from the Jap outposts' ears.

Livermore and his men landed without incident or opposition, to their immense relief. As did the second and third waves later that morning. Sergeant Joseph E. deLongpre, commanding a mortar squad in E Company, came in with the third wave. No one was shooting at them as they approached the beach, and he decided that, at least in the short run, he and his men had more to fear from the US Navy than from any Japanese defenders:

> The Navy man that was operating the Higgins Lander stopped up against a rock about 50 feet from shore and ordered everyone off, then dropped the front ramp gate. The water was black because it was so deep. Because we were so heavily loaded [with mortars and ammunition] I knew we would lose a lot of men in that deep water. I ordered the Coxwain to back off and go around the rock closer in, but he refused. I raised my M1, chambered a round and asked him to reconsider or I would blow his head off. He turned out to be smarter than he looked and turned out around the rock to head on into shore. Not a man in the boat got his feet wet when we landed on shore.

By midday, when Harold Bradley Benedict's 133rd Signal Company Detachment was approaching its designated landing site, army engineers had constructed a rock and gravel pier extending out into the water. The contrast between what he had expected and what he encountered in the landing was "diametrical." There was neither machine gun fire nor the "sickening noise and confusion of a contested landing." Instead, Benedict wrote, their landing craft "actually idled about twenty yards off shore to wait our turn at the narrow rock pier!"

———

When the first wave landed at dawn, the weather was clear. The men in the landing craft could see all the way from the narrow beaches to the ridgeline, 1,800 feet above sea level, that they were assigned to capture. Lieutenant George F. Earle had been an art student at Syracuse University and at Yale before enlisting in the 87th the day after Pearl Harbor. He brought brushes and paint with him in his gear, and viewed Kiska with an appreciative and painterly eye: "The island was rimmed like a castle with cliff-walled shores, and when occasionally visible, a bright green matting of waist-high tundra and deep lush mosses. This great green sponge of slopes rose to a rocky-knife edge crest nearly 800 feet [high that] zig-zagged its backbone ridge-line toward the seldom-visible 4,000 foot cone of the volcano."

Had the visibility held, the invasion might have ended well. But in the Aleutians, visibility never held. By midday the customary fog, along with icy rain and high winds, rolled in from the sea. Hour after hour the men of the 87th climbed the steep slope, passing through the mossy muskeg bogs which made walking difficult to the rocky talus above, in ever-thickening chill and gloom. There were no sheltering trees or brush at all on the bare slopes. Vague shapes suddenly loomed out of the mist. Uncertain whether they were looking at men (their own? the enemy?) or just rocks, the troopers called out the official password, "long limb"—words chosen because it was assumed Japanese speakers would be unable to pronounce them properly. Sometimes they got the correct response, sometimes they heard nothing back. Riflemen walked with weapons at ready, safeties off, fingers on the triggers of their M1s.

It took Floyd Erickson, H Company, twelve hours to reach the ridgeline, because in addition to his personal gear he was burdened with two heavy boxes of .50-caliber machine gun ammunition. It was pouring rain as he and his company dug shallow foxholes in the stony soil. "It was a terrible night, that first one," he recalled. "You couldn't see ten feet in front of you. We just sat in our foxholes waiting, for as yet we didn't know there weren't any Japs here."

Shortly before dark, shots began to ring out. The regimental command post on the beach below received radio reports of sporadic attacks along the ridgeline by Japanese soldiers. Because the shots were scattered up and down the hillside and along the ridgeline, it was easy for the inexperienced soldiers to imagine they were surrounded, being attacked from all sides.

Captain Roger Eddy, who commanded L Company that night on the ridgeline, recalled the increasing chaos over which he had little control, though he did not excuse himself from responsibility. Every man in the company, including its commander, was "green" and "scared stiff," and as a result, each time "a helmet poked up through the fog everyone let go," and a lot of times they fired simply "because they thought they saw Japs in the murk." They all "expected to die" before the night was over.

Private Arthur C. Delaney of L Company shared a foxhole with his buddy Art Hilger. They were told that the enemy was out in front of them and that they should shoot anything that moved. "Art and I squat in our hole, take out our ammunition and grenades and check our pieces," Delaney wrote soon afterwards. "We then eat our D-ration bars, arrange a system for sleeping. We decided upon an hour on & hour off system." Delaney took the first shift, and when Hilger relieved him, he tried to get some sleep, curled up in the muddy foxhole. But not for long. "Hilger called me from my half sleep. A bullet had bounced about three inches over his head. I crawled into position and strained my eyes looking for something but no luck." There was no more sleep for two tired troopers that night:

> Towards morning things began to pop. Shots were glancing off our parapet, we didn't know which way they were coming from . . . Art and I had to stay low as the shots were coming close. I heard a mortar shell burst and I really buried myself in the sod. It was becoming light now and the firing had ceased. I saw Joe Jones get out of his foxhole. He came over to us and said, Sgt. [Harvey J.] Nokleby was dead. He had been shot through the helmet in the side of the head. This was a shock . . . It was hard to believe that "Nock" was gone.

"Nock" Nokleby had been Hilger and Delaney's squad leader, in the third platoon of L Company. None of the men in the little squad had ever seen the corpse of a man killed in combat by the enemy, let alone a man they knew well, liked, and respected. That was hard enough to accept. But then it turned out "Nock" hadn't been killed by the enemy.

When mountain troopers bumped into one another on the ridgeline, or into groups of Rangers, who they hadn't been told were also up there, they had only a few seconds to decide whether to open fire. Sometimes caution prevailed and lives were spared. Sometimes not.

Of all the units in the 87th on Kiska, I Company was hardest hit that night. Its commander sent a platoon out to locate the elusive Japanese attackers. They were caught in a fusillade of friendly fire and five men died as a result, including the platoon leader, Second Lieutenant Wilfred J. Funk. Funk was the son of the president of the venerable publishing firm Funk and Wagnalls, publisher of the well-known dictionary of the same name. A talented sculptor, before the war he helped carve the great stone presidential faces on Mount Rushmore. He was Earl Clark's best friend, ever since the two of them served together in I Company.

Another of Funk's good friends in the regiment was Captain Roger Eddy of L Company, who remembered his slain comrade as "the original hero type — clean cut, enthusiastic, intelligent." Eddy was deeply shaken by the night's deaths, including Funk's, but especially that of Sergeant Nokleby, who was under his command: "I can remember bending over one of my sergeants who had been shot between the eyes. And while I looked at him he died. The next morning, when we realized what had happened, we felt as if we'd been on an all-night drunk. We were exhausted, disgusted, and ashamed. And we knew we'd done all the killing ourselves."

In the morning, some men still insisted they had killed attacking Japanese soldiers the night before, but no dead enemy bodies could be found to corroborate their accounts. Several days of patrols after that first bloody night established beyond doubt that the Japanese were gone. Sensing a public relations disaster, the military brass kept a tight lid on news from Kiska. It was over a week before reports of the landings made it into print in the United States, and then in a heavily sanitized version: "2 Killed at Kiska," the *New York Times* reported on August 24, in a brief story that attributed the deaths to Japanese land mines and booby traps. In reality, twenty-eight Americans and Canadians died on Kiska, only four of them from mines and booby traps, most of the rest from friendly fire. Of the dead, nineteen were mountain troopers. The 87th also suffered a number of wounded. (Although the exact number is difficult to know, estimates range from five to fifty-five.)

Harder to disguise was the fact that the Japanese had hoodwinked the American navy by slipping in and out of Kiska Harbor at the end of July, and that no one in high command realized it in the nearly three weeks that followed. "The circumstances surrounding the evacuation of Kiska ought to make someone's face red," Hanson Baldwin, the *New York Times'* chief military correspondent, observed in his account of the landings. *Life* magazine ran a photo-essay about the Kiska operation that attempted to sound upbeat, but most of the troops who appeared in the pictures looked glumly damp instead of happily victorious. The Kiska fiasco branded the entire Aleutian campaign with an image of futility, one of the reasons why it disappeared from popular memory after the war.

In the by now well-established tradition of the 87th, the mountain troopers soon came up with a satirical musical commentary about the folly of their recent mission, titled "Kiska Blues." It was sung to the tune of a bawdy barroom ballad, "No Balls at All," and commenced:

> *I'll tell you a story as well as I can*
> *Of the biggest dry run of the Ski Trooper clan*
> *They trained in the winter, they trained in the fall*
> *Then came to an island with no Japs at all!*
>
> *What? No Japs at all? Yes, no Japs at all!*
> *We learned how to ski and we learned how to climb*
> *We learned how to stay out in any ol' clime*
> *We jumped on our skis when they gave us the call*
> *Then came to an island with no Japs at all!*

There were jokes as well as songs (the Kiska operation was an example of "optical Aleutians," troopers liked to say), but the irony left a bitter aftertaste. It wasn't all that funny, being part of a military joke—"JANFU." They had risked their lives, and seen friends die, in as pointless an operation as any in the entire war. In the months that followed the landings, as they waited impatiently for their own evacuation from their dismal encampments on Kiska (some for as long as four months), the men of the 87th were restrained in what they could say in letters to family and friends because of war zone censorship. When Denis Nunan finally got back to the States at the start of the new year and no longer had to submit his correspondence to an army censor, he instructed his mother to disbelieve everything she had read in newspapers and magazines about the Kiska misadventure:

> Did any of those pictures in *Life* show how we lived in Kiska? Did they show the food we ate? Did they show the boys being blown sky high by booby traps and land mines? Did the stories tell that the fog was so dense that we shot and killed our own men as they loomed out of the fog? There were no Japs there so they don't show the graves of our boys — but I have friends buried on Kiska . . . No, you can't rely on the papers, movies, radio, etc. One has to see first hand the horrible waste of War, the bungling, red tape, inefficient management — one has to live the life of a ground force soldier to realize how rotten war is. And to think I learned all this without a Jap on the island.

That civilians were naïve and misled, all too willing to accept whitewashed accounts of military blunders like Kiska, was hard enough to take. Even harder to accept was that their fellow mountain troopers back at Camp Hale could not seem to understand what they had been through. The Kiska veterans endured unsympathetic taunts from soldiers from other regiments, the cruelest of which was "buddy-killer."

Of the 3,897 members of the 87th who were dispatched to Kiska, far fewer died than expected, but far more than circumstances required. The attrition by transfer that followed had an even greater impact on the regiment. From the time the 87th returned to Camp Hale at the end of 1943 and the start of 1944 until it sailed for its second overseas assignment a year later, 2,148 Kiska veterans left its ranks, a 55 percent departure rate in a single year, suggesting a profound degree of demoralization.

But Sergeant Denis P. Nunan, for all his bitter reflections on war, the press, and military higher-ups, was not among those departing. Nor was First Lieutenant Earl E. Clark, who had been planning to transfer out of the division even before Kiska. They both left friends buried on the island. They both stayed with the mountain troops — and distinguished themselves in the 10th Mountain Division's coming battles.

Members of the 87th Mountain Regiment pose by a captured Japanese artillery gun bunker on Kiska Island in the Aleutian Islands.
THE DENVER PUBLIC LIBRARY (TMD619)

Tired mountain trooper, end of D Series maneuvers, April 1944.

5

Camp Hale and Camp Swift, 1944

"We'll Be Playing for Keeps before Long"

Get a grip on yourself, soldier; we are plenty hot! We'll be playing
for keeps before long and when that day comes we want to come
out on top, and we will!

— *Corporal Arnold Holeywell, "STICK TO THE FIGHT,"*
Camp Hale Ski-Zette, March 10, 1944

ON MOST DAYS, NINETEEN-YEAR-OLD PFC JOHN PARKER COMPTON
of G Company in the 86th loved life at Camp Hale. He had originally
been assigned to the Mountain Training Group, thanks to his experience
as a skier. Even after his transfer to a rifle company, he still helped out as
a ski instructor from time to time. But by the start of his eighth month at
camp, despite his enthusiasm for the sport and the mountain surroundings, and his usually sunny disposition, he found himself wondering just
what was the point of training men to ski when the army clearly had no
use for skiers. "When and where would we ever use skis?," he asked in
a letter to his parents in May 1944. "How could we use skis? The majority don't ski well enough to be used in combat. There is always binding
trouble or ski trouble. These questions keep popping up in your mind
as you see someone take an awful sitzmark on a simple snow plow." And,
he confessed, after another day spent on the slopes of Cooper Hill, "you
think, 'What a waste of time!!'"

By the spring of 1944, a lot of ski troopers at Camp Hale were think-ing along those lines. Applications for transfer to army units that were actually fighting—the Air Corps, the Airborne—multiplied. Among those transferring out was Charles B. McLane, the very first volun-teer to join the mountain infantry at Fort Lewis, as well as co-lyricist of "Ninety Pounds of Rucksack." By the spring of 1944, after training for over two and a half years, he decided he did not want to sit out the war in Colorado, and in April 1944 he transferred to the Military Intel-ligence Training Center at Camp Ritchie, Maryland.

The war was going on without the men of the 10th, in the island-hopping campaigns in the Pacific, in the mountains of Italy, over the skies of western Europe, and in preparation for the invasion of northern France, and many didn't want to wait any longer to be a part of the ac-tion. Twenty-one-year-old Corporal Arnold Holeywell of Headquarters Company of the 86th decided there was too much griping in the ranks. The 10th's time to contribute to the war effort was coming, he was sure, and all they had to do was be patient a little longer. He conceded, in an editorial comment in the March 10, 1944, *Ski-Zette,* that they had been engaged in "fighting the battle of Colorado for more than a year, " which could be disheartening. But he disagreed with those who believed that the division "would never see combat duty." Holeywell thought other-wise, and believed in the end all the training would pay off when they were deployed overseas: "We've got the stuff and we've got the training, so make the most of every day you undergo."

———

With the return of the 87th Mountain Infantry Regiment to Camp Hale from Kiska in January 1944, and the transfer of the 90th Regiment to Camp Carson in late February (minus a sizeable number of 90th troop-ers who remained at Hale with the other mountain regiments), the 10th Division was in its final form. If and when it shipped out for overseas duty and, indeed, finally got to show its "stuff," the division would con-sist of the 85th, 86th, and 87th Regiments, plus three field artillery bat-talions and other auxiliary units.

Meanwhile, in what turned out to be the last winter at Camp Hale, the men of the 10th carried out some spectacular mountain exploits. Three division medics, Corporal Russell Keene and PFC William Ferguson, both of the 86th, and Private Howard Freedman of the 85th, celebrated Christmas 1943 by setting off on an attempt to make the first winter ascent of the nearby 14,011-foot Mount of the Holy Cross (named for the image of a cross formed by snow lingering on its dark granite northeast face in the summertime). Two previous attempts by soldiers from the 10th had failed, but the three medics, aided by a rare windless day, reached the summit on December 26.

The next day, a party of sixty-eight officers and enlisted men from the 10th Recon and the Mountain Training Group left camp, most on skis, some on snowshoes, and pulled off the first recorded winter ascents of 14,440-foot Mount Elbert, on December 28, and 14,428-foot Mount Massive the following day. "Just returned from a three day trip," Mountain Training Group instructor and veteran Sierra Club climber Glen Dawson recorded in his diary on December 30, "much of it on skis, climbing both Elbert and Massive second and third highest peaks in the U.S. (not counting Alaska)."

At the end of February, Dawson and the elite of the 10th Recon and Mountain Training Group set out again on an extreme adventure, skiing fifty miles in four days from Half Moon Gulch between Elbert and Massive across high passes to Aspen, their thirty-three-strong group led by Captain John Jay including an impressive roster of past and, in the case of twenty-one-year-old Private Fred Beckey, future climbing stars. The mountain regiments had always been better stocked with top-ranked skiers than climbers, and the skiers tended to outrank their mountain climbing comrades in prestige. This trip witnessed a rare open squabble between an expert skier and an equally expert mountaineer over mountain safety — in which, at least according to the climbers, they came out ahead. (That the disagreement was between an officer and an NCO seemed irrelevant.) "The second day," Dawson wrote on his return to Hale on February 25, "we went over a pass some 13,000 feet high. The leader [Captain Jay] picked a poor route up the pass but Sgt. Paul Petzoldt of K2 fame . . . led the end of the line on a variant which proved faster and safer." That unpleasantness behind them, the third day took skiers and climbers over three high passes and the Continental Divide. They enjoyed days of bright sunshine and downhill runs extending for six miles through unbroken powder snow. On the fourth and final day, Dawson wrote, "we travel[ed] a terrific distance but reached Aspen. I broke trail part of the way, a job that had to be traded frequently because the snow was ankle to knee deep all the way, even with skis."

At journey's end, Dawson took a walk around Aspen with Hans Hagemeister of the Mountain Training Group. Hagemeister was born in the United States, but when he was a child, his German-born father took the family back to the paternal homeland. Hagemeister learned to ski at the Schneider school in St. Anton am Arlberg in the early 1930s, and moved to the Austrian mountain resort when the Nazis took over Germany, finally returning to the United States in 1935. Back in Aspen that day, Dawson and Hagemeister noted the decrepit condition of the community, including many boarded-up homes. But they were impressed by the "great ski run coming right down into town." Hagemeister flatly predicted that Aspen would one day become a premier ski resort. The troopers enjoyed the hospitality of the Hotel Jerome that night, sleeping in warm beds and splitting a couple of free bottles of whiskey provided by the proprietor, which represented the sum total of luxuries Aspen had to offer at the time.

The same week in early March when Private Arnold Holeywell exhorted his fellow troopers in the pages of the *Ski-Zette* to "STICK TO THE FIGHT," he wrote home to his mother, Mary, back east on Long Island, preparing her for what he thought would be his imminent departure for war: "About every other day I have to go out on a problem of some sort. All I do is break my back carrying a pack and marching. Then we turn around and come back. They say it's a toughening up program. We are getting ready for combat soon. Around the end of March we are going on maneuvers for a month. Then?"

If the longer-term "then?" remained opaque, the short term was coming into focus: for the first time the entire division would take to the field for maneuvers, practicing tactical operations (attacks and defense), not just winter survival techniques. In its edition for the third week in March, the front-page headline of the *Ski-Zette* reported, "10th Infantry Division Moves Out Sunday on Extensive Field Maneuvers; Rugged, Snow-Capped Rockies to Prove Real Test for General Jones' Men." The maneuvers were scheduled to last for five weeks in April and May. They would prove the most arduous — and physically costly — exercise in US military history. The 1944 maneuvers were called the "D-Series" ("D" for divisional). When the 10th finally went to war, the standard joke in the division became some variation of "If this gets any worse, it'll be as bad as D-Series."

D-Series began as a massive traffic jam as twelve thousand men on skis, plus thousands of heavily burdened mules, were unwisely scheduled to set off en masse from the camp's south gate at 8 a.m. on March 26, 1944. As MPs worked frantically to unsnarl the predictable chaos, soldiers stood motionless in temperatures of twenty degrees below zero, a particularly misery-inducing example of the old army saying "Hurry up and wait." When their turn came to move out, the men shuffled up-hill, bent under ninety-pound rucksacks, bringing PFC Marty Daneman's scrawny unburdened weight of 140 pounds to a robust 230.

For soldiers in the 86th like Daneman, who had missed the Home-stake fiasco the previous year, there was, at least at first, a sense of adventure attached to D-Series. They had been training for a long time for this moment, and as Daneman recalled, for "the first couple of days we were full of piss and vinegar."

Not so for those unfortunates of the 87th, some of whom had suffered through the earlier maneuvers, and all of whom had deployed to and subsequently endured months of hardship on Kiska. Denis Nunan had been in the country less than three months when the orders came to strap on skis and head for the hills. It did not improve the dark mood he had brought back from the Aleutians. "They are trying to kill us and the boys are going 'over the hill' in droves," he wrote to his mother a week into D-Series. "Well, why have maneuvers? That's what gets us, 'cause we *aren't* learning anything! We are taking this beating so the *brass hats* can get a bit of practice at handling a division in the field!"

Senior officers did not help morale in any of the regiments by riding up into the mountains in covered Weasels, and from the warm and cozy interiors of their mechanized thrones exhorting enlisted men on foot, or skis, or snowshoes to get the lead out. (Ordinary soldiers who did not get to ride in Weasels learned to huddle around the exhaust pipes of idling vehicles for the welcome warmth they provided.) Division commander Lloyd Jones, beset with chronic bronchitis, was little seen in weeks to come by the shivering men plodding up steep hills in blizzard conditions. Radios worked sporadically, and whole companies and even battalions got lost in the back country. That meant they couldn't be resupplied in the field, and men went hungry as a result. Those lucky enough to have C-rations, which included cans of stew, ate them cold (and often frozen solid), since fires were forbidden in the mock-combat "tactical conditions" of the maneuvers. Units temporarily rotated back to Camp Hale had to sleep outside, since barracks, with their minimal creature comforts, were ruled off-limits.

Back at her post in the Camp Hale hospital, Jean Cummings monitored rumors of disaster unfolding in the surrounding mountains by speaking to evacuated casualties. "Last week," she wrote to her in-laws on April 3, "190 fellows (I think that was the figure) from the 87th alone went over the hill (AWOL) including several officers. The 87th is the regiment that was at Kiska so they realize that even battle conditions don't call for all the hardships they have to go through here in these maneuvers."

Another army wife, the writer Kay Boyle, had moved with her children to a hotel in Leadville in the winter of 1944 to be near her husband, exiled Austrian baron, Kiska veteran, and Mountain Training Group instructor PFC Joseph von Franckenstein. She wrote to a friend back east at the end of March: "Joseph has disappeared as completely as if he had been wiped off the glistening, white world up here. No news since I left him in the midst of a blizzard at midnight Saturday outside the gates to camp. But we can hear cannon booming over in the mountains, which is as much of him as I can get close to at the moment." On April 1 she wrote again, reporting that she had seen Joseph at Camp Hale, where he was temporarily excused from maneuvers. She was shocked at his condition:

He said there was simply no way of describing what they had been through: 35° below for three nights, no tents, no fires, no hot food. I can't think of anywhere in the world where they would be sent to fight where it would be that cold — except Russia perhaps. Joseph was the only one of his rank and age [he turned 34 years old in 1944] who did not fall out, and his toes are one mass of blisters from freezing . . . Joseph's mouth was swollen unrecognizably from sun and wind-burn, and he sat at table with a group of boys who had been with him. In the hospital were Joseph's two best friends — one who may have to have a foot amputated, the other with a frozen lung. I have never seen Joseph so near collapse.

Back in Leadville, she said, the streets were filled with drunken soldiers who had gone "over the hill" to escape the maneuvers, and several hundred military police were in town to round them up and return them to Camp Hale. (After the war, Boyle wrote a novel based on Franckenstein's experiences in the 10th, *His Human Majesty,* published in 1949.)

Jean Cummings's husband, Stan, up in the hills with the men of A Company of the 85th, tried to make the best of things. When he finally got the chance to write to his parents on April 12, he told them of the hardships but added: "Even maneuvers have their bright spots. Say you've been hiking steadily for 18 hours with no meals and few breaks. Then you have time to brew a canteen cup of hot chocolate. Nothing again will ever taste as delicious as that chocolate." And the mountains, when they were visible, which wasn't often since it snowed every day, were beautiful to behold. "If you could hike around Colorado under no one's orders but your own it would truly be a worthwhile vacation."

Most of the men were probably dreaming of warmer vacation spots during D-Series. By the time the maneuvers dragged through a second week, insubordinate if not mutinous sentiments began to spread. Sergeant Hugh Evans, a recent graduate of Phillips Exeter Academy who turned twenty only a few days before the start of D-Series, was in C Company of the 85th, commanding a platoon. He too was feeling the physical effects, with mildly frostbitten fingers, toes, and ears — not bad enough, however, for a ticket back to the camp hospital. Thus at three o'clock in the morning on April 7, he had to rouse his exhausted men for a company field exercise. After hastily gulped cups of lukewarm coffee, they started hiking uphill — and didn't stop for five straight hours. Finally, his platoon rebelled and demanded a rest stop.

Evans halfheartedly tried to encourage them to keep moving, but when they wouldn't, he went forward in the line to speak to the com-

Sergeant Hugh Evans drying his socks and innersoles in bivouac area, April 1944.
THE DENVER PUBLIC LIBRARY (TMD432)

pany commander about taking things a little slower. The captain not only was unsympathetic but also demanded that Evans tell him the names of the rebels. Courage takes many forms, depending on circumstance—and sometimes unbending adherence to orders and authority is not its best measure. The young sergeant refused to name names, even when threatened with being busted in rank and being told that if they were in combat, the captain could have him shot on the spot. Evans lost his stripes (although only temporarily as it turned out) and was transferred to C Company in the 85th. His experience was not unique: an officer in C Company of the 85th, Thornton Race, who dared criticize the regimental commander for setting too fast a pace, kept his lieutenant's bars but was soon transferred out of the division.

Easter fell on April 9 that year, and everyone agreed in retrospect that it was the low point of D-Series. Private Robert Ellis of L Company of the 86th, writing home "after the worst physical ordeal of my entire life," recounted the weekend's events for his parents:

> Saturday night we started on a march on snowshoes and skis through snow that was up to our waists. We hiked until 1:30 A.M., then crawled into our bags and fell asleep exhausted in the snow. We were awoken at 4:00 A.M., and had to pack in a snowstorm (it snowed every day we were out) . . . For four hours we climbed in that blizzard. Finally soaked clear through, completely exhausted, and almost frozen, I and another fellow fell out. We hiked back to the temporary base camp after rescuing a fellow who had fainted in the snow and taking him to an aid station. I never thought we could make it; you could hardly see 15 yards ahead.

Since Ellis was not considered sick enough to be hospitalized, the next day he was sent out again, and went thirty-six hours without food or any water except the snow he ate while on the march. By the time he got back to Camp Hale, he had lost seventeen pounds.

There were some redemptive moments that Easter weekend. PFC John Parker Compton wrote to his parents afterwards:

> I walked on a three-man patrol across a huge open side of this mountain (13,000 ft. high) from midnight to 2 a.m. Good Friday night. I have never seen such a beautiful sight!!! We could see 100 miles in all directions. The full moon glistened silvery on the surrounding country. Precipitous Mt. Elbert (second highest in the U.S.), Mt. Massive, Mt. Homestake, and others poked their huge selves into the sky. Every once in a while a great greyish cloud passed *beneath* us. Twice one of these clouds passed right through us. The snow whirled all around. I couldn't see my hand in front of my face. We were so impressed with the gorgeousness of the scene, we forgot our worries. Not even a picture could give that scene. It left you breathless.

Of what turned out to be three weeks of maneuvers (rather than the five originally planned), Private Harris Dusenbery of C Company of the 86th would write, "the first was the coldest, the second was the worst, and the third was anticlimax." On Friday, April 15, at the end of the third week, General Jones called off the rest of the scheduled maneuvers, and the battered veterans of D-Series headed back to Camp Hale on what were now, after a week of spring thaw, muddy trails. Private Marty Daneman, no longer quite so full of piss and vinegar, limped along on badly blistered feet, and a half-dozen men in his outfit took turns lugging his pack, skis, and rifle to spare him the ninety-pound burden for those last few miles to camp. According to official statistics, almost certainly an underestimate, there had been 195 cases of frostbite and 340 other injuries that left soldiers incapacitated in the course of the maneuvers.

Afterwards, the mountain troopers wondered if it had all been worth it. Few lessons learned in those three weeks in late March and early April 1944 would be of direct practical use in the combat they would see a year later. Nevertheless, Harris Dusenbery decided, D-Series veterans "gained something in that misty realm of the spirit that the army calls morale." The mountain troopers now had a standard by which to measure the hardships that were to come. And they strengthened their bonds with the men with whom they shared icy dugouts and frozen rations. Thereafter, the rifleman's squad, platoon, and company, Dusenbery wrote, "was composed of his comrades whom he could not let down and before whose eyes he could not turn back."

Not that the men of the 10th didn't bear some grudges after D-Series, particularly against their rarely seen division commander. Following the maneuvers, General Jones flew to Washington, DC, to discuss the results with Lieutenant General Lesley J. McNair, commander of Army Ground Forces. On his return to Camp Hale in May, Jones praised the men of the division for their "fortitude" in having survived what he called the "toughest training" ever undergone by American soldiers. Whatever good effect his praise might have had on the 10th's morale was undercut by what came next, a series of belittling comments about the men who went AWOL, or fell out and went back to camp, pleading to be medically excused from the maneuvers. They'd let their buddies down, he said, and lacked "that sense of personal pride and achievement which rewards those who completed 100% of the series." It saddened the general to think that "a certain number of individuals just don't have what it takes to perform the arduous job of a soldier of the 10th Division."

Private Ellis of the 86th, one of the men who had "fallen out" from exhaustion and been sent back the next day for more maneuvers, bridled at the general's "obvious contempt" for the men under his command. The division commander was derided behind his back as "old lady Jones." Later that year, at a gathering to watch a boxing match, Jones was booed by the angry crowd of mountain troopers when he rose to present a trophy, a serious breach of discipline but a good measure of the division's sentiments. If they were ever to see combat, General Jones was not the man they wanted to lead them.

At National Ski Patrol headquarters in New York, Minnie Dole was barraged with complaints about D-Series from acquaintances at Camp Hale, and pleas that he use his influence to secure a combat assignment for the division. On April 19, once again he boarded a train for Washington with associate John Morgan to meet with General George C. Marshall. Dole told the army chief of staff that the 10th needed a mission — and a new commanding general.

Marshall had nothing to say on the latter question, but on the former assured his visitors that he remained committed to finding a combat assignment for the mountain troops that suited their specialized training. He admitted they could have been used to good effect the previous winter in the fighting to take Monte Cassino in Italy, the anchor of the German Gustav Line in the mountains south of Rome. Lieutenant General Mark Clark, commander of the 5th Army, the Allied forces besieging Monte Cassino, actually had mountain-trained troops under his command, including the 1st Special Service Force, which, after taking part in the invasion of Kiska with the 87th Mountain Infantry Regiment, was shipped to Italy and helped to seize a number of German strongholds on the southern approach to Cassino. There was also the Corps de Montagne of the French Expeditionary Force in Italy, French-officered Moroccan troops rightly feared by the Germans for their fierce fighting qualities, who would be credited with seizing five mountain peaks that allowed Allied forces to outflank German defenses and opened the road to Rome in May 1944. Clark's 5th Army, like the 10th, also made extensive use of mules for resupplying troops in the field, with ten thousand of the animals in service by the spring of 1944. But oddly enough, when initially offered the services of the American mountain troops, Clark turned the offer down, considering the unit hopelessly "elitist." Marshall then offered the 10th to General Dwight Eisenhower for use in the invasion of western Europe, but Walter Bedell, Ike's chief of staff, had replied: "All those mules? Hell no!"

What Dole did not know was that Army Ground Forces observers reporting on the results of D-Series to General Marshall were preparing a report, to be delivered the following month, that advocated converting the 10th to a standard flatland division. The Mountain Division was judged too weak in numbers and equipment to be of much use. It was inconvenient, administratively, to maintain a highly specialized unit like the 10th in the field. Standard infantry units, Army Ground Forces argued, had proved their ability to fight successfully in Italy's mountains (a dubious reading of the evidence from Cassino). The experiment with mountain troops, they believed, had been a failure. It was time to bring it to a close. The future of the 10th, at least as mountain troops, was in jeopardy.

When news of the D-Day landings in Normandy arrived on June 6, it electrified the camp on what was otherwise just another training day. "It was the greatest day in the Army as yet," Corporal Donald Potter wrote home to his mother on D-Day plus one, June 7. "Morale hit a new high and men worked like they never wanted to before. Everyone hung on the radio from the first time the c.q. [man appointed to be Charge of Quarters] yelled in the morning until way after lights at night."

The men at Hale viewed the invasion's prospects optimistically, their own less so. With the invasion of Normandy, the war in Europe was clearly coming to its climactic moment. Robert Ellis, writing home two days after the invasion, predicted, "It will be over in Europe before the end of autumn."

If that was the case — and for the moment it seemed a genuine possibility — there wouldn't be anyplace with mountains (Norway, Italy) for the 10th to be sent to liberate in Europe. But Burma had mountains, if not snow — a battlefront few mountain troopers hoped to visit. Jean Cummings wrote to her in-laws on D-Day, relaying the impact of the news on the men at Camp Hale: "The invasion seems to be going as well as could be expected, doesn't it ... Some people are awfully optimistic, but I think it will still take some time to crack the Germans. However, most [of] the boys think now that they will be used in Burma or some such place ... Probably the Germans will be beaten this year and all the boys come home from Europe and Stan will be stuck in Burma and thereabouts for two or three years yet before the Japs are finished."

On the day after D-Day, the mountain troopers learned that the entire division was being shipped to Camp Swift in Texas, to spend the summer in preparation for scheduled maneuvers in Louisiana come fall. After having endured the hardships of a Colorado winter, including the misery of D-Series, it seemed an especially cruel fate to have to leave Camp Hale just as the last snow was disappearing and the Rocky Mountain columbine bloomed and scented the air. "We are all having fits," Jean Cummings wrote her in-laws on June 12. "Can you imagine sending these boys who have become acclimated to this high cold atmosphere and altitude to a place like Texas." And it wasn't just weather and altitude. The move seemed to portend something even worse than assignment to Burma, which was the imminent end for the mountain troops as a distinctive unit: "We don't know just what they are going to Texas for ... flat land infantry training, or — what I fear — airborne infantry training." Or perhaps even being broken up as a division, and sent piecemeal as replacements for other units.

The end of the 10th's Camp Hale days came quickly. The men packed their gear — or some of it. They left the ski equipment and clothing behind. Between June 20 and June 25, units of mountain troopers paraded through the camp grounds to the Pando train station, where they boarded passenger trains equipped with bunk beds stacked three high for the two-day trip to Texas. The camp's band played patriotic airs, and civilian workers, WACs, and children lined the way to cheer the troops. "Good luck, kids," three young WACs called out as L Company of the 86th marched by, and Robert Ellis long remembered his feelings of pride and gratitude.

Not everyone felt that way. A postcard addressed to Minnie Dole at the NSPS office in New York arrived a few days after the 10th's final march through the streets of Camp Hale. It read as if dictated through gritted teeth: "Emphasized stupidity. A lousy outfit. Two years wasted."

At Camp Hale, a warm summer day might mean temperatures in the mid-sixties. When the mountain troopers arrived at Camp Swift, near Bastrop, Texas, some thirty miles southeast of Austin, it was closer to one hundred degrees (and in the months that followed, the temperature sometimes reached 120). They were still dressed for the mountains in their woolen OD uniforms when they disembarked and had to hike a mile from the train depot to the base, carrying their heavy barracks bags. Almost immediately men began collapsing along the route. It was like revisiting the early days at Camp Hale, except in reverse: this time, instead of high altitude and the "Pando Hack," men were felled by the heat and humidity of low-altitude Texas. And just as in the early days at Camp Hale, acclimatization could be a drawn-out process. Writing to his wife on July 1, eight days after his regiment reached Camp Swift, Harris Dusenbery reported: "When we were standing rifle inspection this morning, one of the boys in our platoon, Turner, fainted. He fell flat on his face and hit the pavement with his jaw . . . About three minutes later another man flopped in the third platoon. He went straight back and now has a large lump on his head where he hit the pavement. This by the way is a fairly cool day."

Camp Swift, constructed in 1942, was much bigger than the division's previous camp, home to ninety thousand soldiers and ten thousand German POWs at its peak, and the facilities, which included outdoor swimming pools, were far more luxurious than those available at Hale. Weekend passes were also doled out more generously than at Hale. Austin, a city featuring, among other attractions, thousands of resident University of Texas co-eds, was an hour's bus ride away. But such advantages were outweighed in the minds of many of the men of the 10th by the Texas heat, and the host of noxious pests that thrived in it, including bedbugs, cockroaches, sand fleas, mosquitoes, gnats, and scorpions, not to mention poisonous coral and copperhead snakes. Shortly after arriving at Swift, in the midst of a nighttime training exercise, Sergeant Paul Petzoldt was sitting in his foxhole when a wriggling snake fell into his lap from the tree above. That had not been a problem during D-Series. The very next day Petzoldt arranged to be transferred to a position as an instructor at Fort Benning, where he spent the rest of the war. So many men applied for transfer to airborne units (desperately in need of replacements after D-Day) that the division shut down the transfer option. Adding to the dissatisfaction was the stricter attention to military dress and discipline prevailing at Swift. No more slopping around in every conceivable kind of uniform. Spit and polish was the order of the day, and closed collars and neckties added to the troopers' discomfort and discontent as they stood at attention or paraded in the broiling sun.

The training was intense, with hikes up to twenty-five miles (usually done at night to cut down on the number of cases of heat exhaustion). The men were limited to one quart canteen of water, even on the longest hikes. On the shorter hikes, they moved at a much faster pace, being expected to complete five miles in an hour and nine miles in two hours. They swallowed six salt tablets a day to replace what they sweated out.

Soldiers of the 10th Mountain Division training with Browning automatic rifle, Camp Swift, Texas, 1944. THE DENVER PUBLIC LIBRARY (TMD617)

For a few hundred 10th Division men, their time at Camp Swift was cut short by a new opportunity. The Officer Candidate School quota for the division was raised dramatically in midsummer. Donald Potter, who had been trying to get into OCS for months without any luck, got his orders for transfer to Fort Benning on July 18. "Last week they shipped out over a hundred candidates, and tomorrow I believe about the same number are going," he wrote his mother with the good news. Of course, he reflected, his good news came at the expense of others' bad news. "I guess the need for infantry officers has sharply increased due to overseas casualties."

At Fort Benning the pressure of the training was relentless, and every week candidates washed out and were sent back to the ranks. Of the 206 men who started with Potter in a training company in late July, only 133 were left to graduate with him in November. The training also gave the twenty-one-year-old mountain trooper the feeling that the past eighteen months of his military service, for all its hardships, had been a little sheltered. In October, a month short of receiving his lieutenant's bars, he got to watch a battlefield exercise unlike anything ever staged at Camp Hale: "This last week we had a million-dollar demonstration of an attack on pill boxes and permanent installations. Tanks, airplanes, antitank guns, demolitions, every explosive the infantry had ever heard of was shown us. It was *very* impressive, especially to us in the 10th Light Division where we're used to a lone sniper with a bee-bee gun up on the side of a cliff."

Back at Camp Swift, there were abundant signs that summer that the 10th's identity as a mountain division was being phased out of existence. The division lost the designation "Alpine." Now it was just the "10th Light Division." The troopers also learned that their former home, Camp Hale, was to be abandoned and torn down — which meant the army had no intention of training any more mountain troops, either as a new unit or as replacements for casualties in the 10th. The Mountain Training Group was formally disbanded, its members reassigned to other units in the division. Two thousand newcomers, without any mountain training, joined the outfit, bringing the 10th's total strength to the newly authorized level of 14,101. Battalions, composed of three rifle companies of 180 men each, also included a heavy weapons company, wielding for the first time .50-caliber machine guns and 81 mm mortars, more lethal than the .30-caliber machine guns and 60 mm mortars the division had trained with before (and were still being used by the weapons platoon in each infantry company). While they were in the United States, the standard (or "organic") artillery for the division's three field artillery battalions remained the 75 mm pack howitzer, rather than the heavier 105s and 155s employed by regular infantry divisions.

Two things happened that fall that cheered up the troopers. One was the cancellation of the Louisiana maneuvers originally scheduled for September, which meant no wallowing around in swamps. And the second, far more consequential, came on November 6, just a week or so short of the third anniversary of the formation of the 1st Battalion (Reinforced), 87th Infantry Mountain Regiment at Fort Lewis in mid-November 1941. The 10th Light Division was officially renamed the 10th Mountain Division. Members of the division were now authorized to wear a curved cloth tab above their crossed bayonet shoulder patch inscribed in white letters on a blue background with the word "MOUN-TAIN"—akin to the "AIRBORNE" and "RANGER" patches of other elite units. Morale soared (although no "MOUNTAIN" patches were available to sew onto uniforms until many months later). Word came down to the men that it was time to wrap up their personal affairs—and to write their wills. Realizing that the changes meant a real assignment was in the offing, the men began singing "Over There" as they marched to and from their daily training assignments. It's not entirely clear what lay behind the 10th's change in fortunes, but it may be that the decisive role of French Moroccan mountain troops in the spring fighting in Italy swung opinion in the Pentagon and at 5th Army headquarters in Italy in favor of employing the division as originally intended, that is, as specialized mountain infantry. And having seen so many divisions transferred from Italy to France after D-Day, Lieutenant General Mark Clark could no longer afford to be all that choosy about available infantry divisions, elitist or not.

And then a final gift to the 10th Mountain Division—delivered on Thanksgiving Day, no less—a new commander, Major General George Price Hays. Hays was fifty-two years old when he arrived at Camp Swift to take command of the 10th Mountain Infantry, a seasoned soldier with impressive combat experience in two wars. He was born in China in 1892, the son of Presbyterian missionaries, educated in Oklahoma before enlisting in the US Army in 1917. In France in 1918, a first lieutenant serving as a forward artillery observer with the 10th Field Artillery Regiment of the 3rd Division, he earned the Congressional Medal of Honor for horseback heroics during the Second Battle of the Marne. On Bastille Day, July 14, 1918, he rode back and forth across the battlefield delivering messages to batteries under heavy German shelling, having seven horses shot out from under him and being severely wounded by the end of the day. In the Second World War, he served as commander of artillery units in both Italy (during the Battle of Monte Cassino) and France (landing on Omaha Beach on D-Day plus one). General Marshall, an old friend, held him in high regard.

Ahead of his arrival at Camp Swift, Hays had been warned of the 10th's morale problems by Minnie Dole (at a chance meeting in the Pentagon) and others. He knew only one man in the division, David Ruffner, who commanded the division's artillery. Moving quickly to establish his own leadership, he had the division's officers and noncoms assembled in the camp's field house on November 25 for a pep talk. A short, wiry figure with a prominent nose and ears, a classic dog-faced soldier in appearance despite the star on his collar, he made a good impression, especially since, as his listeners knew, only two weeks earlier he had been with men on the front lines fighting in France. And then there was the Congressional Medal of Honor ribbon he wore on his short battle jacket. "We are going to have good times as well as bad times in our combat overseas," he told the men, "and as far as possible it will be my policy to make everyone as comfortable and to have as good a time as possible as long as we accomplish our mission . . . If you're going to risk your life, you might as well do it in good company."

The "good times and bad times" line was soon being repeated in conversations throughout the division, and left a favorable impression of the new commander. As did his visits to smaller gatherings of enlisted men over the next few days. "What amazed us," Robert Ellis recalled, "was that he said he'd heard a lot about us over in France, and the story was we're a crack outfit." A little praise from a genuine war hero went a long way to ease the bruised feelings of a division that had come to feel, in Minnie Dole's phrase, like "the Army's bastard child."

Three days after General Hays's pep talk, the 86th Mountain Infantry Regiment began to board trains — headed for where, no one was telling them. Harris Dusenbery, who had transferred to HQ Company of the 1st Battalion of the 86th in July, posted a letter to his wife, Evelyn, before his departure on November 27. "This may be my last uncensored letter . . . Honest, I don't have the least idea where we are going. I doubt whether the 86th officers know." His next letter was postmarked December 3 and, now subject to official censorship, was even less informative: "We've arrived at another camp but I'm not permitted to say where or what or when."

The men of the 86th were followed three weeks later, to wherever it was they were going, by those of the 85th and 87th. Second Lieutenant Donald Potter, H Company of the 85th, wrote to his mother on Christmas Day from an unidentified location, reporting that he had attended a Christmas Eve service the night before: "Christmas carols were sung with quite a bit more meaning that most of us have ever put into them and then to end it up we sang 'Onward Christian Soldiers' until every beam and rafter in the chapel was standing on end. I've never heard anything like it before." Marty Daneman, also of the 85th, posted a final stateside letter to his fiancée, Lois, on New Year's Eve 1944: "Happy New Year darling . . . My letters will stop without notice soon too, but please don't worry about it . . . I'll miss you sweet, & think of you every minute."

What would the new year, 1945, bring for mountain troopers Dusenbery, Potter, and Daneman, and the other 14,098 men of the 10th Mountain Division? Whatever and wherever it was, it was now clear they would be playing for keeps.

View of Riva Ridge, stretching from Mount Serrasiccia on the right to Mount Mancinello on the left, February 21, 1945.
THE DENVER PUBLIC LIBRARY (TMD374)

6

Italy, December 23, 1944–February 18, 1945

"Still Green"

I have been up in the front lines. I don't wish to sound like I know it all now because I am still about as green as a combat Infantryman can be but life in the front lines isn't as bad as I expected . . . [I]t isn't a Hollywood hell of living in fox holes under constant fire etc.

— *Private Stuart E. Abbott to his family,*
February 6, 1945

THE TRAINS CRAWLED EAST FROM TEXAS TOWARD THE ATLANTIC, SO it was almost certain that the 86th Mountain Infantry Regiment was not bound for Burma. But with the exception of regimental commander Colonel Clarence M. (Tommy) Tomlinson and a few select staff officers, no one in the 86th knew their ultimate destination. On December 2, three days after leaving Swift, the mountain troopers arrived at Camp Patrick Henry near Newport News, Virginia. The camp, constructed in 1942, served as a temporary home for waves of soldiers headed for the European theater in World War II. Over 700,000 GIs had passed through its gates before the 86th arrived at the start of December. The troopers were kept under tight security, forbidden to reveal their location to anyone, all passes denied, correspondence censored. The 10th, a little over three years after its activation at Fort Lewis in December 1941, was the next-to-last US Army division scheduled to ship out to Europe.

On December 10, 1944, at the nearby Hampton Roads Port of Embarkation, the 86th boarded the USS *Argentina,* a passenger liner converted to a navy transport troopship at the start of the war. At 8 a.m. the *Argentina* pulled away from the dock, and in the widening bay fell in line with the other ships of its convoy, including destroyers on patrol against enemy submarines. The relative equality among the ranks that the mountain troops had enjoyed in Camp Hale days was not a feature of life aboard the *Argentina.* Officers were housed in staterooms, crowded by prewar cruise ship standards, but nothing like the tightly packed quarters the enlisted men occupied below them in fetid holds where tiers of bunks were stacked many levels high. Three times a day officers sat down at tables to have their meals served to them, complete with linen and silver. In contrast, enlisted men got two meals a day, each requiring waiting in line for hours, and eaten standing up.

Many men soon lost interest in any meals at all, since, unaccustomed to ocean travel, they found it impossible to keep food down, and in that regard at least, a degree of egalitarian misery united the ranks. Harry Robert (Bob) Krear, a private first class in L Company, was sick for all but the last two days it took to reach their destination. During the daytime he stayed on deck as much as possible, where there was fresh air and the opportunity to vomit as needed over a railing into the ocean. "Just the smell of food produced retching," he recalled, "as did the smell of coffee, diesel fuel, and especially the smell of the toilets."

PFC Harris Dusenbery, HQ Company, 1st Battalion of the 86th, had a better voyage, facing its trials, including intermittent seasickness, with his usual detached equanimity. He spent his time peeling potatoes on KP and reading a biography of Walt Whitman. As he wrote to his wife, Evelyn, after a week at sea: "We've been having a good trip so far and for an Atlantic crossing in mid-December I'd say the weather has been very good. A warm south wind has been steady and sometimes blowing at gale force. So we've had white caps and a choppy sea but our ship rides smoothly . . . Life on a troop ship is crowded and monotonous but my reading keeps me occupied and interested."

By the time the coast of Africa and the Rock of Gibraltar loomed into view, the men on board the *Argentina* had been told they were bound for Italy, news that met general approval. They were, at long last, headed back to mountains. The decision to send the 10th to the Mediterranean was made in Washington in early November, and the assistant division commander, Colonel Robinson E. Duff, was sent with a small advance party to Italy in mid-November to oversee arrangements for the division's deployment.

As the *Argentina* sailed into calmer waters east of Gibraltar, Bob Krear finally stopped retching and recovered his "zest for life," able to enjoy "the spectacular beauty of the Mediterranean Sea, which was of a lovely blue color compared to the dark Atlantic." The classically educated Harris Dusenbery was reminded of "ancient Greek legends, of Roman triremes, and of Moorish galleys." The last two days of the voyage became something like a sightseeing cruise for the *Argentina*'s passengers, most of whom had never before traveled abroad. Flying fish darted away from the ship's wake. The sunsets were glorious, and a warm breeze blew up from Africa. The soldiers crowded the bow of the boat to watch for landmarks like the Isle of Capri and Mount Vesuvius. The *Argentina* finally arrived in the port of Naples on December 23, thirteen days after departing from Virginia.

Elsewhere in Europe, while the 86th was making its ocean crossing, the Germans had broken through American lines in Belgium and besieged the crucial crossroads city of Bastogne. General George S. Patton's 3rd Army was driving north from France to relieve the encircled Americans in Bastogne, including the 101st Airborne Division, but the outcome of what became known as the Battle of the Bulge was still in doubt when the *Argentina* docked in Naples. By then the 85th and 87th Mountain Infantry Regiments had departed Camp Swift by train for Camp Patrick Henry. When they boarded the USS *West Point* (another converted passenger ship) on January 4, 1945, the troopers had no idea where their brothers in the 86th had landed. Given the news from the Belgian front, many believed that was their own destination. But two days into the voyage, they too learned they were bound for the Mediterranean and Italy. The 10th's ultimate destination was still an official secret, although more effectively preserved in the United States than elsewhere. "Welcome Men of the 10th Mountain Division," German propaganda leaflets delivered by artillery shell to American lines mockingly greeted the division in its early days in Italy. "It's a long way from Camp Hale."

The *West Point* was fast enough that it made the ocean crossing without convoy. It was a bigger ship than the *Argentina* — not that that made any difference to the soldiers aboard, since its holds were crowded with two mountain regiments instead of one. "The ship used to be a luxury liner, tho it's hard to tell that right now," Corporal Marty Daneman, HQ Company, 2nd Battalion of the 85th, wrote to fiancée Lois mid-voyage. "There are 80 of us in a compartment only twice as big as our living room." Private Robert Ellis, F Company of the 85th, started keeping a diary (although diaries in combat zones were forbidden by army regulations, that proved a commonly violated rule) on the day the *West Point* set off from Newport News. After three days at sea he noted that he was reading the poetry of Alan Seeger, an American volunteer with the French Foreign Legion in the First World War who was killed on the western front in 1916, and whose most famous poem was prophetically titled "I Have a Rendezvous with Death." Other men, choosing not to think about such things just yet, were more interested in the continuous high-stakes craps games available on the ship's stairway landings. Ellis noted in his diary that one member of his company, Charles A. Eitel, won a thousand dollars just before they reached Naples — serious money for a private earning $50 a month (though all ranks received a 20 percent pay raise for overseas duty as soon as they shipped out). The *West Point* arrived in Naples harbor on January 13, nine days after its departure from the States.

The mountain troopers' first glimpse of Italy was of a city that had had a bad war. Arriving troopships had to wend their way around half-submerged hulks in the harbor, sunk by Allied bombing raids or scuttled by the Germans before they pulled out. Little improved upon their landing. Norman Lewis, a British intelligence officer, had kept a diary during the previous winter of 1943–44, when he was based in Naples. "It is astonishing," he wrote, "to witness the struggles of this city, so shattered, so starved, so deprived of all those things that justify a city's existence, to adapt itself to a collapse into conditions which must resemble life in the Dark Ages. People camp out like Bedouins in deserts of brick. There is little food, little water, no salt, no soap."

Conditions had not changed much in the fifteen months that separated the city's liberation in October 1943 from the arrival of the first units of the 10th in December 1944, except that a thriving mafia-controlled black market had sprung up. Lewis estimated that by the spring of 1944, "the equivalent of the cargo of one Allied ship in three unloaded in the Port of Naples is stolen." Eric Sevareid, a war correspondent for CBS Radio stationed in Naples in 1944, spent as little time as he could in the city, describing it as a sinkhole of corruption where well-connected Allied officials were "making more money than they had as civilians, inhabiting finer homes . . . entertaining lavishly and being entertained."

Little of that ill-gotten bounty benefited ordinary Neapolitans. As the men of the 10th disembarked from their ships, they were surrounded by scenes of poverty and degradation. Stan Cummings, newly commissioned second lieutenant and serving as a platoon leader in B Company of the 85th, was sickened to see men fighting over the cigarette butts and apple cores the Americans discarded. "I feel like J. P. Morgan," he wrote in his first letter home to wife Jean, "and I'm ashamed of it." In Naples, "the people either work for us, beg, steal, prostitute themselves, or starve," Marty Daneman wrote to Lois in his own first letter from Italy. "There simply is nothing else to do."

Long before the 10th Mountain Division shipped overseas, it had become a cliché in the American press to label the war in Italy the "forgotten front." Congresswoman Clare Booth Luce, returning from an official visit to the Italian front in December 1944, described the American troops fighting there as "forgotten men."

If the Italian front and the men who fought there tended to be forgotten at home in 1944, it was due in part to Italy's relative unimportance in the final outcome of the war; the decisive battles were clearly being fought in eastern and northwestern Europe. But the neglect also reflected the fact that the Allied campaign in Italy did not fit the uplifting wartime narrative favored in American newspapers, newsmagazines, and Hollywood movies — one of steady, heroic, and inexorable progress toward total victory. "The war in Italy was tough," war correspondent Ernie Pyle wrote in 1944, before the arrival of the 10th. "The land and the weather were both against us. It rained and it rained. Vehicles bogged down and bridges washed out. The country was shockingly beautiful, and just as shockingly hard to capture from the enemy."

In the most famous passage of Ernest Hemingway's *Farewell to Arms*, set in an earlier war in Italy, the novel's American protagonist confesses his embarrassment at hearing in speeches and official proclamations "the words, sacred, glorious, and sacrifice." Overused and drained of meaning, they were inadequate to describe the blood-spattered shambles of life and death on the front lines. In the end, Hemingway's war-weary ambulance driver concludes, "Only the names of places had dignity." In Italy since 1943 there had been plenty of sacrifices and, as any reader of Pyle's dispatches from the front knew, a lot of courageous dignity, but victories were hard-won and always incomplete.

"I feel like a fugitive from th' law of averages."

Cartoon by Bill Mauldin, Stars and Stripes *(Mediterranean edition), November 2, 1944.* © 1944 BY BILL MAULDIN. COURTESY OF BILL MAULDIN ESTATE LLC

The names of places in Italy where Americans fought in 1943–44 — the Rapido River, Cassino, Anzio beachhead — increasingly evoked a sense of bloody futility, a war of attrition in which there was neither strategic nor dramatic payoff. Frontline infantry units were in the war for the duration, and individual soldiers increasingly felt like fugitives "from th' law of averages," as Willie says to Joe in a Bill Mauldin cartoon that ran in *Stars and Stripes* in November 1944. No outfit better exemplified the "law of averages" in the Mediterranean theater than the US Army's 34th (Red Bull) Division, a National Guard unit from the north-central states, and the first US division sent to fight the Nazis. After first being bloodied in North Africa, the 34th landed in Italy in September 1943 and fought at both Cassino and Anzio. By war's end, the unit had spent 517 days on the front line, more than any other US Army division, with killed, wounded, captured, and missing soldiers totaling over twenty thousand, for a casualty rate of more than 150 percent.

Following a winter in which the US 5th Army as a whole suffered 55,000 casualties, a joint offensive of the 5th and 8th Armies, code-named "Diadem," broke through the German Gustav Line south of Rome in mid-May 1944, capturing Cassino at long last and advancing up the Liri Valley, followed soon after by a breakout from the Anzio beachhead to Rome's west. But even with the Allies finally advancing, there was little sense of exhilaration. "Battles were large or small; points at issue were vital or of minor consequence; but always and everywhere procedure and pattern were monotonously the same," correspondent Eric Sevareid wrote in a postwar memoir:

> In the big push in the spring of 1944, German guns betrayed their presence. We called our planes to bomb them, and we concentrated our own artillery . . . Thereupon the infantry flowed slowly ahead. At each strong point or village there were always a few snipers to be blasted out, always mines which exploded a number of vehicles, always booby traps which filled a few rooms with smoke and mortal cries. Bulldozers would clear the rubble, engineers would fill the craters, the medical troops would set up their aid stations, a few half-starved Italian families would be rooted out of evil-smelling cellars, and while silent men hoisted limp bodies into trucks the news would go out to the world that the place was "liberated."

Press releases from 5th Army publicists always used the term "General Mark Clark's 5th Army" to describe the advance toward Rome. Some disgruntled subordinates took to referring to their imperious commander as "Marcus Aurelius Clarkus." Clark was obsessed with having the Americans beat the British 8th Army to the city, which they finally accomplished on June 4. The event dominated headlines back home for all of a day before being pushed off the front page by the invasion of Normandy. And while the 5th Army commander had his picture taken making a triumphal entry into Rome in his personal jeep with the three stars of a lieutenant general on its front fender, that photo opportunity came at a cost. Clark's decision to order Major General Lucian Truscott's VI Corps to turn toward Rome in late May after its breakout from Anzio, instead of attempting to cut off the retreat of the German 10th Army from the Gustav Line, allowed a formidable enemy to escape to fight another day.

For a few months in the summer of 1944, the war in Italy was fought on relatively flat and open ground, terrain that favored the Allies with their preponderance of armor and air power. Allied leaders concluded that the war in Italy was all but over. General Sir Harold L. G. Alexander, commander of 15th Army Group, which included both the American 5th Army and the British 8th Army, wrote to Prime Minister Winston Churchill following the fall of Rome to report that "morale is irresistibly high" in the Allied armies in Italy. "Neither the Apennines nor even the Alps should prove a serious obstacle," he predicted. And in fact, his counterpart Field Marshal Albert Kesselring, supreme commander of German forces in the Mediterranean, a general known for his optimism and cheerful demeanor (dubbed "Smiling Al" by his own troops and Allied soldiers alike), briefly contemplated a withdrawal all the way to the Alps. But Adolf Hitler flew into a fist-waving rage whenever any of his generals suggested pulling troops back from conquered lands — Italy, Norway, the Balkans — to protect the homeland. Instead, German forces in Italy were ordered to make a stand along a newly constructed line of mountain defenses in the northern Apennines, designated the Gothic Line (Gotenstellung).

The northern Apennine range stretches unbroken for 140 miles between the narrow coastal plains to its east and west. It is fifty miles in width, with peaks as high as seven thousand feet, and in 1944 it was penetrated by only a few roads. The valleys and passes across which those roads snaked lay below high ground controlled by the Germans. There was little cover for attacking troops, who were confronted not only by minefields and artillery but also by sheer cliffs and steep slopes leading to the ridgelines above them. Tanks were of limited use in that terrain, and supplies often had to be carried on the backs of mules and men if they were to reach the front. And in the winter, there was snow and ice to hinder ground troops, and fog and clouds to hinder air operations.

The Gothic Line guarded the approach to the Po Valley, which was both the agricultural breadbasket of Italy and its industrial heartland. In the flat, broad expanse of the valley, Allied military forces would again be at a tactical advantage (armor and airpower), which, they hoped, would carry them all the way to the Alps and into Austria. A British drive along the eastern Italian coast and an American drive to the west into the mountains in August and September made some gains. At the point of its farthest advance, the 5th Army was a mere ten miles from Bologna, gateway to the Po — "one long stride from success," in the words of General Clark. But there was no breakthrough, no success. By late October, after considerable losses, and with the weather turning bad, the Allied offensive halted. In the 5th Army sector, the Germans still had a secure hold on the northernmost line of peaks of the North Apennines, now known as the Winter Line (although still often referred to as the Gothic Line). In a setback for the Germans, "Smiling Al" was sidelined by injuries suffered in an auto accident in late October. Kesselring returned to command in Italy in mid-January 1945, but in March was transferred to western Germany to replace Field Marshal Gerd von Rundstedt as commander of military forces fighting a doomed effort to halt the American and British advance into the German heartland. Command of Army Group C, the German and Italian Fascist forces in Italy, passed to General Heinrich von Vietinghoff.

The Winter Line was the destination for the fourteen thousand men of the US Army's 10th Mountain Division who landed in Naples in December and January. The first to reach the front lines were men of the 86th Mountain Infantry Regiment. They spent their first two nights in Italy in an unheated orphanage in the Neapolitan suburb of Bagnoli, with cold marble floors to sleep on. On Christmas Day, the 1st Battalion traveled northward by train (in boxcars), followed the next day by the rest of the regiment, who made an overnight trip up the Italian coast in the freighter *Sestriere* to the port of Livorno (or Leghorn, as the Americans called it), a major port on the western coast of Tuscany. The 86th might have spent more time in Naples, but the Germans had launched a series of probing attacks in late December in the Serchio Valley along the western coast forty-five miles north of Livorno, pushing back demoralized units of the ill-used and segregated African American 92nd Division. Fifth Army commanders, worried that the Germans might attempt a surprise offensive in northern Italy comparable to the ongoing Battle of the Bulge, were eager to have fresh troops available on the Pisa plain to plug any holes in their lines. There would be no Italian "Bulge," however. The offensive was halfhearted and soon abandoned; the German command understood their army's best hope in Italy lay in a determined defense of the high ground they already held.

From Livorno the 86th was trucked to Pisa, where troopers encountered the first Italian landmark most of them could identify, the eponymous Leaning Tower. There, they encountered something else new to them. "We could now hear the rumble of artillery and see its flashes at night," recalled First Lieutenant David R. Brower, who was serving as S-2 (intelligence officer) for 3rd Battalion of the 86th. At a staging area outside Pisa, the former hunting grounds of King Victor Emmanuel III, they pitched their tents and spent the next five days sorting through their equipment. The mountain troopers were dismayed to discover that much of the specialized cold weather gear and clothing they had been equipped with at Camp Hale never made it to Italy, apparently through the whim of an army quartermaster. (Some wound up in a warehouse in Boston, where it sat until it was sold as surplus after the war.) Mountain boots, parkas, mountain pants, and skis would be in short supply in Italy. What the men particularly missed were the sleeping bags that had kept them warm on those twenty-below nights in the Rockies. Instead they made do with two thin army blankets. As one historian of the war in Europe commented, "Winter always seemed to catch the U.S. Army by surprise." This must have been particularly frustrating to a unit that was used to being well equipped when sent out in the cold. Jack R. Smolenske, a private in HQ Company of the 3rd Battalion of the 85th, who arrived in Pisa a few weeks later, wrote home to complain: "I've never spent such miserable nights in my life. You just can't keep warm at night. We were issued two more blankets that make 4, but it is not much warmer. If only we had some of the equipment we had in Hale, we would be alright."

The 86th's next move, by truck convoy on New Year's Eve, was to Quercianella, a seaside town and training encampment a few miles south of Livorno. The regiment was now officially part of IV Corps of the US 5th Army. Commanded by Major General Willis D. Crittenberger, IV Corps was a patchwork of nationalities — South African and Brazilian as well as American. As for the 5th Army, of which IV Corps was a part, it had a new commander, Lucian K. Truscott Jr., who had been promoted to lieutenant general in September 1944. Following the capture of Rome, Mark Clark had been awarded command of the Allied 15th Army Group in Italy, which included both the US 5th and the British 8th Army.

The war in Italy proved a graveyard for many a general's reputation, but Lucian Truscott proved an exception. Unusual among top-ranking American officers, he was not a West Pointer, or a graduate of any other military academy. Nor, unlike some of his peers, was he a publicity hound. He was a tough old cavalryman, a workhorse general who got the job he was given done, and was much admired by the men he commanded. Truscott was pleased to have the 10th coming under his command because he had a mission in mind for them for which they were uniquely suited.

The 86th took its first casualties on January 6, just two weeks after the regiment disembarked at Naples and before it even reached the front. These proved the worst single-day casualties it or any other unit of the 10th suffered until nearly the end of February. A soldier on guard duty on the perimeter of the 86th's bivouac area in Quercianella wandered into an enemy minefield, despite posted signs warning the area was off-limits. He triggered a German "S" mine (or "Bouncing Betty"), which flew into the air beside him before exploding in a rain of deadly steel pellets. Medics, ordinary soldiers, and a Catholic chaplain, First Lieutenant Clarence J. Hagan, rushed to give aid to the dying man and set off more mines. In a moment, seven men, including four medics and Father Hagan, were dead. Six more were wounded, one of whom died a few days later. (Hagan was one of three 10th Mountain chaplains who died in the war.)

Medic Arthur G. Draper also came to help but stopped short of the minefield when he saw that "bodies were strewn around in grotesque positions." He wondered if it might be a training exercise for a moment, then realized this was war, and the harbinger of more deaths to come. The 10th had suffered other deaths, on Kiska and in training accidents at Camp Hale, but these were the first battlefield deaths inflicted by the enemy.

On January 7–8, 1945, the 86th moved to the front, in trucks that carried them back through Livorno and Pisa, then on the broad *auto-*

strada along the bank of the Arno River, before turning north at Pistoia on narrow and twisting Highway 64 into the province of Bologna and the heart of the northern Apennines. (The city of Pistoia, nineteen miles west of Florence, was a place that many men of the 10th would soon become better acquainted with. It served as IV Corps headquarters, and was home to the tent city of the 16th Evacuation Hospital, where those wounded in the mountains were taken for preliminary treatment.) Once in the mountains, all signs of rank were banished from helmets, collars, and sleeves to prevent German sharpshooters from targeting officers and NCOs; saluting was forbidden for the same reason.

The 86th was assigned to a temporary division-sized unit called Task Force 45, commanded by the 10th Mountain's assistant division commander, General Robinson E. Duff. "We were soon in snow-covered mountains with a cold snowstorm in progress," First Lieutenant David Brower noted, "and we could think back to Camp Hale and D-Series." There was indeed some resemblance to D-Series, even if they weren't at a particularly high altitude. With several feet of snow on the ground, the roads became impassable, and some of the men in the regiment were forced to march the last eighteen miles. The three battalions of the 86th were spread out along a front of about 11,800 yards, or a little under seven miles, roughly along a northeast-southwest axis that ran through the narrow valleys. On the right flank they were linked to the division-sized Brazilian Expeditionary Force. To their left there was heavily mountainous terrain, and a twenty-five-mile gap to the next Allied units. They would remain in that position until relieved by the 85th and 87th regiments on February 2.

In the first days at the front, the 86th's 1st Battalion, commanded by Lieutenant Colonel Henry J. Hampton, was stationed farthest north, with its command post in Vidiciatico, a hilltop village a few miles south of a 3,800-foot mountain called Mount Belvedere. Second Battalion, commanded by Lieutenant Colonel Dured E. Townsend, was headquartered north of San Marcello. Third Battalion, commanded by Major John H. Hay, occupied the town of Bagni di Lucca, another few miles farther south. First Battalion held the ground of most interest to 5th Army planning staff because of its proximity to Belvedere, a key terrain feature blocking any possible Allied advance in the region. The mountain, topped by the ruins of a medieval castle, loomed over the valley and surrounding ridges, spurs, and gorges. Its slopes were relatively gentle; it reminded New Englander Bob Livermore of stubby Mount Monadnock in southern New Hampshire (which is actually higher than Belvedere).

To the west of Belvedere, across the valley, lay a somewhat higher and, on the side facing the Americans, much steeper three-and-a-half-mile-long ridgeline. This was the left flank of the 10th Mountain Division's position. Initially referred to by military intelligence as the Mancinello-Campiano Ridge, it later became known as Riva Ridge, for one of the peaks along the ridgeline, 4,672-foot Monte Riva ("Riva Ridge" was a lot easier for Americans to say than "Mancinello-Campiano"). From the Dardagna River (actually a small stream), which flowed along the base of the ridgeline, the climb to its summits up the east face was roughly 1,600 feet at the northern end and 2,500 feet at the southern end. German soldiers from the 1045th Grenadier Regiment were heavily entrenched on Belvedere; Riva Ridge was more lightly occupied by soldiers from the 1044th Grenadier Regiment and the 232nd Fusilier Battalion. The regiments were severely understrength, with only about three fifths of their full complement. The 29th Panzer Grenadier Division was held in reserve.

The Germans had the advantage of holding the high ground and commanding sweeping views of the valley and villages below. Both Riva Ridge and Mount Belvedere were, in those days, largely denuded of vegetation, except for some groves of pine and chestnut trees on Belvedere. The defenders, in well-prepared and camouflaged bunkers and trenches, were difficult to spot, either from the ground or from the air, although American and Italian partisan patrols helped reveal the disposition of some of them. The Germans had an easier time keeping track of their opponents, at least during daytime. Lieutenant Colonel Hampton likened the 1st Battalion's position in and around Vidiciatico to sitting "in the bottom of a bowl with the enemy sitting on two-thirds of the rim looking down upon you. There was about as much concealment as a goldfish would have in a bowl."

The soldiers were billeted in stone farmhouses, barns, hotels, schoolhouses, and other buildings in the villages below Belvedere and Riva Ridge. These dwellings were usually poorly lighted and heated (if at all), but were preferable to the tents occupied by soldiers farther back from the front line. The thick stone walls and tiled roofs of the village houses kept some of the cold and damp of the Apennine winter at bay. Those closest to the German lines sandbagged their windows and doorways. The rooms in private homes were requisitioned, not rented, but soldiers were generous with spare rations, so the Americans were welcome tenants. Sergeant Denis Nunan of C Company of the 87th wrote home to report that when his unit moved out of the house they had been staying in for a new billet, the family they shared it with "thanked us very sincerely for the food and soap we gave them and the Mother even cried. Made a guy feel that maybe if given the same chances we Americans get, the Italians would be an okay bunch."

The villages provided the men of the 10th a different view of Italy from the one they first encountered in Naples. Families were intact, friendly to the newcomers, but protective of their children. Ragged little boys did not tug on the troopers' coat sleeves, pandering for their sisters. The single village girls were seen mostly in chaperoned circumstances. "Last night the Italians gave a dance in town," Harris Dusenbery wrote his wife in January. "They had two accordions and a clarinet to provide the music, and there were about five men for every woman . . . Everyone seemed to be having a good time and oblivious to the fact that the Germans were not too far off."

The villagers, although usually desperately poor, worked very hard to survive, and knew how to make the most of a scenic but unforgiving mountain environment. "The terracing of the hills surrounding each town is a prominent feature," PFC John Parker Compton wrote to his family in January. "The trouble the Italian goes to in order to cultivate the smallest tract of land is amazing." A lively and mutually beneficial commercial economy sprang up, as villagers washed the soldiers' clothes, cut their hair, and fed them, with the going price for most services a pack of cigarettes, the preferred local currency.

Relations often went beyond the cash (or cigarette) nexus. There was little love for Mussolini or the *tedeschi*, the Germans, in the Italian mountains. Many village men fought with the partisans. The Americans were welcome allies and protectors. There were ghost villages in the surrounding valleys and hills, like Ca Berna in the Dardagna valley, where the Germans killed twenty-nine people on September 27, 1944, and Ronchidoso, two miles northeast of Mount Belvedere, where they killed sixty-eight more on September 28–29 in retribution for a partisan attack, sparing neither women nor children. Those villagers the Germans didn't kill, they robbed. Second Lieutenant William Putnam, L Company of the 85th, soon learned a standard phrase, "*Tedeschi portati tutti via*," the Germans took everything.

The army issued Italian phrase books to the soldiers, but some of the troopers already spoke fluent Italian because they had been raised in Italian American families, or were Italian refugees. Others, even without knowing Italian, came to regard the village families as surrogates for faraway relatives. Second Lieutenant Donald Potter, H Company of the 85th, lived for a while with the Barattini family. "These people are typical of the hard pressed but never say die Italians of the mountain region," he wrote in a letter to his mother in January. "Senora [Signora] Burratini [Barattini] is a wonderful woman and really keeps the house and her five children on the go; her husband works at what ever he can and that's very little because most of the people live from the land." The Barattini parents, children, and Potter, when he wasn't on duty, spent evenings playing the Italian version of gin rummy.

During the daytime, the Americans mostly tried to keep out of sight and not attract shelling from the surrounding hills. After dark, giant searchlights located out of artillery range shone their lights into the clouds above the mountains, obscuring the enemy's vision while providing the soldiers below an artificial moonlight. The men came out of their shelters into the eerily illuminated night and learned the rudiments of what it meant to be frontline soldiers.

It proved a gentler initiation than what would have been their experience had they been shipped to Belgium and thrown into the bloody effort to push back the Germans in the Battle of the Bulge. Private Stuart Abbott of L Company wrote to his family in early February, after the 86th had been relieved by the other two mountain regiments and was enjoying a few days behind the lines. Abbott, the former Chicago Boy Scout and aspiring naturalist who had been so thrilled by the opportunity to go camping and hunting in his off-hours when he arrived at Camp Hale as an eighteen-year-old in 1943, was still full of boyish enthusiasm. He mentioned having been under small arms fire, and was proud to have earned his Combat Infantryman Badge. (The decoration, authorized midway through the war as a way to improve infantry morale, and awarded to all infantrymen who had actively engaged the enemy in ground combat, also brought with it an additional $10 monthly pay.) For Private Abbott war was an adventure, and not even a particularly arduous one for a survivor of D-Series: "Anyway I got enough to eat and got enough sleep to get by and while their [sic] were bad moments they were the exception."

The only real hardship he had experienced thus far was homesickness. "I'm living for the day," he wrote home in another letter, posted four days after his twentieth birthday, "when I can curl up in an easy chair with a good book & an entire pan of hot buttered popcorn for the whole evening." Of course, as a well-meaning son, Abbott would not have wanted to burden family members back home with alarming accounts of the dangers he faced. But those first few weeks on a quiet front encouraged men in the 10th to think that their war might be different from what they had read about in Ernie Pyle dispatches or seen depicted in Bill Mauldin's Willie and Joe cartoons. Second Lieutenant Francis X. Limmer of A Company in the 86th wrote to his father in Boston in mid-January, "I am now able to say that I have been at the front but if things are like it was up there all the time this war will be easier than I ever imagined it could be." The war that the 10th encountered in Italy up until the middle of February was an experience unlike any the soldiers had known before, but in its novelty seemed manageable, even intriguing.

The mountain troopers suffered some casualties. On January 19, PFC Charles G. Norton of B Company of the 86th was the first in his regiment to die (apart from the mine casualties at Quercianella on January 6). Sergeant Harold J. Hall, also of B Company, was mortally wounded while taking a patrol into enemy territory on January 21, but managed to lead his men out of an ambush before he died. He was posthumously awarded a Silver Star for bravery.

But neither the Americans nor the Germans were wasting much ammunition shelling each other's lines in January. They were saving it for more consequential days to come. Nevertheless, for troops coming under fire for the first time, even the occasional artillery explosion could leave a lasting impression. Stan Cummings, now serving as supply officer for Headquarters Company of the 85th Regiment, was uninjured when a shell from a German 88 mm gun exploded nearby shortly after his arrival at the front. But, covered in mud, he became acutely aware of his own vulnerability. "An 88 shell is the worst thing I've run up against," he reported to his wife, Jean. "I have never felt fear like that before." After the explosion, he confessed, "I lay there for half an hour completely out of breath."

The closest the 86th came to a large-scale engagement during its first weeks on the front line was in the early morning hours of January 25. Even soldiers who had gone through rigorous training, in many cases for a year or two, still had a lot to learn when they found themselves in combat for the first time. L Company of the 86th was stationed in the tiny abandoned village of Querciola (nicknamed "Coca-Cola" by the troopers), which consisted of nine house and a little church, and was located about three miles north of Vidiciatico, just below Mount Belvedere's bare southern slope. Coca-Cola was as far to the front as the Americans could go without actually scaling the mountain. They had set up a defensive perimeter in outlying farmhouses and foxholes, connected by a field telephone system, and were on the alert for enemy infiltrators. On the evening of January 24, two German deserters came into the village to surrender and warned of an impending attack.

Despite that advance warning, when the men on guard on the outer perimeter spotted several dozen Germans infiltrating the position around 3 a.m. on the twenty-fifth, they held their fire. There were whispered conversations on the field telephones as to what they should do, but by the time the order came back to open fire, the intruders had disappeared. PFC Bob Krear, who would soon be embroiled in the fight, later speculated that a combination of reluctance to give away their positions and moral qualms about gunning down other men without warning were both to blame for the sentries' passive response. After all, none of the Americans on the front line "had ever shot at or killed anybody before," Krear noted.

The sentries' failure to shoot could have been disastrous and was not without consequences. Inside American lines, the Germans attacked first one and then another of the farmhouse strongpoints, though they were driven back in each case. Krear's platoon was in reserve in Querciola, and his squad was sent up to the front to reinforce one of the farmhouses, code-named "Lion." Krear and Sergeant Artur Argiewicz were ordered to take positions in abandoned foxholes in front of the strong point. (Why the foxholes were abandoned was something else Krear wondered about later on.) Krear made it to his foxhole safely, but Argiewicz was cut down by a sudden burst of automatic weapon fire before he reached shelter. Then American artillery shells began crashing down just in front of Krear's foxhole, and the Germans were driven back to their lines, apparently taking some casualties of their own. "After the Germans had withdrawn," Krear remembered, "the real tragedy of this operation was revealed . . . As I expected, Argiewicz was dead, and the tragedy was magnified by the fact that he was not killed by the Germans, but rather was shot in the back by Thompson submachine gun fire by one of the men manning the Lion outpost."

The well-liked Argiewicz, twenty-two years old when he died, had as a teenager been a rising star in Sierra Club climbing circles in California before the war, and was co-author with David Brower of the army's official field manual on mountain warfare. The man who shot him was one of his best friends, and was so shaken by what he'd done that he had to be sent to the rear. The next time they came in contact with the enemy, the men of L Company would not be reluctant to kill. "The hardening process," Krear later wrote, "which would remain part of us for the rest of our lives, was beginning."

Another revealing first-encounter-with-the-enemy story came from 85th medic Bud Lovett, who went along on a patrol in late January. In the hills above the American-occupied village of Bagni di Lucca, the Americans encountered a German soldier on skis, wearing a white camouflage uniform. The patrol had orders to bring back a prisoner, and it looked like they had acquired one. "We ordered him to put his hands on his head and come on in," Lovett recalled. "He stood and looked at us, and then he did a jump turn and skied right down that thing," as if schussing the headwall in Tuckerman Ravine back home in New Hampshire. "Nobody shot at him; I think most of us were impressed by his skiing." It seems unlikely that, had the circumstances been reversed, veteran German soldiers would have proved as sportsmanlike.

Patrols helped season the troopers, who sometimes brought back prisoners and valuable information, and in one case a grateful Royal Air Force Spitfire pilot shot down behind German lines two weeks earlier. At last the weeks spent on Cooper Hill seemed to be paying off. But there is some dispute about just how many times the "ski troops" of the

10th actually skied once they reached the front. One early account, by 10th veteran Hal Burton, claims no more than three times. Other sources suggest that was an underestimate. But skis were certainly of limited use to the mountain troopers once they were in Italy. First of all, because they hadn't brought any, and had to scrounge ski equipment from local sources, swapping them between different units as needed. Second, because snow conditions were bad — too deep when they first reached the mountains in January, and then all but gone once the weather warmed in February. And finally, because skis proved largely impractical for the terrain and tactical situation in the North Apennines. This wasn't like Finland, where, on relatively flat ground with thick forest cover, Finnish ski troopers could swoop down on road-bound formations of an enemy who were in the open and unprepared for winter fighting. The terrain in the North Apennines was steep and the enemy entrenched and experienced.

Staff Sergeant Dick Nebeker, A Company of the 85th, had been a civilian ski instructor as a teenager in Alta, Utah, and a military ski instructor at Camp Hale. He was certainly well qualified to go out on a ski patrol. He arrived in Bagni di Lucca in late January and was sent on patrol on January 26. It was a large combat patrol — ten officers and 133 enlisted men from the regiment's 1st Battalion, led by C Company commander Charles P. Smith. Its mission was to destroy a German artillery observation post at a place called Ramosceta, high on a ridgeline above Montefegatesi. Leaving after dark, they traveled partway by jeep, then on foot, led up the mountain by an Italian partisan guide. Finally, at about 2 a.m., they strapped on their skis and made their way stealthily toward the collection of stone houses that was their objective. But someone hit an enemy trip wire, alerting the German defenders, who fired their "burp guns" (Schmeiser machine pistols firing .30-caliber ammunition) in the direction of the sound:

> We tried to creep and crawl under fire with skis on, a brand new experience. The guns would fire, and we would scramble laterally on our bellies to find some low spot. The tails of our skis made a give away noise, like dragging a stick along a picket fence. Brrrpp Brrpp fired the gun. Clack, clack, clack went our skis. The German gunner was firing in the fog at the noise made by our skis. Instantly everybody realized how noisy

and immobile we were, and all the skis came off. I remember laying my skis carefully down by a rock wall, where I thought I'd retrieve them later. We managed to swarm around and into the stone house, killed one German and took four prisoners. I never did find that pair of skis and never worried about it.

Nebeker never fought on skis again. "Two winters at Camp Hale trained us for 10 minutes of creeping and crawling under enemy fire with skis on," he commented drily in a postwar memoir.

The 85th suffered its first fatality of the war in that raid when PFC Walter van Boven of A Company was killed. In its first month and a half on the front line, up to mid-February 1945, the three regiments of the 10th Mountain Division lost twenty-four dead and fifty-four wounded, along with a number of men taken prisoner. Some were lost on patrols, others to artillery and sniper fire, others to mines, several to friendly fire. The losses certainly stung. But for comparison's sake, twenty-eight men died on Kiska the first night of the invasion, nineteen of them mountain troopers from the 87th Regiment, and that was on an island with, famously, "no Japs at all."

For some young soldiers in the 10th, war was still an exciting if risky adventure, an opportunity to display some boyish derring-do. "Crazy as it may sound," Marty Daneman, still two months short of his twentieth birthday, wrote to his fiancée in late January, "I'm *almost* anxious to get into a hot spot, out of simple curiosity how I'll react. I'd like to prove to myself whether or not I can take it."

Unlike on Kiska, there were enemy soldiers in Italy, twenty-seven divisions of Germans, nearly 350,000 men, along with six Italian Fascist divisions. The Italian divisions were of little consequence, but the Germans were veteran soldiers, skilled at defensive fighting though hampered by lack of aircraft, motorized transport, and fuel. The question for Allied commanders in Italy in the winter of 1944–45 was what to do about them once spring returned and permitted a new offensive.

Everyone from the lowliest private to the highest general in the US Army in the European theater of operations understood that the war was going to be decided in Germany itself and probably in the near future. PFC Harris Dusenbery wrote to his wife in mid-January, when 2 million Red Army soldiers were poised to cross the border into East

Prussia: "The Stars and Stripes [newspaper] brings us news of the new Russian offensive in Poland. It sounds good to me. I hope it's the drive that breaks the German resistance." Two weeks later, First Lieutenant Earl E. Clark, a Kiska veteran now serving as S-4 (logistics officer) for HQ Company, 1st Battalion, of the 87th, wrote to his mother: "All of us are anxiously watching the Russian drive toward Berlin with our fingers crossed and a prayer on our lips! Things could happen so perfectly and the war in Europe could end so suddenly that the entire world would be amazed, so go you Russians!!!" The February 1 issue of the 10th's divisional newspaper, now renamed *The Blizzard,* reported in a front-page headline, "Berlin 68 Miles Away, Say Russians." And with the American and British armies back on the offensive after pinching off the "Bulge" in Belgium in January, it was clear that a classic pincer operation would soon crush German resistance in the homeland.

Given the circumstances, it was not unreasonable to ask why anyone should care about the Germans remaining in Italy. The Supreme Allied Commander in Europe, General Dwight Eisenhower, certainly didn't. He had stripped the American 5th Army of some of its best fighting units in the lead-up to the invasion of Normandy in June 1944, and of southern France in August 1944, including Lucian Truscott's VI Corps; the 5th Army's 250,000 soldiers in the summer of 1944 had been reduced to a mere 150,000 by December. Other units had been taken from the British 8th Army to occupy Greece following the German withdrawal from that country. The US Army in northwestern Europe fought its biggest and costliest campaign of the war, the Battle of the Bulge, in December 1944 and January 1945, months in which the Italian front lay dormant and irrelevant. In the winter and spring of 1945, Italy did not figure into Eisenhower's calculations of what it would take to secure final victory.

The initial invasion of Italy in September 1943, along with the drive up the boot that secured the ports of Naples and Bari and the airfields at Foggia, served useful strategic ends. The invasion knocked Italy out of the war as a belligerent power and awarded the Allies absolute air and naval superiority over the Nazis in the Mediterranean, as well as providing advance air bases to intensify bombing attacks on southern Germany and central Europe. From October 1943 to the end of the war, however, the rationale for continuing the costly drive north grew increasingly strained. For war correspondent Eric Sevareid, looking back, "it was all a frightful waste of lives and machines which could have been put to more fruitful use somewhere else . . . [S]urely it made no sense to attack beyond Rome; perhaps we would have done as well to stop near Naples, on the Volturno line."

Once it became clear in late 1943 that the Germans were not giving up the rest of Italy without a determined fight, the justification for continuing offensive action became one of tying down as many enemy divisions as possible, making sure that they were not available to fight on the eastern front or in France when the invasion was finally launched. The problem with that rationale is that Allied troops who could have fought elsewhere were also tied down in Italy; when Rome was captured in June 1944, the Anglo-American forces in Italy outnumbered their German opponents two to one.

Whatever ordinary soldiers in Italy thought about letting the war be fought to its bloody conclusion on another front ("go you Russians!!!"), that was not how their commanders saw things. The fighting in the Mediterranean between 1942 and 1945 illustrated the truth of the maxim that war has its own momentum: the invasion of North Africa, reluctantly agreed to by American military commanders, led inexorably to the invasion of Sicily, and then to southern Italy, and then northward to Rome and, ultimately, the Alps. As US Army historian Ernest F. Fischer observed in his magisterial history of the Mediterranean theater in World War II, military campaigns, "like other human enterprises, once undertaken, often claim their advocates long after the undertaking has served its purpose. That was the case [at the end of 1944] in Italy."

No senior Allied commanders in Italy, including Generals Mark Clark and Lucian Truscott (who agreed on little else), were content to have their armies sit out the rest of the war. And there were fears that the Germans might mount a last-ditch resistance even after Berlin was captured. Nazi propagandists boasted of plans to establish an *Alpenfestung* (an Alpine fortress or redoubt) in the Austrian Alps, from where they could fight on indefinitely. There were reports of arms being stockpiled and troops being shifted to the redoubt. The 300,000 German soldiers in northern Italy, it was feared, might be withdrawn through the Brenner Pass to reinforce the effort. None of it was true; Kesselring himself referred to the phantom Alpine redoubt as "merest make-believe." Allied intelligence was divided over how seriously to take the threat, the British tending to be more skeptical than the Americans. Allied bombing of the railroads linking Austria and Italy, plus dwindling fuel stocks, made large-scale withdrawal of German forces into the Alps increasingly unlikely. Still, prudence seemed to dictate that the rumored redoubt not be completely discounted, especially after the surprise offensive in the Ardennes in December. That meant the Germans would have to be tied down in Italy.

Accordingly, when spring came and the roads finally dried, Allied commanders in Italy planned a two-wing offensive. The British-commanded 8th Army would renew its drive along the Adriatic coast, crossing the Santerno River and then swinging northwest into the interior. Then the American-commanded 5th Army (consisting of II Corps and IV Corps) would break through the German Winter Line in the northern Apennines, penetrating the Po Valley, and, having linked up with the 8th Army, would push on to the Alps to cut off the line of retreat for as much as possible of the German army remaining in northern Italy.

As a preliminary measure, the 5th Army's commander, General Truscott, chose the 10th Mountain Division to spearhead an assault code-named "Operation Encore," scheduled for mid-February. The division's mission was intended as a limited offensive to seize Mount Belvedere and several peaks linked to it by a continuous ridgeline, and then, if successful, push on a little farther north. The Belvedere massif was the most prominent feature on the high ground overlooking and paralleling Highway 64 for about eight miles, as the road followed the northeastern course of the Reno River to the east of the mountains. The offensive would be staged in two phases: the first, beginning in mid-February and expected to last two weeks, would concentrate on Belvedere and adjoining peaks; the second, in March, would move northward with the goal of capturing a number of other peaks concluding with Mount della Spe. From the summit of Belvedere it was possible to see the Po Valley twenty miles to the north. From the summit of della Spe, it was only fifteen miles to the valley.

General George P. Hays, commander of the 10th Mountain Division, did not accompany his men to Italy by troopship. Instead he went to Washington for consultations and then flew to Naples, arriving on January 11. He met immediately with the 5th Army's commander to receive his orders. Truscott gave the 10th the assignment to capture Belvedere and the high ground beyond, supported by the Brazilian Expeditionary Force. The 10th would also be supported on the ground by separate field artillery, tank, and tank destroyer units, to increase its firepower in the assault, as well as air support from the fighter-bombers of the Mediterranean Allied air forces. Three mule pack companies, made up of a mix of American and Italian mules (the latter a much smaller breed, but still capable of bearing heavy loads), led by green-clad Italian Alpini troops, with their distinctive Tyrolean hats, would bring up supplies. Italian partisans would serve as guides. There was even a war dog platoon.

Hays rejoined his division at the front lines, where he studied the terrain, aerial photographs, and maps. He quickly made what proved a crucial decision. In late October, and again in November, there had been two costly and failed attempts to capture Mount Belvedere by 5th Army troops. In both cases the attackers had ignored Riva Ridge. Although Mount Belvedere remained the main objective, Hays decided he had to do something about the enemy soldiers on Riva Ridge. From the ridgeline they had a clear view of the approaches to and summit of Mount Belvedere, which allowed them to call in accurate artillery fire on any attackers. The 10th's commander foresaw "terrific casualties" if he had his men attempt to seize Belvedere unless he did something first about Riva Ridge. But to take the ridge, they needed to scale a steep set of cliffs rising from the floor of the valley below. The German defenders considered that so unlikely, they didn't bother to keep that side of the ridgeline under regular observation.

General Hays ordered the commander of the 86th Regiment, Colonel Tommy Tomlinson, to have his men scout possible approach routes directly up the cliffs that lined the eastern edge of the ridgeline. The patrols came back to report that there was no practical way to get up the ridge, given the steepness of the cliffs, their icy conditions, and the crumbling limestone underfoot. Tomlinson, a regular army officer with no rock climbing experience of his own, communicated the bad news to his commander. But Hays was not persuaded. All that training at Camp Hale could not have been for nothing. "This is a mountain division," Hays told Tomlinson. "Surely they can find how to climb up that ridge."

So the patrols went back and took another look. On January 15 a squad from B Company of the 86th led by Staff Sergeant Carl Casperson got all the way to the summit of Pizzo di Campiano, the northernmost of the peaks on Riva Ridge and closest to Mount Belvedere. There they bumped into some German soldiers, got into a firefight that left one of the enemy dead, and skittered back down the cliff to safety. It didn't occur to the Germans to wonder what the Americans were doing up there; they apparently decided they were just dealing with a lone over-aggressive patrol. Casperson's route was steep and would require fixed ropes, but it seemed doable. It was designated route 1. Over the next few weeks, other patrols from the 86th, sometimes aided by local partisans, identified four more trails: route 2 going to Mount Capel Buso, just south of Pizzo di Campiano, which could be climbed without ropes; route 3, going to the summit of Mount Serrasiccia, another route requiring ropes; and routes 4, leading to Mount Mancinello's summit, and 5 to high ground south of Mancinello known as Le Piagge, neither requiring ropes. The routes were explored without benefit of ice axes or, for the most part, crampons. Soldiers cut steps up icy approaches with their bayonets.

At the end of January, most of the 86th, apart from a small contingent assigned to find trails and fix ropes as needed, was withdrawn from the front line to Bagni di Lucca. The village had formerly been a resort with an international clientele, well known for its thermal baths, but the men from the 86th would not be enjoying a restful stay. Instead, soldiers from the regiment's 1st Battalion, along with Company F from 2nd Battalion, underwent rigorous training in rock climbing in a local marble quarry while carrying the rucksacks and weapons they would take with them on the night of the attack on Riva Ridge. They studied a sand table model of the ridge and aerial photographs, memorizing the routes and their objectives. The attack force would include some of the elite skiers and climbers in the 10th, including two company commanders assigned to be in the vanguard, Captain Percy Rideout of Dartmouth ski team fame and Captain Bill Neidner, a racer and jumper from the University of Wisconsin. But many of the men under their command had never been on skis, since nearly a third of the troopers in the assault force had joined the 10th after its departure from Camp Hale. Because neither skis nor snowshoes would be used to climb the ridgeline, it was decided that there was no need to handpick mountain-trained soldiers; everyone would go.

General Hays's plans for the assault on Riva Ridge was called "audacious" by one of the officers assigned to carry it out; that seems, in retrospect, an understatement. Hays was ordering green troops, undertaking their first major combat mission, to advance in the dark, up steep and treacherous trails, to assault experienced enemy troops who were entrenched on the high ground. Army intelligence estimated that forty to fifty Germans were on top of the ridgeline at any one time, with several hundred more in close reserve down the gentler west slope, supported by artillery and mortars. The Germans were well dug-in, their outposts positioned to be mutually supporting with good fields of fire.

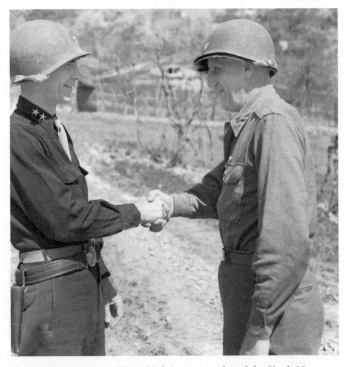

General George P. Hays (right), commander of the Tenth Mountain Division in Italy, shakes hands with Colonel Clarence Tomlinson, commander of the 86th Mountain Infantry Regiment, Italy, 1945. THE DENVER PUBLIC LIBRARY (TMD94)

The 10th's divisional artillery, the 605th and 616th Field Artillery, equipped for the first time with new, heavier 105 mm howitzers as well as the standard 75 mm, and supported by the 34th Division's 175th Field Artillery Battalion, equipped with 105 mm and 155 mm guns, was in position in the valley below to support the attack on Riva Ridge, and then on Mount Belvedere. But in order to maintain the element of surprise, the artillery would open fire on German positions only after the infantry had seized the heights. That meant that lightly armed troops had to go ahead on their own, with no supporting artillery fire in their initial attack. Should a single soldier slip and fall on the icy trails, a shout or the clatter of equipment could alert the enemy above to their approach and bring down a lethal hail of machine gun fire and hand grenades. The separate columns moving up to the ridgeline would need to arrive within a few hours of one another, and all before daylight, lest an isolated unit be surrounded and cut off by counterattack. Everything would have to go exactly as planned for the operation to succeed, and there were very few battles in history in which that could be said to have happened.

The men from 1st Battalion of the 86th, Rifle Companies A, B, and C, and heavy weapons company D, along with F Company from 2nd Battalion, all under the command of Lieutenant Colonel Henry Hampton, would set off up four of the five established trails to the summit of Riva Ridge after darkness fell on Sunday night, February 18. (Trail 4 to Mount Mancinello wasn't used in the end.) The remainder of the 86th, commanded by Colonel Tommy Tomlinson, along with the men of the 85th, commanded by Colonel Raymond C. Barlow, and those of the 87th, commanded by Colonel David M. Fowler, some twelve thousand men, would set off shortly before midnight on Monday, February 19, to seize Mount Belvedere and adjacent peaks. The Brazilian Expeditionary Force, not highly regarded by American officers in the 10th, was assigned the subsidiary mission of capturing neighboring Mount Castello. To minimize the possibility of an accidental and premature discharge of gunfire alerting the enemy to their presence, or resulting in friendly fire deaths, the men assaulting Belvedere would make the climb with unloaded weapons. If they ran into opposition, they could use grenades or bayonets, but they were not allowed to load and fire before daybreak. No one was very happy about carrying an unloaded weapon, but they were good soldiers and, grumbling apart, did as they were told. They had faith in their leaders, and faith in one another.

One year earlier, the mountain troopers had been at Camp Hale, wondering if they would ever get into the war. The issue of the divisional newspaper, the *Ski-Zette*, published on February 18, 1944, reported that Sergeant Torger Tokle of the 86th had taken first place in the ski-jumping contest at the 31st annual Steamboat Springs Winter Ski Carnival the previous weekend, with a jump of 226 feet. A new musical comedy, "Hale and Hearty," written expressly for the 10th Mountain, and featuring songs with titles like "It's So Cold in Colorado," was about to have its premiere performance. A dance, a USO show, and a table tennis meet were also upcoming.

That now seemed a very long time ago, in a world hard to remember, as the men cleaned their weapons one more time and packed their ammunition (ninety-six rounds per rifleman, twice the usual field issue), and over several days moved into position, always at night to avoid tipping off the enemy. Eight hundred men from the 86th's 1st Battalion and Company F of the 2nd Battalion moved on foot on the night of February 17 from the Castelluccio Ridge, east of Bagni di Lucca, on a fourteen-mile march that got them to the base of Riva Ridge before daylight. They took cover in stone farmhouses and barns spread out across the five villages at the base of the ridge and stayed out of sight the next day. Jumping-off time for the assault on Riva Ridge was set for just after darkness fell, at 7:30 p.m., the evening of February 18. Casualties were expected to be heavy; Albert H. Meinke, battalion surgeon for the 86th's 3rd Battalion, heard, unofficially, that the doctors of the 1st Battalion had been warned of the possibility of a 90 percent casualty rate among the initial assault force.

Meanwhile, twelve thousand men from the remaining regiments had to make their way to their jumping-off point below Belvedere. Stan Cummings was one of the junior officers charged with moving supplies up to the 85th's line of departure. In the final stretch, everything was carried on the backs of the tough but diminutive mules the division acquired in Italy. "Night after night we brought mules right up to the point where the men intended to start fighting," Cummings wrote to wife Jean some days later. "Then one night hundreds — thousands — of shuffling feet tramped up our trails. The next morning I'm sure the Tediski [*tede-schi*] saw nothing unusual in the valley, but the men were there!"

Marlin Wineberg, a mortarman in D Company of the 85th, was one of the troopers who gathered for General Hays's memorable farewell "always forward" address on February 16, three days before the scheduled attack on Mount Belvedere. "This has been a historic day," he noted in an account written largely in present tense but set down shortly after the end of the fighting. "The General spoke to us telling us we were selected for assault troops on an unnamed mountain." On the afternoon of February 18, D Company packed up and, after dark, headed toward their objective by truck. An hour before midnight the trucks came to a halt and the men dismounted, as Wineberg recounted: "Then we unloaded, packed the mules, and hiked into position. It is muddy and raining. Everybody is being very cautious as we are directly below the German. All sounds are muffled as we dig in."

While the men of the 85th and 87th were quietly digging in along the road east of Querciola that night, across the valley their comrades from the 1st Battalion of the 86th had set out from their hiding places, crossed the Dardagna River, found the trails at the base of Riva Ridge, and were cautiously making their way upward. It had been just over seven weeks since the 86th had disembarked from the troopship in Naples harbor. Now their real war was about to begin.

From south to north along the ridgeline, F Company, commanded by Captain Percy Rideout, with squads from 2nd Battalion's heavy weapons H Company, would attack Lo Piage via trail 5; A Company, commanded by Captain William Neidner, would attack Mount Mancinello, also via trail 5; C Company, commanded by Captain Worth McClure, with some heavy weapons squads from D Company, would attack Mount Serrasiccia via trail 3; B Company, commanded by Captain Kenneth Seigman, with attachments from D Company, would attack Mount Cappel Buso via trail 2. This column would carry with them four .50-caliber machine guns, the heaviest weapons on top of the ridgeline until a 75 mm howitzer could be brought up the same trail later by mule pack. Trail 2 was the only route a mule could traverse. (By this point 1st Battalion had also acquired two of the T-29 tracked Weasels they had trained with in Colorado, but neither could be used on the narrow tracks to the ridgeline.)

A lone platoon, detached from A Company and commanded by Second Lieutenant James W. Loose, would attack the northernmost peak, Pizzo di Campiano (the lowest peak on the ridge and the one closest to Mount Belvedere), via trail 1. The orders to all of the columns climbing those narrow trails that night were clear: they were to take the ridgeline from its defenders in the early morning hours of February 19, defend it against any German counterattacks, and support by fire and aid by observation the men who would be assaulting Mount Belvedere over the next several days.

The trails were only wide enough to allow the men to move single file. The February thaw left the rocks the troopers climbed slick and treacherous underfoot. Their uniforms were soon soaked, both from sweat and from icy water pouring down from above. On routes 1 and 3 they clipped into and followed fixed ropes over especially steep or slippery sections of the trail. Each column included a five-man wire team, who laid down telephone wire as they climbed, and reported back to battalion headquarters below about the progress of the advance every hour. No radio was used, to avoid alerting the enemy. As the men climbed the four trails, a dense fog settled in over the ridgeline, a great advantage since it hid the attackers from German eyes, but also making it more difficult for the advancing soldiers to see where they were going. They kept their eyes on the strips of white adhesive tape applied to the back of the helmet of the man ahead of them, a beacon in the darkness. The constant rushing sound of the Dardagna River, though ever farther below, helped to mask the occasional noise of their movement. It took six or more hours of steady climbing for the advance guard to reach their respective summits, which, unlike the trails, were still snow-covered. First up was the lead (or "assault") platoon of B Company, which gained the summit of Mount Cappel Buso shortly after 1 a.m. The troopers from B Company were met by scattered machine gun and machine pistol fire from German defenders but held their own fire. One soldier, PFC Ellery J. Potter, was wounded. But the Germans, unable to see much of anything in the dense fog, and again probably thinking they were dealing with only a lone patrol, soon withdrew. Adding to the defenders' confusion, the American attack came as soldiers of the German 1044th Grenadier Regiment were in the midst of being relieved by others from the 232nd Fusilier Battalion, so many men were not in position or on alert.

All of B Company was on the summit and digging in before 3 a.m. A Company was on top of Mount Mancinello by 1:30 a.m. They met no resistance and found no Germans. By 4 a.m. the four southernmost peaks on Riva Ridge were in American hands; only Pizzo di Campiano still belonged to the enemy. Wire teams lay field telephone lines up from the valley floor and then along the ridgeline. At 4:15 a.m. Captain Neidner of A Company was talking on the phone to Colonel Tomlinson at Battalion Headquarters in the valley, reporting on their situation. Tomlinson asked if he knew what had happened to Loose's platoon, but Neidner had no word of them.

Actually, Loose's men — or at least some of them — had reached the ridgeline of Pizzo di Campiano about fifteen minutes earlier. Their climb had not gone as well as that of the other assault parties. Loose and a dozen men in the front of the column lost touch with the other thirty soldiers in their unit. Shortly before reaching the summit, as they noisily crossed a steep scree slope, they were attacked by Germans hurling grenades and firing at them. They fired back, and their attackers withdrew. As on Cappel Buso, the Germans apparently decided they were being confronted only by a wayward patrol, not a general assault. At 4 a.m. Loose and his men reached the top and were amazed to find their complacent enemies asleep in their foxholes and a lean-to. They killed two and drove off the rest without suffering any casualties of their own. At 5:45 a.m. they reported to Battalion that they had reached their objective, although not in strength. Finally, at about 6:30 a.m., the other thirty men in the platoon reached the top, and Loose organized his small defending force to fight off the expected counterattacks.

As the sun rose on the morning of February 19, the Germans remained oblivious to what was taking place along Riva Ridge. The 10th Mountain Division had taken the ridgeline without the loss of a single life, and with only one man wounded. Against all odds, General Hays's plan had been carried out flawlessly by the men of the 10th. Not bad for still green troops.

F Company, 86th Mountain Infantry Regiment, Riva Ridge, February 1945.
THE DENVER PUBLIC LIBRARY (TMD712)

7

Italy, February 19–April 13, 1945

"Front Line Soldiers"

When it was over I shook for 3 days, jumped at every noise, & couldn't hold a meal. And came out with a hate for war I'll never lose. I don't think anyone except a front line soldier, who has endured the mental agony of shelling, seen the gaping, ragged shrapnel wounds in flesh; seen his buddies die before him & smelled the sickly odor of dead men can develop the hate of that I now have.

— Corporal Marty Daneman to his fiancée,
March 9, 1945

IN THE THIRD WEEK OF FEBRUARY 1945, THE 10TH MOUNTAIN DIVISION ceased being green troops. Roughly two hundred men in the division died in the space of five days; hundreds more were wounded. The survivors learned to hate war. They also learned to kill. They became frontline soldiers.

On Riva Ridge, the Germans assigned to defend the heights remained unaware of the American presence on the ridgeline as the fog lifted in the late morning of February 19. At noon, men from A Company of the 86th Regiment atop Mount Mancinello spotted a snow-covered bunker a few hundred yards downhill on the western slope of the ridge. Technical Sergeant Torger Tokle led his platoon in a textbook assault on the bunker, killing four and capturing eight bewildered German soldiers. Tokle came away with a German pistol, a highly valued souvenir for American soldiers fighting in Europe.

An hour later, a German patrol approached C Company on Mount Serrasiccia. They waved to the dug-in Americans, assuming they were comrades. The Americans waved back encouragingly, hoping to lure them closer, but one man (until recently a cook) got nervous and fired. The Germans fled. Now that the enemy knew their true identity, C Company came under counterattack twice over the next several hours. They took some casualties, including a medic who was shot dead while bent over a wounded man, despite the clearly visible red cross painted on his helmet. But they held their ground.

Along the ridgeline that afternoon, more firefights broke out in what became the 10th's first sustained battle. The German 4th (Edelweis) Mountain Battalion joined the counterattack. The rattle of machine guns, the crump of mortars, and the scream of artillery shells (the dreaded German 88s) sounded intermittently through the day and into the night. The men felt exposed on top of the ridge, sometimes having nothing more than a hole dug in the snow for shelter. But for the first time since arriving in Italy, they had the advantage of holding the high ground. This made the difference.

It also helped that the Germans trying to take back Riva Ridge were not the Wehrmacht's finest warriors. As the official history of the 86th Regiment noted, the prisoners taken on the ridge were of two classes: "the elite mountain troops of the 4th Mountain Battalion, who were mostly Austrian and Bavarian; and a sad-looking lot of old men and kids from the 1044th Regiment."

The one place mountain troopers were in serious danger of being pushed off the heights was on Pizzo di Campiano, held by the forty-odd men of the platoon commanded by Second Lieutenant James Loose. They confronted two German companies, several hundred men all told. Asked by a historian after the war why so few soldiers had been sent to hold the vital northern prow of the ridgeline, Lieutenant Loose replied, "The army made a mistake."

For a day and a half, Loose's men were surrounded by the enemy, cut off from supplies and reinforcements on their bare and rocky hilltop. They repelled six counterattacks, supported by American artillery fire from the valley below. Loose and his men conducted an active defense, raiding German positions down the slope, killing and driving off the enemy, capturing and disabling mortars and machine guns. As the hours passed on February 19–20, the little band of American soldiers ran out of food and water, and came perilously close to running out of ammunition. In the midst of one counterattack, Loose called for an artillery strike just yards from where his men were dug in. Colonel Albert H. Jackman, executive officer of the 604th Artillery, thought Loose must have miscalculated where he wanted the barrage to fall. "Do you realize that you are asking for fire exactly on your position?" he asked Loose by field telephone. "I do," the lieutenant responded coolly, "but if we don't get artillery support, you'll have nothing to support."

Reinforcements and supplies finally reached the heroic platoon at about 4 p.m. on February 20, when 1st Battalion commander Lieutenant Colonel Henry L. Hampton personally led a relief force to their position. (Hampton, unlike most senior commanders, had taken the rock climbing course at Camp Hale.) "My god," one of Loose's men cried out in a combination of disbelief and gratitude at the sight of Hampton at the head of the column. "It's Hank!" Loose and his men headed back to American lines later that night. In their two days on the mountaintop they had killed twenty-six Germans and captured seven; their own losses were two dead and six wounded. Loose received a Silver Star for his defense of his lonely outpost, while the rest of his platoon received Bronze Stars.

The Germans' counterattacks all along the ridge proved fruitless and cost them dearly. Casualties for the 10th on Riva Ridge in those first two days of fighting were seventeen dead, fifty-odd wounded, and three missing.

One of the dead was twenty-six-year-old First Lieutenant John A. McCown, a platoon leader in C Company. McCown, an experienced climber and member of the Mountain Training Group, had been in charge of training rock climbers at Seneca Rock, West Virginia, in 1943–44. He had helped scout the trails to the summit of Riva Ridge in the weeks before the attack. In the first day of fighting on the ridgeline, McCown had volunteered to lead a patrol to retake a forward position on Serrasiccia. Some of the German defenders stood up, apparently surrendering. But it was a feint, one in what became an all too familiar series of "white flag ruses." When the Americans exposed themselves, the Germans, who had had their hands in the air, dropped to their knees and opened fire. They killed three Americans, including McCown, and wounded another half dozen. When C Company finally took the position, they captured several prisoners. One was a wounded officer, an SS lieutenant in some accounts, and in all accounts surly and uncooperative. The troopers in C Company were in no mood to put up with badly behaved prisoners after the death of Lieutenant McCown. The officer was turned over to two men to take to the rear. They hadn't been gone long when a single gunshot was heard. No one saw that prisoner again. It was becoming that kind of war.

On February 20, in its first brief account of the capture of Riva Ridge, the division's newspaper, *The Blizzard,* reported, "The enemy believed the position impossible to assault, but the attackers used expert rock-climbers to fix ropes up which the column ascended." A week later the soldier-reporters of *The Blizzard* declared proudly, "The taking of the ridge, a remarkable military feat whether or not it gets into the history books, wasn't luck." In a companion article, the February 27 *Blizzard* noted another unprecedented feat accomplished on Riva Ridge: the construction of an aerial tramway up to the ridgeline by the men of D Company of the 126th Engineer Mountain Battalion, while the battle was still raging.

Evacuating the wounded from the front lines in alpine warfare in Italy had proved difficult and costly in previous battles. It could take hours to move badly wounded men on stretchers or loaded onto mules down the steep, twisting mountain trails, and blood loss, shock, or a misstep could prove fatal.

The men of the 126th Engineers, unlike their comrades in the mountain infantry, were not prewar skiers or mountaineers. They came with other kinds of specialized knowledge and skills from backgrounds in construction or mining, building roads, bridges, and artillery emplacements, and clearing minefields and rubble. At Camp Hale, and again in Italy, they practiced building aerial tramways, devices that worked in principle the same way as the ski lifts that were beginning to appear at American mountain resorts before the war.

At 4 a.m. on February 19, with the assault columns still making their way to the summit of Riva Ridge, a reconnaissance party from the 126th's Company D, led by Captain Fred A. Nagel, a mining engineer and 1940 graduate of the Colorado School of Mines, moved forward to the base of the ridge. They decided to run the tramway line about halfway up the side of 3,798-foot Mount Cappel Buso, terminating at a point easily accessible from the top. At 8:30 a.m. three platoons of engineers began construction, and by 5:30 p.m. they had the tramline up and running, a full eighteen hours ahead of schedule. Their creation was 1,700 feet in length and ran six hundred vertical feet up the side of the ridge. The tram, powered by a gasoline engine, was propelled by a quarter-inch cable, and its carriage ran between two A-frames designed to bear a ten-ton stress. The tram cars could haul up to 350 pounds — a casualty and a medic going down, counterbalanced by a load of ammunition, food, or water going up. The wounded could be delivered from the ridgeline in a matter of minutes instead of hours. Thirty were evacuated on the first day of the tram's operation, three fifths of all the Americans wounded on top of Riva Ridge. Without the skill and ingenuity of the 126th's engineers, the number of American dead on the ridge would certainly have been much higher. And the tramway also carried five tons of supplies to the troopers on top of Riva Ridge over the next few days, helping them withstand German counterattacks.

Meanwhile, a mile or two to the west, men from the 85th and 87th Regiments could hear the sound of firing on Riva Ridge. By sunset on February 19 they were cheered by the news that the ridge had been captured. It meant there would be no German artillery observers along the ridge to call in shells on them as they advanced toward their own objectives that night and in days to come. What's more, the 10th's attack on Belvedere would now be supported by .50-caliber machine guns and two 75 mm pack howitzers laboriously hauled up to the top of the ridge after its capture.

During the long wait on February 19, only an occasional German artillery shell crashed into the little village of Querciola, crammed with concealed American troops. But the Germans on the Belvedere massif, men from the 1045th Regiment of the 232nd Grenadier Division, could

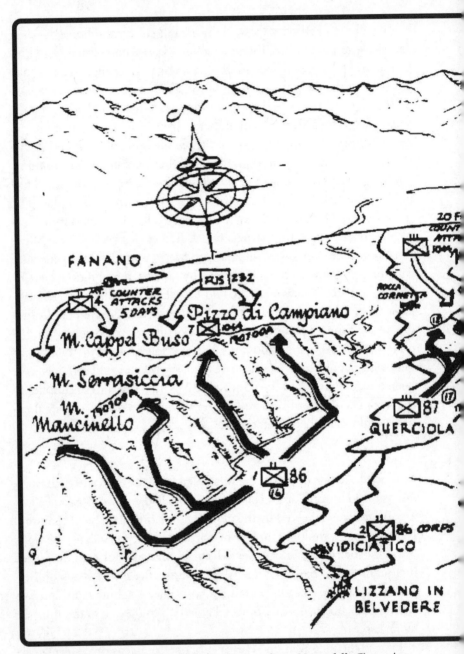

Map of Riva Ridge, Mount Belvedere, Mount Gorgolesco, Mount della Torraccia.
THE DENVER PUBLIC LIBRARY (ARMAND CASINI PAPERS, TMD113)

Map No. 1
Riva Ridge - M. Belvedere -
M. Della Torraccia

also hear the firing going on to their west, where their comrades from the 1044th Regiment were fully engaged, and must have understood that their positions were likely to be the next American target. Stealth and surprise had contributed significantly to the capture of Riva Ridge by the 10th; in the absence of either of those factors, sheer determination would have to suffice in the coming battle.

Mount Belvedere is the first in a line of peaks, all in the three-thousand-foot range, stretching northeast from Querciola and arrayed along a three-and-a-quarter-mile ridgeline. The most prominent of these peaks, south to north, are Belvedere itself, Mount Gorgolesco, and Mount della Torraccia, along with Mount Castello standing apart and a little to the east. The 10th's plan of attack on the German positions on the high ground was complex and multipronged. Starting an hour before midnight on February 19, the 87th Regiment would swing northeast along Belvedere's lower slope, with the 1st Battalion given the assignment of clearing the enemy off of the Valpiano Ridge on Belvedere's western slope, while the 2nd Battalion would capture the German-occupied village of Polla, a key point on the German defensive line between Riva Ridge and Belvedere. The 1st and 3rd Battalions of the 85th Regiment would set off at the same time to make a frontal assault on Belvedere and Gorgolesco, as well as taking a fortified farmhouse called Mazzancana, a German stronghold on the eastern slope. The 3rd Battalion of the 86th Regiment would move up the lower slopes of Belvedere to a position on the shoulder of Gorgolesco. When Gorgolesco was secured, the 2nd Battalion of the 85th, initially held in reserve, would push on to Mount della Torraccia. Meanwhile the Brazilian Expeditionary Force would capture Mount Castello. General Hays hoped that the attackers in the initial wave would be able to slip through the German lines on the lower slopes, so when dawn came they would be on high ground, securing what in mountain warfare is called "ground advantage." They would then be able to fire down on the German defenders below, with only a short way remaining to the summit.

———

Hugh Evans, in C Company of the 85th, the Exeter graduate who had lost his stripes ten months before at Camp Hale for refusing to turn in the names of discontented soldiers under his command during D-

Series, was a sergeant again by the time he reached Italy. Along with Lieutenant Loose on Riva Ridge, he was about to become one of the more celebrated soldiers in the 10th. After the war, he published one of the first accounts of the battle for the Belvedere massif by a participant: "Our attack was to begin a couple of hours before dawn. In other words, we were to carry out a night attack on a division scale, which means superb organization and timing on the part of the higher-ups. A night attack also requires trained troops because men must not fire their rifles, must keep quiet, and need skill in keeping contact. We had been keyed to this high pitch in all our training. We were ready."

At precisely 11 p.m., the order was given for the men of the 85th and 87th Regiments to fix bayonets and move out from the line of departure (the official term for the starting point of an attack). Among those passing on the order to advance was Second Lieutenant George J. Hays of B Company of the 87th, son and namesake of the division commander. He had been lightly wounded by artillery fire earlier in the day but returned to duty in time to take part in the attack. His company was the first to come under enemy fire that night, shortly after midnight.

Marlin Wineberg, mortar squad leader in D Company of the 85th, recalled that at first everything went precisely according to plan, with no confusion, and no sounds to be heard "except some muffled cursing" and creaking gear. Rifles were carried unloaded, as ordered. The regiment walked uphill in two long single files. The weather was cold and clear, and a half moon was rising in the sky. As usual, searchlights from far down the valley played on the mountaintops. Despite the chill February air, the men were soon sweating from exertion, especially the seven-man mortar crews in D Company laden with their .81 mm mortars and ammunition. Each mortar's tube, mount, and base plate, carried separately, weighed in at a total of 136 pounds; mortar shells weighed between six and eleven pounds each.

Wineberg was reminded of the night assault problems he and the men in his squad used to practice at Camp Hale. But that memory was dispelled by the first explosion of a German grenade. More grenades followed, then the sound of burp guns, and finally mortars and artillery:

The forward movement is more jerky now as we have to wait for the more forward elements to overcome enemy resistance. Contact breaks behind me . . . We pass through shelled areas. Trees are snapped off. We halt again for perhaps a half hour. The enemy's artillery and mortars are searching out the draws. They haven't touched the one we are in as yet. One man keeps saying, "Stay here long enough and they'll get us"; another man shuts him up. The General's words come back, "When in artillery and mortar fire, drive ahead!"

They drove ahead, remembering General Hays's injunction, "always forward," while leaving a trail of dead and wounded comrades.

Much the same thing happened around the base of Mount Belvedere in the early morning hours of February 20. Private Robert Krear, L Company of the 86th, carried a twenty-one-pound Browning automatic rifle, along with an additional twenty pounds of ammunition, up the lower slopes of Gorgolesco on the first night's assault. He was accompanied by Private Gene Sisler, a former Idaho cowboy who joined the 10th as a replacement in Italy and who carried additional ammunition for the Browning along with his own rifle. Both lived through the night, but many of those with whom they set off hours before didn't. Krear's platoon came under fire from German machine guns and mortars as it crossed open pastures on a farm below Gorgolesco. The men toiled through the deep snow in the pasture, which slowed their advance and made them even more vulnerable to the machine gun fire. But the snow proved advantageous in one respect. As Krear recalled, "The mortar shells would not explode until they had penetrated all the way to the ground level," which meant that most of the shrapnel and concussion was absorbed by the snow cover. "If it had not been for the snow, many more of us might have been casualties."

One of those in L Company who did not survive the day's fighting was Private Stuart E. Abbott, the aspiring naturalist from Chicago who had turned twenty at the start of February. Shortly after his birthday he had assured his family that "life in the front lines isn't as bad as I expected." In his last letter home, dated February 15, he warned, "Again you must except [sic] lapses in my mail," while apologizing for the brevity of the note. Abbott's squad leader, Staff Sergeant Paul Anderson, wrote to Abbott's mother several months later to report the circumstances of her son's death. As was true of most such messages, he didn't dwell on upsetting details. Abbott, he wrote, "met his death as easily as any soldier could. There was a sniper on our left flank which was unknown to us at the time until one shot rang out and Stuart fell. I can say truthfully that to my knowledge he did not suffer at all. When we could get to him he was gone." Anderson himself was wounded a short time afterwards and spent the remainder of the war hospitalized.

One after another, the dark silent columns of mountain troopers making their way around and up Belvedere and Gorgolesco crashed into German fire. In addition to grenades, machine guns, mortars, and artillery, there were, for the first time in the experience of the 10th, enemy rockets (known as the "moaning minnies," or "screaming meemies," for the unnerving sound they made as they descended). And, even more terrifying, exploding mines. The mines usually either killed their victims outright or left feet, legs, intestines, and genitalia mutilated. Sometime that night, advancing up the slopes of Mount Gorgolesco, Captain Charles Page Smith, commander of the 85th's C Company, tripped a wire to a stake mine. He proved one of the lucky ones. The explosion broke both his legs but inflicted no permanent damage. He lay for some time on the battlefield unconscious. When he awoke, his first feeling was of "enormous relief... The war was over for me and I had survived." The next afternoon, as he observed the envious glances of soldiers heading into combat while he was carried to safety on a stretcher, other feelings came to the fore: guilt for surviving, and regret that he had "abandoned the company" he had led since taking command at Camp Hale in August 1943. Those feelings remained with him long after the war ended. (He wasn't the only company commander to become a casualty; in the 85th alone, two were killed and another wounded by the second day of fighting.)

On Riva Ridge, there had been no minefields to contend with, no shelling, hardly any resistance to speak of on the first night. On Belvedere, in contrast, there was no chance for the Americans to reach the summit before the enemy knew they were coming. Although the official history of the 85th Regiment described the attack as a "complete surprise" to the Germans, that's not how soldiers who set off that night for the dark, looming summits remembered it. Sergeant Kenyon Cooke, C Company of the 85th, was a few days short of his twentieth birthday when the attack began and was uncertain whether he would live to mark that occasion. "We might have surprised them as to the exact day" of the attack, he concluded, "but they sure gave us a big reception."

Everywhere there was death, blood, hideous wounds, and men screaming in pain and shock. Private Jack R. Smolenske, HQ Company, 3rd Battalion of the 85th, wasn't in the initial assault, assigned instead to operate a radio in Querciola. But early on the morning of February 20, as wounded soldiers were beginning to be brought down to the battalion aid station, he realized he wasn't prepared for what he was witnessing. "When I saw the first casualty, a fellow with his ear torn off, I felt sick, dizzy, I thought I was going to throw up." The next one was "one of my pals, that I had lived with for about a year, with his right hand torn just about off. Another with shrapnel in his chest, another with a terrible gash in his buttocks, and on and on."

The 1st Battalion of the 87th was the first to come under fire around Belvedere that night, with B Company pinned down by machine guns just a few minutes after midnight. The two battalions of the 87th involved in the attacks were also first to reach their objectives, with B and C Companies of the 1st Battalion lodged on Belvedere's Valpiano Ridge by 4:30 in the morning, while A Company secured the village of Corona shortly after dawn. Meanwhile 2nd Battalion's F and G Companies captured the village of Polla and the surrounding area by 10:35 a.m. The 87th included in its ranks many veterans of the "no Japs at all" invasion of Kiska a year and half earlier. For them, the fighting on the western slopes of Belvedere on February 20 wiped away the memory of what some had perceived as a stain on the regiment's honor. Although it continued to take casualties, for a total of eighteen dead and ninety-one wounded by the end of the day, the regiment's part in the fighting on February 20 was essentially over by mid-morning, the 87th having secured all its initial objectives. Among the dead was PFC Lee H. Chew of A Company, one of the few Chinese Americans in the 10th, who died charging a German machine gun nest during the fight for Corona. He was posthumously awarded the Silver Star.

Another Silver Star went to Staff Sergeant Conrad Anthien of F Company, who, despite being wounded three times, led a four-man squad in an attack on a German bunker. The thirty-odd Germans inside the bunker, convinced they were outnumbered, took advantage of a lull in

Men of the 87th Regiment digging in under shell fire, Corona, Italy.
THE DENVER PUBLIC LIBRARY (TMD249)

the firing to surrender. Sergeant Anthien remembered that the prisoners were quite put out when they discovered that their captors were this little band of mountain troopers. Anthien refused to go for medical aid until he was hit a fourth time, by shrapnel. All told, the 87th took over a hundred prisoners that day and was credited with killing another hundred Germans.

The fiercest fighting on February 20 took place around and on top of the summits of Belvedere and Gorgolesco, the former the objective for the 85th's 3rd Battalion, the latter for the regiment's 1st Battalion. By 1 a.m., the 3rd was meeting resistance below the summit of Belvedere, and by 3 a.m., the 1st Battalion was engaged on Gorgolesco.

C Company of 3rd Battalion were in the forefront of the assault on Gorgolesco, which they attacked after fighting their way across the east ridge of Mount Belvedere. (Belvedere's summit was taken between 3:30 a.m. and 5:30 a.m. by troopers from L, K, and I Companies of the 3rd Battalion.) Second Lieutenant Herbert Wright, who was C Company's executive officer, remembered taking shelter in a wooded slope below Gorgolesco when the Germans discovered their location. Then "all hell broke loose" as "artillery, mortars, 'screaming meemies,' and ma-

chine gun fire enveloped us." Wright feared that the entire company had
been destroyed. He got word that somewhere up ahead Captain Charles
Page Smith, the company commander, had been wounded by a mine.
"I crawled forward," he recalled, "and found C.P. lying on the ground
with his usual crooked smile, both legs broken, waiting to be evacuated."
Now Wright was in command, "a responsibility I really didn't want."
(Wright survived the battle, was promoted captain, and was himself
badly wounded a month later.)

February 20, 1945: Two soldiers from the Tenth Mountain Division, 85th Regiment, 1st Battalion, walk in front of a wounded soldier on a litter.
THE DENVER PUBLIC LIBRARY (TMD367)

C Company stayed in the lead, fighting its way uphill. Around 7 a.m.
on February 20, Sergeant Hugh Evans and his squad, mixed with men
from other squads and platoons, found themselves just short of and
downhill to the right of the final German stronghold on the summit of
Gorgolesco. It had been eight hours since they crossed the line of departure, and given the night they had lived through, they must have found

it surprising to see the sun come up. In the early morning light, Evans spotted his platoon sergeant and close friend Technical Sergeant Robert Fischer lying on the ground, next to Private Malcolm Mackenzie, who was holding his hand, trying to comfort him. Fischer was badly wounded, with a bullet through his lungs, and kept repeating: "Oh God. Please not now. Please not now."

Evans thought he could save Fischer by putting a bandage over the chest wound, and began tearing a strip of cloth off a jacket for that purpose. But Fischer's cries stopped, and then his breathing, before Evans could apply the bandage. "Bob was 20," Evans recalled. "I got up and left, my eyes filled with tears of anger. He was the first person I had seen die."

Enraged, determined to avenge his friend, Evans raced uphill toward the German machine guns, calling for men to follow him. Some did and, amazingly, for a few crucial seconds there was no fire from above, which would have cut Evans's brave little band to pieces. When he was a few feet from the German fortifications, Evans and two men with him hurled grenades toward the enemy, then jumped into their trench, landing on the backs of two dead Germans. "For the next ten minutes, I just kept moving," he recalled, "throwing grenades and firing my machine pistol. The last German who got up and yelled '*Kamerad!*' I held with an empty gun. The toll in Germans was about eight dead and twenty captured. Our objective was taken."

Walking back down the ridge afterwards, he fell in beside another C Company man, Eugene Savage. Savage and his brother Irving had trained with Evans at Camp Hale. As they moved downhill, they passed a dead American soldier, unrecognizable to Evans because the top of his head had been blown off. To the young sergeant's amazement, Savage's reaction to seeing the corpse was to mutter, "That's my brother," and keep walking. It was becoming that kind of war.

When he got back to the rest of the company about noon, Evans learned that he had inherited Bob Fischer's post as platoon sergeant. He also found Captain Smith, who was still awaiting evacuation. Smith asked Evans how C Company had done. "When I responded that we had knocked the damn Germans off the mountain, he smiled and said: 'Nice going.'" Evans turned his head away and walked off, weeping. C Company of the 85th lost seven men killed and twenty-three wounded in the capture of Gorgolesco. For his actions on February 20, Sergeant Evans received a Silver Star.

The twenty Germans who surrendered to Sergeant Evans on top of Gorgolesco were fortunate to escape with their lives. Around the same time, shortly after dawn on February 20, two German soldiers on Belvedere faked a surrender to lure Staff Sergeant William F. Murphy, leader of a machine gun squad, and several other men from C Company of the 87th into the open. Another hidden German opened fire, killing Murphy and wounding several more Americans. Afterwards, it became the unspoken policy of C Company never to take another German prisoner. "The Krauts fought to the last bullet and then gave up," Sergeant Denis Nunan of C Company wrote to his parents. "To see them marching to our rear and safety, after killing and maiming our men, made one want to kill them in cold blood."

But German doggedness in fighting to the last bullet could be seen in another light. Some Americans came away from this first major battle with a grudging respect for the men they were trying to kill. "The German is a fantastic person," Lieutenant Earl Clark, S-4 (supply officer) for the 1st Battalion of the 87th, wrote his mother three days after his regiment helped capture Belvedere. "He fights like hell even though they know that they have lost. That makes them rather tough to whip." As successive peaks along Riva Ridge and the Belvedere massif fell to the 10th, however, it must have been increasingly tempting for the Germans to surrender rather than die for a lost cause. Army intelligence acquired a German officer's diary (whether from a prisoner or a corpse is unclear), and translated excerpts were published in the division newspaper, *The Blizzard,* soon afterwards. By the fourth day of the February offensive, the officer despaired that the end of the battle and the war was near, with German defeat a certainty: "23 Feb. 45 — It is 2000 hours . . . The whole neighborhood is alive with crashes. The bunker is shaking. The air pressure is blowing out the carbide lamp, and exerts pressure on the ears . . . The 1044 [Infantry] Regiment is almost completely destroyed." Two whole companies from the regiment, he recorded, had "gone over to the enemy" as prisoners. "This war is terrible," he concluded. "Whoever has not gone through it as a frontline infantryman cannot possibly picture it." Albert Meinke, surgeon for the 3rd Battalion of the 86th, saw many prisoners being escorted to the rear. "All of them," he recalled, "seemed to be relieved that they had been captured and were still alive."

The Allies' absolute control of the skies over the battlefield also significantly contributed to declining German morale. As long as daylight lasted, starting on February 20 and continuing through the coming days of battle, American P-47 fighter-bombers and British Spitfire fighters (the latter flown by both Royal Air Force and South African pilots) buzzed overhead, directed to their targets by Air Corps and 10th Mountain ground spotters collectively dubbed "Rover Joe."

The planes bombed, rocketed, napalmed, and strafed any German soldiers or guns spotted in the open. "The air corps finally arrives late," Private Dan L. Kennerly of D Company of the 85th, recorded laconically in a diary entry for February 20. "Probably had a second cup of coffee with their ham and eggs. Nevertheless, I'm glad to see them." Private Jack R. Smolenske wrote more enthusiastically about the Air Corps' contribution, telling his parents that the arrival of the planes at dawn on February 20 was "the most welcome sight a person could see . . . Every man's heart skipped a beat as they came roaring down to strafe the enemy. Now the tables were turned, we had them on the go." Spotters on Riva Ridge also called in devastating barrages from field artillery on German counterattackers. And as engineers slowly cleared paths for them through the heavily mined hillsides, Sherman tanks began to roll into position to support the mountain infantry. Weasels, the tracked snow vehicles familiar from Camp Hale days, supplemented the mule trains in carrying supplies up the mountains to the soldiers on the front lines. Territory won with grenades and bayonets by the mountain troopers was now being consolidated with the full material advantages of the Allied side.

The battle was by no means over as the sun set on February 20. And the grim and still dangerous task of retrieving the dead was beginning. It was not a welcome assignment, as Private Smolenske reported to his parents: "The next day [February 21] I had the detail to go and pick up the dead." The first corpses they came upon were "two of the 'Nazi Supermen' lying there, covered with blood and a horrible look on their faces." They spat on them and went on. "We located several of our dead and started to go over to the other side. Jerry saw us on the skyline and so they dropped about five or six in on us. We were covered with dirt,

but unhurt . . . We carried four of our men down. One had set off a mine.
Both hands were torn off, one knee was blown away. It was horrible."

Corpses on Mount Belvedere, February 20, 1945.
THE DENVER PUBLIC LIBRARY (TMD252)

An even more graphic account of the carnage encountered on the
battlefield was recorded by Dan L. Kennerly in his diary. Crossing the
saddle connecting Mount Gorgolesco and Mount Belvedere on February 21, he came across the mangled corpses of men from B Company of
the 85th, lying where they fell in the assault on Gorgolesco the previous
day. As in Smolenske's letter, "horrible" was again the operative word:

They are lying everywhere, "frozen" in many different positions, instant
rigor mortis. Some have their arms or legs sticking straight up, nothing is
supporting them . . . They all have a pale yellow, waxy color, like artificial
fruit. There is a strong scent. At first I cannot place it, now it comes to
me, it's the odor of a slaughter house. What I'm smelling is blood. Near
the low point of the crest are eleven bodies in a row . . . [The] bodies
have been chopped to pieces and lying in every type of grotesque position. One has the top of his head shot off, his brains have spilled out onto
the ground. Glancing into the cavity, I recognize the stump of the spinal

cord. It reminds me of a watermelon with all the meat gone. This is the most horrible sight I've ever seen. I'm gripped with fear. I feel sick and want to vomit.

While most of those who retrieved corpses were reluctantly following orders, there were a few volunteers, Marty Daneman and Stan Nelson among them. At dawn on February 23, the two men, both assigned to HQ Company of the 85th's 2nd Battalion, set out to retrieve the bodies of Johnny Dolan and Edwin Nedoszytko, Daneman's two closest friends from Camp Hale days, both killed on the ridgeline between Gorgolesco and the as yet untaken Mount della Torraccia. They found the men, arm in arm in a foxhole, rigid in death and bloated. Before they could fit the corpses in the mattress covers used as body bags, they had to release the gas bloating the bodies. The only practical way to do that was to puncture their friends with their bayonets. "Their bodies," Daneman recalled, "deflated like grotesque balloons." Weeping, they carried the bodies back to 2nd Battalion's command post at a small hamlet known as Ronchidos di Sopra, about a half mile below the ridgeline.

Daneman made no mention of that experience in his usual newsy letters to his fiancée, Lois. But once he brought himself to write about the battle, he left little else out. "I've been keeping something from [you], and I think that I'd better tell you," he wrote on March 9. "I think you must have read in the papers about the attack on Mt. Belvedere . . . I was in on it darling — & the story I'll tell you about it isn't pretty." Shortly after midnight on the second night of fighting, he recounted, he and his commanding officer headed up the slope of Belvedere to find their battalion's advanced command post. Soon after they arrived, the Germans launched a counterattack:

> I managed to get in a dugout during part of the shelling, but when the Krauts started to assault us, I got in a shallow slit trench & started firing. I spotted one Kraut running across a gully I was covering & shot him. I'd always wondered how I'd feel shooting a man & I found out quick enough. I felt no remorse doing it, almost pleasure. In one short period of time I learned to hate as I never thought I could. I saw enough blood & torn flesh & death to last forever. I came near to it a few times myself — shells landing all around, machine gun bullets flying etc. — but the clos-

est shell was about 25 yds. I left my hole after that to carry a stretcher. I came back to find that an 88 had landed right on it . . . But I came out whole and we did it — 4 outfits tried it before, & we did it. But we paid a price. Stan Nelson & I ran across a wounded Kraut in a dugout & killed him. I guess hate does things to the mind.

Daneman, having just turned twenty, was no longer the callow youth who only a month or so earlier had been "anxious to get in a hot spot." Now he was coming to grips with a new and hard-won maturity growing out of his experience and identity as a frontline soldier. The sights and smells he encountered on Belvedere had left him with an abiding hatred of war. That and a conviction that the war he was fighting was nonetheless necessary and just: "I still say — better to have it happen here than back home. I still say that the tragic price we pay is worth it and I would live thru it again & again to insure the fact that you & our kids won't have to endure another war. And so my 20th birthday rolled around & I feel 30."

Belvedere was a mountain of death, littered with the bodies of American and German fighters. As the mountain troopers pushed into villages long controlled by the Nazis, they found still more bodies, this time civilian, a reminder of the nature of the enemy they were fighting. Second Lieutenant Stan Cummings, HQ Company of the 85th, checked out a shed in the ruined village of Ronchidoso on the flank of Belvedere on February 21, hoping it could be used as an ammunition dump. Inside, he reported to wife Jean, he found the burned remains of seven people, three of them children, their bones clad in scraps of civilian clothes, "all with either a bullet hole in their skull or their skull bashed in . . . What the real story is I don't know if anyone will ever know." They buried the bones, and marked the graves with crosses fashioned from ration crates. Eventually another sixty-one bodies were uncovered in Ronchidoso — the victims of the SS massacre of the village inhabitants the previous September in retaliation for local partisan activity.

With the capture of Mounts Belvedere and Gorgolesco and the villages on their flanks on February 19–20, and the subsequent capture of Mount Castello by the Brazilian Expeditionary Force on February 21, the first phase of Operation Encore was three quarters completed, on time and at relatively low cost in lives. But the most difficult and prolonged phase of the battle was just beginning as the 2nd Battalion of the 85th Mountain Infantry, under the command of Lieutenant Colonel John Stone, moved through the advanced American lines below Gorgolesco to cross the saddle linking the mountain to the final objective, Mount della Torraccia.

As they moved into position on the night of February 20, crossing the peaks already seized from the Germans, the soldiers of the 2nd Battalion had to step aside to let a succession of mules pass in the opposite direction, each carrying a single dead GI slung over its back. Sergeant Jack Leslie, a squad leader with F Company, remembered fifty or more mules laden with that grim cargo passing by on his squad's way up Belvedere, which contributed nothing to their morale as they prepared for combat. Then, in the last hundred or so yards to the summit of Gorgolesco, Leslie remembered, "we stepped over and around our dead, which were yet to be collected."

En route they began taking casualties from mines and booby traps. By 9 p.m. they were dug in on a forested ridge short of the summit of della Torraccia. Private Robert B. Ellis, who had read Alan Seeger's "I Have a Rendezvous with Death" while on the ocean crossing to Naples, was part of a machine gun squad in F Company. He left a tersely dramatic narrative in his war diary of the night and days that followed:

> Dug in on crest of ridge with [Turman] Oldman. Scared to death. Cold. No bags or blankets . . . 3 of us left in my squad. 9 in platoon of 32 men. Horrible slaughter. Moved over ridge in morning and 1st [platoon] captured 3 Huns. MG's [machine guns] popping all around. Held at edge of ridge . . . [Harlon] Jensen killed 10 yds. from me. Dug in fast. 88's pounded us terribly. Slept that night and captured 14 Germans by yelling at them and firing machine gun. Killed my first Jerry on the ridge (Division objective). Moved the gun up to a new position and 1 minute later a mortar hit my old foxhole and wounded [Laverne] Staebell and [Leonard] Giddix . . . Counterattack surrounded us. Prayed in my foxhole and read my Bible. Shrapnel dropped on my stomach. Can't take it any longer.

The Germans threw in fresh soldiers from the 741st Infantry Regiment, and the 2nd Battalion had to beat off five counterattacks the night of February 21–22. Colonel Stone reported to General Hays that his battalion was crippled by casualties and lack of supplies. Hays ordered him to keep up the attack, and sent a pack train of supplies, but no reinforcements. The pounding the battalion took from German artillery was decimating the ranks and demoralizing the survivors. PFC Thomas R. Brooks of G Company, later a pioneering historian of the 10th and the war in Italy, was standing with two friends when a German shell exploded nearby. Brooks was unscathed, although covered in blood. His two friends were dead. The blood covering Brooks was theirs. He didn't move until his platoon sergeant, seeing him standing there and realizing he was in shock, thrust a shovel into his hands and ordered him to dig in. Brooks was still a few months shy of his twentieth birthday.

By the evening of February 22, 2nd Battalion was reduced in size to some four hundred men. The beleaguered unit even lost its surgeon, Captain Morton E. Levitan, when he left the aid station, perhaps to look for wounded soldiers, perhaps in shock himself, and was captured by the Germans. He was the only officer of the 10th to be captured in the entire campaign, and was liberated in Germany months later. The soldiers of the 2nd Battalion displayed no shortage of heroism in the battle for della Torraccia; at least five were awarded Silver Stars for their actions, one posthumously. But the Germans proved fiercely determined to retain their last strongpoint on the Belvedere massif. And Colonel Stone, at least according to some accounts by men who served under him (Marty Daneman's was particularly scathing), did not distinguish himself in combat. He was relieved of command by General Hays in April, the only senior officer in the 10th during the fighting in Italy to suffer that fate.

Robert B. Ellis recorded in his diary what happened on the 2nd Battalion's last night below della Torraccia: "All nite we sweated out the relief... Capt. [Charles] King [Company Commander] crying [Timothy] Prout knocked senseless. Chaplain cried. Pulled out at 5 AM. Followed by 88's till we reached the town. Then the heartbreaking reunions and experiences were exchanged. 16 dead and 48 wounded [out of company]. Prout wept with his arms around me as did Wally and Larry. Rode back to Campo Pizzoro (rest camp). Wonderful here but our hearts are heavy. God saved my life." With so many losses, many enlisted men moved up in rank in the days and weeks to come, including Ellis, who was promoted to sergeant.

On the night of February 23–24, the 2nd Battalion was relieved by the 86th's 3rd Battalion, under the command of Major John Hay Jr. The twenty-eight-year-old Hay, a former national park ranger from Montana, was one of the most respected officers in the regiment. The line of departure for the next day's attack was only four hundred yards from the summit of della Torraccia. The men of the 86th's 3rd Battalion, who had yet to fight in a sustained battle, could see the bodies of dead Americans from the 85th in the gap between their own line and the German advance positions, just two hundred yards away. General Hays came up to the front line early that morning to observe the attack. At 6:50 on the morning of February 24, artillery from the valley below began bombarding the German position on the summit of the mountain. Ten minutes later, 3rd Battalion's I and K Companies moved forward, taking casualties from machine gun and artillery fire, but seizing the summit shortly before 9 a.m. in hand-to-hand fighting, and then moving forward to capture some subsidiary peaks. Counterattacks by the Mittenwald Mountain Battalion started in the late afternoon on February 24 and continued through the night. Around 1 a.m. on February 25 a concerned officer back at the regimental command post telephoned Hay to ask if his battalion needed reinforcements. He replied: "Hell no, we don't need any help here. We're doing all right." At dawn the counterattacks ceased, and the survivors of one German company, forty men including their captain, surrendered to the Americans. Mount della Torraccia, the final objective of the first phase of Operation Encore, was under American control.

The Belvedere massif was secured, but the victors were still at risk. Among the last Americans to die on Mount della Torraccia was Captain Ralph R. Bromaghin of HQ Company, 3rd Battalion, the former Sun Valley ski instructor who, three years earlier at Paradise Valley on Mount Rainier, had been co-founder of the 87th Regimental Glee Club and shared credit for the lyrics to "Ninety Pounds of Rucksack." He was killed on the otherwise peaceful morning of February 26, drinking coffee in his foxhole, when a mortar shell exploded ten feet away. Bromaghin had turned twenty-seven a month earlier. He received the Bronze Star posthumously.

The capture of the Belvedere massif cost the 10th Mountain Division a total of 923 casualties: 192 killed in action, 730 wounded, and one prisoner of war. With 470 killed and wounded, the 85th Mountain Infantry suffered over half the total American casualties in the battle. German casualties are unknown, but over four hundred were taken prisoner. Original plans for the offensive, perhaps influenced by grim memories of the prolonged campaign to capture Cassino, had envisioned it could take as long as two weeks to drive the Germans off Belvedere and adjoining peaks; instead it took the 10th five days.

As American bodies were retrieved from the battlefield, the appropriate casualty notification forms were filled out and made their way through channels to the War Department in Washington, DC. It took several weeks for family members back home to learn the fate of loved ones who had suddenly gone silent in Italy. Mrs. Hallie E. Murphy in Albuquerque, New Mexico, received a telegram on March 5, 1945, notifying her of her son's death in the battle to take Mount Belvedere:

THE SECRETARY OF WAR DESIRES ME TO EXPRESS HIS DEEP REGRET THAT YOUR SON SERGEANT WILLIAM F. MURPHY WAS KILLED IN ACTION TWENTY FEBRUARY IN ITALY CONFIRMING LETTER FOLLOWS. J A ULIO THE ADJUTANT GENERAL.

Mrs. Murphy's son William, victim of the white flag ruse on Mount Belvedere on February 20, was posthumously awarded the Silver Star.

———

The famous ski troops were in the news again, although in the first published reports of the fighting in the North Apennines they appeared incognito, since the 10th's presence in Italy was still an official secret (just not to the Germans). "American troops of the Fifth Army have regained 3,760-foot Mount Belvedere," the *New York Times* reported on February 22, "and obtained their firmest grip yet on the worst Apennine ridge due north of Pistoia, official reports said today."

Reading between the lines, Minnie Dole guessed who was responsible for the success of the attack, his supposition confirmed by a confidential phone call from someone at the Pentagon. By the time the fighting ceased on Mount della Torraccia on February 25, it was no longer forbidden for journalists to mention the whereabouts and role of the 10th. "The recent successes of the Fifth Army in the area around and including Mount Belvedere, west of the Bologna-Pistoia road, were achieved by the American Tenth Mountain Division, which has been in action only a few weeks and which could not be identified until today," the *Times* reported on February 25. "Made up of especially trained fighters, many of whom were formerly skiers, mountain-climbers and forest rangers, the division from Monday through yesterday secured not only the key feature of Mount Belvedere itself but also Mount Gorgolesco and the Mount della Torraccia bridge. Elements under Maj. Gen. George P. Hays, the division's commander, also took the rocky village of Pol[l]a, Valpiana and Mazzancana and were officially credited with greatly facilitating the supporting attack by Brazilian troops that led [to] the seizure of Mount Castello."

This kind of news was seldom heard from the "forgotten front" in Italy, where there had been no significant Allied progress over the past four months. That it was the already vaunted, glamorous 10th in the vanguard of the Allied advance made the story irresistible. The ascent of Riva Ridge in particular caught the imagination of copywriters and editors. Thus *Time* magazine, in its snappy colloquial style, celebrated the attack as historic and potentially war-winning: "Using tactics old when General James Wolfe scaled Quebec's heights in 1759, Major General George P. Haye's [*sic*] 10th Mountain Division was jolting the German loose from the Apennine positions upon which he had based the center of his line."

Articles recounting the praise the 10th was receiving from higher-ups became a staple of *The Blizzard* in the days to come, including General Hays's personal message of commendation on February 25, in which he saluted the mountain troopers for "your courage, determination, fighting spirit, and the professional workmanship you have displayed in all your actions." (If the men of the 10th respected General Hays before the fighting in February, they revered him thereafter, not least for his commitment to visiting wounded troopers in field hospitals, something few other division commanders did on a regular basis. As 5th Army commander General Lucian Truscott wrote in a postwar memoir, "Hays, one of the ablest battle leaders I ever knew, fit the [10th Mountain] Division like a well-worn and well-loved glove.") Further congratulatory messages came from Truscott himself, from Field Marshal Alexander, supreme commander of the Mediterranean theater, from Lieutenant General Mark Clark, commanding the 15th Mountain Group in Italy, and other higher-ups. One other general's admiring appraisal of the US mountain infantry would not be revealed for some years. That belated praise came from former German field marshal Albert Kesselring in his 1953 memoir: "To my surprise—in deep snow—the remarkably good American 10th Mountain Division launched an attack against the left flank of the 'static' 232nd Infantry Division, which speedily led to the loss of the dominating heights of Monte Belvedere."

With a quickly won if costly victory and so much praise coming their way, it's not surprising that the men of the 10th were proud of their unit, especially now that they were finally allowed to wear their crossed-bayonet division patches (forbidden while their presence in Italy supposedly was being kept secret). And the curved "MOUNTAIN" tabs, authorized back at Camp Swift, but unavailable, would soon arrive as well. (None had been shipped from the States as of late February, so an Italian company was commissioned to manufacture them.) Lieutenant Joseph Berry, C Company of the 85th, wrote to his parents in Reno, Nevada, on February 24, while the fighting on the Belvedere massif was still going on, exulting in the 10th's triumph: "I've been busy as hell lately, and as you have probably read in the papers, very successful. I am proud to be a part of such a splendid bunch of men as this Division. I've never seen such driving, hard hitting, coldhearted boys when the chips are down . . . We mowed those Jerry bastards down like wheat in a hail storm—man it was good to see them hit the dirt."

Neither the 10th's esprit de corps nor its ability to attract favorable publicity exactly endeared the division to other American soldiers in Italy who had been fighting there far longer. The European edition of *Yank*, the Army's weekly magazine, featured 10th Mountain soldiers on its cover for the issue of March 16, 1945. Inside, a lavishly illustrated five-page story carried the subhead "Cocky, Special Trained Troops of the U.S. 10th Mountain Division Blast the Nazis from 'Impregnable' Mt. Belvedere Less Than a Month after They Arrive in Italy." *Yank's* correspondent went on to note, with some measure of awe, and a remarkable tin ear for the likely effect of his prose: "Because the division was drawn largely from the social class of men who could afford the rather expensive sport of skiing in civilian life, it has more swank than the usual Infantry outfit. It is quite normal to hear one of its lieutenants say, 'My platoon sergeant is a Princeton graduate, cum laude,' or to get challenged in its area by a sentry with a Harvard accent."

That provoked some predictably sarcastic responses, including letters to the editor from GIs in less "swanky" units. "I suppose we should feel it is an honor and a privilege to have such a highly trained and educated group of blue bloods alongside us," Corporal Renzo Guy and eight other enlisted men commented in their response to the article:

> The publicity they got certainly overshadowed all other divisions in this theater although the 10th Mountain was in combat for a short period. Not that we care for the glory but we think it unfair to those many average GIs who fight up there with much less publicized divisions. We also feel that high IQs don't mean much up here. The Krauts don't ask the GIs what their IQs may be . . . When you mention their being cocky, they certainly are. They feel superior to the average GI who may not have been educated in any college but is a fighter as good as any of the 10th Division men.

Both the original *Yank* article and the responses it provoked exaggerated the social homogeneity of the 10th, which also included a good many men without Harvard accents. (And did any lieutenants really brag to reporters about the Ivy League credentials of their platoon sergeants?) In any case, the most important social distinction in the army in the Italian (or any) combat zone, apart from rank, was between those who served as frontline soldiers and those who didn't. In March, Dan Kennerly, D Company of the 85th, who had indeed gone to college before he joined the 10th (although at the University of Georgia, not Harvard or Princeton), was sent on an errand to regimental headquarters, located at a safe remove from the front line. He wrote afterwards in his diary: "Rear echelon troops sure have it made, good duty, good food and sleep without fear of sudden death. Everyone at regiment is neatly dressed. By contrast my clothes are baggy, muddy and torn. I have several days growth of beard. My helmet is dented and scarred. My boots look as if I've been standing in cow shit for a week. If there was ever a live model for Willie or Joe in a Bill Mauldin cartoon I'm it."

*"That can't be no combat man. He's
lookin' for a fight."*

Cartoon by Bill Mauldin, Stars and Stripes *(Mediterranean
Edition), July 13, 1944.* © 1944 BY BILL MAULDIN. COUR-
TESY OF BILL MAULDIN ESTATE LLC.

There was one other social distinction worth noting at the front.
That was between veterans and replacements. Following the fighting in February, hundreds of new men, with no memory of Camp
Hale or Camp Swift, and no specialized mountain training, joined the
10th Mountain Division. Often, they weren't around very long. Of the
eleven replacements who joined C Company of the 85th Regiment
on February 27, one would be killed and two wounded in the next ten
days. Also joining the 85th, as a new platoon leader for I Company, was
Second Lieutenant Robert "Bob" Dole, a twenty-one-year-old Kan-
san who, like many of the replacements, had never skied or climbed a
mountain in his life. He too was wounded within a few days of joining
the 10th, catching a grenade fragment in the leg while on a night patrol
on March 18 (from a grenade that he threw himself, he would later rue-
fully acknowledge), but would soon return to duty. Dole was liked by
his men for his modesty; he wrote that he stood out among the veter-

ans in his unit in one particular aspect: "I was the one with a clean uniform."

After the guns fell silent on Mount della Torraccia on Sunday, February 25, there were five days of relative peace that followed in the North Apennines, although German shelling continued. The weather was getting warmer and the snow was melting. Some lucky troopers were sent back from the front to nearby rest camps, where they could shower, obtain clean uniforms, and eat something other than C- or K-rations. Hot food sometimes made it to the front lines; Dan Kennerly happily recorded a meal served to his company on February 28 in their new position below Belvedere of "hot slices of canned corn beef, mashed potatoes, corn, English peas, bread and butter, slices of pineapple and some sort of punch. It's damned good." Skier Debbie Bankart, famed in the lore of the 10th for her recruitment tours on its behalf back in Camp Hale days, now showed up in the division's sector as a Red Cross "doughnut girl" and raised morale by her presence as well as her pastries; "Debby Dishes Out Doughnuts, Skiing Chatter, and Feminine Charm," read an appreciative headline in *The Blizzard*. Several other doughnut girls soon joined her, and soldiers in the 10th were sometimes astonished to see them handing out their wares dangerously close to the battlefront.

All this proved a temporary respite. The killing resumed on Saturday, March 3, in the second phase of the 10th's Operation Encore offensive. General Truscott wanted to widen the salient that the 10th's offensive had gained with the seizure of Riva Ridge and Belvedere, as well as advance the 1st Armored Division, which had been held in reserve all winter, northward on Route 64 toward Bologna, all in preparation for the April offensive. There was high ground five or so miles ahead and to the northeast, around the crossroads town of Castel d'Aiano. In American hands, those heights, overlooking another important road junction at Vergato on the far side, would cut the German line of supply and communication to the Po Valley and provide an ideal jump-off for a breakout from the North Apennines. Getting there required taking the intervening peaks from the Germans, as well as several fortified villages. It couldn't be accomplished in a day, and there would be no element of surprise or cover of darkness. This would be, from the first day, a daylight offensive.

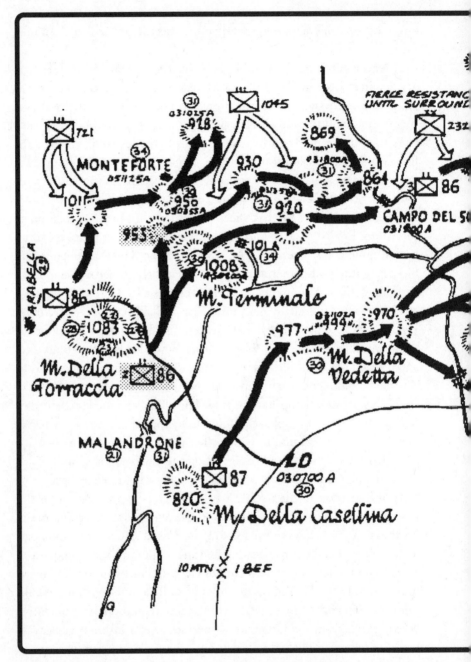

Map of Mount Grande d'Aiano, Castel d'Aiano, and Mount della Spe.
THE DENVER PUBLIC LIBRARY (ARMAND CASINI PAPERS, TMD113)

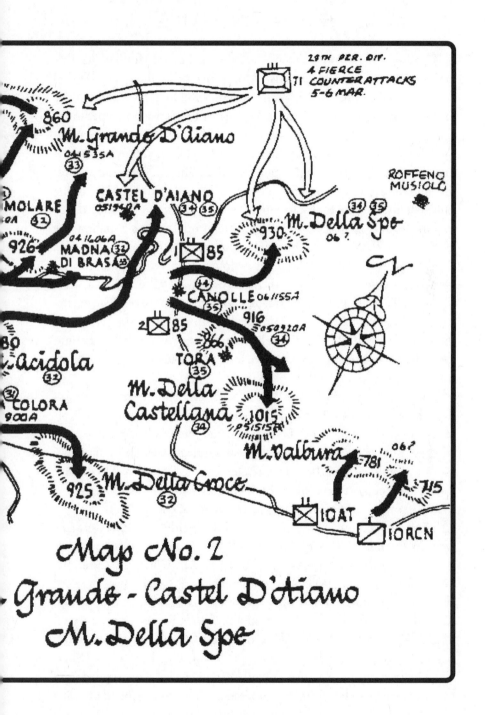

860
M. Grande D'Aiano
041535A
33
MOLARE
40A 41
926
041606A
MADNA 32
DI BRASA 33

CASTEL D'AIANO
051540A
34 35

29TH PER. DIV.
71 4 FIERCE
COUNTERATTACKS
5-6 MAR.

ROFFENO
MUSIOLO

930 M. Della Spe
06?
34 35

1 85

CANOLLE 06 1155A
35
916
050210A
34

ROFFENO MUSIOLO

80
Acidola
33

34
COLORA
900A

2 85

066
TORA
35

M. Della
Castellana
34

1015
PSISISA

M. Valbura 781 06?

715

925 M. Della Croce
32

10AT

10RCN

Map No. 2
Grande - Castel D'Aiano
M. Della Spe

The line of departure this time ran from the base of Mount della Torraccia to another peak to its east, Mount della Casellina. The Americans were pulled off Riva Ridge, Belvedere, and Gorgolesco, their place on those hard-won heights taken by part of the Brazilian Expeditionary Force. The initial attack would be made by the 86th Regiment on the left flank and the 87th Regiment on the right flank, moving abreast in a widening sweep through complicated terrain, up, over, and around the intervening mountains and hill towns. They would face some of the same enemy soldiers they had fought in February, from the 1043rd and 1045th Regiments, backed up by the Mittenwald Training Battalion, the 114th Recon Battalion, and the 721st Regiment. The principal objectives for the 86th were Mount Terminale, Mount della Vedetta, and Mount Grande d'Aiano. For the 87th, the objectives were Mount della Croce, Mount della Castellana, and Castel d'Aiano, which would bring the Americans to the foot of a long ridge called Mount della Spe. The 85th, the regiment hardest hit in the February fighting, would follow behind the other two regiments until it came time to take the German positions on della Spe, which was their objective.

The skies were overcast on March 1, the day chosen for the start of the offensive. General Hays wanted air support and postponed the attack until the next day, and then again when the weather remained unsuitable. But the forecast for March 3 was for clear skies, and at 6:30 that morning, gunners from IV Corps artillery opened fire. A half hour later the 1st and 2nd Battalions of the 86th on the left and the 3rd Battalion of the 87th on the right stepped forward toward the enemy.

The 10th's second battle started well. Coincidentally, the Germans were in the midst of relieving some of their frontline units, and their guard was down. Rover Joes called in air strikes, which prevented the enemy from launching effective counterattacks. E Company of the 86th secured the regiment's first objective of the day, the summit of Mount Terminale, in little over an hour and a half, then moved on to the next objective, the town of Iola. There they had to fight a house-to-house battle, but they had help from the 751st Tank Battalion, whose Shermans blasted out the German defenders, and leveled a good portion of the town and its church in the process. In a notorious incident, men from E Company gunned down what they thought were two German soldiers who inexplicably exposed themselves in the street. When they got closer they saw that the dead were actually Italian women, dressed in German uniforms and forced into the street to draw fire from the Americans. The fight for Iola was brutal, but there and throughout the day Germans were readily surrendering, with hundreds giving themselves up by nightfall. The 86th captured five of its seven objectives on the first day of fighting and advanced a full two miles from its starting point.

The 86th's success on March 3 was all the more remarkable given that, for some of its soldiers, it was their first day of serious combat. Back in February, 1st Battalion of the 86th had seized Riva Ridge, and 3rd Battalion had captured Mount della Torraccia. But in the regiment's 2nd Battalion, only F Company, which took part in the Riva operation, had previously been in battle; the other companies had remained in reserve.

Among the men of G Company, 2nd Battalion, about to undergo their initiation as frontline soldiers was PFC John Parker Compton. Compton, a child of privilege with his Westchester upbringing and Exeter and Princeton education, loved being in the 10th. Back in the States, he had turned down the opportunity to attend OCS at Fort Benning, not wanting to risk being assigned to a different division on graduation. And according to his platoon leader, Second Lieutenant Fred Wendorf, Compton had recently passed on the opportunity to become a general's aide, preferring to remain with his friends in G Company. Wendorf remembered the private as a "tall slim young man . . . , twenty-two years old [actually twenty] and intelligent." He was carrying a Browning automatic rifle on March 3 as his platoon joined the assault on Iola when he was shot in the head by a sniper and died instantly. In his last letter home, dated February 23, "Eagle" Compton hadn't said anything at all about the war, beyond reporting, "I'm still in the land of olives and signorinas, and feeling fine," and thanking his parents for sending a package with two pairs of wool socks.

The fighting around Iola also took the life of the best-known enlisted man in the 10th Mountain Division, Technical Sergeant Torger Tokle of A Company, the Norwegian émigré and world champion ski jumper. Since joining the newly established 86th at Camp Hale in 1943, he had been admired for his extraordinary physical prowess by fellow soldiers; in Italy, Tokle established an equally sterling reputation for fearlessness and leadership in battle, time and again volunteering for dangerous assignments. On March 3 he and his platoon were on a wooded ridge above Iola, pinned down by a German machine gun. Tokle along with bazooka man Sergeant Arthur K. Tokola (a fellow émigré, born in Finland) moved to an exposed position to get a shot at the machine gun when they were hit by shellfire, detonating the bazooka rounds that Tokola was carrying and killing both men instantly. Enraged, the men of A Company vowed to take no prisoners that day and pushed on relentlessly past Iola. When the news of his death was announced two weeks later in the United States, the *New York Times* ran a two-column article, "Foe Kills Tokle, Skiing Champion," complete with a prewar photo of him holding a pair of skis, and a detailed listing of his championship jumps. The publicity given Tokle's death was disturbing not only to the soldiers of the 10th but also to their families and friends back home, who had to wonder if the next such news to arrive from Italy would involve their own loved ones.

One other notable casualty from the 86th that day was Pete Seibert of F Company, a champion New England ski racer in his teenage years, who survived but was told he could never walk let alone ski again. An exploding shell left him with wounds to the head, torso, arms, and legs. His teeth were knocked out from catching a piece of shrapnel in the jaw, and his right kneecap was blown off. He spent the next year and a half recovering in the hospital, his survival a testament to the skill of army doctors, and to the resilience, at least in his case, of the human body.

On the right flank on the first day of battle, led by its 3rd Battalion, the 87th captured several hilltops and routed the enemy sheltering in farmhouses or behind stone walls and haystacks. Second Battalion captured the town of Pietra Colora, suffering only a single man wounded, and taking thirty prisoners. By day's end the 87th had advanced two miles while capturing over four hundred prisoners. The worst loss the regiment suffered came when its aid station in the village of Abetaia blew up from a booby trap the Germans had left behind before their evacuation. It killed many of the patients and medical staff, and two of the regiment's three chaplains, Captain Harry Montgomery and Captain William S. Contino.

The second day's fighting was largely a repeat of the first twenty-four hours, with both the 86th and 87th gaining ground and scooping up many more prisoners. The 86th captured the town of Sassomolare by 11:30 a.m., and shortly before 3:30 p.m. was on top and in control of Mount Grande d'Aiano, the regiment's final objective. Lieutenant Colonel Henry J. Hampton, commander of 1st Battalion, who had a reputation for leading from the front lines as he had in the relief of Lieutenant Loose's platoon on Riva Ridge, was badly wounded in the attack on Sassomolare and was evacuated. Meanwhile, the 87th captured Mount Acidola and a hilltop called Madonna di Brasa, overlooking the town of Castel d'Aiano, while its 3rd Battalion captured Mount della Croce. The Brazilians, in a supporting role, advanced west of Highway 64.

———

The attack had gone on schedule and according to plan on the first two days of the offensive. But German resistance stiffened on March 5, thanks to reinforcements, and the return of bad weather, which limited Allied air cover. The 87th continued its drive to capture Castel d'Aiano. Soldiers from the regiment's 1st Battalion, supported by tanks from the 1st Armored Division, took the town that afternoon, with its vital road network. And Castel d'Aiano was only twenty-two miles from Bologna.

The 85th was now back in the battle. While the regiment's 2nd Battalion captured its objective, Mount della Castellana, by midday, it took the 1st Battalion all day to take the main objective, Mount della Spe, finally gaining control of the summit a little after 6 p.m. The troops dug in, expecting German counterattacks, which began shortly after midnight and continued until 5 a.m. Field Marshal Kesselring threw in his strategic reserve, the 29th Panzer Grenadier Division (a motorized infantry unit, which included a tank component), against the Americans on della Spe. It was one of his last acts as commander of German forces in Italy; on March 9 Hitler transferred him to the crumbling western front in Germany. Fighting on della Spe that night was sometimes hand-to-hand. First Sergeant Harry J. Porzio of B Company found himself in a shell hole with two German soldiers; one he bayoneted and the other he shot. Sergeant Werner von Trapp of B Company (and also of the von Trapp family singers) overheard a Nazi officer giving instructions in German for an assault on his unit and alerted the company. Concentrating their fire on the draw where the Germans were approaching, they inflicted many casualties and beat back the attack. Dan Kennerly of D Company spent much of the night swiveling his heavy machine gun back and forth at enemy soldiers only a grenade toss away. In the morning, exhausted Americans still held the hill. Kennerly scribbled in his diary, "I believe the Germans want this dung heap we've taken from them."

Sergeant Dan Kennerly's 85-D Machine Gun Squad, June 1945. From left: Paul Eley, Dan Kennerly, Francis Starkey, Theodore Tarala, Oliver Love, Gerald Adams. THE DENVER PUBLIC LIBRARY (TMD351-2017-1999)

The 1st Battalion's ordeal on Mount della Spe was only beginning, as the new owners of the mountain were battered nearly every day by artillery fire from the former owners. It was like being at Anzio, if not for quite so long a duration, enduring life under relentless shelling as helpless, exposed targets. Lieutenant Stan Cummings, B Company of the 85th, was spared the shelling, assigned temporary duty at battalion headquarters, but from friends learned what it was like: "B Co was on a bare knoll in full view of the enemy and took unbelievable barrages day after day for almost three weeks. Several went off their nut and a couple shot off their toes to get out of it. They never came out of their foxholes during the day and rarely at night. At the end ... many were so weak they could hardly walk. Practically their only exercise was in digging. You never saw deeper or more elaborate foxholes! It was these sandbag covered holes that saved them."

The newspaper stories back in the United States showed the line on the map advancing an impressive five miles from Mount della Torraccia to Mount della Spe in three days, and that, not the ordeal that followed for the men on top of della Spe, shaped the coverage of the fighting. Once again, plaudits showered the victorious 10th Mountain Division, for the past month the most consistent (and really the only) source of positive news coming out of Italy. "A three-day offensive by the American Tenth Mountain Division, aided by Brazilian troops, had resulted in gains up to five miles as of yesterday afternoon and greatly improved the Fifth Army's positions southwest of Bologna," the *New York Times* reported on March 8. "Although the attack was described as directed at a 'limited objective,' it was considered a notable success — probably the greatest since the smashing of the Gothic Line in October."

News of the 10th's latest triumph in Italy, however heartening, could not compete with the stories coming from elsewhere in Europe in early March. On March 7, Americans captured an intact bridge over the Rhine at Remagen, Germany, gaining a critically important beachhead in the Nazi heartland. Three days later, the last German forces west of the Rhine retreated across the river. Meanwhile, the Russians drove on, bloodily, inexorably, toward Berlin.

The mountain troopers did not seem at all dismayed by being pushed off the front page by the Remagen story. "The crossing of the Rhine is of course the big news over here and all of us are watching that front with a prayer on our lips," First Lieutenant Earl E. Clark of 1st Battalion of the 87th wrote to his mother in mid-March, little more than a week after his regiment had captured Castel d'Aiano. "With fate and God on our side, the break needed to end the war is now in sight."

Although overshadowed by events elsewhere (including the Battle of Iwo Jima, being waged simultaneously on the other side of the world), the 10th's battles in the North Apennines in February and March were not inconsequential. In the three-day March offensive, the division captured ten mountains and a number of unnamed hills, adding up to some thirty-five square miles of enemy territory, along with taking over a thousand prisoners. Overall German casualties had been staggering; Field Marshal Kesselring admitted in his memoirs that after the March fighting, the 29th Panzer Grenadiers "suffered such serious losses that they lost their value as a strategic reserve."

Thanks to the 10th's advance to Mount della Spe, and the additional length of Route 64 opened to the 1st Armored Division as a result, the US 5th Army was now poised for a breakthrough into the Po Valley. The Germans remained entrenched on high ground overlooking Highway 64 from the village of Vergato north toward Bologna. General Hays was in favor of continuing the attack from the northern slopes of Mount della Spe to push the Germans off those heights, but General Truscott ordered a delay, not wanting to signal to the enemy the direction in which he intended to attack in April. The cost to the 10th had been high. Between March 3 and March 6, the division had lost 146 killed and 512 wounded, with three POWs.

For five weeks the mountain troopers remained in place. The dead were buried, the wounded were evacuated, and more replacements arrived to fill the vacancies in the ranks. Civilians, who had kept out of sight during the fighting, now reappeared, including many fleeing German-occupied villages for safety behind American lines. The area around the shattered town of Castel d'Aiano was now filled with refugees, many of them tending herds of pigs, goats, cattle, and horses. Spring arrived in the mountains, gloriously. A reporter from *The Blizzard* in early April returned to Mount della Torraccia and found the foxholes full of water, with primroses, forget-me-knots, and violets springing up around them. On the hillside farms, at least those where the fields had been cleared of mines, farmers were plowing and sowing spring crops. "It was too quiet and spring like for one to believe that men had fought and died in this area a few weeks ago," the reporter concluded.

Most soldiers got at least a few days off the front lines, sent to rest camps like the ones at Montecatini or Campo Tizzoro, both near Pistoia, or to cities like Florence or Rome. For the first time since early

February, soldiers could write home about experiences that did not include death and destruction. Marty Daneman got to visit both Montecatini and Florence. From Montecatini he wrote to fiancée Lois on March 23: "The place is littered with bars, shops, movies (6 of them), baths, and most important, people. It seems so strange to see hundreds of people walking around — some of them are even clean with good clothes on their backs. And it was even stranger to see all the little kids on the way to school in the morning and coming out at noon. It's good to see civilization, and what could almost be considered a normal life."

Easter Sunday fell on April 1, and *The Blizzard* reported the next week in a headline whose joke was best understood by veterans of Camp Hale days, "Division Celebrates Easter in Spring Setting — For Once."

———

Apart from the German shelling, the last weeks in March and the first weeks in April definitely weren't as bad as D-Series. Medic Arthur B. Draper had earned a Bronze Star (the first of two he was awarded that spring) for the courage he displayed treating wounded soldiers in the assault on Mount della Torraccia; he was also promoted to staff sergeant. "This has been one of those delightful Spring days," he wrote to his mother on April 2, in a letter that said nothing about his heroism or his medal, "when for no reason at all one suddenly finds himself emitting strange bleating noises . . . The fruit trees are in blossom. Little flowers, dandelions and daisies, are in bloom. A few birds are around singing. It's really pleasant, especially if one can let his eye skip over the signs of war."

Back in his observation post on Mount della Spe after enjoying leave in Rome, Second Lieutenant Donald Potter, H Company of the 85th, wrote his mother on April 8: "Except for the routine exchange of artillery and an Easter serenade the valleys are quiet and the mountains are peaceful. The trees are budding and the grass is green; sheep graze on the hillsides and yesterday I heard a couple of children laughing and playing around their farm. Best darned sound in the world."

———

Flowers, children, Easter, normal life: such were the preoccupations of the soldiers of the 10th in early spring 1945. Yet they knew their respite was coming to an end. In 1944 the Allied spring offensive had begun on May 11. Had the generals in Italy waited that long in 1945, there would have been no need for another offensive. But by the start of April, ordinary soldiers could clearly read the signs that told them they were about to be sent back into action. Their platoons, companies, and regiments were up to strength. There were no more leaves. Huge dumps of ammunition, fuel, and other supplies were assembled in the rear areas. As the official history of the 87th Regiment recorded, "Tanks, tank destroyers, armored artillery, artillery fieldpieces, and heavy equipment of all types stretched to the rear as far as the eye could see."

The men of the 10th Mountain Division were now frontline soldiers. Though not eager to return to battle, they were certainly prepared to do their duty in the fighting to come. Still, having enjoyed a taste of peace for a few weeks in March and April, they could not help but think of what their lives would be like once the final victory was gained—provided they survived to see it. They remained civilians at heart, as their letters home revealed, often through a touch of sly or rueful humor.

Sergeant Albert Brockman, G Company of the 85th, wrote to his mother on March 13 from atop Mount della Spe: "I have a captured German machine gun in my hole with me. We had Jerry on the run and he left plenty of things behind. I could send you souvenirs but they aren't much and would only remind me of this after I get home. The only thing I want to take home is myself."

Corporal Marty Daneman wrote to Lois on April 2, two days after he returned to the front from Passover leave in Florence: "Another day, another $2.88 & board & meals—neither of which is too hot. If [it] wasn't for the fact that I like to travel I'd quit this job." And then, a few days later, in a more serious vein: "I want to have the wedding as soon as possible dearest—I've found life is too short, + too uncertain to waste waiting. Our love has been proved a thousand times, + it can't be said that we're too young anymore. I want to be with you every moment of my life dearest, + never have to wait."

Sergeant Robert B. Ellis, also back at the front, advised his mother in mid-April, "You probably won't hear from me for awhile after this letter." Then he added: "I think these years in the Army have given me my fill of mountains. From now on I'll simply be content to ride thru them, very rapidly, in a car." Ellis's letter was dated April 13. As he predicted, it turned out to be awhile, twelve eventful days in his case, before he had the chance to write again. The 10th Mountain Division's final offensive in the war began the next morning.

April 6, 1945: A bugler plays taps beside the rows of white crosses during a memorial service held for the dead of the 10th Mountain Division at the newly dedicated American Cemetery in Castelfiorentino, Italy.
THE DENVER PUBLIC LIBRARY (TMD78)

8

Italy, April 14–May 3, 1945

"All Those Fine Young Men"

Last night we heard [the] news we've fought long and terrible battles for, and the dawn has broken through at last . . . I wish all those fine young men who gave their lives in the past few months could be here to rejoice with us. I feel that very much, for many of my oldest and best friends of Camp Hale days have given their lives.

— *Sergeant Robert B. Ellis to his mother,*
May 3, 1945

IN THE LULL BEFORE THE STORM, THE FIVE WEEKS IN THE SPRING of 1945 in the North Apennines between the conclusion of the March offensive and the beginning of the April offensive, men continued to die. The war in the mountains, fought by two opposing armies whose front lines were only a mile or so apart in places, sometimes became highly personalized. One such occasion came the night of March 23, when Second Lieutenant William Lowell Putnam of L Company, 85th Regiment, led a reconnaissance patrol to a small German-occupied village called Pra del Bianco, located in the valley of the same name below Mount della Spe. It was well past midnight when Putnam's men approached the village. They were spotted, and three of the scouts, PFC Lorenz Köhler and two others, were shot by a German sentry. For Köhler, "an inspired soldier" according to Putnam, the war was already personal. He was Jewish and had been forced to flee Nazi Germany with his family, which was why he volunteered for dangerous missions like that night's patrol. He had carved the words *siempre avanti* (a slight misspelling of the Italian for "always forward") on the wooden stock of his submachine gun, and he lived up to the motto that night. Now, badly wounded, he shouted to Putnam to leave him behind; an attempted rescue would only mean losing still more men. Under fire, Putnam had no choice but to pull his men back and hope for the best for his wounded troopers. (Two other members of the patrol were killed by friendly fire as they attempted to cross back into American lines on Mount della Spe.)

The following day, March 24, an artillery spotter saw something strange in the village where the patrol had run into trouble the night before and called Lieutenant Putnam to take a look. Through binoculars, Putnam was shocked to spot Köhler's corpse dangling from the roof beam of a ruined house. The Nazis may have learned that Köhler was Jewish, and German Jewish at that; the letter "H" for "Hebrew" was included on Jewish soldiers' dog tags for purposes of grave registration. He may have died of his wounds, or the Germans may have finished him off. Both sides had killed prisoners; however terrible, there was no surprise there. But however he died, desecrating an American corpse was, to Putnam's eye, a horrifying precedent that could not go unanswered. "Those dirty bastards," he thought. "They couldn't just kill him; they had to hang him out for all of us to see, too."

Putnam brooded and then sought out his company commander, First Lieutenant Kenneth Eggleston. He asked permission to lead another, stronger patrol that night to Pra del Bianco to settle unfinished business. Eggleston was reluctant. "We're winning this war anyway," he told Putnam, "and don't need to do anything foolish just because of what they've done to Köhler." But Putnam was adamant, and Eggleston relented. After dark, Putnam returned to the village with three dozen men, who in addition to carrying their usual weapons brought with them several captured Panzerfausts, German bazookas with a heavy explosive punch, much prized by American soldiers. While some of his men blew up the house harboring a dozen or so Germans, the others, led by Putnam, waited at the end of the village to kill or capture any survivors. Only one German, a sergeant, was left alive to flee, and he was brought down and badly wounded by a fusillade of fire from Putnam's men. General Hays had ordered that combat patrols bring in as many prisoners as possible for interrogation, but that order was not a priority for Putnam's men that night. Although they tried to drag the badly wounded German prisoner back with them, he died before they got to American lines. But the sergeant was carrying a satchel when he was shot down, and Putnam turned it over to military intelligence. The papers found inside pinpointed the disposition of German forces in the immediate area. Putnam's patrol that night delivered both frontier justice and valuable information.

Sempre Avanti, "Always Forward," was the sentiment that Private Köhler carved on his weapon stock, the same that General Hays insisted on in his meeting with the 85th Regiment prior to the attack on Mount Belvedere. It became the motto of the 85th Regiment. Always forward was good tactical advice; in battle, relentless pressure on the enemy during an attack was often key to victory, while delay or hesitation could spell greater losses or even defeat. But was it equally good advice when applied to the larger realm of strategy? Or had the time arrived in Italy when *always forward* ceased to make sense?

On March 26, a few days after Putnam's raid on Pra del Bianco, and on the same day news arrived that General George S. Patton's 3rd Army had crossed the Rhine at Mannheim, Germany, Sergeant Robert B. Ellis of F Company of the 85th wrote home to his mother. All around him preparations were obviously under way for a new offensive, likely to begin sometime in the next few weeks. If so, Ellis didn't see the point. "The news this morning about our crossing the Rhine is certainly great. The papers are so optimistic that I'm beginning to feel that this may well be the end. I just hope that we don't launch some bloody useless drive down here."

A quarter century later, 10th Mountain veteran Hal Burton wrote in his history of the division that the decision to go ahead with a spring offensive in Italy "epitomized the needless gallantry of war, the compulsiveness that drives generals to commit their troops, the irresistible urge to share in a victory that could be earned more prudently by simply standing still." As Burton noted, clandestine peace talks were taking place that winter and spring between SS-Obergruppenführer Karl Wolff, who headed the German police, Gestapo, and intelligence service in Italy, and Allen Dulles, head of the America intelligence operation in Bern, Switzerland, intended to effect an early and separate surrender of the German army on the Italian front.

By mid-April more than half of Germany's territory had already been conquered by Allied forces, with the Americans only fifty-odd miles away from Berlin and the Red Army at the city's gates. The fate of the Nazi regime was decided in Germany by the converging Soviet, American, and British armies. V-E Day, marking Allied victory in the European theater, would not be hastened as much as an hour by renewing the battle in Italy. General Mark Clark, as always, tended to confuse his personal ambitions with strategic vision. As Ernest Fischer argued in the official US Army history of the Mediterranean theater in World War II, Clark could not abide the idea that the Red Army, or even the US 7th Army, might reach the Alpine frontier between Italy and Austria before his forces.

Clark, however, wasn't alone in his wish to be "in on the kill," in Fischer's phrase, a desire shared by all senior American and British commanders in the Mediterranean theater. And as always, the wisdom of hindsight should be handled gingerly. Clark was acting in accordance with principles drilled into US Army officers for generations: American military doctrine since the Civil War stressed the advantage of pressing an enemy on multiple fronts with superior force. Moreover, the Germans had seemed to be on the ropes six months earlier and then pulled off a stunning surprise counteroffensive in the Battle of the Bulge. A similar battlefield reversal for Allied armies on the western or eastern front, however unlikely, could not be ruled out. And then there was the specter of the Alpine redoubt. Drew Middleton, chief military correspondent for the *New York Times*, reported in early April 1945 that there was "still plenty of fight" left in the German army. The final struggle, he predicted, would occur "in the mist-shrouded mountains of southeastern Germany, into which SS units already are reported withdrawing." Reinforcements could be expected from the German army in northern Italy, "the only enemy force still in action which appears to have a chance of finishing the war undefeated in the field."

The defeat of the German army in Italy was not just a matter of gaining a victory. The success of the final offensive would justify the sacrifices made in the long bloody slog up the Italian boot since the 1943 landings at Messina and Salerno. Whether or not, in retrospect, the decision to launch a final Allied offensive was the right one, leaving German forces in Italy "undefeated in the field" was simply unacceptable, even unimaginable, to Allied commanders in the Mediterranean theater in the spring of 1945.

At a meeting at Clark's headquarters on March 18, the generals agreed on plans for that offensive. The operation was designed to break the enemy's lines in the North Apennines, envelop the German armies in the Po Valley, and block any retreat by survivors to the Alps and southern Germany. The plans envisioned a one-two punch, with the 8th Army striking first on the eastern sector of the front, followed a few days later by the second punch on the 5th Army's western sector. (By separating the two, the Allies could devote maximum air support to each attack, in sequence.) The offensive would also be supported by fifty thousand Italian partisans behind German lines.

On the 5th Army front, where the offensive was dubbed Operation Craftsman, the attack would be carried out by two US Army corps, II Corps and IV Corps. The latter, under the command of General Will Crittenberger, covered the front between Bagni di Lucca and Highway 64, and consisted of the 10th Mountain Division, the Brazilian Expeditionary Force, and the 1st Armored Division (which included three infantry battalions, as well as tanks). General Mark Clark still favored an attack centered on Highway 65, the more direct but also more heavily defended route to Bologna, and spearheaded by II Corps, while General Lucian Truscott favored the route along Highway 64, in which IV Corps would lead the way. In the end, largely because of the favorable terrain captured in February and March by the 10th, Truscott prevailed.

In the initial phase of the operation, the mountain infantry would open the attack west of Highway 64, moving down the divide between the Reno and Samoggio Rivers, seizing vital hilltops. The Brazilians would advance on the left and protect the 10th's flank, while 1st Armored Division tanks and infantry, on the right flank, pushed up the highway toward the town of Vergato. Farther east, II Corps would also push forward, but as General Truscott noted in his memoirs, "the 10th Mountain would carry the brunt of the attack to the Po Valley — and beyond."

The Allies enjoyed many advantages over their German adversaries, including overwhelming superiority in the air, as well as in tanks and artillery on the ground. And once the breakout from the Apennines was realized, the geography in which the 5th and 8th Armies would be operating provided an additional advantage. The Po Valley is the only place in Italy where the distance between the eastern and western coasts exceeds 150 miles, spreading out to 350 miles — an expanse much more difficult to defend by the Germans, while its flat and open terrain offered mobile Allied forces welcome opportunity for maneuver and speed. The new supreme German commander in Italy, General Heinrich von Vietinghoff, like his predecessor Kesselring, preferred to withdraw to shorter, more defensible lines farther north, but Hitler remained adamantly opposed to any surrender of occupied territory — and as always and up to the very end, his will prevailed. The Germans had one big advantage of their own: they knew the attack would come as soon as the roads dried and the skies cleared, and they had had all winter to prepare for it.

For five weeks the soldiers of the 10th had held the summit of Mount della Spe. Now they would move down to take the next set of hills to their north. Regimental commanders were briefed on unit objectives on April 1. The 87th Regiment would be in the center position during the attack, flanked on its left by the 85th and on its right by the 86th. The 85th and 87th would step off simultaneously on D-Day, set for April 12, followed later in the morning by the 86th. The 87th's initial objective was the town of Torre Iussi and the heights of Hills 890 and 903. (Those designations on military maps referred to the height in meters of otherwise unnamed hills.) Two battalions of the 86th would remain in reserve on the first day of the attack, but 2nd Battalion would follow the advance of the 87th before turning to its initial objective, the heights of Rocca di Roffeno. The 85th would cross the valley to climb and seize three rocky hilltops, designated on their maps as Hills 915, 909, and 913. None of the jumbled band of hills that were the division's objectives that first day were as steep as Riva Ridge, but some were steeper than Mount Belvedere, with deep draws and rocky outcroppings, as well as chestnut groves and, on some, cleared fields and farmhouses. The approaches would be heavily mined, and the terrain, as always, favored the defenders, who had the ground advantage.

While the 10th Mountain Regiments prepared for their assignments, on April 5 the African American 370th Regiment (part of the reorganized 92nd Division), along with the Japanese American 442nd Regimental Combat Team, launched a diversionary attack along the Ligurian (western) coast of Italy, with the goal of capturing the coastal city of Massa and continuing northward. Although enemy counterattacks slowed the 370th's advance, the Germans were forced to deploy the 90th Panzer Grenadier Division from their dwindling reserves. On April 9, following a massive air and artillery bombardment, the British 8th Army (which included Polish, Indian, and New Zealand as well as British soldiers) smashed into German lines on the Adriatic (eastern) coast, making significant gains, and once again the Germans had to draw on their reserves, in this case the already bloodied 29th Panzer Grenadier Division.

The next and decisive punch was to be delivered by US Army IV Corps on Thursday, April 12, with the 10th in the lead. But the mild, sunny spring weather of preceding weeks gave way to overcast skies on the morning chosen for the attack, which would have hindered tactical air support, so the start was delayed for a day. Bad weather continued the next morning, causing another postponement.

While the men waited, nervous and impatient in their advance positions, news arrived by radio, and a special mimeographed issue of *The Blizzard,* that President Franklin Delano Roosevelt had died the previous day of a stroke. "Funeral arrangements have not yet been announced to a nation plunged into mourning on the eve of victory," *The Blizzard* reported. Roosevelt, who had delivered his first inaugural address a dozen years earlier calling on the nation to set aside fear, was virtually the only president the twenty-year-olds in the 10th had ever known. Thirty-six-year-old First Lieutenant Earl Clark was old enough to remember the pre–New Deal era. Reflecting on Roosevelt's legacy a few weeks later, Clark wrote that FDR had been "more than just a president. He had become in my mind a really great leader, a great man who had made us what we are today. From nothing to everything, from defeat to overwhelming victory, from chaos to serenity . . . It is a great irony that he could not have lived just a little bit longer to see the fruits of his great effort—the overwhelming defeat of Germany and Japan."

Two days after Roosevelt died, the last great offensive in the Italian campaign began, and Lieutenant Clark, along with ten thousand other mountain troopers, went forward once again. How many of those men would live to see the defeat of Germany was a question that many must have thought about that morning. Sergeant Robert Ellis certainly did, scribbling in his field diary: "April 14 — In a few minutes we will attack. It is now 7 a.m. Dawn is breaking and the men are nervous, wondering what lies ahead and who won't come back. Hope my luck stays with me."

Morning fog threatened another day's delay. But it soon burned off, and at 8:30 a.m. over one thousand heavy, medium, and fighter bombers from the United States 15th Air Force dropped over two thousand tons of bombs on German positions across the valley. Fifth Army artillery took over at 9:10 a.m., with two thousand guns firing thousands of rounds into the opposing hills. "We had never witnessed a bombardment to compare with it," Sergeant Ellis recalled. The noise was overwhelming but reassuring. Smoke, dust, and flames obscured the view, and some dared hope that this time the weight of ordnance would be enough to demolish even the famously sturdy German bunkers. At 9:45 a.m. the command was given, "Packs On," and the 85th and 87th Regiments crossed the line of departure and descended into the valley, followed forty-five minutes later by the 2nd Battalion of the 86th.

General Truscott came to the front to observe the first day of the offensive. "From an OP [observation post] on Mount [della] Castellana," he wrote in his memoirs, a position placing him behind the right flank of the American attack, "we watched Hays' 10th Mountain Division scale and capture Mt. Rocco Roffino [Rocca di Roffeno]. Fighting was heavy, opposition was intense in spite of the bombing and artillery barrages, with high explosives and fire bombs. But we watched the Mountaineers reach and clear the top." Truscott, a down-to-earth GI general, was not given to the florid military mythopoesis of some of his colleagues, like General George S. Patton. Still, the general's description of the 10th's attack, while appreciative, was couched in language that obscured as much as it revealed: fighting was "heavy," opposition was "intense," but in the end the mountain infantry prevailed, as they always had. The human cost was implied, but not dwelled upon, as was common in most of the official writing devoted to the war.

PFC Harris Dusenbery also had the privilege, at least for a day, of a spectator's view of the attack, not far from where General Truscott stood. Dusenbery's battalion of the 86th sat out the first day's fighting, so he found a place where he could watch the advance on Torre Iussi and Rocca di Roffeno, using a twenty-power spotting scope to magnify the image of the advancing troopers. In the late morning, he saw soldiers from the 87th fighting their way up Hill 860, near Torre Iussi: "The Germans were reacting strongly with intense artillery fire upon the hill. Sometimes the whole hill would be hidden by the shell bursts. When the smoke would clear away I would see our men rise up and go on." He couldn't help wondering "how many did not rise up after one of those fierce barrages." Still, at day's end, he took satisfaction in what had proved "a spectacular advance for our side, [that] seemed to assure the valley on the first day of our attack."

For the soldiers actually crossing that valley and then climbing up the opposing slopes, their memories of April 14 were not as sanguine. Vague, abstract, and distancing words like "heavy" and "intense" did not feature in their subsequent accounts, nor did celebratory words like "spectacular." Medic Murray Mondschein took part in the 85th's capture of Hill 913. In a letter written in early May 1945 to the girlfriend of a buddy who had been wounded in February and thus missed the April offensive, he wrote, "You can tell him that 913 made Belvedere look like kindergarten." A month after the battle, he still seemed in shock at what he had witnessed and experienced on April 14: "Oh Christ! What's the use — you tell him that he wouldn't recognize the [battalion]. Most everybody he knew are all killed or wounded . . . The fellows died everywhere, beneath the blooming apple blossom trees, along the ridges, the peaks, in their fox holes, on the trails. Tell him the aid station had four direct hits in one afternoon, and to my last day I don't know why we are still alive . . . Tell him I can still hear the guys yelling, 'Medics, medics, medics.'"

———

Decades would pass, and for those who survived April 14 the memories remained similarly vivid and dark. Second Lieutenant Robert Dole, in charge of 2nd Platoon of I Company of the 85th, took part in the attack on Hill 913, and recalled the day in a memoir published sixty years later. As his company descended from Mount della Spe into the cleared land of the Pra del Bianco valley, "the world exploded" as the Germans "started pouring artillery, machine gun, and mortar rounds into the clearing in front of us, mowing down dozens of American soldiers, shredding others, pulverizing still more . . . Guttural grunts, thuds, and screams added to the bedlam." "Mowing down," "shredding," "pulverizing"— this is a different kind of language from that offered in the conventional narratives of victorious battle.

The 10th Mountain suffered what would, in time, become its most famous casualty when Lieutenant Bob Dole was hit by German fire on April 14. Two platoon leaders in I Company, Lieutenants Keith J. Evans and John D. Mitchell, had already been killed when Dole broke cover to drag his badly wounded radioman, William E. Sims, to shelter. Sims died before he could be rescued, and Dole was wounded in the upper back behind his right shoulder. Falling to the ground, he realized with horror that he could not move any of his limbs. Then, mercifully given a shot of morphine, he drifted into semiconsciousness. It was six or seven hours before medics reached him and evacuated him to an aid station. It was thirty-nine months before he was released from army hospitals, with a crippled right arm. Dole was awarded a Bronze Star for his attempt to save his radioman.

Another casualty of April 14 was PFC John D. Magrath of G Company of the 85th, a twenty-year-old from East Norwalk, Connecticut, who had joined the 10th at Camp Hale in the spring of 1943. Finding himself pinned down by machine gun fire with others of his company on Hill 909, and acting on his own, he charged one German machine gun nest, killed two of the gun crew, and wounded three. Dropping his rifle, he grabbed the German machine gun and, firing as he walked, routed two more enemy machine gun positions. Then, circling around the hillside, he surprised another four Germans from behind, killing them all. Private Magrath subsequently volunteered to check on the condition of other platoons on the hillside, but while doing so was killed by a mortar shell. He received the Congressional Medal of Honor posthumously, the only member of the 10th, dead or alive, so honored in the Second World War.

April 14 proved the division's costliest day in Italy, with 553 casualties, including 114 dead. At dusk, the 10th had captured all but one of its assigned objectives, and that was taken the next morning. Meanwhile, the 81st Reconnaissance Squadron of the 1st Armored Division had entered the last important German bastion on Highway 64, the village of

John D. Magrath, a member of G Company,
85th Regiment, at Camp Hale.
THE DENVER PUBLIC LIBRARY (TMD439)

Vergato, seventeen miles southwest of Bologna. And on April 15, the US Army II Corps began its own offensive up Highway 65.

For the 10th, April 15 was a repetition of the day before, with all three regiments moving forward to the command "Packs on," climbing more hills, taking more villages. Staff Sergeant Arthur Draper, a medic with the 86th, wrote his parents that day wondering why, with the Russians closing in on Berlin from one side and the Americans from the other, Germany wasn't "collapsing like a house of cards, especially in her outposts," like Italy. Instead, Draper noted, the German soldiers at the start of the April offensive had to be driven off each hilltop and routed out of each village: "That they should continue fighting, counter-attacking, sniping, maiming and killing, all against such odds, seems ridiculous. After so many years of it one would think the enemy had had their fill. But they keep on at the damnable game."

The damnable game continued over the next several days, on hilltops named Mounts Mantino, Pigna, Croce, and others. The troopers, including high-ranking officers, continued to take casualties; Colonel Tommy Tomlinson, commander of the 86th, was wounded on April 16 and evacuated under fire; Colonel Dured E. Townsend, commander of the regiment's 2nd Battalion, was hit the following day. By the end of April 16, the 10th had lost 286 killed and 1,047 wounded in the first three days of the offensive. Everyone was exhausted. "Wherever the men dropped their packs," the official history of the 86th Regiment noted, "they fell asleep."

Until now, the tanks of the 1st Armored Division had been tied to the one major road in the region, Highway 64. But the 10th's advance into gentler terrain freed the tankers to maneuver in open territory, away from the main roads. Late on April 16, General Truscott ordered 1st Armored to cross from the 10th's right flank on Highway 64 to the division's left flank and move up the Samoggia Valley toward the Po Valley. At the same time, the 85th Infantry Division (the 85th was a reserve division reassigned from II to IV Corps, and not to be confused with the 10th's own 85th Regiment) would take 1st Armored Division's place on the 10th's right flank and continue the push up Highway 64. The 10th's advance was in the middle of these two units, along a broad stretch of low hills between the Samoggia and Lavino Rivers.

Three or four days into the offensive, the men of the 10th sensed a change was coming. The term "breakthrough" began to be heard in conversations between ranking officers. Counterattacks were now fewer, and enemy resistance seemed disorganized. Hundreds of prisoners were taken every day, and proved extremely docile as they were led to holding pens in the rear, dozens of them sometimes guarded by a lone American minder. Albert H. Meinke, battalion surgeon for 3rd Battalion of the 86th Regiment, noted that by the third day of the offensive, his aid station was treating more German than American wounded.

On April 17, the 87th Regiment captured the village of Tolè, and the slopes to the north began to descend toward the Po. The surviving mules were now sent to the rear; their war was over. Ambulances and jeeps, rather than mules or stretcher bearers, were deployed to evacuate the wounded from the front, which saved lives. Tanks and tank destroyers rumbled along beside the advancing columns. All that four-wheeled

German soldiers surrendering to 10th Mountain troops.
THE DENVER PUBLIC LIBRARY (TMD14)

and tracked traffic raised clouds of dust, and men tied bandannas over their noses and mouths. Temperatures rose, medics treated cases of heat exhaustion, and some soldiers stripped down to undershirts. The mountain troopers, always a little unorthodox in dress when they could get away with it, began to resemble an invasion of *banditti,* albeit extremely well-equipped *banditti.* Some sported feathered Alpini hats in place of regulation headgear. As Dan Kennerly, D Company of the 85th, noted in a diary entry, with a kind of rueful pride, "We look like a damn band of Gypsies."

The American attack was taking on a rolling momentum of its own —for the first time heading downhill, with views of an Italy the GIs had until now never glimpsed. On the evening of April 19, the 10th Mountain Division stood at the northern edge of the North Apennines, gazing down at a plain that reminded Philip A. Lunday, D Company of the 126th Mountain Engineers, of California. "Suddenly the mountains were gone," Lunday recalled, "and up ahead the level green Po Valley spread out like a carpet . . . Now suddenly the terrain was flat, full of orchards and blooming cherry trees." It was the same plain, although farther south and west, that Hemingway had described in *A Farewell to Arms* a decade and a half earlier. And once again, as in the First World War, the tramp of marching soldiers along the roads would raise dust to powder the leaves in the orchards. Except this time, the fighting was not going to be restricted to the still distant Alps, but would take place on the plain itself, amidst the flowering trees.

At 6 a.m. on Friday, April 20, six days after the start of the April offensive, A Company of the 85th Mountain Infantry Regiment descended into the Po Valley to seize a crossroads a little less than five miles west of Bologna. It was, coincidentally, Adolf Hitler's fifty-sixth birthday. The 10th Mountain celebrated by fighting its first flatland battle. Private Thomas Hatfield, a scout with the 3rd Platoon, was the first American to step into the Po Valley. A Company captured the crossroads by 8:30 and established a roadblock. They also captured a very surprised German mess sergeant, riding down the road from Bologna on a motorcycle with a load of eggs. The Germans they were intended for would go hungry. The eggs instead provided breakfast for American mountain troopers. The war was definitely taking a turn for the better, in ways small and large.

All three regiments poured down into the valley that morning and afternoon, reinforced by tanks, tank destroyers, and jeeps carrying .50-caliber machine guns, moving ahead of every other Allied unit. PFC Basil L. Lesmeister, lead scout for A Company of the 86th, was the first to reach that day's most important objective, Highway 9, the historic Roman Via Emilia connecting Bologna to the Adriatic and to other northern Italian cities, including Milan. In one week, the 10th had broken the enemy's lines in the northern Apennines and advanced sixteen miles from Mount della Spe to the Po Valley. German resistance, at long last, was collapsing like the proverbial house of cards. Not that the war had ceased to be deadly: April 17 to April 20, the breakthrough moment, cost the 10th 485 casualties, including eighty-five killed in action.

Captain Bob Livermore, serving on division staff, was one of those

10th Mountain Division troops march through the Po Valley as they head
toward the Po River, near Bagazzano, Italy, April 1945.
THE DENVER PUBLIC LIBRARY (TMD289)

who reached the Po on April 20. He had been present at the creation
of the 10th, five and a half years earlier and half a world away, when he
had traded ideas in a cozy Vermont inn with Minnie Dole, Roger Langley, and Alex Bright about the need for the American army to train soldiers who could fight on skis. As he wrote to his wife a few weeks after
the breakthrough: "[If] ever anyone won the war in Italy it was Minnie's
boys . . . I will never be able to tell you the mixture of laughter, grimness,
tears, scorn and joy I felt in that hectic rush, with at last the knowledge
that we had the enemy on the run and that we were conquerors riding
through a liberated land."

On the afternoon and evening of April 20, the division, led by 3rd
Battalion of the 86th Regiment, moved five miles west up Route 9 to the
town of Ponte Samoggia, where a little before midnight troopers captured a bridge across the Samoggia River intact. On the 10th's first day
of fighting in the valley, it had become a motorized division, although
not according to the specifications laid down in the army's table of organization. Dan Kennerly noted in his diary that by the second day in
the Po Valley, the men of the 85th Regiment were going forward in a collection of vehicles that included "German trucks, half-tracks, Volkswa-

gen jeeps, Italian sports cars, motorcycles, bicycles, horses and wagons, carts and a 1936 Ford."

And then there was the cavalry, making its only appearance in an American advance in the Second World War. The 10th Mountain Cavalry Reconnaissance Troop, or 10th Recon, had the most peculiar evolution of any component of the mountain troops. It had been formed at Camp Hale in 1943 with the idea that mounted horsemen could carry out reconnaissance in the mountains where jeeps couldn't go. It turned out that horses couldn't go very far either, certainly not in the deep snow of the Rockies. The unit was then redesigned as a mountain training group, with new personnel, although the "cavalry" designation stuck. At Camp Swift, where no mountain training was going on, it was reconstituted once again as a genuine cavalry unit shortly before the 10th shipped out for Italy. The 10th Recon brought no horses with them to Italy, and operated with jeeps in the mountains until shortly before the Po breakout. Then they were provided a motley collection of poorly trained local horses, most of which were better suited to pulling carts than galloping into battle. General Hays, an old cavalryman, may have liked the idea of having mounted troops under his command one more time. In any case, nearly two hundred strong, they rode into the Po Valley on April 20 to pursue the retreating Germans, where (accounts vary, and the evidence is ambiguous) they may or may not have launched a costly cavalry charge, the last such instance in US Army history. A magnificent military anachronism, they played a colorful though not significant part in the final offensive.

Soldiers in the 10th had expected once they reached the Po that their objective would be to capture Bologna. But that assignment was given instead to Polish troops from the 8th Army and American troops from II Corps, who entered the city on April 21 to find that it was already largely under the control of Italian partisans. On April 22, General Clark, who had a taste for such things, staged what was supposed to be a triumphal entry into Bologna, accompanied by his disgruntled subordinate, Truscott. "What we were supposed to accomplish I do not know," Truscott recorded sourly. "There were few Bolognese about and these did not seem overly enthusiastic."

While Clark was preoccupied with Bologna, 10th Mountain commander George P. Hays kept his eye on the main prize, the German army and the Alps. Once the breakthrough to the valley was accomplished, Clark intended to have the 10th surrender its vanguard role to more conventional flatland infantry and armored divisions. But Hays had other ideas. Inspired by his troops' élan and achievements over the past two months, he was becoming a bit of a freebooter himself in those last weeks of the war. And he was discreetly encouraged to stretch his orders and continue in hot pursuit of the retreating enemy by both 5th Army commander Truscott and IV Corps commander Crittenberger.

In a masterpiece of rapid improvisation, assistant division commander Brigadier General Robinson Duff, on orders from Hays, patched together a task force to spearhead the 10th's advance to the Po River. (Duff, like Hays, was a First World War veteran and non–West Pointer; during the April offensive, he was often seen at the front urging men to keep moving forward.) At 6:30 on the morning of April 21, Task Force Duff was up and running, a force consisting of the 2nd Battalion of the 86th, along with a borrowed tank company and a platoon of tank destroyers. While they raced ahead, the rest of the division followed.

Hays and Duff were throwing away the rule book. Speed, not consolidation, was their main priority. Once again, the watchword was "Always Forward." What at West Point was called the "line of communication," the vital route connecting a military unit in the field with its supply base, would go undefended. Task Force Duff would drive on to the Po River ignoring the enemy, leaving its flanks and rear unsecured, figuring that the Germans were in no condition to launch a serious threat. The rest of the division following behind would mop up isolated pockets of resistance and corral prisoners, who, unless they were snipers, had little to fear when they gave themselves up. PFC Raymond Albert, B Company of the 86th, set off on April 20 for the division stockade in the rear, escorting one prisoner. By the time he reached it, he had sixteen in tow. Asked where the others came from, he explained that they "just accumulated."

If General Clark's reception in Bologna proved lukewarm, such was not the case for the mountain troopers as they pushed northward past villages and farms. Unlike in Naples, where GIs shared their food scraps with starving civilians, in the breadbasket of Italy it was the civilians who had food to share with appreciative soldiers. Jack Smolenske, HQ Company, 3rd Battalion of the 85th, found time to scribble notes in his diary during the hectic advance:

April 21. Thousands of vehicles, everywhere people clapping, throwing flowers. All had white flags from houses. One fellow was hysterical. He had stolen Kraut rifle so they killed his father. Beautiful country. Grape vines and green fields. Stop and go all day. Finally stopped, it was all very impressive.

April 22. Prisoners everywhere without guard. Freed cows from burning barn. Got 6 krauts and a German Jeep which we rode in. Everywhere people with wine & bread & sausage & onions. Girls throwing flowers & kissing & hugging us, wanting us to come live & sleep at their house with them. Women crying out "Bravo Liberator."

At the end of its first day, Task Force Duff had captured a second intact bridge, this one spanning the Panaro River at Bomporto, northeast of Modena. The Germans had placed dynamite charges under the bridge but had been in too much of a hurry to depart to detonate them. With General Hays personally taking a shift directing traffic, the rest of the division crossed the bridge that night and the next day, along with the 85th Division of II Corps. Hays swapped out the infantry battalions in Task Force Duff on a daily basis to be sure of having relatively fresh soldiers at the attack's cutting edge; on April 22, 2nd Battalion of the 85th took the lead. The next objective of Task Force Duff lay twenty-four miles to the north, San Benedetto di Po, a few miles east of Mantua on the southern banks of the Po River. Duff pushed the column along at top speed "like a worried sheep dog," according to one account.

Task Force Duff reached the river at dusk on April 22. But it did so without its leader. About an hour before the column came in sight of the Po, Duff, on foot at the front, was wounded when the lead tank detonated a mine. Brigadier General David Ruffner, whose time in the 10th went back to the early days at Camp Hale, and who commanded the division's artillery in Italy, temporarily replaced Duff as leader of the task force. The 10th had advanced fifty-five miles in two days to reach this objective.

The Po, whose headwaters are in the Alps, flows some four hundred miles eastward across northern Italy before emptying into the

Adriatic Sea near Venice. It is Italy's longest river and, in the stretch near San Benedetto di Po, roughly two hundred yards wide. Ordinarily in April the river was high and fast-flowing, and subject to flooding, but the mild winter and spring of 1945 left it shallower and slower than usual, a lucky break for the men who were about to attempt to cross it.

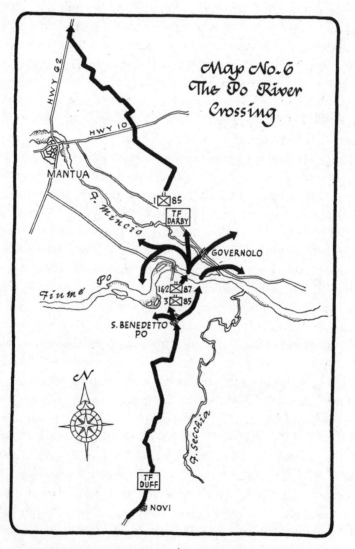

THE DENVER PUBLIC LIBRARY (ARMAND CASINI
PAPERS, TMD113)

This time the Germans did blow the bridge before the Americans arrived. The river would have to be crossed by boat. A shipment of assault boats was in fact en route at that very moment — except they were intended for the use of the 85th Infantry Division, which was then making its own way, more slowly than the 10th, toward the river. That was in accord with General Clark's plans for the 10th to play a secondary role in the race across the Po Valley to the Alps. But the 10th *banditti* struck again. Lieutenant Fritz Benedict and Warrant Officer Glenn Heller of the 126th Engineers, dispatched to the rear by General Hays to secure boats, came across the five-truck convoy carrying fifty canvas-sided boats for the 85th Division. Thinking fast, the two engineers deviously offered to guide the convoy to the Po — and took them to the 10th's assembly point at San Benedetto di Po, where at midnight the boats were unloaded. The truck drivers may have been persuaded that the 10th's 85th *Regiment* and the 85th *Division* were one and the same, or maybe they just didn't care and wanted to get back to their billets and go to sleep. In any case, the 10th now had the means to get across the Po.

Colonel David Fowler's 1st Battalion of the 87th leapfrogged to the front of the line. This battalion included some of the 10th's longest-serving officers and enlisted men, including its executive officer, John Woodward, who had helped train the very first ski troops in the winter of 1940–41 on Mount Rainier and in the Olympics. At noon on April 23, A and B Companies clambered into the assault boats — six infantrymen and four engineers to a boat, all of them paddling as hard as they could against the current to get across to the northern bank. Not knowing who or what awaited them on the far bank, the soldiers were ordered to fix bayonets. Since this was the 87th Regiment, many of the men were also veterans of the 10th's only previous amphibious landing, on Kiska in August 1943. That time they had been unopposed; this time they were being shelled by German 88s and flak guns. Amazingly, none of the boats was hit, although some troopers waiting on the southern bank of the river for their turn to cross were killed or wounded. Technical Sergeant George Hurt, whose service in the 10th stretched back to the days at Mount Rainier, where he had sung "Ninety Pounds of Rucksack" with the regimental glee club, was the first to step off the boat onto the north bank of the Po. Hurt was wounded by a sniper a few minutes later, but the landings met only light resistance; it was safer to stand on the Po's north bank that afternoon than on its south bank. After depositing their human cargo, the engineers from D Company of the 126th Engineers then brought the boats back to the south side for more men. Soon the entire 87th was across, followed by the 85th Regiment.

While this was going on, General Truscott arrived at the river in a Piper Cub airplane (piloted by daredevil Special Forces leader Colonel William Darby, whose Ranger unit had been cut to pieces during the Anzio campaign, and who was temporarily and unhappily without a combat command). "What are you doing, George?" Hays recalled General Truscott asking. "You know I don't have any troops to support you if you are attacked across the river." Hays pointed out that his men were advancing across the river in boats, dry, organized, and with their weapons ready. The Germans retreating across the river elsewhere were swimming. (German general Fridolin von Senger, commander of the XIV Panzer Corps, whose troops had encountered the 10th before on Riva Ridge and Mount Belvedere, found himself trapped on the south bank of the Po; he would later tell General Hays that he made it to safety on the north bank only because he chose to swim.) Hays asked rhetorically if he should bring his troops back across to safety on the south bank. Truscott told him no. He knew the 10th's qualities and wasn't going to call a halt when they had the enemy on the run.

By the next day, all three regiments were across the river, some of them ferried in newly arrived army DUKWs (amphibious vehicles, capable of traveling on land and water, called "ducks"), while engineers had constructed a cable ferry across the river. The engineers were also working on a nine-hundred-foot pontoon bridge. When completed on the afternoon of April 25, it allowed tanks and heavy artillery to cross to the northern beachhead, along with the motley collection of Volkswagens, Italian Fiats, and other captured vehicles. Farther east, the 88th and 85th Divisions made their own crossings of the Po. By April 24, the 5th Army controlled sixty miles of the southern bank of the river.

With the main drama being played out in Germany, the fighting in Italy was, as usual, given short shrift in American newspapers. Except for the 10th, who as always made good copy. The *New York Times* reporter who covered the crossing of the Po described it as "the Remagen of this campaign, even if no bridge was involved." And in an editorial comment, the *Times* noted: "Three days ago the Tenth American Mountain

Major General Willis D. Crittenberger and other officers watch the 5th Army,
1554th Engineering Heavy Pontoon Battalion, complete the first pontoon bridge
built across the Po River at San Benedetto di Po, Italy.
THE DENVER PUBLIC LIBRARY (TMD611)

Division, in the face of concentrated German fire, fought its way across the Po. That advance across 200 yards of water ended any hope the enemy may have had of holding a river line in Italy."

There was little time for the soldiers to write home in the midst of the 10th's hectic progress, but Sergeant Robert Ellis managed to dash off a V-mail letter to his mother from somewhere north of the Po: "This is the first chance I've had to write. You've probably read about our rapid advance and the 10th Mt. has really been going to town . . . It looks as tho we'll still have some stiff fighting tho if these Heinies hole up in the Alps."

Once the 10th was across the river, General Hays appointed the fortuitously arrived Colonel Darby, an old friend, as assistant division commander, leading what was now renamed Task Force Darby. As the armor crossed the river on April 25, advance elements of the 10th headed north again.

On that same day, the Italian resistance called for a general insurrection throughout northern Italy. Milan and Turin fell to the partisans on April 25, Genoa two days later. Farther north, the Red Army completed its encirclement of Berlin, cutting off escape for its defenders and inhabitants. Meanwhile, Soviet forces linked up with the US 1st Army on the Elbe River at Torgau, joining the eastern and western fronts for the first time in the war. On the other side of the world, the Battle of Okinawa was in its third week, with no end in sight. And in the United States, the newly elevated American president, Harry Truman, addressed the opening session of the United Nations conference in San Francisco.

The 1st Battalion of the 85th was ordered to capture the airport at Villafranca, forty miles to the north. They met only scattered resistance and captured their objective by late afternoon on April 25. The most notable event that day came at 10 p.m., when a German Focke-Wulf 190 fighter, out of gas, made an emergency landing on the airfield's runway. When the pilot, after initially heaving a sigh of relief, noticed that ownership of the runway had changed hands, he jumped out of the plane and escaped into neighboring woods.

Task Force Darby, which now included the 86th Regiment, sped off from the Po beachhead around 4:30 p.m. on April 25, fully motorized, with trucks to carry the troops, along with tanks, tank destroyers, and self-propelled howitzers. Again there was little resistance; the Italian civilians they encountered along the way told them, "*Tedeschi tutta via*" ("The Germans are all gone"). They rendezvoused with the troopers from the 85th at the Villafranca airfield around midnight, and then pressed on to take Verona ten miles to the north, another city already largely controlled by the partisans by that time.

For once the 10th wasn't at the tip of the Allied spearhead. The 85th Infantry Division had beaten it to Verona. And then the 88th showed up, and the men of the 10th, who had arranged comfortable billets in private homes, were told they had to vacate the city. They were trucked to a muddy field outside Verona, where they slept outdoors, in the rain, which did little to improve inter-divisional relations on the front.

General Crittenberger of IV Corps decided the mountain troopers could be put to better use than jostling alongside flatland divisions. He gave the 10th a new objective on April 26 that once again would see the division on its own and leading the way: Lake Garda, which lay to the west of Verona. Its capture would put the 10th in position to cut the last German escape route to the Brenner Pass in the Alps. And the division would be back in the mountains, on the terrain for which it was trained.

In the seven days of the 10th's Po Valley campaign, it lost ninety-one killed and 414 wounded.

Lake Garda is Italy's largest lake, carved out by glaciers, and some thirty-odd miles long. Its broad southern end opens to the Po Valley, while the narrower northern end is surrounded by snowcapped mountains. Its waters, when the sun shines, are a spectacular deep blue. Human habitation along its shores stretches back to early Etruscan settlements around 500 BC. The lake and its surroundings occupy a strategic passageway between northern and southern Europe; the Romans fought a battle against Germanic tribes on its shores in AD 268, and there were many more battles to come between then and 1945. With its natural beauty and mild climate, Lake Garda also attracted those interested in more peaceful pursuits. Saint Francis of Assisi founded a monastery on an island in the lake in the thirteenth century. It inspired poets and writers from the time of Catullus to that of Shelley and Goethe. In the nineteenth century, the American artist John Singer Sargent and the Austrian Gustav Klimt both came to paint the vistas along its shores.

The Fascists also liked Lake Garda. In 1943 the Nazis installed Benito Mussolini as the nominal leader of the puppet Repubblica Sociale Italiana in Salò on Lake Garda's western shore. Mussolini lived for the next year and a half in considerable splendor if declining health in a villa in nearby Gargnano, his mistress Claretta Petacci discreetly housed not far away in Il Vittoriale, with her own private SS guard. In April 1945, with partisan uprisings brewing and the Allied advance pushing the Nazis out of the North Apennines, Mussolini knew his time was running out. He traveled to Milan on April 18, hoping, irrationally, to work out a deal with the resistance. When that failed to happen, he made a break for the Swiss border on April 25. Traveling in a German military convoy, Mussolini was captured by partisans on April 27 and executed the following day along with the unfortunate Claretta. The partisans brought their corpses back to Milan on and contemptuously dumped them in a square near the city's train station, where anti-Fascist prisoners had been executed the year before. To provide a better view to a jeering crowd, the dictator and his mistress wound up being hung upside down from meat hooks on a girder in a half-built service station, along with other executed Fascists. There were some in the Allied camp who regretted the grisly execution of the first Axis leader to fall from power, but their number did not include the editors of the division newspaper, *The Blizzard.* The lead headline for the issue of April 30 read, "MUSSOLINI IS DEAD, EXECUTED BY ITALIAN PATRIOTS." Sergeant Ellis wrote home that same day, and mentioned in passing, "The Italian Partisans help a lot and according to the news last night caught Mussolini and hung him."

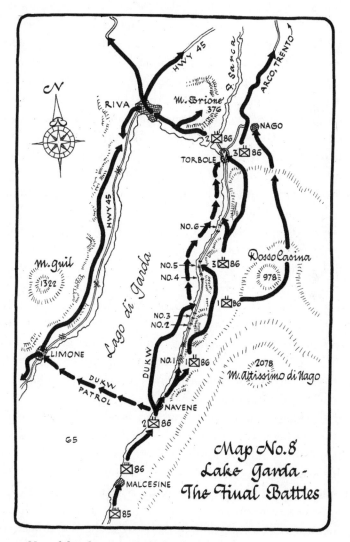

Map of the advance on Lake Garda. THE DENVER PUBLIC LIBRARY (ARMAND CASINI PAPERS, TMD113)

Hays intended to drive up the eastern shore of Lake Garda to the towns of Torbole and Riva at the northern tip of the lake, where he could cut the road that led to Trento, Bolzano, and the Brenner Pass. His plan was to systematically swap out the division spearhead every eight hours, regiment by regiment. While one regiment led, a second would be resting in the rear, and a third would be trucked forward to replace the attacking force at the front. In theory, at least, the fighting day would take the form of the workday: eight hours on, sixteen hours off. That way maximum pressure and momentum could be maintained for however many days it took to reach the final objective. But stiff German resistance, and physical obstacles, disrupted the schedule. Along Lake Garda, the 10th would be confronting one of the last German units in Italy maintaining cohesion and resolve, General von Senger's XIV Panzer Corps. (The regimental history of the 87th called them "'fighting' Germans of the quality encountered during the initial phase in the mountains.")

Task Force Duff, with the 3rd Battalion of the 87th Regiment initially in the lead, captured the town of Lazise, on the southeastern shore of Lake Garda, on the morning of April 27. There was no fighting, and as in the Po Valley, the residents turned out to greet the liberators with wine and flowers, while the church bells pealed. That proved the last such celebration in the Lake Garda campaign until the very end.

The heady days of racing through the Po Valley were over. It kept raining. Lake Garda's blue waters turned black and choppy, and the advance up its lakeshore proved a soggy one. Orders came down that all the remaining German and Italian trucks, cars, and motorcycles had to be turned over to the division ordnance officer, doubtless to the disappointment of their temporary owners.

The 87th fought a short, sharp battle to drive SS troops out of Garda, where the lake begins to narrow. In another firefight north of Garda, the mountain infantry and the accompanying tank destroyer unit got into a squabble over who should take the lead. Each wanted the other to have that honor. The regimental history of the 87th recorded that when the tank destroyers were ordered to advance, their commander refused to enter the next village unless the troopers went ahead and made sure it was safe to proceed. "After much bickering, name-calling, and threatening," the regimental historian reported, the tank destroyers finally "went

A group of soldiers from the 10th Mountain Division, 86th Infantry Regiment,
C Company walk in a loose formation along the banks of Lake Garda.
THE DENVER PUBLIC LIBRARY (TMD384)

forward and hit a German half-track, a 20-mm gun, an 88-gun, and set
fire to an ammunition dump."

The narrow road the task force followed now ran directly along the
lakeside, beneath the sheer cliffs of Mount Baldo above. Ahead lay six
tunnels between Navene and Torbole cutting through cliffs that came
directly down to the waterside. On the morning of April 28, with 2nd
Battalion of the 86th in the vanguard, the Germans blasted the first,
southernmost tunnel along the road to Torbole. There was no going
through the tunnel, or any way to advance by climbing above it. General Hays had anticipated this tactic and arranged for a convoy of
DUKWs to accompany the division's advance. Seven of the DUKWs
were launched on the lake and, despite harassing German artillery fire
from the opposite shore, shuttled the men from the 86th to the road beyond the demolished tunnel. All day, the 86th pushed forward in that
manner, and by night controlled four of the six tunnels and the roads

between. The tunnels were used to shelter the advanced units of the division at night.

Tunnel at north end of Lake Garda, April 1945.
THE DENVER PUBLIC LIBRARY (TMD295)

Meanwhile, a second prong of the 10th's attack moved forward in the hills above the eastern shore, toward the village of Nago, a mile northeast of Torbole, carried out by the 1st Battalion of the 86th. Before they could capture the village, they were bombed by a German plane; nine men from B Company were killed. PFC Harris Dusenbery's unit passed by the site of the bombing the next morning and saw that someone had filled "a gunny sack of arms and legs with the grisly ends sticking out." Dusenbery surmised that the unlucky men from B Company "had simply been blown to bits." They may have been the only casualties the 10th suffered from German aircraft while in Italy, although there had been friendly fire casualties on Belvedere and in the Po Valley from American planes bombing or strafing their own men.

On April 29, 3rd Battalion of the 86th seized the last two tunnels on the eastern shore, numbers five and six. They now had an open road to Torbole at the head of the lake. But before they got there, a lucky shot from a German gun in Riva penetrated the northern entrance of tunnel number five, which was filled with American soldiers. The blast, and rock and shell splinters in the confined space, cut a bloody swath through the men in the tunnel. Five soldiers from the 86th were killed outright, one of them Captain Lawrence Ely, H Company commander, and many others were badly wounded. The tunnel was already filled with the bodies of dead Germans, killed earlier when the demolition charges they were placing detonated prematurely. Captain Meinke, the battalion surgeon, had seen a lot of blood and gore by that point in the war, but when he reached the tunnel to care for the wounded, he decided that this was the worst he had ever encountered, a scene that "looked as if it should have been in a nightmare or a horror movie."

The Germans held on in Torbole, and soon the pretty resort town, which had survived a long war unscathed, took on the desolate, shattered look of so many other Italian communities to the south. But the end was clearly in sight. On the night of April 29, the Germans pulled out of the villages of Nago and Spiazzi. Torbole fell on the morning of April 30, followed later in the day by the capture of Riva del Garda. The Germans' door to the Brenner Pass swung shut.

Also on April 30, in the early morning hours, troopers from K Company of the 85th, accompanied by a heavy machine gun platoon from M Company, climbed into a fleet of DUKWs on the eastern shore and crossed the four-mile-wide lake to seize the town of Gargnano. They met no resistance and blocked the road up the western shore against any further German traffic. (A horse-drawn convoy the previous day along the western shore road had come under attack from American field artillery and P-47s.) The men of K and M Companies had landed what turned out to be a choice assignment. Tired, dirty, and wet mountain troopers made themselves at home in Mussolini's luxurious villa. Some took naps in the dictator's giant four-poster bed. Opportunities for souvenir hunting were not overlooked. First Lieutenant John A. Kaytis of K Company recalled that within a week the villa was stripped of "everything moveable and mailable." James Henry Francis, also of K Company, made off with several of Mussolini's black tasseled hats (one of which is on display in the West Point Military Academy museum). Another K Company trooper, Donald F. Todd, went joy-riding in Mussolini's personal convertible ("We must have been doing 90 easy," he bragged to his brother), but didn't manage to take it home with him.

On that last day of April, seventeen days since the men of the 10th had descended from Mount della Spe into the bloody Pra del Bianco valley, the scent of victory was in the air. The 10th was 115 miles north of its starting point, as measured in a straight line on the map — although they had traveled many more miles on the ground to reach Riva del Garda.

Rumors of a complete German surrender in Italy began to be heard, though no one knew whether to take them seriously. Some expected that the 10th would soon be given orders to capture the Brenner Pass. If so, the division would need to be reequipped with the warm clothing and mountain gear they left behind in the North Apennines, as well as mules, and Weasels. Another problem in moving on to the Alps was posed by the increasing proportion of men in the division who had joined as replacements (nearly half by the end) and had no mountain training at all.

On April 30 Marty Daneman found time to write his first letter home to Lois in nearly a month: "Rumors of peace have been flying around here thick & fast — we don't know what to believe any more. If only one thing seems sure, it's a matter of days, or perhaps only hours that this mess is over." Robert B. Ellis was enjoying a day off from fighting on April 30, billeted in a hotel in Malcesine, the most luxurious accommodations he had enjoyed since coming to Italy. But creature comforts did nothing to soften his gloomy view of his own prospects for surviving the war. "The news is sensationally good," he wrote his mother that day, "but men are still dying in this theatre and the load will be lifted from none of our soldiers until the last shot is fired. I keep thinking of the man in *All Quiet on the Western Front* who reached out of his trench on the day of the Armistice [November 11, 1918] to catch a butterfly and was shot by a sniper."

As Ellis's letter suggested, a heightened sense of fear for personal safety loomed large: any death in war is a loss, but a death on the last day of war somehow seems worse. And it was the 10th's fate to suffer several dozen such deaths on April 30. Late that afternoon, Colonel William Darby was conferring in Torbole with 86th Regimental staff and Brigadier General David Ruffner, head of division artillery, about a proposed advance the next day to Bolzano, en route to the Brenner Pass. Darby stepped outside at the end of the meeting, pausing for a moment before climbing into his jeep. Darby's aide, Second Lieutenant Kenneth Templeton, wondered whether it was a good idea to linger in the open in a town that was still being hit by the occasional German shell, but thought that a combat commander as experienced as Darby must know what he was doing. But an alert German artillery spotter took advantage of Darby's moment of carelessness. A salvo of 88s crashed into the waterfront, killing Colonel Darby and 86th Regiment Sergeant Major John Evans.

Another tragedy took place later that evening when a DUKW loaded with two 75 mm howitzers and men from the 605th Field Artillery Battalion headed for Riva del Garda across the lake. No one in charge of planning for the Italian campaign ever imagined that mountain troops would find themselves needing life preservers, so none were provided to the men in the overloaded DUKW. And when it overturned before reaching Riva, there would be only a single survivor, Corporal Thomas E. Hough. The twenty-five men who drowned in the choppy waters of Lake Garda on the night of April 30 were the last of the 333 casualties the 10th Mountain Division suffered in the four days of Lake Garda fighting, including sixty-three dead.

And as it turned out, they were the last men in the 10th to die in combat in Italy. Fighting subsided around Lake Garda on May 1. A few patrols went out, and some prisoners were taken, but there was little shooting, and no casualties. On the following day, May 2, at 6:30 p.m., a radio broadcast announced that the German armies in Italy had surrendered to the Allies, the clandestine Wolff-Dulles negotiations in Switzerland having finally paid off. Orders were given to all regiments to cease firing except in self-defense. Church bells rang, and local partisans fired their guns in the air to celebrate. Overall, though, the mood among the men of the 10th was subdued. Some wept. That night jeeps drove the roads around Lake Garda with their headlights on, the first time that had been permitted since the division reached the northern Apennines. Marty Daneman, whose letters home to Lois had taken on an uncharacteristically somber tone since Belvedere, reverted to his earlier, cheerful self when writing her on the evening of May 2: "The news reached us this afternoon — for us it's all over in Italy. The Kraut has thrown in the towel. You have no idea how it hit us — all the tension is gone. No more worries about not coming home. All there is now is waiting & waiting & waiting, but better than fighting . . . No more 88's, or 105's or 170's to land in our midst, no foxholes, blackouts — its over at long last darling . . . I'm very happy about the whole thing."

———

On the morning of May 3, General Hays, standing atop a DUKW, spoke to several hundred 10th Mountain soldiers in a public square in Torbole. "We have achieved final victory over all German armies in this theater and in southern Austria," the general announced. The nineteen days between April 14 and May 2, he told them, "will go down in history. I'm proud to be associated with this fine body of troops."

Standing in a piazza in Torbole, Italy, 10th Mountain Division troops learn of the final victory from General George P. Hays.
THE DENVER PUBLIC LIBRARY (TMD91)

Anthony Mascaro, C Company of the 86th, was one of those listening in the crowd. He wrote in his diary afterwards that C Company "marched to Torbole at 1100 to hear Gen. Hayes speak about the end of the war. He told us how good we were and how proud he was to have a Div. like the 10th. The men didn't do much celebrating, not near as much as they thought they would, but it was a great relief to have it over."

General Hays had a busy day on May 3. He met with most of the rest of the division that afternoon in Malcesine to congratulate them on their victory. That evening he accepted the surrender of General Fridolin von Senger, commander of the German IV Panzer Corps. General Senger had driven down to Lake Garda that day from his headquarters in Bolzano and was escorted to General Hays's headquarters farther down the lake. The two men drove to Verona and then flew to Florence for the formal surrender. Senger described his meeting with Hays in his postwar memoir: "About 9 p.m. we reached the battle H.Q. of the US 10 Alpine Division . . . The divisional commander, General Hays, escorted me in his large Packard, and we exchanged our impressions of past fighting, in which his division had been my most dangerous opponent. It was this division that had achieved the breakthrough that separated my corps from LI Corps."

———

Five days later the remainder of the German army surrendered, ending the war in Europe. The Italian campaign was the longest the US Army fought in World War II. From the landings at Salerno on September 9, 1943, to the German surrender on May 2, 1945, 602 days passed, twenty months of battle. The US Army counted 234,874 deaths in battle in all theaters in the Second World War; one in every ten, or 23,501, lost their lives in Italy. Total US casualties in Italy, including killed, wounded, captured, and missing, were 120,000. Total Allied casualties were 312,000.

Because the US Army couldn't figure out what to do with the strange new outfit that took shape on Mount Rainier and at Camp Hale between 1942 and 1944, with their skis and all those mules, the 10th Mountain Division arrived late to the war, the last to be sent to Italy. And it wasn't there long. Just four months and one week separated the arrival of the first regiment of the 10th in Naples on Christmas Eve from the moment when the Germans surrendered the day after May Day. "Our stint in combat was short," William Lowell Putnam would write, "though frighteningly severe." In terms of the percentage killed per day in combat, the 10th suffered the highest casualty rate of any US division in the

Italian campaign. A total of 20,635 men served in the 10th in Italy, including 6,415 combat replacements or temporarily attached individuals who joined between January and May. Total casualties for the division during that time were 983 killed, 3,900 wounded, and twenty taken as prisoners of war.

Now that they had time to take stock, those 983 missing comrades were much on the minds of the survivors. Wallace Arnheiter, A Company of the 85th Regiment, wrote home three days after the German surrender: "It's all over here. It has been over a few days and yet it is hard to believe it . . . We are all just coming out of the fog now — for the last month we've been all "sweating it out" — just praying it would end before the law of averages caught up with us. So many of my buddies died and so many more were hurt . . . You wonder why God let you walk thru all that hell, and come out unscratched, and took so many finer, better men."

———

In the spring of 1945, the bodies of the 10th Mountain soldiers killed in Italy were buried in a cemetery at Castelfiorentino, located some twenty-five miles southwest of Florence. After the war, American families who had lost soldiers abroad could have the bodies brought back to the United States for reburial, or could leave them in military cemeteries in the countries in which they died. In 1959 the Florence American Cemetery and Memorial was completed, just south of the city of Florence, near the village of Tavarnuzze. Its seventy acres are the final resting place for 4,402 US servicemen killed in the fighting in Italy. Of those, 326 died while serving in the 10th Mountain Division.

PFC John Parker Compton, G Company of the 86th Regiment, who died on March 3, 1945, in the assault on Iola, is one of the 326 mountain troopers buried in the Florence cemetery. About nine months before his death, in June 1944, as the 10th prepared to ship out from Camp Hale to Camp Swift, Compton wrote his parents expressing regrets at having to leave the Colorado Rockies behind: "I looked up at the mountains this afternoon as I was crossing Eagle River. The sun seemed to intensify the green of the firs and the aspen foliage . . . I'll always remember that panorama. I felt the vastness and majesty of the feeling one gets after traveling days and days on the ocean without sight of land."

What parents reading a letter like that from their twenty-one-year-old son wouldn't be touched? What a fine young man he's become, they might think, with justifiable pride. One can also imagine Compton's parents rereading the same letter a year later and wondering if their boy might have had a premonition that day at Camp Hale that he would not be returning to the Colorado mountains.

Among the 10th's souvenirs.
THE DENVER PUBLIC LIBRARY (TMD351-2017-1893)

Epilogue: "Among My Souvenirs"

There's nothing left for me — I'll never learn to ski,
I fell and broke my knee and tore off both my ears.
The thing I tried to do was follow after you —
The things that I've been through
Will leave me scarred for years.

> *— sung to the music of "Among My Souvenirs,"*
> *10th Mountain drinking song*

AMONG THE SOUVENIRS THEY BROUGHT BACK WERE ALPINI HATS, Nazi flags, and German Lugers, although, contrary to legend, the famous Luger was not the most sought-after souvenir weapon; the men who knew their pistols preferred the Walther P38. Radioman James H. Roberts, HQ Company, 1st Battalion of the 86th, acquired one of the latter on Riva Ridge on February 19, 1945, and described it fondly in a letter home a few days later as "a beautiful weapon rated as the best in its class. It is shaped similarly to the German luger but does not have the odd breech action."

They also brought back stories, a lot of which, not surprisingly for a group of young men at war, involved the consumption of alcohol — American beer and whiskey, Italian vino and grappa, and, in the end at Lake Garda and in the Alps, champagne confiscated from German military warehouses. The champagne was distributed free to the soldiers of the 10th; since American-imported beer still cost twenty cents a bottle, it was remarked that only the wealthy drank beer.

In a postwar memoir, General Mark Clark told a drinking story that involved the 10th, although in his story they weren't the ones getting drunk. Following the German surrender, Clark billeted a group of high-ranking Wehrmacht captives in a comfortable villa that, unknown to its new inhabitants, had been surreptitiously wired with listening devices. In the basement, a contingent of German-speaking intelligence officers and stenographers listened in to their guests' conversations among themselves. After several days, with nothing interesting recorded, Clark sent the German generals a couple of cases of whiskey with his compliments. Within hours, the stenographers were finding it hard to keep up with all the information being revealed, including, as Clark noted, the Germans' "amazement at the offensive power in the mountains" displayed by American divisions in the final months of the war, "particularly the 10th Mountain Division." *In vino veritas.*

Despite the relatively short time that the 10th had been in combat, 114 days all told, a surprising number of German generals, along with their soldiers, had direct experience of fighting against the division. In mid-May 1945, General George P. Hays, writing to the father of one of his junior officers, listed the German units his men had encountered since January. They included the 232nd Infantry Division, 114th Jaeger Division, 29th Panzer Grenadier Division, 334th Infantry Division, 90th Panzer Grenadier Division, 94th Infantry Division, 8th Mountain Division, 65th Infantry Division, and 305th Infantry Division, adding up at one time or another to 100,000 enemy troops.

As the number and variety of opponents the 10th met in battle suggests, the division's experience of combat differed from that of most of the American infantry who fought in Italy in 1943–44. The mountain infantry fought a war of movement, not of position or attrition. They never set out to take an objective only to fail and have to go back and try to take it again. Nor were they ever driven back from an objective they had captured. Although they paid heavily for the gains they made, the 10th's history in Italy was truly one of going Always Forward. The attempted crossing of the Rapido River in January 1944 by the US Army's 36th Infantry Division cost over two thousand casualties, decimating two regiments, with not so much as an inch of territory gained. There was nothing comparable in the 10th Mountain Division's experience. When they lost men, whether on Mount Belvedere, Mount della Spe, the breakthrough to the Po, or Lake Garda, they always had in their possession the objective they set out to capture to show for it afterwards.

Of course, the mountain troopers were lucky to be fighting an enemy that, although still dangerous, was running low on material resources and strategic options. And they knew it. "If you got to go to war," Lieutenant Colonel John H. Hay Jr., commander of 3rd Battalion of the 86th Regiment, would later say, "it's a good way to go. Get there last and get home first." On the one hand, had the 10th been sent to Italy in 1943 or early 1944, when they were certainly eager to go, their casualties, say at Monte Cassino, would have been much higher. On the other hand, it's possible that the deployment of mountain infantry could have dramatically shortened the campaign to capture Cassino. In the nature of counterfactuals, we will never know.

Back in 1940, when Minnie Dole and his friends first envisioned the creation of American ski troops, they looked to the Finns in their winter war against the Red Army as "a perfect example of men fighting in an environment with which they were entirely at home and for which they were trained." The 10th was trained to fight their own version of the winter war. Outside of a few patrols in January 1945, however, their training as skiers was of minimal importance to the victories in the North Apennines in the winter and spring of 1945. Rock climbing skills proved of greater utility — but only on a single occasion, the capture of Riva Ridge. And in the race across the Po Valley, and the capture of Lake Garda, the 10th fought on territory for which their specialized training on Mount Rainier and at Camp Hale was irrelevant.

And yet, all that ski training and those high-altitude maneuvers did bring the division to a finely honed combination of fitness, endurance, self-confidence, and unit cohesion. Minnie Dole proved to be right about the potential contribution of ski troops to the war effort — just not for the reasons he originally thought. The 10th's identity as ski troops, of being an elite unit like the airborne divisions, had everything to do with its success in battle. After Riva Ridge and Mount Belvedere, General Mark Clark sent a congratulatory message to the 10th, saying that it had "acquitted itself with the courage and daring of a veteran combat unit." The mountain infantry went into their first full-scale battle certainly aware that they were "green" and had much to learn, but came out of it a few days later as frontline soldiers, comparable in battle prowess to any other division in the theater. D-Series, the "MOUNTAIN" patch, even the exuberantly boyish drinking songs had something to do with that. "We are plenty hot!," twenty-one-year-old Corporal Arnold Holeywell had proclaimed in the *Camp Hale Ski-Zette* in the spring of 1944, and so it proved in the spring of 1945. Technician Fifth Grade Holeywell would return from Italy with a Bronze Star among his souvenirs, one of 4,647 issued to men of the 10th. Four hundred and forty-six mountain troopers would be awarded Silver Stars, four received the Distinguished Service Cross, and one the Medal of Honor.

Just when and under what circumstances they would return home from Italy was much on the minds of all American soldiers in the European theater in the spring and summer of 1945, and certainly those in the 10th. "You can only expect me home after the war is over both in Europe and Japan which is still quite aways off," Sergeant Hugh Evans wrote to his mother a day before the start of the April offensive. Maybe a year, he thought, or eighteen months. "At least mother," he joked, "I'll get a trip around the world." Mrs. Evans, one suspects, would not have found that particularly consoling.

With the end of the war in Europe, the War Department devised a "points system" to determine if and when soldiers could return to the United States for discharge. The magic number was eighty-five, with points assigned for months in service, additional points for months overseas, and for other factors, like number of dependent children, military awards, and so forth. Because they had been abroad so briefly, very few mountain infantry men qualified. And as Hugh Evans suspected, although it had yet to be officially announced, the entire division was slated for transfer to the Pacific theater to take part in the planned November invasion of Japan.

In the meantime, with the German surrender, the 10th was assigned to secure the border passes between Italy and Austria. Then, in late May, the division was sent to patrol Italy's northeastern border to forestall any attempt by the new communist rulers of Yugoslavia to annex the Italian city of Trieste. The mountain infantry and the communist partisans warily eyed each other for several weeks, although with no shots exchanged, an episode offering a preview of Cold War tensions to come. During the deployment, the 87th Regiment's command post was located at Caporetto, site of the famous Italian defeat by the Austrians in 1917.

———

The men of the 10th got used to being clean-shaven and wearing clean uniforms again, along with polishing their boots, saluting officers, and practicing close order drill. But there was an abundance of leisure time that spring and early summer of 1945, and easy access to Alpine slopes. "To the creaking and groaning of joints and muscles long unused to skiing," *The Blizzard* reported in early June, "F/Sgt. Walter Prager, HQ Co., 3rd Bn., 87th, led the field in the Mountaineers' first ski meet since May 1944," a slalom race on 8,027-foot Mount Mangart in the Julian Alps. "By the time they were halfway down the course almost all the skiers showed their lack of training by developing rubber legs." Some headed for the French Alps for climbing or skiing or both. First Lieutenant David Brower climbed the famous Charmoz-Grépon Traverse on the Mont Blanc massif, while First Lieutenant Donald Potter climbed to Mont Blanc's summit and then skied down. In a letter home, Potter described Chamonix, the resort town at the base of the mountain, as "a replica of a high class Lake Placid with three times the mountains and three times the prices."

And then, finally, orders arrived in mid-July for the 10th to make the return voyage to the United States. On arrival, they would have a month's furlough before returning to duty at Camp Carson, Colorado. There they would train for the invasion of Japan.

The 86th boarded the SS *Westbrook Victory* in Livorno on July 26 and arrived at Newport News, Virginia, on August 7. The 85th boarded the SS *Marine Fox* on July 31 in Naples, arriving at New York on August 11. The 87th boarded the SS *Mount Vernon* on August 2 in Naples, docking at Newport News on August 11. By the time they disembarked, the world, and their future prospects, had changed. Hiroshima was destroyed by an atomic bomb on August 6, followed by Nagasaki on August 9. On August 14, Japan surrendered, ending the Second World War. Three and a half months later, on November 30, 1945, the 10th Mountain Division was inactivated, and most of its members were discharged from military service shortly afterwards.

What next for the men of the 10th? The *Camp Hale Ski-Zette* tried its hand at forecasting the future in its second issue, in late April 1943, two years before the mountain troopers fought their final battle on Lake Garda: "Men, released from the army, will know much better how to take care of themselves in the mountains and on the ski slopes. Many of them will undoubtedly have been infected by the ski bug, which is a most virulent animal. They will pass on their knowledge to civilians, who have not had their training and will form a nucleus whose enthusiasm will convert many new recruits to the sport of skiing."

That proved an excellent prophecy. The 10th Mountain Division was the only unit in the history of the US military to use wartime skills to promote a civilian pastime. Another elite division, the 101st Airborne, made its last combat jump in Europe in September 1944. In civilian life, few airborne veterans ever jumped out of a plane again. But the men of the 10th, returning from the slopes of the Apennines and the Alps, turned to the slopes of the Rockies, the Cascades, the Sierras, the Adirondacks, and the White and Green Mountains. Over the next several decades, they played a leading role in the postwar expansion and transformation of the outdoor winter sports industry.

After 1945, a soaring civilian economy, increasing leisure time for middle-class households, the phenomenal growth in car ownership, and the creation of the interstate highway system brought Americans to the mountains in unprecedented numbers for both summer and winter recreation. That, plus the 100,000 pairs of skis declared army surplus and offered for sale to civilians at rock-bottom prices, jump-started the postwar ski industry. Tenth Mountain veterans played a central role in changing skiing from an elite pastime to a mass participation sport. "We were the original ski bums," Dick Wilson, M Company of the 85th Regiment, and among the first to be wounded in the assault on Mount Belvedere, told a reporter from the *New York Times* in 2006. Wilson became the editor of *National Skiing Magazine,* forerunner of *Skiing* magazine.

"We were entrepreneurial types, too, but mostly we couldn't get skiing out of our blood. We wanted to teach the country to ski. And we did." Literally thousands of 10th veterans were employed, one way or another, in the postwar ski industry, the majority as skiing instructors. And some did quite a bit more.

Friedl Pfeifer, A Company, 87th Regiment, who, on his first visit to Aspen, Colorado, in June 1943, felt "an overwhelming sense of my future before me," came pretty close to not having any future at all: wounded in the chest and lungs on the first day of the April offensive, he was expected to die by the doctors at the field hospital. Instead, he survived, moved to Aspen in the fall of 1945, and with other 10th veterans over the next several years helped transform the town from a failed mining camp to America's premier ski resort.

Pete Seibert, F Company, 86th Regiment, who had his right kneecap blown off in the fighting on March 3 and was told he would never walk again, also came to Aspen, resumed skiing, and in 1948 finished third in the giant slalom event at the US national ski competition. He taught at the Aspen Ski School, then managed the Loveland Ski Area, also in Colorado. In 1957 he climbed to the summit of a mountain in Vail, Colorado, only a few miles from the former site of Camp Hale, and had the vision to see the potential for a major ski resort. Working with other 10th veterans, he set out to make it happen. Vail opened in 1962. Its longest ski run is named "Riva Ridge"; another is "Minnie's Mile." In 2000, *Ski* magazine rated Seibert third in a list of the one hundred most influential skiers of all time.

Walter Prager, HQ Company, 3rd Battalion of the 87th Regiment, returned to Dartmouth to coach the ski team, and went on to coach the 1948 US Olympic ski team, which included three 10th veterans on its roster. He also directed the ski school at Squaw Valley, and later was a partner in ski shops in Vermont and upstate New York. The list of 10th veterans making their mark as coaches, instructors, ski resort operators, ski equipment developers and promoters, and others goes on and on.

The veterans made their mark in other outdoor-related fields as well. David Brower, S-2 (intelligence officer) for the 3rd Battalion of the 86th Regiment, became the first executive director of the Sierra Club and oversaw its transformation from a small, regional outdoors club to the nation's most influential environmental advocacy group. Gerry Cunningham, a medic with the 86th Infantry, founded a small mountaineering equipment business with packs of his own design in 1945, then moved the business to Colorado the following year, where Gerry Mountaineering grew into a retail giant. (Edmund Hillary and Tenzing Norgay slept in a two-man Gerry tent the night before they made the first ascent of Mount Everest.) Bill Bowerman, S-4 (logistics officer) for the 86th Regiment, coached the powerhouse University of Oregon track team for a quarter century, coached the 1972 US Olympic track team, co-founded the Nike athletic shoe and sports apparel manufacturing empire, invented the waffle-sole running shoe, and sparked the jogging craze in the 1970s.

And many excelled in indoor as well as outdoor pursuits. Charles Page Smith, commander of C Company of the 85th Regiment, whose legs were shattered by a German mine during the assault on Mount Gorgolesco, became an American historian, teaching at the University of Santa Cruz, winning the prestigious Bancroft Prize for his two-volume biography of John Adams in 1962 and writing a popular eight-volume "People's History" of the United States. Bob Dole, badly wounded on April 14, 1945, went on to be elected a US senator from Kansas and nominated as the Republican presidential candidate in 1996. Ed Fancher, S-2 for 1st Battalion of the 86th Regiment, was co-founder of the *Village Voice* in 1955. Noting that his co-publishers, Dan Wulf and Norman Mailer, were also World War II veterans, he told a reporter in 2017 that as veterans they shared "a feeling that there should be an open society, and that would require an open sort of newspaper, which *The Village Voice* was."

Some of the men highlighted in the preceding account went on to lead less famous but still noteworthy lives. Among them were Marty Daneman, who arrived in New York Harbor on August 11, 1945, and married his beloved Lois two weeks later in Chicago. They remained happily married for seventy years until Daneman's death in 2015, and had four sons. After graduating from DePaul University, and a career in sales and sales management, Daneman became active in Republican Party politics and was Texas state co-chair of Veterans for Dole in 1996.

Marty and Lois Daneman's wedding photo, 1945.
COURTESY OF THE DANEMAN FAMILY

Another such was Robert B. Ellis. Ellis turned down an appointment to attend the US Military Academy at West Point in the spring of 1945. As he explained in a letter to his mother, he had no taste "for a course of life I despise every part of, and living that monastic, pseudo-disciplinary hell for four long years. Having been thru numerous vicious battles I don't think I could do that." Instead he got a master's degree in international relations from the University of Chicago and began a twenty-year career with the Central Intelligence Agency. After retiring from the CIA, he became a wildlife photographer and environmental activist.

And, finally, there is the example of Harris Dusenbery, the classically minded Reed College graduate, who returned to his family in Portland, Oregon, after the war. He resumed his prewar job with the Social Security Administration, retiring in 1969. For the next four decades, he and his wife, Evelyn, traveled as often as they could, eventually visiting eighty-two countries (including six trips back to the northern Apennines). "Travel teaches tolerance and respect for other people, for their heritage, and their practices," Harris told his college alumni magazine shortly before his death in 2015 at age 101. "It made me realize that humanity is really one community on the surface of the earth, and it's a community of equals, at least in terms of who we are as human beings."

For the most part, the men of the 10th returned to lives of personal fulfillment and professional achievement in the years following the war. They kept up with one another through the National Association of the 10th Mountain Division, which held regular and well-attended reunions into the first decades of the twenty-first century, and through the pages of the association newsletter, *The Blizzard.* Beginning in the 1960s, many returned to Italy on tours sponsored every three years by the association, walking the battlefields of their youth. Many more visited the Tennessee Pass Memorial Monument in Colorado, erected in 1959, which lists the names of one thousand 10th Mountain men who were killed in action on Kiska and in Italy.

Of course, the men most active in the association, and most likely to show up for reunions and tours, tended to be those who made the best adjustment to postwar life. Inevitably, there were those who were "scarred for years" by their wartime experiences, and not in the lighthearted sense suggested by the old 10th drinking song. Some, undoubtedly, never found ways to restart their lives as civilians. Even among those who came home to successful careers and happy marriages, like Marty Daneman, there were burdens acquired in the first four months of 1945 never to be shed. "On sleepless nights," Daneman wrote in the concluding pages of his 2012 memoir, "my head still fills with the war." In particular, he remembered his friends from the 85th Regiment, Johnny Dolan and Edwin Nedoszytko, killed on the ridgeline between Gorgolesco and della Torraccia in February 1945. He remembered them alive and unharmed, in "immaculate khaki," not as the ghastly remains he came across on the ridgeline and carried, weeping, to the village of Ronchidoso. But in his dream, in a haunting detail, the three friends could never bring themselves to make eye contact: "We avoid each other's direct, accusative stares." Trauma, guilt, and regret were also among the souvenirs packed home by the veterans in 1945.

Along Riva Ridge, and the ridgeline connecting Belvedere, Gorgolesco, and della Torraccia today, there aren't many reminders that a great and terrible battle was fought there within living memory: a few memorials, a few markers, some shallow depressions in the earth that were once bunkers or foxholes. The barren mountainsides of 1945 are now heavily wooded. In the springtime, the hills are dark green, except where the canopy of leaves is embroidered by flowering chestnut trees. Visible on the lower hills, the little towns like Querciola and Vidiciatico are bigger now, and prosperous, the time of hunger, rubble, and violent death long gone if not forgotten. There is a "Piazza 10th Mountain Division" on a quiet side street in Querciola that invites appreciative reflection in the shadow of Belvedere. The views from Riva Ridge and Mount Belvedere today are of a beautiful and peaceable landscape in an imperfect but better world. The men of the 10th helped to make it so. *Sempre Avanti.*

Acknowledgments

I incurred many debts in research and writing, for which I can offer only the meager compensation of personal gratitude and public acknowledgment. First on the list is Keli Schmid, director of the 10th Mountain Division Resource Center of the Denver Public Library. During my three visits to the Center between 2016 and 2017, she patiently and skillfully aided my exploration of the vast archive she oversees. And for two summers in succession, she took me along to the annual picnic gathering of the 10th Mountain Division Descendants Rocky Mountain Chapter, where, on the second occasion, I had the pleasure of listening to Dick Over (110th Signal Company), Hugh Evans (C Company of the 85th Regiment), and Marlin Wineberg (D Company of the 85th Regiment) deliver a stirring rendition of the 10th Mountain's favorite drinking song, "Ninety Pounds of Rucksack."

Sandra Djikstra, my agent, Alexander Littlefield, my editor, and assistant editor Olivia Bartz were a joy to work with, professionally and personally.

Others deserving gratitude and acknowledgment, included in alphabetical order:

Antonia Ambrose, for Italian translation services.

Thomas Duhs, for sharing his deep knowledge of the 10th's history on a visit to the Camp Hale site.

McKay Jenkins, author of the excellent 2003 history *The Last Ridge: The Epic Story of America's First Mountain Soldiers and the Assault on Hitler's Europe,* for answering questions on the history of the 10th.

MacGregor Knox, Emeritus Professor, the London School of Economics and Political Science, for steering me to sources on Italian and German military history in the Second World War, and for helping me decipher some of the mysteries of military terminology.

Reid S. Larson, reference librarian at Hamilton College, for the invaluable services he has provided again and again in the course of my research on this book, and several others.

Jeff Leich, Executive Director, New England Ski Museum, for steering me to valuable sources on the history of American skiing, and for reading and correcting the first draft of my manuscript.

David Little, historian for Tenth Mountain Division Foundation, for answering *innumerable* questions on 10th Mountain history, and for reading and correcting the first draft of my manuscript.

Charles J. Sanders, author of the excellent 2005 history *The Boys of Winter: Life and Death in the U.S. Ski Troops During the Second World War,* for answering questions about the 10th.

Katie Sauter, Director of the American Alpine Club library in Golden, Colorado, for steering me to materials on the history of the 10th in the AAC archives.

Massimo Turchi, my knowledgeable and congenial guide to the battlefields in the North Apennines, who also corrected my many spelling errors in Italian.

And last, and most certainly not least, Flint Whitlock, co-author of the excellent 1992 history *Soldiers on Skis: A Pictorial Memoir of the 10th Mountain Division,* who took me on a tour of the Camp Hale site, who read and corrected errors in the first draft of my manuscript, and who throughout the writing of my book encouraged and inspired its creation.

To those I've forgotten to mention, my apologies. Any factual errors in the book are, as always, my fault alone.

Maurice Isserman
Keene, New York
November 2018

Notes

Introduction: "Always Forward"

page

xi   *"the finest troops"*: Quoted in John Imbrie and Hugh Evans, eds., *Good Times and Bad Times: A History of C Company, 85th Mountain Infantry Regiment, 10th Mountain Division, July 1943 to November 1945* (Quechee, VT: Vermont Heritage Press, 1995), p. 226.

xii *"You must continue to move forward"*: Quoted in Imbrie and Evans, *Good Times and Bad Times,* p. 226.

"The General would make": "The War Diary of Dan L. Kennerly, Company D, 85th Mountain Infantry Regiment, 10th Mountain Division," Dan L. Kennerly folder, box 1, TMD309, 10th Mountain Division Collection, Denver Public Library. Selections from Kennerly's diary, which he expanded after the war, are reprinted in Imbrie and Evans, *Good Times and Bad Times,* pp. 225–37, and in Dan L. Kennerly, "'You have come a great distance from Colorado to die': A 10th Mountain Division Diary of War in Italy," *Colorado Heritage* (Spring 2004): 2–25. Also see accounts of General Hays's speech in Peter Shelton, *Climb to Conquer: The Untold Story of World War II's Tenth Mountain Division Ski Troops* (New York: Scribner, 2003), p. 129; and McKay Jenkins, *The Last Ridge: The Epic Story of the US Army's 10th Mountain Division and the Assault on Hitler's Europe* (New York: Random House, 2003), pp. 164–66. Following the war, Kennerly became a science teacher and football coach at an Atlanta high school, retiring as director of athletics for the Atlanta school system in 1982. *Tenth Mountain Division* (Paducah, KY: Turner Publishing, 1998), p. 140.

"It looks bad": Diary, Jack R. Smolenske Papers, box 1, TMD70, 10th Mountain Division Collection, Denver Public Library.

xiii *"my most dangerous opponent":* General Frido von Senger und Etterlin, *Neither Fear Nor Hope* (New York: E. P. Dutton, 1964), p. 307.

xiv *unmatched level of detail:* Email to the author from Keli Schmid, director of the 10th Mountain Division Resource Center, Denver Public Library, August 30, 2018.

"end the goddam suspense": Martin Daneman to Lois Miller, March 9, 1945, Martin L. Daneman Papers, TMD25, 10th Mountain Division Collection, Denver Public Library.

1. Origins, 1940–41: "Soldiers Out of Skiers"

2 *National Ski Patrol System:* For the Orvis Inn, see Edwin L. Bigelow and Nancy Otis, *Manchester, Vermont: A Pleasant Land Among the Mountains, 1761–1961* (Manchester, VT: Northshire Bookstore, 2008), p. 289. The Orvis Inn still stands, forming part of the Equinox Golf Resort & Spa in Manchester. http://www.equinoxresort.com/history.

territorial concessions to the Soviet Union: For an overview of the Finnish-Soviet war, see Robert Edwards, *White Death: Russia's War on Finland, 1939–40* (London: Weidenfeld & Nicolson, 2006). Also see Stephen Bull, *World War II Winter and Mountain Warfare Tactics* (Oxford: Osprey, 2013), pp. 9–16; and Hal Burton, *The Ski Troops* (New York: Simon and Schuster, 1971), pp. 20–23.

"a perfect example": "Finns Beat Back a Quarter of Million Russians in Biggest Offensive of the War," *Burlington Free Press,* February 8, 1940; Minnie Dole, "Birth Pains of the 10th Mountain Division," in *Tenth Mountain Division* (Paducah, KY: Turner Publishing Co., 1998), p. 49. This was a speech that Dole wrote for the first national reunion of 10th Mountain veterans in 1946. Also see Charles Minot Dole, *Adventures in Skiing* (New York: Franklin Watts, 1965), pp. 90–91; and Thomas R. Brooks, "10th Mountain Division History," in *Tenth Mountain Division,* p. 15.

3 *Caporetto:* Gordon L. Rottman, *US 10th Mountain Division in World War II* (Oxford: Osprey, 2012), p. 3; Gordon Williamson, *German Mountain and Ski Troops, 1939–45* (London: Osprey, 1996), p. 3; MacGregor Knox, *Hitler's Italian Allies: Royal Armed Forces, Fascist Regime, and the War of 1940–43* (Cambridge: Cambridge University Press, 2000), pp. 18–19.

individual initiative in battle: Dole quoted in Flint Whitlock and Bob Bishop, *Soldiers on Skis: A Pictorial Memoir of the 10th Mountain Division* (Boulder: Paladin Press, 1992), p. 3. For a wartime assessment of the qualities of German mountain divisions, see "Some Notes on German Mountain Warfare," *Intelligence Bulletin,* March 1944, http://www.lonesentry.com/articles/gemtwarfare/. Also see Rottman, *US 10th Mountain Division in World War II,* p. 3; Williamson, *German Mountain and Ski Troops,* pp. 4, 51. For a debunking of the stereotype of German automaton soldiery, see MacGregor

Knox, "The 'Prussian Idea of Freedom' and the Career Open to Talent: Battlefield Initiative and Social Ascent from Prussian Reform to Nazi Revolution, 1807–1944," in *Common Destiny: Dictatorship, Foreign Policy, and War in Fascist Italy and Nazi Germany* (Cambridge: Cambridge University Press, 2000), pp. 186–226.

4   *"tropical army":* Dole, "Birth Pains," p. 49. On the outsized role that cavalry held in the esteem and outlook of high-ranking US Army officers up to 1940, see Russell F. Weigley, *Eisenhower's Lieutenants: The Campaign of France and Germany, 1944–1945* (Bloomington: Indiana University Press, 1981), p. 2.

North American soil: While Dole and his companions were most concerned with the possibility of a German invasion from Canada down the Champlain Valley, outdoorsmen in other parts of the country came up with similar apocalyptic scenarios for their own regions. See, for instance, the article by Richard Leonard, a prominent member of the Sierra Club and pioneering Yosemite climber, imagining an invasion of the High Sierras by unnamed foreign ski troops, which appeared in the monthly magazine of the California Chamber of Commerce a year before Pearl Harbor. Richard Leonard, "War in the Snow?," *California: Magazine of the Pacific* 30 (December 1940): 24, 40.

polite dismissal: Dole, *Adventures in Skiing*, p. 91; Dole, "Birth Pains," p. 49.

5   *their mastery of the sport:* John Jay, *Ski Down the Years* (New York: Universal Publishing, 1966), pp. 49–67.

6   *Thomas vigorously promoted skiing:* Allen Adler, *New England & Thereabouts — A Ski Tracing* (Barton, VT: Netco Press, 1985), p. 15. For Buchmayr's role at Peckett's, see Jeffrey R. Leich, "Winter Work: The CCC and New England Skiing," *Journal of the New England Ski Museum*, no. 61 (Autumn 2004): 5; Burton, *The Ski Troops*, pp. 30–31, 39–42. For Harriman's role in the development of Sun Valley, see Rudy Abramson, *The Life of W. Averell Harriman: 1891–1986* (New York: William Morrow, 1992), pp. 221–32. Lowell Thomas first encountered skiing in Italy in 1917, where as a war correspondent he covered the Alpini troops. Mitchell Stephens, *The Voice of America: Lowell Thomas and the Invention of 20th Century Journalism* (New York: St. Martin's Press, 2017), pp. 88–89.

"The balance and poise": Lincoln A. Werden, "12,000 Cheer Ski Jumpers at Garden Exhibition: Leaps into Space Thrill Big Crowd," *New York Times,* December 11, 1936; Friedl Pfeifer, *Nice Goin': My Life on Skis* (Missoula, MT: Pictorial Histories Publishing, 1993), pp. 51–52. For an overview of Schneider's life and influence, see Gerard Fairlie, *Flight Without Wings: The Biography of Hannes Schneider* (New York: A. S. Barnes, 1957). Also see Jay, *Ski Down the Years,* pp. 84–86, 245.

7   *multiple novices:* For contemporary works describing the Arlberg technique,

see Frank Harper, *Military Ski Manual: A Handbook for Ski and Mountain Troops* (Harrisburg, PA: Military Service Publishing Co., 1943), pp. 388–92; and two works by Schneider associations: the 1930s-era manual by émigré Czech Benno Rybizka, *The Hannes Schneider Ski Technique* (New York: Harcourt, Brace, 1938); and, by Austrian émigré Otto Lang, *Downhill Skiing* (New York: Henry Holt, 1936). Also see "The Man Who Started It All: Otto Schneibs," *Skiing Heritage* 8 (Fall 1996): 10–11.

"The day that I performed": Dole, *Adventures in Skiing*, p. 41.

8   *Edson died shortly after:* Dole, *Adventures in Skiing*, pp. 50–53; McKay Jenkins, *The Last Ridge: The Epic Story of the US Army's 10th Mountain Division and the Assault on Hitler's Europe* (New York: Random House, 2003), pp. 19–20; Burton, *The Ski Troops*, pp. 53–56.

wounded soldiers: For example, see the illustrated instructions for improvising traction splints for shattered arms and legs in Charles Minot Dole et al., *The National Ski Patrol System Manual* (New York: National Ski Patrol System, 1941), pp. 64–66; Gretchen R. Besser, *The National Ski Patrol: Samaritans of the Snow* (Woodstock, VT: Countryman Press, 1983), pp. 27–31; Janet Nelson, "National Ski Patrol Celebrates 50 Years," *New York Times*, March 3, 1988; Jenkins, *The Last Ridge*, pp. 19–21.

9   *"It was Minnie's persuasiveness":* Quoted in Besser, *The National Ski Patrol*, p. 30. Also see Burton, *The Ski Troops*, p. 57. For a brief biography of Livermore, see *Harvard Class of 1932: Twenty-fifth Anniversary Report* (Cambridge: Harvard University Printing Office, 1957), pp. 724–25. For Livermore's feats on Mount Washington, see Jeffrey R. Leich, *Over the Headwall: Nine Decades of Skiing in Tuckerman Ravine* (Franconia, NH: New England Ski Museum, 2011), pp. 38–46. For his experiences at the 1936 Olympics, see Guy Walters, *Berlin Games: How the Nazis Stole the Olympic Dream* (New York: William Morrow, 2006), pp. 65–75.

Likewise, Hal Burton: Burton, *The Ski Troops*, 65. For Burton's role in the development of Whiteface Mountain as a ski resort, see Pete Nelson, "Hal Burton's Peak," http://www.adirondackalmanack.com/2012/09/lost-brook-dispatches-hal-burtons-peak.html.

"the American Army will probably be": Captain Christian Clarke's discouraging letter of July 2, 1940, is reprinted in Dole's *Adventures in Skiing*, p. 92.

"a hundred guys a day": Colonel Curt R. Simonson, "Creating the 10th Mountain Division: The National Ski Patrol's Role" (United States Army War College, 2015), pp. 2–7; Dole, "Birth Pains," p. 49; Burton, *The Ski Troops*, pp. 69–70. Also see Historical Section, Army Ground Forces, *History of the Mountain Training Center*, study no. 24 (1948), p. 1, although the chronology of Governors Island meetings given in that account is inaccurate. The quotation regarding guns that can shoot around corners can be found in Dole, *Adventures in Skiing*, p. 96.

10 *"unusual and untried ideas":* Charles M. Dole to President Franklin D. Roosevelt, July 18, 1940, Charles Minot Dole Papers, box 9, WH1001, Western History Collection, Denver Public Library. As a good salesman, Dole neglected to point out that of the "2,000,000 skiers" in the United States, many were women and children, more were over military age, and very few were truly expert skiers.

"new opportunities for play": Roosevelt quoted in Douglas Brinkley, *Rightful Heritage: Franklin D. Roosevelt and the Land of America* (New York: Harper, 2016), p. 403. Also see Sarah Baker, *Timberline Lodge: The History, Art, and Craft of an American Icon* (Portland, OR: Timber Press, 2009); Burton, *The Ski Troops*, p. 46. In New England, the New Deal's Civilian Conservation Corps (CCC) cut trails in Vermont, New Hampshire, and Massachusetts, including a ski run on the side of the Berkshires' Mount Greylock in 1934, which became known as the Thunderbolt Trail and was soon a favorite of the region's elite skiers. Jonathan Mingle, "Skiing Old Trails of the New Deal," *New York Times*, February 15, 2013; Leich, "Winter Work," pp. 1, 4–20; Charles J. Sanders, *The Boys of Winter: Life and Death in the U.S. Ski Troops During the Second World War* (Boulder: University Press of Colorado, 2005), pp. 3–4.

11 *White House aide informed:* James Rowe Jr., Administrative Assistant to the President, to Charles M. Dole, July 24, 1940, Charles Minot Dole Papers, box 9, WH1001, Western History Collection, Denver Public Library.

secure a meeting for Dole: For the meeting with Stimson's aides, see Dole, *Adventures in Skiing*, pp. 97–98. For the contribution of American Alpine Club members to the creation of the 10th Mountain Division, see Maurice Isserman, *Continental Divide: A History of American Mountaineering* (New York: Norton, 2016), p. 262; Robert Bates, *The Love of Mountains Is Best: Climbs and Travels from K2 to Kathmandu* (Portsmouth, NH: Peter E. Randall, 1994), p. 165; and Jenkins, *The Last Ridge*, pp. 27–28.

ushered into Marshall's office: Dole, *Adventures in Skiing*, pp. 98–99.

12 *fifteen minutes of his crowded day:* Dole, *Adventures in Skiing*, p. 99. On George C. Marshall's qualifications as a leader, see Richard Overy, *Why the Allies Won* (New York: Norton, 1995), pp. 272–74. On Marshall's confrontation with President Roosevelt, see Ed Cray, *General of the Army: George C. Marshall, Soldier and Statesman* (New York: Norton, 1990), pp. 154–155. Also see Andrew Roberts, *Masters and Commanders: How Four Titans Won the War in the West, 1941–1945* (New York: Harper, 2009), p. 29.

Much hinged: Kent Roberts Greenfield, Robert R. Palmer, and Bell I. Wiley, *The Organization of Ground Combat Troops* (Washington, DC: Department of the Army, 1947), p. 245; George F. Howe, *The Battle History of the First Armored Division* (Washington, DC: Combat Forces Press, 1954), pp. 3–11; Weigley, *Eisenhower's Lieutenants*, pp. 12–13.

"an interesting question": Dole, *Adventures in Skiing*, p. 100.

13 *Graybar Building:* Dole, *Adventures in Skiing,* pp. 100–101; Simonson, "Creating the 10th Mountain Division," pp. 9–10.
"an army on skis": "Army's New Ski Patrol Practices on the Snowy Slopes of Mount Rainier," *Life,* January 20, 1941, p. 8; Simonson, "Creating the 10th Mountain Division," p. 11.
14 *crossing many of its glaciers: History of the Mountain Training Center,* pp. 4–5.
"I believe that ski training": Quoted in *History of the Mountain Training Center,* p. 3. Also see Burton, *The Ski Troops,* pp. 84–85.
Europe and the Pacific: Dole, "Birth Pains," p. 51; Simonson, "Creating the 10th Mountain Division," pp. 11–12; Albert H. Jackman, "The Tenth Mountain Division: A Successful Experiment," *American Alpine Journal* (1946); Peter Shelton, *Climb to Conquer: The Untold Story of World War II's Tenth Mountain Division Ski Troops* (New York: Scribner, 2003), pp. 20–22.
15 *"thousands of experienced skiers":* David Bradley to Charles Minot Dole, February 18, 1941, Charles Minot Dole Papers, box 9, WH1001, Western History Collection, Denver Public Library. The first writer to highlight Bradley's importance in the background to the creation of the 10th Mountain Division was a veteran of the division, Hal Burton, in *The Ski Troops,* p. 22. Bradley had an interesting and varied career thereafter. As a US Army medical officer, he was assigned to monitor radiation levels during postwar atomic tests on Bikini Atoll in the South Pacific. His sober account of what he witnessed, *No Place to Hide,* published in 1948, proved a pioneering and best-selling anti-nuclear jeremiad. While pursuing both a medical and a political career, he also designed several score ski-jumping hills in the Northeast, and managed the US Nordic ski team at the Olympic Games in Squaw Valley, California, in 1960. Margalit Fox, "David Bradley, 92, Author, Antinuclear Advocate, Champion Skier and State Legislator, Is Dead," *New York Times,* January 30, 2008.
"initiative and self-reliance": Besser, *The National Ski Patrol,* p. 38.
"So many of the conclusions": Charles Minot Dole to David Bradley, February 24, 1941, Charles Minot Dole Papers, box 9, WH1001, Western History Collection, Denver Public Library.
16 *some quarters of the military establishment:* Charles J. Sanders, "Dartmouth and the 10th Mountain Division," in *Passion for Skiing,* ed. Stephen L. Waterhouse (Lebanon, NH: Whitman Communications, 2010), pp. 128–29.
17 *"This is a distinct type":* Quoted in *History of the Mountain Training Center,* p. 10.
But McNair disagreed: Quoted in *History of the Mountain Training Center,* p. 11. Also see Jenkins, *The Last Ridge,* p. 31; Burton, *The Ski Troops,* p. 91.
Greek defeat: Mario Cervi, *The Hollow Legions: Mussolini's Blunder in Greece, 1940–1941* (Garden City, NY: Doubleday, 1965).
Gerow concluded: Quoted in *History of the Mountain Training Center,* p. 11. Also see Shelton, *Climb to Conquer,* pp. 24–25.

18 *87th Mountain Infantry Regiment: History of the Mountain Training Center*, p. 12; Rottman, *US 10th Mountain Division in World War II*, p. 6.
Secretary of War Henry Stimson: Secretary of War Henry L. Stimson to Charles M. Dole, October 24, 1941, Charles Minot Dole Papers, WH1001, Western History Collection, Denver Public Library.
"qualified people": Frank Elkins, "Ski Slopes and Trails," *New York Times,* December 29, 1941.

19 *"Lad," the major is said:* The exact wording of the punch line in this origins story varies from one published account to another; in some versions it's a sergeant rather than a major delivering the line. The version offered here seems the most reliable, since it is based on McLane's own account, written not long after the event. See Charles B. McLane, "Of Mules and Skis," *American Ski Annual* (1943): 22. Also see Burton, *The Ski Troops,* p. 94; Brooks, "10th Mountain Division History," p. 16; Shelton, *Climb to Conquer,* p. 25; and Sanders, *The Boys of Winter,* p. 54. Most accounts put the date of McLane's arrival at Fort Lewis on December 7, 1941. But in interviews with Charles Sanders, and in a Dartmouth alumni newsletter, McLane makes it clear that he arrived sometime before Pearl Harbor. John Henry Auran, "The First of the 10th," *'41 Newsletter,* Dartmouth College, February 1992. On the McLane clan's prominent role in Dartmouth history, including its skiing history, see Waterhouse, *Passion for Skiing,* p. 125.
118 former Dartmouth students: Sanders, "Dartmouth and the 10th Mountain Division," pp. 127, 131; Whitlock and Bishop, *Soldiers on Skis,* p. 6; Edward A. Nickerson, "Mountain Men," *Dartmouth Alumni Magazine,* January–February 1941, pp. 50–55; "Tenth Mountain Division," *Dartmouth Alumni Magazine,* April 1994, p. 46. Six of the Dartmouth alumni who served in the 10th during the war were killed in action.
"we guessed at the odds": McLane, "Of Mules and Skis," p. 22. Also see George F. Earle, "History of the 87th Mountain Infantry in Italy" (1945), p. 1, https://www.scribd.com/document/94745160/WWII-87th-Infantry-Division. McLane and Earle differ on the number of troops gathered at Fort Lewis in the second week of December, this account following McLane's estimate.

20 *hundreds of applications:* Dole, "Birth Pains," p. 53.
Not surprisingly: Larry Jump's NSPS questionnaire is reprinted in Jeffrey R. Leich, *Tales of the 10th: The Mountain Troops and American Skiing* (Franconia, NH: New England Ski Museum, 2003), pp. 38–40. After the war, Jump helped create the Arapahoe Basin ski area in Colorado.
status as volunteers: History of the Mountain Training Center, p. 12; Simonson, "Creating the 10th Mountain Division," p. 17; Shelton, *Climb to Conquer,* p. 54.
Dole professed distaste: "Minnie's Ski Troops," *The New Yorker,* February 21, 1942, p. 10.

21 *"Through these portals"*: McLane, "Of Mules and Skis," p. 32; Jenkins, *The Last Ridge*, pp. 37–38. For Rolfe's Hawaii service, see "Norse Speaking Soldiers Train at Pando Camp," *Denver Post*, December 20, 1942. The "beautiful girls" sign adorned the Earl Carroll Theater at 753 Seventh Avenue in Manhattan's theater district and another theater that opened in the late 1930s on Sunset Boulevard in Hollywood. Nicholas von Hoogstraten, *Lost Broadway Theatres* (New York: Princeton Architectural Press, 1997), p. 214. *Paradise and Tatoosh Lodges*: Shelton, *Climb to Conquer*, p. 30.

22 *"I don't think Pinkie"*: Dole, *Adventures in Skiing*, p. 113.

"a little bell mare": Dole, *Adventures in Skiing*, p. 113; McLane, "Of Mules and Skis," pp. 32–33.

2. Training, 1942: "Ninety Pounds of Rucksack"

26 *The outcome of the war:* According to an official account written just after the war, American military planners in 1941 came to fear a joint German-Japanese attack on Alaska. A month after the start of the Nazi invasion of the Soviet Union, a "German citizen" informed the American ambassador to Switzerland that "one of the principal objectives of the German campaign . . . was the establishment of a bridge to Japan and the Vladivostok–eastern Siberian region from which war could be carried to the United States." This fear, naturally, further contributed to the army's growing interest in mountain and cold weather warfare. Captain Thomas P. Gowan, *The Army Ground Forces Training for Mountain and Winter Warfare*, study no. 23 (Washington, DC: Historical Section, Army Ground Forces, 1946), p. 6. Also see McKay Jenkins, *The Last Ridge: The Epic Story of the US Army's 10th Mountain Division and the Assault on Hitler's Europe* (New York: Random House, 2003), pp. 34–35.

"more like a college reunion": Hal Burton, *The Ski Troops* (New York: Simon and Schuster, 1971), p. 100.

27 *Dartmouth skier:* As the official history of the mountain troops noted of the recruits, "They liked their fellow-soldiers, many of whom they had known in pre-war days, and an unusual comradery grew up among the volunteers." Historical Section, Army Ground Forces, *History of the Mountain Training Center*, study no. 24 (1948), p. 62. Also see Burton, *The Ski Troops*, p. 137; John Jay, *Skiing the Americas* (New York: Macmillan, 1947), pp. 223–24.

Three such regiments: Gordon L. Rottman, *US 10th Mountain Division in World War II* (Oxford: Osprey, 2012), p. 22; William Lowell Putnam, *Green Cognac: The Education of a Mountain Fighter* (New York: AAC Press, 1991), pp. 28–29.

28 *"we are mountain troops"*: Quoted in *History of the Mountain Training Center*, p. 16.

"It will interest you to know": Minnie Dole to Private Robert Livermore, September 11, 1942, Charles Minot Dole Papers, WH1001, Western History

Collection, Denver Public Library. For Livermore's military record, see *Harvard College Class of 1932, Quindecennial Report* (August 1947), p. 235; and Robert Livermore Personal Report, *Records of the Harvard University War Records Office,* UAV 874.1269, box 157, Harvard University Archives.

29 *As Dole saw it:* Charles McLane, "Of Mules and Skis," *American Ski Annual* (1943): 24; Peter Shelton, *Climb to Conquer: The Untold Story of World War II's Tenth Mountain Division Ski Troops* (New York: Scribner, 2003), pp. 21, 23.

   Soldiers on skis: Charles C. Roberts Jr. and Seth Masia, "The 10th Mountain Division Ski Technique of World War II," *Skiing History* (November–December 2017): 13.

30 *whacked in the head:* Charles C. Bradley, *Aleutian Echoes* (Fairbanks: University of Alaska Press, 1994), p. 10; Charles J. Sanders, *The Boys of Winter: Life and Death in the U.S. Ski Troops During the Second World War* (Boulder: University Press of Colorado, 2005), p. 65; *History of the Mountain Training Center,* p. 16.

   thick woolen socks: Georgiana Contiguglia, "Searching for the Perfect Ski Gear: Equipment Development for the Tenth Mountain Division," *Colorado Heritage* (October 1992): 7–12; Burton, *The Ski Troops,* p. 105.

31 *ear flaps:* Contiguglia, "Searching for the Perfect Ski Gear," pp. 6–8; *History of the Mountain Training Center,* p. 99. On the paratroopers' problems skiing with standard army overcoats, see Dick Nebeker, "My Experiences in the Ski Troops," typescript, p. 1, in author's possession.

   Army Quartermaster Corps: History of the Mountain Training Center, pp. 6–8; Bradley, *Aleutian Echoes,* pp. 14–15. For Bestor Robinson's climbing achievements, see Maurice Isserman, *Continental Divide: A History of American Mountaineering* (New York: Norton, 2016), pp. 207–8, 213–15.

32 *"waffle-stompers":* Carter, fluent in German and other languages, also translated scores of prewar foreign mountain warfare manuals and articles, which he passed along to the Equipment Committee and US Army G-2. Some of Carter's translations are preserved in the H. Adams Carter Papers, TMD3, 10th Mountain Division Collection, Denver Public Library. Also see Putnam, *Green Cognac,* pp. 20–21; Burton, *The Ski Troops,* p. 106; Maurice Isserman and Stewart Weaver, *Fallen Giants: A History of Himalayan Mountaineering from the Age of Empire to the Age of Extremes* (New Haven, CT: Yale University Press, 2008), p. 228. Along with other leading lights of the Harvard Mountaineering Club in the 1930s, Adams was profiled in David Roberts, "Five Who Made It to the Top," *Harvard Magazine,* January–February 1981, pp. 31–40.

33 *cold weather survival:* Robert Bates, *The Love of Mountains Is Best: Climbs and Travels from K2 to Kathmandu* (Portsmouth, NH: Peter E. Randall, 1994), pp. 183–215; Burton, *The Ski Troops,* p. 106; *History of the Mountain Training Center,* pp. 76–78; Isserman, *Continental Divide,* pp. 231–35, 245–51, 262–65.

34 *They were the precursors:* Charles Minot Dole, *Adventures in Skiing* (New York: Franklin Watts, 1965), pp. 114–15; Minnie Dole, "Birth Pains of the 10th Mountain Division," in *Tenth Mountain Division* (Paducah, KY: Turner Publishing Co., 1998), p. 51; Rottman, *US 10th Mountain Division in World War II*, p. 20; *History of the Mountain Training Center*, pp. 78–79; Jay, *Skiing the Americas*, pp. 228–42. The Weasel was developed under top secret conditions in 1942 as part of a somewhat far-fetched scheme favored by British prime minister Winston Churchill to drop the vehicles from the air in support of a raid by Norwegian paratroopers on German "heavy water" plants in the interior of Norway. Royal Air Force leaders thought the plan was insane, and it was scrapped for a more conventional (and successful) commando raid, accomplished on foot. But the Weasels proved valuable in the mountain fighting to come in Italy. Burton, *The Ski Troops*, pp. 101–2; Shelton, *Climb to Conquer*, p. 95.

35 *frozen footwear:* Putnam, *Green Cognac*, p. 24; Contiguglia, "Searching for the Perfect Ski Gear," p. 13; *History of the Mountain Training Center*, pp. 98–99. Bad ideas, like pemmican, never seemed to stay discredited; at Camp Hale in January 1943, soldiers were again sent out on maneuvers with nothing to eat but pemmican in their rucksacks. Jenkins, *The Last Ridge*, pp. 59–60.

The most dramatic: "Biographical Information: Albert H. Jackman," Nicholas B. Clinch Collection, American Alpine Club Papers, box 7, American Alpine Club Library, Golden, CO.

They took twelve days: Shelton, *Climb to Conquer*, p. 51.

"a great ski run": Bradley, *Aleutian Echoes*, p. 30; Shelton, *Climb to Conquer*, pp. 39–42; *History of the Mountain Training Center*, pp. 75, 98–99.

36 *"Our faces grew dark":* McLane, "Of Mules and Skis," p. 27.

"I do not believe": Quoted in *History of the Mountain Training Center*, p. 21. Also see Shelton, *Climb to Conquer*, p. 34.

traditional military expectations: Shelton, *Climb to Conquer*, p. 38; Jenkins, *The Last Ridge*, p. 41; *History of the Mountain Training Center*, pp. 16, 22.

37 *"snow up to my head":* Quoted in Sanders, *The Boys of Winter*, p. 59. Konieczny is one of three 10th Mountain veterans profiled in Sanders's history of the division. Also see Burton, *The Ski Troops*, p. 100.

"very little that is natural": Charles B. McLane, "Address to the College," *The Dartmouth*, June 14, 1941, p. 7.

"Success in combat demands": *Basic Field Manual, Military Training*, FM 21-5 (Washington, DC: United States Government Printing Office, 1941), p. 19.

"The purposes of drill": *Basic Field Manual, Infantry Drill Regulations*, FM 22-5 (Washington, DC: United States Government Printing Office, 1939), p. 2. Also see Robert Palmer, Bell I. Wiley, and William R. Keast, *United States Army in World War II: The Procurement and Training of Ground Com-*

bat Troops (Washington, DC: Center of Military History, United States Army, 1941), p. 445.

38 *Synchronized skiing:* Synchronized skiing was a feature of the 1941 army instructional film *The Basic Principles of Skiing,* produced by Darryl F. Zanuck and directed by Hannes Schneider protégé Otto Lang. The ten skiers featured in the film, skiing in white camouflage, performed beautiful synchronized maneuvers on the slopes of Galena Pass, near Sun Valley. Their number included some of the top ski instructors in the United States, including Walter Prager. Williams College ski team captain John Jay, then a private in the Army Signal Corps, was another of the skiers. But ordinary ski troopers could never have pulled off a similar display. The film was probably more useful for recruiting than it was for instruction. John Jay, *Skiing the Americas* (New York: Macmillan, 1947), pp. 208–17; Shelton, *Climb to Conquer,* pp. 49–50; Sanders, *The Boys of Winter,* pp. 53–54.

"The better a person skis": Benno Rybizka, *The Hannes Schneider Ski Technique,* 2nd ed. (New York: Harcourt, Brace, 1946), pp. 41–42. On Rybizka's role in popularizing the Arlberg technique in the 1930s, see Jeffrey R. Leich, *Over the Headwall: Nine Decades of Skiing in Tuckerman Ravine* (Franconia, NH: New England Ski Museum, 2011), p. 59.

"A good squad": McLane, "Of Mules and Skis," p. 32.

39 *"But where are the mountains":* Quoted in Burton, *The Ski Troops,* p. 35. Following his arrest, Schneider was accused in the Nazi press of being a Jew himself, which he was not. Gerard Fairlie, *Flight Without Wings: The Biography of Hannes Schneider* (New York: A. S. Barnes, 1957), p. 207. In any case, his opposition to anti-Semitism was unusual, and not just in Austria. As Hal Burton notes, a casual anti-Semitism, which included barring Jewish patrons from many guest lodgings, pervaded the prewar skiing world, at least in the northeastern United States. Burton, *The Ski Troops,* pp. 49–50.

"I had a very interesting talk": Adams Carter to Joel Fisher, February 1, 1942, H. Adams Carter Papers, TMD3, 10th Mountain Division Collection, Denver Public Library. Joel Fisher was treasurer of the American Alpine Club in 1942.

40 *"one of the singingest outfits":* Charles C. Bradley, "A Mountain Soldier Sings," *American Ski Annual* (1945): 38. The McLane-Bromaghin songwriting team had already come into existence at Fort Lewis in the weeks before Pearl Harbor, when, with a couple of other Dartmouth alumni, they formed the Latrine Quartet. Charles J. Sanders, "Dartmouth and the 10th Mountain Division," in *Passion for Skiing,* ed. Stephen L. Waterhouse (Lebanon, NH: Whitman Communications, 2010), p. 131.

"bastard in the Mountain Infantry": Songs of the 10th Mountain Division (10th Mountain Division Association, n.d., souvenir ephemera), 5. Also see Shelton, *Climb to Conquer,* pp. 36–37; Jenkins, *The Last Ridge,* p. 41; Sanders, *The Boys of Winter,* pp. 44–45, 62–63. Interestingly, when Lieutenant Charles

Bradley contributed an article, "A Mountain Soldier Sings," to the 1945 *American Ski Annual* on the songs of the 10th Mountain Division, he neglected to mention or include the lyrics of "Ninety Pounds of Rucksack," perhaps feeling it a little too risqué for civilian skiers.

A schussing bastard: For the anti–snowshoe songs, see the lyrics to "Sven" and "The Heavy Weapons Company," reprinted in Bradley, "A Mountain Soldier Sings," pp. 39–41. Also see Sanders, *The Boys of Winter,* pp. 63–64.

41 *"Goddamned Infantry":* "The American Army of World War II habitually filled the ranks of its combat infantry with its least promising recruits, the uneducated, the unskilled, the unenthusiastic." Russell F. Weigley, *Eisenhower's Lieutenants: The Campaign of France and Germany, 1944–1945* (Bloomington: Indiana University Press, 1981), p. 27. Also see Douglas Porch, *The Path to Victory: The Mediterranean Theater in World War II* (New York: Farrar, Straus & Giroux, 2004), p. 346; Paul Fussell, *Wartime: Understanding and Behavior in the Second World War* (New York: Oxford University Press, 1990), p. 283; Rick Atkinson, *The Guns at Last Light: The War in Western Europe, 1944–1945* (New York: Henry Holt, 2013), p. 19; James T. Patterson, *Grand Expectations: The United States, 1945–1974* (New York: Oxford University Press, 1996), p. 67.

42 *"Very Superior":* Burton, *The Ski Troops,* p. 136; Sanders, *The Boys of Winter,* p. 67.

overqualified corporals and sergeants: Sanders, *The Boys of Winter,* p. 69.

"Maybe it would interest you": Marty Daneman to Lois Miller, May 22, 1943, Martin L. Daneman Papers, TMD25, 10th Mountain Division Collection, Denver Public Library.

43 *103 troopers:* 10th Mountain Division Name Index, Denver Public Library, https://history.denverlibrary.org/sites/history/files/10th_mountain_index_1.pdf; Sanders, *The Boys of Winter,* pp. 151–53. For the ethnically mixed platoon in Hollywood films, see Richard Slotkin, "Unit Pride: Ethnic Platoons and the Myths of American Nationality," *American Literary History* 13 (Autumn 2001): 469–98; Michael C. C. Adams, *The Best War Ever: America and World War II* (Baltimore: Johns Hopkins University Press, 1994), p. 11.

naturalized citizens: Isserman, *Continental Divide,* pp. 219–20, 262; John D. Gorby, *The Stettner Way: The Life and Climbs of Joe and Paul Stettner* (Golden, CO: Colorado Mountain Club Press, 2003), pp. 113–14; Philipp Winter, "Historic Mountain Battles: Battles in the Dolomites During the Last War," *Camp Hale Ski-Zette,* May 26, 1944, p. 2; John Imbrie and Hugh W. Evans, *Good Times and Bad Times: A History of C Company, 85th Mountain Infantry Regiment, 10th Mountain Division, July 1943 to November 1945* (Quechee, VT: Vermont Heritage Press, 1995), p. 122. Pakkala, a member of C Company, 85th Regiment, was killed in action in Italy on April 19, 1945, and is buried in the American Cemetery in Florence. Imbrie and Evans, *Good Times and Bad Times,* p. 152.

"What was encouraging": McLane, "Of Mules and Skis," p. 32.

44 *elite status:* David R. Witte, *World War II at Camp Hale: Blazing a New Trail in the Rockies* (Charleston, SC: History Press, 2015), p. 110.

traditional military values: The best-known source on the paratroopers in World War II is Stephen Ambrose's account of Easy Company. In it he writes of the paratroopers, "They put a premium on physical well-being, hierarchical authority, and being part of an elite unit." Only the first and third of those values can be attributed to the mountain troops. Stephen Ambrose, *Band of Brothers: E Company, 506th Regiment, 101st Airborne from Normandy to Hitler's Eagle's Nest* (New York: Touchstone, 1992), p. 14. Also see Kurt Gabel, *The Making of a Paratrooper: Airborne Training and Combat in World War II* (Lawrence: University Press of Kansas, 1990); Captain Tania M. Chacho, "Why Did They Fight? American Airborne Units in World War II," *Defence Studies* 1 (Autumn 2001): 74–75; Gerard M. Devlin, *Paratrooper! The Saga of U.S. Army and Marine Parachute and Glider Combat Troops During World War II* (New York: St. Martin's Press, 1979), pp. 91–95.

45 *"backbone of the continent":* Walter R. Borneman and Lyndon J. Lampert, *A Climbing Guide to Colorado's Fourteeners* (Boulder: Pruett, 1998), p. 59.

Aspen Mountain: For Leadville's glory days, see Edward Blair, *Leadville: Colorado's Magic City* (Boulder: Pruett, 1980), pp. 163–82; Witte, *World War II at Camp Hale,* pp. 39–40.

highest military establishment: Witte, *World War II at Camp Hale,* pp. 67–68; Burton, *The Ski Troops,* p. 124.

46 *Any and all weapons:* Witte, *World War II at Camp Hale,* pp. 36–42.

Leadville was declared: Witte, *World War II at Camp Hale,* pp. 144–46.

47 *second- and third-highest peaks:* Witte, *World War II at Camp Hale,* p. 83; Jenkins, *The Last Ridge,* p. 49. Also see the map of Camp Hale in Imbrie and Evans, *Good Times and Bad,* p. 271.

coal-burning stoves: Witte, *World War II at Camp Hale,* pp. 43–58; *History of the Mountain Training Center,* p. 37.

48 *Nazi-occupied Norway: History of the Mountain Training Center,* pp. 36, 114–15; Witte, *World War II at Camp Hale,* pp. 98–99, 162–63, 210. The 99th Infantry Battalion (Special) won another distinction when it was chosen to represent Camp Hale at a parade at Camp Carson, Colorado, when President Franklin Roosevelt visited in April 1943. Witte, *World War II at Camp Hale,* p. 120.

"Rocky Elk trails lead": Frank Elkins, "Camp for Skiing Mountaineers Is Near Completion in Rockies," *New York Times,* October 18, 1942.

"in a beautiful valley": Bill Dunkerley, "By a Ski Trooper," *Sierra Club Bulletin,* June 1943, pp. 67–68.

49 *on account of the cold weather:* Witte, *World War II at Camp Hale,* pp. 80–81, 87, 90; *History of the Mountain Training Center,* pp. 37–38.

world distance record: Frank Elkins, "Nation's Skiing Stars Prepare for

Mountaineer Troop Service," *New York Times*, December 15, 1942; "Tokle, Ski Champion, Will Be Inducted Today," *New York Times,* October 1, 1942.

51 *"I could feel the polish oozing":* Robert Livermore to Minnie Dole, April 18, 1943, Charles Minot Dole Papers, WH1001, Western History Collection, Denver Public Library.

3. Camp Hale, 1943: "Heaven and Hell"

54 *"most gorgeous plus country":* Marty Daneman to Lois Zora Miller, April 29, 1943, Martin L. Daneman Papers, TMD25, 10th Mountain Division Papers, Denver Public Library. Daneman offered a different version of the arrival story in his 2012 memoir, but the one based on his letter at the time seems the more likely. Marty Daneman, *Do Well or Die: Memoirs of a WWII Mountain Trooper* (Brule, WI: Cable Publishing, 2012), pp. 9–11. For Camp Hale bus service, see David R. Witte, *World War II at Camp Hale: Blazing a New Trail in the Rockies* (Charleston, SC: History Press, 2015), p. 163.

55 *"Our skis will be issued soon":* Albert N. Brockman to Betty Brockman, February 22, 1943, Albert N. Brockman papers, TMD84, 10th Mountain Division Papers, Denver Public Library.

"We are going to start skiing": Albert N. Brockman to Betty Brockman, March 8, 1943, Albert N. Brockman Papers, TMD84, 10th Mountain Division Papers, Denver Public Library.

"I have been skiing all day": Albert N. Brockman to Betty Brockman, n.d. [March 1943], Albert N. Brockman Papers, TMD84, 10th Mountain Division Papers, Denver Public Library.

"I was one tired soldier": Albert N. Brockman to Betty Brockman, n.d. [March 1943], Albert N. Brockman Papers, TMD84, 10th Mountain Division Papers, Denver Public Library.

56 *"Time after time General Rolfe begged":* Historical Section, Army Ground Forces, *History of the Mountain Training Center*, study no. 24 (1948), pp. 41, 63.

dust on the bottom: Daneman, *Do Well or Die,* p. 13.

"At last we've started basic": Marty Daneman to Lois Zora Miller, May 10, 1943, Martin L. Daneman Papers, TMD25, 10th Mountain Division Papers, Denver Public Library.

57 *"10 out of 50 men collapsed":* Robert B. Ellis to Jessie Ellis, April 16, 1943, Robert B. Ellis Papers, TMD58, 10th Mountain Division Papers, Denver Public Library. Also see Ellis's letter to Jessie on April 29, 1943, where he describes, hour by hour, a typical training day. On the erratic attention paid to the problem of acclimatization at Camp Hale, see *History of the Mountain Training Center,* p. 59.

"camp nearest Heaven": "Colonel L. D. Brogan Extends Welcome to Hale Ski-Zette," *Camp Hale Ski-Zette,* April 21, 1943, p. 1.

"Camp Hell": Letter to "Wendell," January 23, 1943, Charles Minot Dole Papers, WH1001, Western History Collection, Denver Public Library.

58 *It didn't seem to help:* Robert B. Ellis, *See Naples and Die: A World War II Memoir of a United States Army Ski Trooper in the Mountains of Italy* (Jefferson, NC: McFarland, 1996), p. 41; *History of the Mountain Training Center,* p. 41.

59 *"My Pando Hack got better":* John Parker Compton to his grandparents, n.d. [Christmas 1943], and to his parents, January 23, 1944, reprinted after the war in *John Parker Compton, Private First Class* (privately printed), John Parker "Eagle" Compton Papers, TMD42, 10th Mountain Division Papers, Denver Public Library. Also see the letter to "Wendell," January 23, 1943, Charles Minot Dole Papers, WH1001, Western History Collection, Denver Public Library; McKay Jenkins, *The Last Ridge: The Epic Story of the US Army's 10th Mountain Division and the Assault on Hitler's Europe* (New York: Random House, 2003), p. 56.

"headache, nausea": Charles S. Houston, *Going Higher: The Story of Man and Altitude* (Burlington, VT: C. S. Houston, 1983), pp. 98, 103–5.

"A large percentage of men": Harris Dusenbery to Evelyn, Harris Dusenbery Papers, TMD57, 10th Mountain Division Papers, Denver Public Library. Also see William Lowell Putnam, *Green Cognac: The Education of a Mountain Fighter* (New York: AAC Press, 1991), p. 16; Charles J. Sanders, *The Boys of Winter: Life and Death in the U.S. Ski Troops During the Second World War* (Boulder: University Press of Colorado, 2005), p. 86; Witte, *World War II at Camp Hale,* p. 101.

60 *toll on the health and morale:* The 10th Mountain veteran and chronicler Hal Burton noted the gap in altitude between where the division trained and where it fought. Hal Burton, *The Ski Troops* (New York: Simon and Schuster, 1971), pp. 122–23. David Witte notes that the choice of the Pando site may have been influenced by the fact that the mountain troops were originally conceived as a force that would fight in North American mountains to repel a foreign invader. In that scenario, unlikely as it seems in retrospect, it made more sense to have troops acclimatized to an altitude of nine thousand to thirteen thousand feet. Witte, *World War II at Camp Hale,* p. 35.

Homestake Lake: Witte, *World War II at Camp Hale,* pp. 121–22.

61 *Hale was no paradise:* Charles Minot Dole, *Adventures in Skiing* (New York: Franklin Watts, 1965), p. 121.

62 *"What do you guys":* Dole, *Adventures in Skiing,* p. 123; Burton, *The Ski Troops,* pp. 128–29; Sanders, *The Boys of Winter,* pp. 86–87; *History of the Mountain Training Center,* p. 48.

thankfully not engulfing: Dole, *Adventures in Skiing,* p. 123; Burton, *The Ski Troops,* pp. 128–29; Sanders, *The Boys of Winter,* pp. 86–87; *History of the Mountain Training Center,* p. 48.

"retreat from Moscow": Peter Shelton, *Climb to Conquer: The Untold Story*

of World War II's Tenth Mountain Division Ski Troops (New York: Scribner, 2003), pp. 59–63; Jenkins, *The Last Ridge,* pp. 60–61; Witte, *World War II at Camp Hale,* pp. 124–25; Sanders, *The Boys of Winter,* p. 87.

63 *In his postwar memoir:* Dole, *Adventures in Skiing,* p. 122.
"*rank happy*": Quoted in Shelton, *Climb to Conquer,* p. 64. Also see Witte, *World War II at Camp Hale,* p. 125.
"*The statement I heard*": Frank H. Howard to Charles Minot Dole, April 5, 1943, Charles Minot Dole Papers, WH1001, Western History Collection, Denver Public Library.
"*The large proportion*": General McNair's letter is reprinted in Captain Thomas P. Govan, *Training for Mountain and Winter Warfare,* study no. 23 (Washington, DC: Historical Section, Army Ground Forces, 1946), pp. 11–12; and in *History of the Mountain Training Center,* p. 49. Also see Burton, *The Ski Troops,* pp. 129–30; Jenkins, *The Last Ridge,* p. 61.
Two things happened: Burton, *The Ski Troops,* pp. 135–36.

64 *As for Pinkie Rolfe:* Witte, *World War II at Camp Hale,* p. 126; Jenkins, *The Last Ridge,* pp. 61–62; Flint Whitlock and Bob Bishop, *Soldiers on Skis: A Pictorial Memoir of the 10th Mountain Division* (Boulder: Paladin Press, 1992), p. 10; Hanson Baldwin, "Amchitka Victor Runs Camp Hale," *New York Times,* November 1, 1943, p. 5.

65 *morale-builder:* Gordon L. Rottman, *US 10th Mountain Division in World War II* (Oxford: Osprey, 2012), pp. 6–7; Witte, *World War II at Camp Hale,* pp. 160–61; *History of the Mountain Training Center,* pp. 112–13.
"*lots uff fun*": James A. Goodwin, *And Gladly Guide: Reflection on a Life in the Mountains* (privately published, n.d.), p. 74.
"*Almost any Eagle scout*": George Trevor, "Mountain Troops Need Skiers," *New York Sun,* January 22, 1943, clipping in Charles Minot Dole Papers, WH1001, Western History Collection, Denver Public Library; *History of the Mountain Training Center,* pp. 53–55.

66 *one of the 10th's best recruiters:* Burton, *The Ski Troops,* pp. 142–43; Shelton, *Climb to Conquer,* pp. 53–54.
"*Tough Triple-Threat Men*": Ralf Myers, "Troops Training at Camp Hale Are Tough Triple-Threat Men," *Denver Post,* January 13, 1943.
the cover was used: Saturday Evening Post, March 27, 1943, cover; Shelton, *Climb to Conquer,* p. 52; Witte, *World War II at Camp Hale,* pp. 116–20. I'm grateful to Flint Whitlock for pointing out to me the *Saturday Evening Post* cover's technical inaccuracies.
"*the average American citizen*": *History of the Mountain Training Center,* pp. 56–57; Shelton, *Climb to Conquer,* p. 50.

67 "*superb physical specimens*": "They're Taking the 'High' Way to Berlin," *Collier's,* March 18, 1944, p. 28; "Hell-Bent for Victory," *Saturday Evening Post,* January 8, 1944, p. 64.
"*At first most of the men*": Glen Dawson, "Hurry Up and Wait," entry for

November 17, 1943, typescript, Glen Dawson Papers, 10th Mountain Division Personal Papers, TMD309, 10th Mountain Division Collection, Denver Public Library. For "Pineapple Boys," see Dawson entry for May 8, 1944; Putnam, *Green Cognac,* p. 66; Ellis, *See Naples and Die,* p. 44. For Dawson's distinguished climbing career, including the first ascent of the east face of Mount Whitney at age nineteen, see Jill Leovy, "Glen Dawson Dies at 103," *Los Angeles Times,* March 28, 2016.

"it is easy to get lost": Marty Daneman to Lois Miller, n.d. [December 1943], Martin L. Daneman Papers, TMD25, 10th Mountain Division Papers, Denver Public Library.

68 *Petzoldt supervised:* "Petzoldt Finds Mountain Climbing 'His Meat' — He's Only World's Champ, You Know," *Camp Hale Ski-Zette,* November 5, 1943, p. 1; Raye C. Ringholz, *On Belay! The Life of Legendary Mountaineer Paul Petzoldt* (Seattle: The Mountaineers, 1997), pp. 154–57.

69 *"overwhelming sense of my future":* "Friedl Pfeifer, One-Time Head of Sun Valley, Joins Skiers," *Camp Hale Ski-Zette,* July 16, 1943, p. 2; Friedl Pfeifer, *Nice Goin': My Life on Skis* (Missoula, MT; Pictorial Histories Publishing, 1993), pp. 96–98, 105–7, 111; Burton, *The Ski Troops,* p. 144; Sally Barlow-Perez, *A History of Aspen* (Aspen, CO: People's Press, 1991), p. 44.

a welcome addition: "First WAAC Contingent Arrives at Camp Hale; Company of 140 Is Expected Here in About a Week," *Camp Hale Ski-Zette,* June 2, 1943, p. 1; Witte, *World War II at Camp Hale,* pp. 131–42.

Not so another group: Some sources date the arrival of the POWs to early December 1943, but contemporary letters from 10th Mountain soldiers suggest they were already in camp by September.

"About 300 German prisoners": Ellis, *See Naples and Die,* p. 51.

"The boys say that those prisoners": Harris Dusenbery to Evelyn Dusenbery, October 26, 1943, Harris Dusenbery Papers, TMD57, 10th Mountain Division Papers, Denver Public Library. For fantasies of killing the POWs, see Jenkins, *The Last Ridge,* p. 112. Also see Allen W. Paschal, "The Enemy in Colorado: German Prisoners of War, 1943–1946," *History Colorado* (1979): p. 125.

Fraternization between the two groups: Some in Camp Hale felt otherwise. Private Dale Maple of the 620th Engineer General Service Company (a labor company reserved for soldiers whose loyalty was suspect) not only fraternized with the POWs but also, in February 1944, helped two of them escape from the camp. He and the two escapees were apprehended in Mexico and returned to prison in the United States. Maple was sentenced to death for desertion and treason, but his sentence was commuted to a life sentence by President Roosevelt, and he was released from prison in 1951. The tale of the escape has been told recently and completely in Paul N. Herbert, *Treason in the Rockies: Nazi Sympathizer Dale Maple's POW Escape Plot* (Charleston, SC: History Press, 2016). Also see Jenkins, *The Last Ridge,* pp. 112–15.

"receive the finest ski instruction": Frank Elkins, "Ski Slopes and Trails," *New York Times*, January 26, 1943.

70 *"Well, this starts 5th week"*: Arnold C. Holeywell to May Holeywell, April 3, 1943, Arnold C. Holeywell Papers, TMD62, 10th Mountain Division Papers, Denver Public Library.

"This was really living": Dick Nebeker to Glen Hines, Richard H. Nebeker Papers, M2168, 10th Mountain Division Archives, Denver Public Library.

71 *"G.I. skiing is regular snow plow"*: Donald Potter to Carol [sister], "Night Before Easter" [April 24, 1943], Potter family collection.

72 *"We have steep slopes"*: Frederick C. Miller to Dorothy Miller, February 18, 1943, Frederick C. Miller Papers, TMD333, 10th Mountain Division Papers, Denver Public Library; Witte, *World War II at Camp Hale*, p. 105. The Canadian-born Arthur Doucette, who, after being a ski instructor at Hale, served with the Headquarters Company of the division's Quartermaster Corps, had moved to New Hampshire as a teenager, taught himself skiing from a book, and was good enough to be hired by Benno Rybizka in 1936 as an instructor at the new Arlberg technique school in North Conway. In 1937 he was sent to St. Anton am Arlberg to train with Hannes Schneider for a month, and was thus one of the few North Americans in the 10th trained directly by the master. Karen Cummings, "Ageless Racer Arthur Doucette," *Mountain Ear Chronicles*, December 28, 1984, https://www.mtearchronicles.com/single-post/2016/08/26/Ageless-Racer-Arthur-Doucette.

73 *"with the best of them"*: Daneman, *Do Well or Die*, pp. 23–26. For the cry of "Bend zee knees!," see Gerald Buckley Cullinane, "From Student to Soldier: My War Years, 1941–1945," typescript, Gerald Buckley Cullinane Papers, TMD38, 10th Mountain Division Papers, Denver Public Library. For the late-night skiing, see Dick Nebeker to Glen Hines, Richard H. Nebeker Papers, M2168, 10th Mountain Division Archives, Denver Public Library.

"This comes in very handy": Harris Dusenbery to Evelyn, May 29, 1944, Harris Dusenbery Papers, TMD57, 10th Mountain Division Papers, Denver Public Library.

74 *Among the best-known climbers*: David R. Brower, "It Couldn't Be Climbed," *Saturday Evening Post*, February 3, 1940, pp. 24–25, 72–79; Maurice Isserman, *Continental Divide: A History of American Mountaineering* (New York: Norton, 2016), pp. 216–18.

Brower first arrived: David Brower, *For Earth's Sake: The Life and Times of David Brower* (Salt Lake City: Gibb-Smith, 1990), pp. 87–93; Robert Wyss, *The Man Who Built the Sierra Club: A Life of David Brower* (New York: Columbia University Press, 2016), pp. 48–51; *History of the Mountain Training Center*, pp. 58–59, 70; Sanders, *The Boys of Winter*, p. 84; Shelton, *Climb to Conquer*, pp. 84–88. For the field manual Brower contributed to, see *War Department Field Manual, Mountain Operations*, FM 70-10 (Washington, DC: War Department, December 1944). Another 10th Mountain veteran contributing to the field manual's section on rock climbing was Artur Argiewicz Jr., killed in Italy on January 25, 1945, on the outskirts of the village of Querciola while serving in L Company, 86th Mountain Infantry Regiment, one of the first men of the 10th Mountain Division to die in Italy. His contribution to the field manual is noted in Brower's introduction to the second edition of the *Manual of Ski Mountaineering* (Berkeley: University of California Press, 1947), pp. viii–ix.

Fred Beckey: Fred Beckey enlisted in the US Army in April 1943 at Fort Lewis. He was honorably discharged on January 12, 1945, at Fort Lewis, a week after his regiment departed for Italy from Newport News, Virginia. The circumstances surrounding his discharge are obscure but may be cleared up in a forthcoming biography by Megan Bond, who provided me with copies of pages from Beckey's wartime diary.

75 *"future of mountaineering":* Lieutenant John W. James, "We're in the Army Now," *The Mountaineer* 36 (December 1943): 11; Robert D. McFadden, "Fred Beckey, Conqueror of North American Peaks, Dies at 94," *New York Times,* October 31, 2017.

"Once a soldier and his animal": Charles W. Webb, *Field Artillery, the King of Battle: A History of the 616th Field Artillery (Pack)* (self-published, 1996), pp. 28–29, 37, 42; Whitlock and Bishop, *Soldiers on Skis,* pp. 14–15, 36, 38.

"By the end of the week": Martin L. Daneman to Lois Miller, n.d. [December 1943], Martin L. Daneman Papers, TMD25, 10th Mountain Division Papers, Denver Public Library.

"I had not even uttered": H. Robert Krear, *The Journal of a U.S. Army Mountain Trooper in World War II* (Estes Park, CO: self-published, 1993), p. 11; "H. Robert Krear, Ph.D.," *Estes Park News,* January 3, 2018, http://www.estesparknews.com/local_obituaries/article_3d18c802-f0bf-11e7-aba6-4f2427db796d.html?utm_medium=social&utm_source=email&utm_campaign=user-share.

76 *"several thousand new cuss words":* Earl E. Clark to "Mom, Nana, and All," June 3, 1943, Earl E. Clark Papers, TMD8, 10th Mountain Division Papers, Denver Public Library. Also see Ellis, *See Naples and Die,* pp. 54–55. Some men also received training in dog handling, and still others in the use of pigeons for sending messages. The dogs performed well but were left behind when the 10th Mountain departed Camp Hale in 1944. And the pigeons were a failure, since they couldn't cope with the altitude and preferred walking to flying. *History of the Mountain Training Center,* pp. 70–73; Witte, *World War II at Camp Hale,* p. 114.

"Through rain, snow, and sleet": John Parker Compton to Jim Compton, October 23, 1943, John Parker "Eagle" Compton Papers, TMD42, 10th Mountain Division Papers, Denver Public Library.

Sometimes it was so cold: History of the Mountain Training Center, p. 41.

77 *"When you first climb"*: Albert N. Brockman to Mr. E. W. Brockman, n.d. [1943], Albert N. Brockman Papers, TMD84, 10th Mountain Division Papers, Denver Public Library.

Brown Palace Hotel: Witte, *World War II at Camp Hale*, pp. 148–49.

78 *"a beautiful resort town"*: Ellis, *See Naples and Die*, p. 41.

bars and brothels: Daneman, *Do Well or Die*, p. 36; Sanders, *The Boys of Winter*, p. 81; Witte, *World War II at Camp Hale*, pp. 146–47; Blair, *Leadville*, pp. 234–36.

"an amazing place": Donald Potter to "Mom," n.d. [summer 1943?], Potter family collection.

79 *"What fun"*: Arnold C. Holeywell to May Holeywell, September 5, 1943, Arnold C. Holeywell Papers, TMD62, 10th Mountain Division Papers, Denver Public Library. Also see Witte, *World War II at Camp Hale*, p. 148.

only black soldier: "Jinx Falkenburg, Hollywood's 'All American Girl,' to Make Personal Appearance Here Thursday, Friday," *Camp Hale Ski-Zette*, May 5, 1943, p. 1; "Lovely Jane Wyman, Hollywood's Own Hot Blues Singer, Will Make Personal Appearance at Camp Hale Theater, July 22," *Camp Hale Ski-Zette*, July 16, 1943, p. 1; "Joe Louis & Co. Thrill GIs at Boxing Show," *Camp Hale Ski-Zette*, October 22, 1943, p. 1; Webb, *Field Artillery*, pp. 57–58.

80 *"The Himalayas sure are terrific"*: "Mountain Climber Tells Soldiers of Perilous Trips," *Camp Hale Ski-Zette*, April 21, 1943, p. 4; Donald Potter to "Mom," n.d. [April 1943], Potter family collection. Some months later, Camp Hale's resident K2 veteran, Paul Petzoldt, gave a talk in which he predicted that Mount Everest would be climbed after the war: "Everest Is Only World's Highest Peak, but Petzoldt Sees Its Conquest Near," *Camp Hale Ski-Zette*, November 12, 1943, p. 1.

"all your dreams": Stuart E. Abbott to "Bob," December 18, 1943, Stuart E. Abbott Papers, TMD50, 10th Mountain Division Papers, Denver Public Library; "Fishing Season Opens Next Month; Privileges Given to Service Men," *Camp Hale Ski-Zette*, April 21, 1943, p. 4.

81 *"some of the worst skiers"*: Jean Cummings to "Dear folks," September 28, 1943, and January 3, 1944, Stan and Jean Cummings Papers, TMD7, 10th Mountain Division Papers, Denver Public Library. Also see Jean Cummings, "An Army Wife," *Blizzard* 36, no. 2 (2007): 8.

82 *rival Sun Valley:* Barlow-Perez, *A History of Aspen*, pp. 43–44; Tom Washing, "West: Development of Skiing in the Western US," in *Passion for Skiing*, ed. Stephen L. Waterhouse (Lebanon, NH: Whitman Communications, 2010), pp. 174–75; Sanders, *The Boys of Winter*, p. 75.

"the boys in Africa": Denis P. Nunan to Mrs. M. G. Nunan, January 11 and February 15, 1943, Denis P. Nunan Papers, TMD33, 10th Mountain Division Papers, Denver Public Library. Also see Jenkins, *The Last Ridge*, p. 64; Sanders, *The Boys of Winter*, p. 86. On the fighting in North Africa, see Rick Atkinson, *An Army at Dawn: The War in North Africa, 1942–1943* (New York:

Henry Holt, 2002), pp. 340–90; Douglas Porch, *The Path to Victory: The Mediterranean Theater in World War II* (New York: Farrar, Straus and Giroux, 2005), pp. 384–92.

attrition rate: John Parker Compton to parents, November 1, 1943, John Parker Compton Papers, TMD42, 10th Mountain Division Papers, Denver Public Library; Martin Daneman to Lois Miller, n.d. [December 1943], Martin L. Daneman Papers, TMD25, 10th Mountain Division Papers, Denver Public Library. The attrition statistics were compiled by David Little and come from a database of 10th Mountain personnel records: 10th Mountain Division Database, 10th Mountain Division Database Records, TMD2, 10th Mountain Division Resource Center, Denver Public Library.

83 *Historians have long debated:* For a discussion of the "primary group cohesion" versus larger war aims debate, see Captain Tania M. Chacho, "Why Did They Fight? American Airborne Units in World War II," *Defence Studies* 1 (Autumn 2001): 59–94.

"This morning we saw a picture": Marty Daneman to Lois Miller, n.d. [December 1943], Martin L. Daneman Papers, TMD25, 10th Mountain Division Papers, Denver Public Library.

84 *Of course, the mountain troops:* Joan Gearin, "Movie vs. Reality: The Real Story of the Von Trapp Family," *Prologue Magazine,* Winter 2005, p. 1, https://www.archives.gov/publications/prologue/2005/winter/von-trapps. html. In addition to Norwegians and Norwegian-Americans serving in the mountain troops, another unit with the odd designation the 99th Battalion (Separate) trained at Camp Hale, and consisted entirely of soldiers of Norwegian descent. The unit was created at Camp Ripley, Minnesota, in the summer of 1942, with the idea that it would be deployed in commando actions behind enemy lines in Norway. The 99th arrived at Camp Hale in mid-December 1942. In September 1943 the 99th shipped out to England, and the following spring it took part in the invasion of Normandy, landing on D-Day plus sixteen, June 22. For an overview of the 99th's history, including its time at Camp Hale, see Gerd Nyquist, *The 99th Battalion* (Oslo: H. Aschehoug & Co., 1981).

firsthand accounts: "Remember? VIENNA . . . 1938," *Camp Hale Ski-Zette,* April 28, 1943, p. 2; "When Vienna Was Not So Gay," *Camp Hale Ski-Zette,* May 5, 1943, p. 2; "The Nazi Way — Every Tenth Man," *Camp Hale Ski-Zette,* May 12, 1943, p. 2; "Out of Darkness — to America," *Camp Hale Ski-Zette,* May 19, 1943, p. 2.

Marcus Aurelius: Harris Dusenbery, *Ski the High Trail: World War II Ski Troopers in the High Colorado Rockies* (Portland, OR: Binford & Mort, 1991), pp. 8–9; Marcus Aurelius, *Meditations* (Chicago: Henry Regnery, 1970), p. 61. In a letter to his wife in early 1944, Dusenbery wrote that he "did some reading today . . . in the Meditations of Marcus Aurelius. The latter made me feel that here was a kindred spirit. He wrote this philosophy while on military campaigns against the Germans. He was no Christian, but his philosophy is remarkably close to that of Christianity. In many ways he was the greatest Roman Emperor—perhaps the greatest Roman of all." Harris Dusenbery to Evelyn, February 22, 1944, Harris Dusenbery Papers, TMD57, 10th Mountain Division Papers, Denver Public Library.

85 *"The army tries to teach us"*: Harris Dusenbery to Evelyn, December 19, 1943, Harris Dusenbery Papers, TMD57, 10th Mountain Division Papers, Denver Public Library.

Mussolini's overthrow: Carlo D'Este, *World War II in the Mediterranean, 1942–1945* (Chapel Hill, NC: Algonquin Books, 1990), pp. 61, 70, 74–77; Porch, *The Path to Victory*, pp. 454–58.

86 *Salerno landings:* "General Clark Leads American British Troops at Landing at Naples; Nazi Resistance Stiff," *Camp Hale Ski-Zette*, September 10, 1943, p. 1; Rick Atkinson, *The Day of Battle: The War in Sicily and Italy, 1943–1944* (New York: Henry Holt, 2007), pp. 179–318.

"pretty optimistic": Letter from Robert Ellis, September 19, 1943, reprinted in Ellis, *See Naples and Die*, p. 51.

end of October: Porch, *The Path to Victory*, p. 468.

87 *"there are so many mountains":* Todd DePastino, ed., *Willie and Joe: The WWII Years*, vol. 2 (Seattle: Fantagraphics, 2008), p. 39; Hanson Baldwin, "Eisenhower Holds War in Italy Sound," *New York Times*, December 24, 1943. Also see John Keegan, *The Second World War* (New York: Penguin, 1989), p. 353.

"there's too much over-optimism": John Parker Compton to his parents, November 14, 1943, reprinted in *John Parker Compton, Private First Class*, John Parker "Eagle" Compton Papers, TMD42, 10th Mountain Division Papers, Denver Public Library.

4. Kiska, 1943: "This Little Expedition"

89 *"I would prefer anything":* Earl E. Clark to "Mom, Nana, and All," June 3, 1943, Earl E. Clark Papers, TMD8, 10th Mountain Division Papers, Denver Public Library.

90 *"My mountain knowledge":* Earl E. Clark to his mother, August 29, 1943, Earl E. Clark Papers, TMD8, 10th Mountain Division Papers, Denver Public Library.

91 *"had done a Kiska on us":* Samuel Eliot Morison, *History of United States Naval Operations in World War II*, vol. 7, *Aleutians, Gilberts, and Marshalls, June 1942–April 1944* (Boston: Little, Brown, 1951), p. 155.

Kiska foul-up: "Battle of the Pacific: Janfu," *Time*, August 30, 1943, p. 38.

B-17 bombers: Dean C. Allard, "The North Pacific Campaign in Perspective," in *Alaska at War, 1941–1945, The Forgotten War Remembered*, ed. Fern Chandonnet (Fairbanks: University of Alaska Press, 2008), p. 3.

92   *"jumping off place":* Allard, "The North Pacific Campaign," p. 4; Major Matthew Scott Metcalf, "The Battle of Attu and the Aleutian Island Campaign" (School of Advanced Military Studies, United States Army Command and General Staff College, Fort Leavenworth, KS, AY 2014-001), p. 10.

    fogbound shores: Brian Garfield, *The Thousand Mile War: World War II in Alaska and the Aleutians* (Garden City, NY: Doubleday, 1983), pp. 28, 96–98; Del C. Kostka, "Operation Cottage: A Cautionary Tale of Assumption and Perceptual Bias," *Joint Force Quarterly* 76 (2015), http://ndupress.ndu.edu/Media/News/News-Article-View/Article/577595/jfq-76-operation-cottage-a-cautionary-tale-of-assumption-and-perceptual-bias/; Metcalf, "The Battle of Attu," p. 3; George L. MacGarrigle, *Aleutian Islands: The US Army Campaigns of World War II,* Pub. 72-6 (Washington, DC: US Government Printing Office, US Army Center of Military History, 1992), pp. 5–9.

93   *beginning in September:* MacGarrigle, *Aleutian Islands,* p. 12.

    cold and damp: Allard, "The North Pacific Campaign," p. 8; Fern Chandonnet, "Recapture of Attu," in Chandonnet, *Alaska at War,* pp. 81–85; Garfield, *The Thousand Mile War,* p. 297; Morison, *Aleutians, Gilberts, and Marshalls,* pp. 44–50; Metcalf, "The Battle of Attu," pp. 5, 18–19; MacGarrigle, *Aleutian Islands,* pp. 17–23, 26; Hal Burton, *The Ski Troops* (New York: Simon and Schuster, 1971), p. 109.

    "I should have sent alpine troops": Quoted in Peter Shelton, *Climb to Conquer: The Untold Story of World War II's Tenth Mountain Division Ski Troops* (New York: Scribner, 2003), p. 71.

94   *their final destination:* Shelton, *Climb to Conquer,* p. 70.

    "Just a line tonight": Earl E. Clark to Lillian Clark, August 3, 1943, Earl E. Clark Papers, TMD8, 10th Mountain Division Papers, Denver Public Library.

95   *Operation Cottage:* Garfield, *The Thousand Mile War,* pp. 314–15, 323–27; Morison, *Aleutians, Gilberts and Marshalls,* pp. 58–59.

    "wet and muddy": Denis Nunan to his mother, January 1, 1944, Denis Nunan Papers, TMD33, 10th Mountain Division Papers, Denver Public Library.

    The invasion armada: The Aleutians Campaign, June 1942–August 1943 (Washington, DC: Naval Historical Center, Department of the Navy, 1993), p. 123; Shelton, *Climb to Conquer,* p. 71; Flint Whitlock and Bob Bishop, *Soldiers on Skis: A Pictorial Memoir of the 10th Mountain Division* (Boulder: Paladin Press, 1992), pp. 19–21. For a more detailed breakdown of units involved in the invasion of Kiska, see Gordon L. Rottman, *US 10th Mountain Division in World War II* (Oxford: Osprey, 2012), pp. 15–17.

    high ridgeline: McKay Jenkins, *The Last Ridge: The Epic Story of the US Army's 10th Mountain Division and the Assault on Hitler's Europe* (New York: Random House, 2003), p. 90; Whitlock and Bishop, *Soldiers on Skis,* p. 23.

96   *"it's up to God":* Nunan quoted in Jenkins, *The Last Ridge,* p. 91. For ex-

pected casualty rates see Jenkins, *The Last Ridge,* p. 87; Garfield, *The Thousand Mile War,* pp. 329–30.

"Jap outposts' ears": Quoted in Burton, *The Ski Troops,* p. 113.

97 *"Not a man in the boat":* Joseph deLongpre, "Service in the US Army," typescript, Joseph deLongpre Papers, TMD309, 10th Mountain Division Papers, Denver Public Library.

"narrow rock pier": H. Bradley Benedict, *Ski Troops in the Mud: Kiska Island Recaptured* (Littleton, CO: H. B. & J. C. Benedict, 1990), p. 114.

"The island was rimmed": George F. Earle, *Birth of a Division* (Syracuse, NY: Signature Publications, 1995), p. 5.

98 *"It was a terrible night":* Floyd H. Erickson, notes, typescript, 10th Mountain Division Personal Papers, TMD309, 10th Mountain Division Resource Center, Denver Public Library.

inexperienced soldiers: Whitlock and Bishop, *Soldiers on Skis,* pp. 24–25.

99 *"Japs in the murk":* Quoted in Burton, *The Ski Troops,* p. 114. Hal Burton's account identifies Eddy as commander of K Company, but that is not borne out by regimental records, according to David Little's examination of 10th Mountain personnel records: 10th Mountain Division Database, 10th Mountain Division Database Records, TMD2, 10th Mountain Division Resource Center, Denver Public Library.

"This was a shock": "Kiska Diary," Arthur C. Delaney Papers, TMD19, 10th Mountain Division Papers, Denver Public Library.

When mountain troopers bumped: Burton, *The Ski Troops,* p. 114; Whitlock and Bishop, *Soldiers on Skis,* p. 26; Charles J. Sanders, *The Boys of Winter: Life and Death in the U.S. Ski Troops During the Second World War* (Boulder: University Press of Colorado, 2005), p. 90.

100 *"I can remember bending over":* Quoted in Burton, *The Ski Troops,* p. 115. Also see George F. Earle, "Kiska: Birth of a Division," in Chandonnet, *Alaska at War,* p. 106.

estimates range from: The numbers of the 87th's dead and wounded vary widely in published accounts. I'm relying on statistics compiled by David Little that come from a database of 10th Mountain personnel records: 10th Mountain Division Database, 10th Mountain Division Database Records, TMD2, 10th Mountain Division Resource Center, Denver Public Library.

101 *Kiska fiasco:* "2 Killed at Kiska," *New York Times,* August 24, 1943; Hanson W. Baldwin, "Encircling Japan: Reoccupation of Kiska Draws Closer Strategic Net About Foe in Pacific," *New York Times,* August 23, 1943; "Allied Troops Retake Deserted Kiska," *Life,* September 13, 1943, pp. 25–32. Also see Garfield, *Thousand Mile War,* p. 333.

"I'll tell you a story": Quoted in Jenkins, *The Last Ridge,* p. 95; Burton, *The Ski Troops,* p. 118.

There were jokes: Sanders, *The Boys of Winter,* p. 91.

102 *"Did any of those pictures":* Denis Nunan to his mother, January 1, 1944,

Denis Nunan Papers, TMD33, 10th Mountain Division Papers, Denver Public Library.

"buddy-killer": Sanders, *The Boys of Winter,* p. 92.

stayed with the mountain troops: The 87th's attrition statistics, both on Kiska and afterwards, were compiled by David Little and come from a database of 10th Mountain personnel records: 10th Mountain Division Database, 10th Mountain Division Database Records, TMD2, 10th Mountain Division Resource Center, Denver Public Library.

5. Camp Hale and Camp Swift, 1944: "We'll Be Playing for Keeps before Long"

105 *"When and where":* John Parker Compton to his parents, May 8, 1944, John Parker Compton Papers, TMD43, 10th Mountain Division Papers, Denver Public Library.

106 *Camp Ritchie:* McLane would be dispatched to France as an interpreter shortly after the D-Day landings. For McLane's transfer from the 10th, see John Henry Auran, "The First of the 10th," Dartmouth College *'41 Newsletter,* February 1992; "Charles B. McLane," https://catalog.denverlibrary.org/search/title.aspx?ctx=1.1033.0.0.6&cn=739467; April 17, 1944, Morning Report, 10th Mountain Division database records, TMD2, 10th Mountain Division Resource Center, Denver Public Library.

"We've got the stuff": Corporal Arnold Holeywell, "STICK TO THE FIGHT," *Camp Hale Ski-Zette,* March 10, 1944, p. 2.

the division would consist of: David R. Witte, *World War II at Camp Hale: Blazing a New Trail in the Rockies* (Charleston, SC: History Press, 2015), p. 173.

107 *rare windless day:* "Mt. Holy Cross, Conquered by Three Medics," *Camp Hale Ski-Zette,* January 21, 1944, p. 2; Walter R. Borneman and Lyndon J. Lampert, *A Climbing Guide to Colorado's Fourteeners* (Boulder: Pruett, 1998), p. 65.

"a three day trip": Glen Dawson diary, 10th Mountain Division Personal Papers, TMD309, 10th Mountain Division Papers, Denver Public Library; "10th Recon, MTG Make Ascents to Mts. Elbert, Massive, Second and Third Highest Peaks in This Country," *Camp Hale Ski-Zette,* January 7, 1944, p. 1; Witte, *World War II at Camp Hale,* pp. 169–70.

108 *"ankle to knee deep":* Glen Dawson diary, 10th Mountain Division Personal Papers, TMD309, 10th Mountain Division Papers, Denver Public Library; "Make Rugged 50-Mile Ski Trek to Aspen," *Camp Hale Ski-Zette,* March 3, 1944, p. 1; Peter Shelton, *Climb to Conquer: The Untold Story of World War II's Tenth Mountain Division Ski Troops* (New York: Scribner, 2003), pp. 98–101; Witte, *World War II at Camp Hale,* p. 172; Charles J. Sanders, *The Boys of*

Winter: Life and Death in the U.S. Ski Troops During the Second World War (Boulder: University Press of Colorado, 2005), pp. 98–100.

sum total of luxuries: Glen Dawson diary, 10th Mountain Division Personal Papers, TMD309, 10th Mountain Division Papers, Denver Public Library; Wolfgang Lert, "Hans Hagemeister Brought Us Good Things to Ski With," *Skiing Heritage* (Fall–Winter 1996): 35–36.

"About every other day": Arnold C. Holeywell to his mother, March 7, 1944, Arnold C. Holeywell Papers, TMD62, 10th Mountain Division Papers, Denver Public Library.

"Real Test": "10th Infantry Division Moves Out Sunday on Extensive Field Maneuvers; Rugged, Snow-Capped Rockies to Prove Real Test for General Jones' Men," *Camp Hale Ski-Zette*, March 24, 1944, p. 1.

109 *"If this gets any worse":* Harris Dusenbery, *Ski the High Trail: World War II Ski Troopers in the High Colorado Rockies* (Portland, OR: Binford & Mort, 1991), pp. 156–57; Sanders, *The Boys of Winter*, p. 102.

"piss and vinegar": Marty Daneman, *Do Well or Die: Memoirs of a WWII Mountain Trooper* (Brule, WI: Cable Publishing, 2012), pp. 42–44; Witte, *World War Two at Camp Hale*, pp. 175–80.

"They are trying to kill us": Denis P. Nunan to his mother, April 1, 1944, Denis P. Nunan Papers, TMD33, 10th Mountain Division Papers, Denver Public Library. Nunan did concede things could be worse: "But we shouldn't kick I suppose, cause we'll live through this whereas the boys in Italy are taking a hellafa beating that really kills."

110 *ruled off-limits:* McKay Jenkins, *The Last Ridge: The Epic Story of the US Army's 10th Mountain Division and the Assault on Hitler's Europe* (New York: Random House, 2003), pp. 116–19; Robert Ellis, *See Naples and Die: A World War II Memoir of a United States Army Ski Trooper in the Mountains of Italy* (Jefferson, NC: McFarland, 1996), pp. 68–69; Daneman, *Do Well or Die*, p. 53; Dusenbery, *Ski the High Trail*, pp. 44, 145.

"all the hardships": Jean Cummings to "folks," April 3, 1944, Stan and Jean Cummings Papers, TMD7, 10th Mountain Division Papers, Denver Public Library. Also see Jenkins, *The Last Ridge*, pp. 116–19.

"Joseph has disappeared": Kay Boyle to Ann Watkins, March 29, 1944, reprinted in *Kay Boyle: A Twentieth-Century Life in Letters*, ed. Sandra Spanier (Champaign-Urbana: University of Illinois Press, 2015), p. 402.

"there was simply no way": Kay Boyle to Ann Watkins, April 1, 1944, in Spanier, *Kay Boyle*, p. 404.

111 *Back in Leadville:* Spanier, *Kay Boyle*, p. 405; Kay Boyle, *His Human Majesty* (New York: McGraw-Hill, 1949). After D-Series, Franckenstein was determined to get out of the mountain troops and transferred to the Office of Strategic Services. Sent behind enemy lines in Austria, he was captured but survived the war. Sandra Spanier, *Kay Boyle: Artist and Activist* (Carbondale: Southern Illinois University Press, 1986), p. 150.

"a worthwhile vacation": Stan Cummings to "folks," April 7, 1944, Stan and Jean Cummings Papers, TMD7, 10th Mountain Division Papers, Denver Public Library.

112 *Evans lost his stripes:* John Imbrie and Hugh W. Evans, *Good Times and Bad Times: A History of C Company, 85th Mountain Infantry Regiment, 10th Mountain Division* (Quechee, VT: Vermont Heritage Press, 1995), p. 6; Jenkins, *The Last Ridge,* pp. 117–18.

113 *lost seventeen pounds:* Ellis, *See Naples and Die,* pp. 69–70.

"walked on a three-man patrol": John Parker Compton to his parents, April 15, 1944, John Parker Compton Papers, TMD43, 10th Mountain Division Papers, Denver Public Library.

114 *"the first was the coldest":* Dusenbery, *Ski the High Trail,* p. 13.

According to official statistics: Daneman, *Do Well or Die,* p. 56; "General Jones Praises Fortitude of 10th," *Camp Hale Ski-Zette,* May 19, 1944, p. 1; Witte, *World War II at Camp Hale,* p. 181; Sanders, *Boys of Winter,* p. 102.

Thereafter, the rifleman's squad: Dusenbery, *Ski the High Trail,* pp. 156–58.

It saddened the general: "General Jones Praises Fortitude of 10th," *Camp Hale Ski-Zette,* May 19, 1944, p. 1.

115 *General Jones was not the man:* Ellis, *See Naples and Die,* pp. 71, 74; Jenkins, *The Last Ridge,* pp. 126–27; Gordon L. Rottman, *US 10th Mountain Division in World War II* (Oxford: Osprey, 2012), p. 24.

At National Ski Patrol headquarters: Some earlier histories of the 10th say that Dole visited Camp Hale during D-Series, as he had in the previous year's Homestake maneuvers, but nothing in Dole's own writings supports that. Hal Burton, *The Ski Troops* (New York: Simon and Schuster, 1971), p. 139.

116 *"All those mules":* William Lowell Putnam, *Green Cognac: The Education of a Mountain Fighter* (New York: AAC Press, 1991), p. 78; Jenkins, *The Last Ridge,* p. 122; Mark W. Clark, *Calculated Risk* (New York: Harper and Brothers, 1950), p. 348; Joseph A. Springer, *The Black Devil Brigade: The True Story of the First Special Service Force* (Pacifica, CA: Pacifica Military History, 2001), pp. 68–130; Edward L. Bimberg, *The Moroccan Goums: Tribal Warriors in a Modern War* (Westport, CT: Greenwood Press, 1999), pp. 43–67; Thomas R. Brooks, *The War North of Rome: June 1944–May 1945* (New York: Da Capo Press, 2003), pp. 5, 33, 36: Rick Atkinson, *The Day of Battle: The War in Sicily and Italy, 1943–1944* (New York: Henry Holt, 2007), p. 513.

The future of the 10th: Kent Roberts Greenfield, Robert R. Palmer, and Bell I. Wiley, *The Organization of Ground Combat Troops* (Washington, DC: Department of the Army, 1947), pp. 348–49; Thomas R. Brooks, "10th Mountain Division History," in *Tenth Mountain Division* (Paducah, KY: Turner Publishing Co., 1998), pp. 24–25; John Imbrie, "Chronology of the 10th Mountain Division in World War II," p. 10, http://10thmtndivassoc.org/chronology.pdf.

"the greatest day in the Army": Donald Potter to "Mother," June 7, 1944, Potter family collection. Also see "'D-Day' Finds Allies Smashing Inland Along French Coast; Invasion Forces Meet Little Opposition in First Landings; Reinforcements Widen Initial Beachheads," *Camp Hale Ski-Zette,* June 9, 1944, p. 1.

"before the end of autumn": Ellis, *See Naples and Die,* p. 75.

"The invasion seems to be going": Jean Cummings to "folks," n.d. [June 6, 1944], Stan and Jean Cummings Papers, TMD7, 10th Mountain Division Papers, Denver Public Library.

117 *Or perhaps even being broken up*: Jean Cummings to "folks," June 12, 1944, Stan and Jean Cummings Papers, TMD7, 10th Mountain Division Papers, Denver Public Library. Also see Shelton, *Climb to Conquer,* p. 106.

"Good luck, kids": Ellis, *See Naples and Die,* p. 79.

Not everyone felt that way: Dole, *Adventures in Skiing,* p. 126.

118 *"When we were standing rifle inspection"*: Harris Dusenbery to Evelyn, July 1, 1944, Harris Dusenbery Papers, TMD57, 10th Mountain Division Papers, Denver Public Library; Dick Nebeker to Glen Hines, Richard H. Nebeker Papers, M2168, 10th Mountain Division Archives, Denver Public Library; Jenkins, *The Last Ridge,* p. 124.

119 *the broiling sun*: Shelton, *Climb to Conquer,* p. 110; Daneman, *Do Well or Die,* pp. 64–68; Ellis, *See Naples and Die,* p. 81; Sanders, *The Boys of Winter,* pp. 105–6; H. Robert Krear, *The Journal of a US Army Mountain Trooper in World War II* (self-published, 1993), pp. 24–25.

six salt tablets: Gerald Buckley Cullinane, "From Student to Soldier: My War Years, 1941–1945," pp. 27–28, Gerald Buckley Cullinane Papers, TMD38, 10th Mountain Division Papers, Denver Public Library; Ellis, *See Naples and Die,* p. 85.

"over a hundred candidates": Donald Potter to "Mother," July 18, 1944, Potter family collection.

120 *"a million-dollar demonstration"*: Donald Potter to "Mother," October 23, 1944, Potter family collection.

75 mm pack howitzer: Some earlier books on the 10th erred in reporting that the field artillery units were equipped with either or both of the heavier 105 mm and 155 mm guns while at Camp Swift. They would get the 105s only after they arrived in Italy. I appreciate the guidance provided by David Little's scrutiny of the 10th Mountain Division database: 10th Mountain Division Database Records, TMD2, 10th Mountain Division Resource Center, Denver Public Library. Also see Rottman, *US 10th Mountain Division in World War II,* pp. 21, 23.

121 *Lieutenant General Mark Clark*: Brooks, "10th Mountain Division History," pp. 25–26; Ellis, *See Naples and Die,* p. 90; Imbrie and Evans, *Good Times and Bad Times,* p. 130.

122 *"as well as bad times"*: George P. Hays, "Personal Memoirs of Lt. General

George Price Hays, 1892–1978," typescript, p. 31, George P. Hayes Papers, TMD61, 10th Mountain Division Papers, Denver Public Library; Brooks, "10th Mountain Division History," pp. 25–26; Imbrie and Evans, *Good Times and Bad Times*, p. 9; Charles Minot Dole, *Adventures in Skiing* (New York: Franklin Watts, 1965), p. 126; Minnie Dole, "Birth Pains of the 10th Mountain Division," in *Tenth Mountain Division* (Paducah, KY: Turner Publishing Co., 1998), p. 52; Burton, *The Ski Troops*, pp. 139–40; Rottman, *US 10th Mountain Division in World War II*, pp. 24, 33.

"What amazed us": Ellis, *See Naples and Die*, p. 91; Shelton, *Climb to Conquer*, p. 115.

"my last uncensored letter": Harris Dusenbery to Evelyn, November 27 and December 3, 1944, Harris Dusenbery Papers, TMD57, 10th Mountain Division Papers, Denver Public Library.

123 *"Christmas carols were sung"*: Donald B. Potter to his mother, December 25, 1944, Potter family papers.

"Happy New Year darling": Marty Daneman to Lois, December 31, 1944, Martin L. Daneman Papers, TMD25, 10th Mountain Division Papers, Denver Public Library.

6. Italy, December 23, 1944–February 18, 1945: "Still Green"

125 *next-to-last US Army division:* William Reginald Wheeler, ed., *The Road to Victory: A History of Hampton Roads Port of Embarkation in World War II*, vol. 1 (Newport News, VA, and New Haven, CT: Yale University Press, 1946), p. 20.

126 *enlisted men got two meals:* On the departure of the *Argentina*, see Harris Dusenbery, *The North Apennines and Beyond with the 10th Mountain Division* (Portland, OR: Binford and Mort, 1998), p. 5. On dining arrangements, see Stan Cummings to Jean Cummings, January 7, 1945, Stan and Jean Cummings Papers, TMD7, 10th Mountain Division Papers, Denver Public Library. Also see Flint Whitlock and Bob Bishop, *Soldiers on Skis: A Pictorial Memoir of the 10th Mountain Division* (Boulder: Paladin Press, 1992), p. 61. After the war, Richard M. Calvert, HQ Company, 2nd Battalion, 86th Regiment, put together two scrapbooks documenting his military experience. In one he pasted a copy of the officers' menu for breakfast, lunch, and dinner aboard the *Argentina*. The dinner menu included salmon and steak entrees. Calvert penciled in a parenthetical comment, "We got garbage & only twice daily." Scrapbook A, Richard M. Calvert Papers, TMD189, 10th Mountain Division Papers, Denver Public Library.

"Just the smell of food": H. Robert Krear, *The Journal of a US Army Mountain Trooper in World War II* (self-published, 1993), p. 29; Whitlock and Bishop, *Soldiers on Skis*, p. 61; Charles Wellborn, "History of the 86th Mountain Infantry in Italy" (Denver: Bradford-Robinson Printing Co., 1945), p. 1.

"We've been having a good trip": Harris Dusenbery to Evelyn, December 17, 1944, Harris Dusenbery Papers, TMD57, 10th Mountain Division Papers, Denver Public Library. Also see Dusenbery, *The North Apennines and Beyond*, pp. 5–7.

127 *Colonel Robinson E. Duff:* Whitlock and Bishop, *Soldiers on Skis*, p. 60.

"Moorish galleys": Dusenbery, *The North Apennines and Beyond*, p. 9.

The Argentina *finally arrived:* Krear, *The Journal of a US Army Mountain Trooper*, pp. 30–31; Dusenbery, *The North Apennines and Beyond*, pp. 10–11; David R. Brower, ed., *Remount Blue: The Combat Story of the Third Battalion, 86th Mountain Infantry* (Berkeley, CA, 1948), pp. 1–2. There is some dispute among published sources as to when the *Argentina* docked in Naples, with dates variously given as December 22, December 23, or Christmas Eve. Official records of troopship departures and arrivals were for some reason destroyed after the war. This account relies on Wellborn, "History of the 86th Mountain Infantry in Italy," p. 1.

"It's a long way": Whitlock and Bishop, *Soldiers on Skis*, p. 61; Peter Shelton, *Climb to Conquer: The Untold Story of World War II's Tenth Mountain Division Ski Troops* (New York: Scribner, 2003), p. 123; Robert B. Ellis, *See Naples and Die: A World War II Memoir of a United States Army Ski Trooper in the Mountains of Italy* (Jefferson, NC: McFarland, 1996), p. 96; Gerald Buckley Cullinane, "From Student to Soldier: My War Years, 1941–1945," typescript, p. 38, Gerald Buckley Cullinane Papers, TMD38, 10th Mountain Division Papers, Denver Public Library.

128 *"used to be a luxury liner"*: Marty Daneman to Lois Zora Miller, n.d. [January 1945], Martin L. Daneman Papers, TMD25, 10th Mountain Division Papers, Denver Public Library.

Ellis noted in his diary: Ellis, *See Naples and Die*, pp. 96–99; John Imbrie, "Chronology of the 10th Mountain Division in World War II," p. 10, http://10thmtndivassoc.org/chronology.pdf, p. 12.

"It is astonishing": Norman Lewis, *Naples '44: A World War II Diary of Occupied Italy* (New York: Carroll & Graf, 1978), p. 43.

Conditions had not changed much: Lewis, *Naples '44*, p. 122.

Eric Sevareid, a war correspondent: Eric Sevareid, *Not So Wild a Dream* (New York: Knopf, 1958), p. 375.

129 *"I feel like J. P. Morgan"*: Stan Cummings to Jean Cummings, January 15, 1945, Stan and Jean Cummings Papers, TMD7, 10th Mountain Division Collection, Denver Public Library.

"the people either work for us": Marty Daneman to Lois Zora Miller, January 17, 1945, Martin L. Daneman Papers, TMD25, 10th Mountain Division Papers, Denver Public Library. Shortly after the 10th reached Italy, their divisional newspaper, now called *The Blizzard*, began publishing a weekly edition from an office in Florence. An early issue included an article highlighting tourist attractions in the division's port of entry. Naples was truly a city of con-

trasts, according to *The Blizzard*'s reporter, with "its breathtaking architecture" combined with "barefoot children tugging at your sleeve and pandering for their sisters." "Beauty and Dirt—That's Naples," *The Blizzard*, February 17, 1945, p. 3. Also see Douglas Porch, *The Path to Victory: The Mediterranean Theater in World War II* (New York: Farrar, Straus and Giroux, 2004), pp. 516–20.

Long before the 10th Mountain Division: Thomas R. Brooks, *The War North of Rome: June 1944–May 1945* (New York: Da Capo Press, 2003), p. 331. The term "forgotten front" even turned up in official publications of the 15th Army group. Allied Forces, 15th Army Group, *Finito! The Po Valley Campaign, 1945* (Milan: Rizzoli, 1945), p. 5.

"The war in Italy was tough": Ernie Pyle, *Brave Men* (New York: Henry Holt, 1944), p. 37. Pyle's most famous dispatch from Italy, "The Death of Captain Waskow," dateline January 10, 1944, was not about victory but about a beloved young company commander's death in combat, and was reprinted in *Brave Men*—a book published shortly before the 10th's departure for Italy.

130 *"Only the names of places":* Ernest Hemingway, *A Farewell to Arms* (New York: Charles Scribner's Sons, 1929), pp. 177–78.

131 *more than 150 percent:* Brooks, *The War North of Rome*, p. 332; Porch, *The Path to Victory*, p. 521; "History of the 34th Division: World War II, 1941–1945," http://www.34thinfantry.com/history/history-34th.html.

"In the big push": Sevareid, *Not So Wild a Dream*, p. 389. Wartime censorship prevented Sevareid and other correspondents from sharing this grim perspective with readers at home during the five months he spent in the Mediterranean theater in the spring and summer of 1944. But after he left Italy for London, Sevareid offered a witheringly critical view of the Italian campaign in the liberal *Nation* magazine: "The Allied peoples—and history—may well ask whether the bloody Italian campaign has been a 'victory,' whether, indeed, it has accomplished anything of a decisive nature." Eric Sevareid, "The Price We Pay in Italy," *The Nation*, December 9, 1944, pp. 713–14.

132 *allowed a formidable enemy:* Rick Atkinson, *The Day of Battle: The War in Sicily and Italy, 1943–1944* (New York: Henry Holt, 2007), pp. 548–49; Carlo D'Este, *World War II in the Mediterranean, 1942–1945* (Chapel Hill, NC: Algonquin Books, 1990), pp. 166–77; Porch, *The Path to Victory*, pp. 551, 559–60.

"morale is irresistibly high": Quoted in Rick Atkinson, *The Guns at Last Light: The War in Western Europe, 1944–1945* (New York: Henry Holt, 2013), p. 578.

German forces in Italy: The Germans later renamed it the Green Line (Grüne Linie), but to the Allies it remained the Gothic Line. Ian Kershaw, *Hitler, 1936–1945: Nemesis* (New York: W. W. Norton, 2000), p. 759; Andrea and Guiliano Gandolfi, *Sulle Orme di Mio Padre* (Bologna: Edizione Re Enzo, 2006), p. 16.

133 *General Heinrich von Vietinghoff:* Clark quoted in John Imbrie and Thomas R. Brooks, *10th Mountain Division Campaign in Italy, 1945* (Forest Hills, NY: National Association of the 10th Mountain Division, 2002), p. 3; Brooks, *The War North of Rome,* pp. 156–93; Mark Clark, *Calculated Risk* (New York: Harper and Brothers, 1950), pp. 376–78, 391; Dwight D. Oland, *North Apennines, 10 September 1944-4 April 1945,* Pub. 72-34 (Washington, DC: US Government Printing Office, U.S. Army Center of Military History, n.d.), pp. 4–22, http://www.history.army.mil/brochures/nap/72-34.htm.

134 *The offensive was halfhearted:* Wellborn, "History of the 86th Mountain Infantry in Italy," p. 2; Brooks, *The War North of Rome,* p. 90; Charles J. Sanders, *The Boys of Winter: Life and Death in the U.S. Ski Troops During the Second World War* (Boulder: University Press of Colorado, 2005), p. 118. For the history of the 92nd, see Daniel K. Gibran, *The 92nd Infantry Division and the Italian Campaign in World War II* (Jefferson, NC: McFarland & Co., 2001).
"We could now hear the rumble": Brower, *Remount Blue,* p. 4.
"Winter always seemed to catch": Atkinson, *The Guns at Last Light,* p. 337.
"I've never spent such miserable nights": Jack R. Smolenske to "folks," January 25, 1945, Jack R. Smolenske Papers, TMD70, 10th Mountain Division Papers, Denver Public Library. Also see McKay Jenkins, *The Last Ridge: The Epic Story of the US Army's 10th Mountain Division and the Assault on Hitler's Europe* (New York: Random House, 2003), p. 149; John Imbrie and Hugh Evans, eds., *Good Times and Bad Times: A History of C Company, 85th Mountain Infantry Regiment, 10th Mountain Division, July 1943 to November 1945* (Quechee, VT: Vermont Heritage Press, 1995), p. 134; William Lowell Putnam, *Green Cognac: The Education of a Mountain Fighter* (New York: AAC Press, 1991), p. 90. Before the 10th shipped out for Italy, Minnie Dole received a letter from an irate officer in the division complaining about the army's decision to leave most of the specialized cold weather gear behind. Whoever was responsible, the officer wrote, "is unfamiliar with the nomenclature of the equipment, and thinks of our boots, ski-mountain, as something the boys use in recreational skiing. That is not the case. I don't care if we never see a ski—the boot is the best all purpose boot the Army ever developed. With this boot, Trench Foot becomes practically extinct . . . The sleeping bag is essentially in the same category. The Mountain (or Arctic Bag) is the only one which is adequate for bitter cold weather . . . Now we have these bags in Boston—but we will not get them . . . In closing I wish to say, the *tragedy* of it all is just this. We have spent three years developing this clothing and equipment. We may now be denied the use of it at a time when we may really need it." Dole forwarded the letter to Army Chief of Staff George C. Marshall, minus the officer's name, but the cold weather gear remained behind. [Name deleted] to Dole, December 6, 1944, Charles Minot Dole Papers, WH1001, Western History Collection, Denver Public Library. Marshall forwarded the letter to the

commander of the 10th, General George P. George Hays, who responded with a curt note directly to Dole telling him to mind his own business. Shelton, *Climb to Conquer,* p. 116.

135 *Following the capture of Rome:* D'Este, *World War II in the Mediterranean,* p. 199.

Truscott was pleased: For biographies of Truscott, see Wilson A. Heefner, *Dogface Soldier: The Life of General Lucian K. Truscott, Jr.* (Columbia: University of Missouri Press, 2010); and Harvey Ferguson, *The Last Cavalryman: The Life of General Lucian K. Truscott, Jr.* (Norman: University of Oklahoma Press, 2015), pp. 256–57. Also see Lieutenant General L. K. Truscott Jr., *Command Missions: A Personal Story* (New York: E. P. Dutton, 1954).

Hagan was one of three: Albert H. Meinke, *Mountain Troops and Medics: A Complete WWII Combat History of the U.S. Tenth Mountain Division* (Victoria, BC: Trafford, 2002), pp. 42–46. The other two 10th Mountain chaplains killed over the next few months were First Lieutenant William S. Contino and Captain Harry Montgomery. Chaplains in general had a surprisingly high mortality rate throughout the military, but even more so in the 10th; a total of twenty-four army chaplains died in the European theater of operations during the war, which means that one in eight of those killed was assigned to the mountain troops. I owe the information on the date, number of casualties, and 10th chaplain casualties to David Little and his scrutiny of the 10th Mountain database: 10th Mountain Division Database Records, TMD2, 10th Mountain Division Resource Center, Denver Public Library. For overall army chaplain casualties, see "The Chaplain Corps," WW2 US Medical Research Centre, https://www.med-dept.com/articles/the-chaplain-corps/.

Medic Arthur G. Draper: Arthur G. Draper, "Doughnuts to Doughnuts with the Mountain Troops," *American Ski Annual* (1945–46): 38; Wellborn, "History of the 86th Mountain Infantry in Italy," p. 3. There were four deaths of Kiska from mines and booby traps, but it's not clear how many, if any, of those were 10th Mountain men.

136 *saluting was forbidden:* Putnam, *Green Cognac,* p. 95; Meinke, *Mountain Troops and Medics,* p. 47.

"soon in snow-covered mountains": Brower, *Remount Blue,* p. 7.

There was indeed some resemblance: Lieutenant Colonel Henry J. Hampton, "The Riva Ridge Operation" (1945), p. 1; Wellborn, "History of the 86th Mountain Infantry in Italy," p. 6.

137 *Mount Monadnock:* Hal Burton, *The Ski Troops* (New York: Simon and Schuster, 1971), p. 158.

29th Panzer Grenadier Division: CSI Battlebook: Operation Encore (Fort Leavenworth, KS: Combat Studies Institute, 1984), pp. 2, 25–26; Brooks, *The War North of Rome,* p. 354: Brooks, "10th Mountain Division History," p. 30.

"in the bottom of a bowl": CSI Battlebook, p. 28; Wellborn, "History of the 86th Mountain Infantry in Italy," p. 3; William Ware, "The Riva Ridge,"

American Alpine Journal (1947), http://publications.americanalpineclub.org/articles/12194620800/The-Riva-Ridge; Hampton, "The Riva Ridge Operation," pp. 1–2.

138 *"Italians would be an okay bunch"*: Denis P. Nunan to Mr. and Mrs. Richard D. Rickard, April 5, 1945, Denis P. Nunan Papers, TMD33, 10th Mountain Division Collection, Denver Public Library.

"the Italians gave a dance": Harris Dusenbery to Evelyn, January 21, 1945, Harris Dusenbery Papers, TMD57, 10th Mountain Division Collection, Denver Public Library. Also see Shelton, *Climb to Conquer*, p. 124.

"The terracing of the hills": V-mail from John Parker Compton to "Family," January 31, 1945, John Parker Compton Papers, TMD42, 10th Mountain Division Collection, Denver Public Library.

A lively and mutually beneficial: For the cigarette pack economy, see Dusenbery, *The North Apennines and Beyond*, pp. 40–41; Marty Daneman, *Do Well or Die: Memoirs of a WWII Mountain Trooper* (Brule, WI: Cable Publishing, 2012), p. 78; Meinke, *Mountain Troops and Medics*, p. 69.

There were ghost villages: Mässimo Turchi, *La Linea Gotica e le Stragi* (Roma: Prospettiva editrice, n.d.), p. 153; Massimo Turchi, "Ca' Berna, Lizzano in Belvedere, 27.09.1944," http://www.straginazifasciste.it/?page_id=38&id_strage=5166.

139 *"Tedeschi portati tutti via"*: Putnam, *Green Cognac*, p. 87.

"These people are typical": Donald Potter to "Mom," January 28 [1945], Potter family collection. The correct spelling of the family's name was pointed out to me by Massimo Turchi. For a similar account of a family-like bond between villagers and soldiers, see Robert Woody, "Charley Red One — Over and Out," in Imbrie and Evans, *Good Times and Bad Times*, 136–38. On Italian-speaking GIs, see Putnam, *Green Cognac*, p. 84. On learning Italian from an army phrase book, see Dusenbery, *The North Apennines and Beyond*, pp. 33–34.

140 *"Anyway I got enough to eat"*: Stuart Abbott to family, February 6, 1945, Stuart E. Abbott Papers, TMD50, 10th Mountain Division Collection, Denver Public Library. On the use of searchlights, see Dusenbery, *The North Apennines and Beyond*, p. 27.

"I'm living for the day": Stuart Abbott to family, February 6, 1945, Stuart E. Abbott Papers, TMD50, 10th Mountain Division Collection, Denver Public Library.

"I have been at the front": Francis X. Limmer to "folks," January 19, 1945, Francis X. Limmer Papers, TMD309, 10th Mountain Division Papers, Denver Public Library. In the official 1945 "History of the 86th Mountain Infantry in Italy," p. 7, Charles Wellborn described the regiment's initial month on the line as almost "too calm and uneventful," saying that "most of the men" expected "something more important, more exciting, more deadly in the future."

mountain troopers suffered some casualties: "Sergeant Hall's Men Won't Forget How He Won the Silver Star," *The Blizzard,* February 17, 1945, p. 1; Wellborn, "History of the 86th Mountain Infantry in Italy," p. 6; Ray King, "North Attleborough Soldiers, Sailors and Marines Lost During WWII," p. 8, http://www.orgsites.com/ma/vfwpost443/NorthAttleboroWWII.pdf.

141 *"An 88 shell is the worst":* Stan Cummings to Jean Cummings, January 22, 1945, Stan and Jean Cummings Papers, TMD7, 10th Mountain Division Collection, Denver Public Library.

PFC Bob Krear: To slaughter an enemy "in cold blood" was, Krear observed, "a lot to ask of sensitive, highly intelligent men, some of whom had just left their university classrooms a few months previously!" Krear, "The Journal of a US Army Mountain Trooper," pp. 37–38.

142 *"As I expected, Argiewicz was dead":* Krear, "The Journal of a US Army Mountain Trooper," pp. 38–39.

"The hardening process": Krear, "The Journal of a US Army Mountain Trooper," p. 40. David Brower also included an account of his friend and fellow climbing instructor Argiewicz's death in *Remount Blue* but failed to mention it was the result of friendly fire. In 1948, when this account was published, that was still too raw and dismaying a reality to be shared in print, although few veterans would have been surprised by the information. Brower, *Remount Blue,* pp. 11–12. Also see Skyler Bailey, "First Blood in the 10th Mountain Division: The Skirmish at Querciola," http://www.skylerbaileyauthor.com/first-blood-in-the-10th-mountain-division-the-skirmish-at-querciola/.

"We ordered him": Quoted in Whitlock and Bishop, *Soldiers on Skis,* p. 67. Flint Whitlock's interviews with several dozen 10th Mountain veterans in his research for his 1992 history are an invaluable resource for anyone interested in retelling the history of the division at a time when most of the veterans are long departed. Also see Shelton, *Climb to Conquer,* pp. 4–5; Sanders, *The Boys of Winter,* p. 126.

Patrols helped season: Brooks, "10th Mountain Division History," p. 10.

But there is some dispute: Burton, *The Ski Troops,* p. 148. Another 10th veteran, Thomas Brooks, repeats the three patrol figure. Brooks, *The War North of Rome,* p. 352. Also see Shelton, *Climb to Conquer,* p. 125.

144 *"Two winters at Camp Hale":* Dick Nebeker to Glen Hines, Richard H. Nebeker Papers, M2168, 10th Mountain Division Archives, Denver Public Library; John B. Woodruff, "History of the 85th Mountain Infantry in Italy, 4 January 1945–31 May 1945" (1945), p. 2. George F. Earle of the 87th suggested another reason why skis were impractical in the conditions found in the northern Apennines: "The Italian snow was corn snow, from all that sunlight. If we'd had nice powder, I'm sure we could have made use of them for patrol work." There were a few attempts at nighttime ski patrols, but "all of them had to withdraw quickly . . . because the Germans could hear them coming. The sound of the skis on the corn snow was quite loud." George F. Earle, "Paint-

ing with the Tenth Mountain," in *Alaska at War, 1941–1945, The Forgotten War Remembered,* ed. Fern Chandonnet (Fairbanks: University of Alaska Press, 2008), p. 55. Also see Sanders, *The Boys of Winter,* p. 120. For a contrary view, arguing that in those first days on the front the term "ski trooper" was well deserved, see veteran Al Field's account, "Combat Ski Patrols," *The Blizzard,* no. 1 (2007): 6.

The losses certainly stung: A list of some of the more significant patrols undertaken by all three regiments of the 10th in the first month and a half on the line is included in Imbrie and Brooks, *10th Mountain Division Campaign in Italy,* p. 4. Imbrie and Brooks report eight men of the 10th were taken prisoner in this period, but Woodruff, "History of the 85th Mountain Infantry in Italy," p. 3, reports nine prisoners taken from that regiment alone on January 30, 1945.

"Crazy as it may sound": Marty Daneman to Lois, January 29, 1945, Martin L. Daneman Papers, TMD25, 10th Mountain Division Papers, Denver Public Library. Also see Daneman, *Do Well or Die,* p. 75.

Unlike on Kiska: "Po Valley 1945," https://history.army.mil/brochures/po/72-33.htm; Porch, *The Path to Victory,* p. 642; Ferguson, *The Last Cavalryman,* p. 303.

145 *"The Stars and Stripes":* Harris Dusenbery to Evelyn, January 17, 1945, Harris Dusenbery Papers, TMD57, 10th Mountain Division Collection, Denver Public Library.

"All of us are anxiously": Earl E. Clark to "Mother, Nana and all," February 3, 1945, Earl E. Clark Papers, TMD8, 10th Mountain Division Collection, Denver Public Library.

"Berlin 68 Miles Away": The Blizzard, February 1, 1945, p. 1. The Soviet winter offensive is chronicled in Anthony Beevor, *The Fall of Berlin 1945* (New York: Viking, 2002), pp. 24–135.

Italy did not figure: Atkinson, *The Guns at Last Light,* pp. 577–78; Ferguson, *The Last Cavalryman,* p. 303; Sanders, *The Boys of Winter,* p. 125.

146 *"a frightful waste of lives":* Sevareid, *Not So Wild a Dream,* p. 427.

Anglo-American forces in Italy: Russell F. Weigley, *The American Way of War: A History of United States Military Strategy and Policy* (Bloomington: Indiana University Press, 1973), p. 327.

"like other human enterprises": Ernest F. Fischer Jr., *The Mediterranean Theater of Operations: Cassino to the Alps* (Washington, DC: US Army Center of Military History, 1977), pp. 373–74.

147 *That meant the Germans:* Atkinson, *The Guns at Last Light,* pp. 591–93; Porch, *The Path to Victory,* p. 642; Fischer, *The Mediterranean Theater of Operations,* pp. 437, 443. A week before the 10th Mountain Division would resume the Allied advance in the northern Apennines, the *New York Times* ran a feature story about the supposed Alpine redoubt. Even after the fall of Berlin, the *Times* reporter wrote, "organized fighting may still go on for another year or more in a last corner of Hitler's defunct European fortress . . . It

would be comparatively easy to defend this 'fortress' for a very long time with some twenty divisions, perhaps much less, behind the formidable barrier of the gigantic chain of central and eastern Alps." Victor Schiff, "'Last Fortress' of the Nazis," *New York Times Sunday Magazine,* February 11, 1945, p. 5. Also see the follow-up story, "Germans Speed Arms to Mountains as Allies Map Their Destruction," *New York Times,* March 24, 1945.

cut off the line of retreat: Porch, *The Path to Victory,* pp. 642–44; Fischer, *The Mediterranean Theater of Operations,* pp. 448–49.

From the summit: Dominick Graham and Shelford Bidwell, *Tug of War: The Battle for Italy, 1943–45* (New York: St. Martin's Press, 1986), p. 390; Fischer, *The Mediterranean Theater of Operations,* pp. 424–27; Brooks, *The War North of Rome,* pp. 305–9, 354.

148 *a war dog platoon: CSI Battlebook,* pp. 23, 25; "Expert Alpini Mule Skinners Are Veterans of Cassino," *The Blizzard,* February 27, 1945, p. 6. For an appreciation of the Italian mules by a 10th soldier, see Linwood Erskine, recollections, TMD309, 10th Mountain Division Personal Papers, 10th Mountain Division Collection, Denver Public Library. Also see Meinke, *Mountain Troops and Medics,* p. 107.

The German defenders: CSI Battlebook, pp. 17–21; Shelton, *Climb to Conquer,* p. 126; Brooks, *The War North of Rome,* pp. 305–9.

"This is a mountain division": George P. Hays, "Personal Memoirs of Lt. General George Price Hays, 1892–1978," typescript, pp. 33–34, George P. Hays Papers, TMD61, 10th Mountain Division Papers, Denver Public Library; Brooks, "10th Mountain Division History," p. 30; Jenkins, *The Last Ridge,* p. 152; Burton, *The Ski Troops,* pp. 151–52.

149 *Soldiers cut steps:* Hampton, "The Riva Ridge Operation," pp. 3–4; Ware, "The Riva Ridge"; Jenkins, *The Last Ridge,* pp. 156–59; Shelton, *Climb to Conquer,* p. 127; Whitlock and Bishop, *Soldiers on Skis,* pp. 74–75.

150 *everyone would go:* Hampton, "The Riva Ridge Operation," p. 5; Jenkins, *The Last Ridge,* pp. 159–60; Burton, *The Ski Troops,* p. 154.

General Hays's plan: Ware, "The Riva Ridge."

151 *very few battles in history:* Hampton, "The Riva Ridge Operation," p. 6; Charles W. Webb, *Field Artillery, the King of Battle: A History of the 616th Field Artillery (Pack)* (Dalton, GA: Charles W. Webb, 1996), pp. 133–34.

152 *They had faith:* Shelton, *Climb to Conquer,* pp. 128–29.

A dance, a USO show: "Hale Skiers Sweep Steamboat Carnival" and "Hale's Own Musical Comedy, 'Hale and Hearty,' Shows February 22–23," *Camp Hale Ski-Zette,* February 18, 1944, p. 1.

90 percent casualty rate: Meinke, *Mountain Troops and Medics,* p. 87; Shelton, *Climb to Conquer,* pp. 131–32.

"Night after night we brought": Stan Cummings to Jean Cummings, February 22, 1945, Stan and Jean Cummings Papers, TMD7, 10th Mountain Division Collection, Denver Public Library.

153 *"All sounds are muffled":* Marlin Wineberg "Diary," Marlin Wineberg Papers, TMD297, 10th Mountain Division Papers, Denver Public Library.
154 *they were to take the ridgeline:* Jenkins, *The Last Ridge,* pp. 166–67; Whitlock and Bishop, *Soldiers on Skis,* p. 77; Ware, "The Riva Ridge."
155 *Neidner had no word:* Hampton, "The Riva Ridge Operation," pp. 7–10; Wellborn, "History of the 86th Mountain Infantry in Italy," p. 10; Jenkins, *The Last Ridge,* pp. 167–73; Sanders, *The Boys of Winter,* p. 133.
Finally, about 6:30 a.m.: Hampton, "The Riva Ridge Operation," p. 10; Ware, "The Riva Ridge."

7. Italy, February 19–April 13, 1945: "Front Line Soldiers"

158 *Tokle came away with:* For soldiers in the Second World War, acquiring souvenirs was a major preoccupation. Tenth Mountain Division commander George P. Hays endorsed the right of his men to keep any German pistols that came their way, even machine pistols, although importing automatic weapons into the United States was illegal. Marty Daneman brought two German pistols and a burp gun back with him in August 1945, only to have the latter confiscated before he was allowed to disembark in New York. Marty Daneman, *Do Well or Die: Memoirs of a WWII Mountain Trooper* (Brule, WI: Cable Publishing, 2012), pp. 159–60; "Burp Gun All Yours Says Top," *The Blizzard,* February 17, 1945, p. 1. General Hays prohibited taking "personal items" from prisoners, such as cash or watches, a rule that seems to have been widely ignored. See, for example, Robert Woody, "Charlie Red One — Over and Out," in *Good Times and Bad Times: A History of C Company, 85th Mountain Infantry Regiment, 10th Mountain Division, July 1943 to November 1945,* ed. John Imbrie and Hugh Evans (Quechee, VT: Vermont Heritage Press, 1995), p. 151. And enemy corpses were definitely regarded as fair game, with one case recorded of a trooper cutting off the finger of a dead German to acquire a ring. See Stan Cummings to Jean Cummings, February 29, 1945 [misdated], Stan and Jean Cummings Papers, TMD7, 10th Mountain Division Papers, Denver Public Library.
But they held their ground: Henry J. Hampton, "The Riva Ridge Operation" (1945), p. 10; McKay Jenkins, *The Last Ridge: The Epic Story of the US Army's 10th Mountain Division and the Assault on Hitler's Europe* (New York: Random House, 2003), pp. 171, 174.
This made the difference: Peter Shelton, *Climb to Conquer: The Untold Story of World War II's Tenth Mountain Division Ski Troops* (New York: Scribner, 2003), p. 136.
"old men and kids": Charles Wellborn, "History of the 86th Mountain Infantry in Italy" (Denver: Bradford-Robinson Printing Co., 1945), p. 11.
"The army made a mistake": Flint Whitlock and Bob Bishop, *Soldiers on Skis: A Pictorial Memoir of the 10th Mountain Division* (Boulder: Paladin Press, 1992), p. 77.

159 *"Do you realize":* "Battle Around Belvedere Spreads to Sector on Right; Enemy Counterattack Repulsed, Our Forces Pushing On," *The Blizzard,* February 21, 1945, p. 1; Jenkins, *The Last Ridge,* p. 177; Hal Burton, *The Ski Troops* (New York: Simon and Schuster, 1971), pp. 155–56; Thomas R. Brooks, "10th Mountain Division History," in *Tenth Mountain Division* (Paducah, KY: Turner Publishing, 1998), p. 30.

"It's Hank!": Burton, *The Ski Troops,* p. 156.

Loose received a Silver Star: "Battle Around Belvedere Spreads to Sector on Right; Enemy Counterattack Repulsed, Our Forces Pushing On," *The Blizzard,* February 21, 1945, p. 1; Hampton, "The Riva Ridge Operation," p. 10; Wellborn, "History of the 86th Mountain Infantry in Italy," pp. 10–11; Whitlock and Bishop, *Soldiers on Skis,* pp. 84–86; Jenkins, *The Last Ridge,* p. 177. For the German and American casualties in the first two days of battle for Pizzo di Campiano, see the "Battalion Journal" reprinted in Harris Dusenbery, *The North Apennines and Beyond with the 10th Mountain Division* (Portland, OR: Binford and Mort, 1998), p. 225.

The Germans' counterattacks: Jenkins, *The Last Ridge,* p. 177. Four more 10th troopers died on Riva Ridge before the German counterattacks ceased on February 25. See John Imbrie and Thomas R. Brooks, *10th Mountain Division Campaign in Italy, 1945* (Forest Hills, NY: National Association of the 10th Mountain Division, 2002), p. 6.

160 *No one saw that prisoner again:* For an overview of McCown's life, see "John Andrew McCown II, 1918–1945," *American Alpine Journal* (1945), http://publications.americanalpineclub.org/articles/12194614500/print. The obituary concluded: "John McCown was elected to the American Alpine Club in 1940, on the basis of four seasons of climbing, much of it in the Teton area, including four ascents of Grand Teton by various routes . . . Had he emerged from the war, his qualities of leadership would undoubtedly have secured him a notable position in expeditionary mountaineering." Also see Whitlock and Bishop, *Soldiers on Skis,* pp. 80–81; Shelton, *Climb to Conquer,* pp. 136–41; Jenkins, *The Last Ridge,* pp. 175–76.

in its first brief account: "Fifth Army Opens Offensive Against Mount Belvedere; Men Using Ropes Take Ridge on Stronghold's Flank," *The Blizzard,* February 20, 1945, p. 1.

A week later: "'I Am Very Proud of You'—The General," *The Blizzard,* February 27, 1945, p. 1.

In a companion article: "Tramway Saves Vital Hours Bringing Wounded Off Peak," *The Blizzard,* February 27, 1945, p. 5. Also see "Casualties Evacuated by Tram," *The Blizzard,* February 22, 1945, p. 1.

161 *And the tramway also carried:* "Tramway Saves Vital Hours Bringing Wounded Off Peak," *The Blizzard,* February 27, 1945, p. 5; Philip A. Lunday and Charles M. Hampton, *The Tramway Builders: A Brief History of Company D, 126th Engineer Mountain Battalion* (self-published, 1994), pp. 46–47, 119;

Imbrie and Brooks, *10th Mountain Division Campaign in Italy,* p. 6; Shelton, *Climb to Conquer,* pp. 138–40; Whitlock and Bishop, *Soldiers on Skis,* p. 88; "Fred Arthur Nagel," *Denver Post,* May 26, 2008. Although not directly engaged in combat, engineers suffered many casualties, including nine killed in action in the Italian campaign. They were often exposed to enemy fire, and their role in clearing mines was both essential and extremely hazardous work. A plaque at the foot of Riva Ridge, in the village of Ca' di Julio, near the base of the slope where the tramway stood, celebrates the engineers' work and sacrifices.

Meanwhile, a mile or two: CSI Battlebook: Operation Encore (Fort Leavenworth, KS: Combat Studies Institute, 1984), p. 40.

164 *sheer determination:* Thomas R. Brooks, *The War North of Rome: June 1944–May 1945* (New York: Da Capo Press, 2003), p. 354; Kenyon Cooke, "C Company in Action," in Imbrie and Evans, *Good Times and Bad Times,* pp. 55–56; H. Robert Krear, *The Journal of a U.S. Army Mountain Trooper in World War II* (Estes Park, CO: self-published, 1993), p. 42; George F. Earle, "History of the 87th Mountain Infantry in Italy" (1945), p. 12, https://www.scribd.com/document/94745160/WWII-87th-Infantry-Division.

Brazilian Expeditionary Force: CSI Battlebook, pp. 41–43; Jenkins, *The Last Ridge,* p. 165; Brooks, *The War North of Rome,* p. 355.

General Hays hoped: Brooks, "10th Mountain Division History," p. 30; John B. Woodruff, "History of the 85th Mountain Infantry in Italy, 4 January 1945–31 May 1945" (1945), p. 7; William Ware, "The Riva Ridge," *American Alpine Journal* (1947), http://publications.americanalpineclub.org/articles/12194620800/The-Riva-Ridge. Although Mazzancana is described as a village in some accounts, it seems to have been a single building. See Albert H. Meinke, *Mountain Troops and Medics: A Complete WWII Combat History of the U.S. Tenth Mountain Division* (Victoria, BC: Trafford, 2002), p. 93.

165 *"Our attack was to begin":* Hugh W. Evans, "What's Behind That Battle Star," *American Alpine Journal* (1946), http://publications.americanalpineclub.org/articles/12194619300/Whats-Behind-that-Battle-Star, reprinted in Hugh Evans, "Baptism on Belvedere," in Imbrie and Evans, *Good Times and Bad Times,* pp. 45–50.

At precisely 11 p.m.: Earle, "History of the 87th Mountain Infantry in Italy," pp. 11–12.

Each mortar's tube: Marlin Wineberg, typescript memoir written shortly after the war, Marlin Wineberg Papers, TMD297, 10th Mountain Division Papers, Denver Public Library; "Pillbox Destroyer," *Popular Science,* August 1943, pp. 118–19.

"The forward movement is more jerky": Wineberg, typescript memoir.

166 *"The mortar shells would not explode":* Krear, "The Journal of a US Army Mountain Trooper," pp. 43–44.

In his last letter home: Stuart E. Abbott to family, February 6 and February 15, 1945, Stuart E. Abbott Papers, TMD50, 10th Mountain Division Papers, Denver Public Library.

167 *"When we could get to him"*: Paul Anderson to Mrs. Abbott, August 27, 1945, Stuart E. Abbott Papers, TMD50, 10th Mountain Division Papers, Denver Public Library.

And, even more terrifying: Shelton, *Climb to Conquer,* p. 148.

"The war was over for me": Charles Page Smith, "Reflections on Company C," in Imbrie and Evans, *Good Times and Bad Times,* pp. 40–41; Whitlock and Bishop, *Soldiers on Skis,* p. 89; Woodruff, "History of the 85th Mountain Infantry in Italy," pp. 8, 11.

168 *"We might have surprised them"*: Woodruff, "History of the 85th Mountain Infantry in Italy," p. 8; Cooke, "C Company in Action," p. 57; Whitlock and Bishop, *Soldiers on Skis,* p. 93.

"When I saw the first casualty": Jack R. Smolenske to parents, March 11, 1945, Jack R. Smolenske Papers, TMD70, 10th Mountain Division Papers, Denver Public Library.

Among the dead: Earle, "History of the 87th Mountain Infantry in Italy," p. 15; "CSI Battlebook," p. 43; "More Than a Hundred Medal Winners Swell Division's Hero List," *The Blizzard,* March 15, 1945, p. 1.

Another Silver Star went to: "Division's List of Heroes Lengthens," *The Blizzard,* March 15, 1945, p. 6; Conrad Anthien to "10th Mountain Men," July 23, 1998, TMD309, 10th Mountain Division Personal Papers, 10th Mountain Division Collection, Denver Public Library; Earle, "History of the 87th Mountain Infantry in Italy," pp. 13–15.

169 *"all hell broke loose"*: Herbert Wright, "Combat: The Beginning—the End," in Imbrie and Evans, *Good Times and Bad Times,* p. 43.

171 *"Oh God. Please not now"*: Evans, "Baptism on Belvedere," p. 49.

"Bob was 20": Evans, "Baptism on Belvedere," p. 49.

"For the next ten minutes": Evans, "Baptism on Belvedere," p. 50.

"That's my brother": Evans, "Baptism on Belvedere," p. 50; Sanders, *The Boys of Winter,* p. 50. Stan Cummings was probably referring to Eugene Savage in a letter to his wife, Jean, written shortly after the war ended: "Did I ever write of a guy on Belvedere that was advancing in the attack when he came upon the body of his dead brother? Well, after that the company had a hard time keeping up with him and he shot everything in a German uniform under any and all circumstances." Stan Cummings to Jean Cummings, May 9, 1945, Stan and Jean Cummings Papers, 10th Mountain Division Papers, Denver Public Library.

C Company of the 85th lost: For C Company casualties, see Imbrie and Evans, *Good Times and Bad Times,* pp. 55, 63.

172 *"Krauts fought to the last bullet"*: Denis P. Nunan to his parents, May 2, 1945, Denis P. Nunan Papers, TMD33, 10th Mountain Division Papers, Denver Public Library. Also see Brooks, "10th Mountain Division History," p. 31.

"The German is a fantastic person": Earl E. Clark to his mother, February 23, 1945, Earl E. Clark Papers, TMD8, 10th Mountain Division Papers, Denver Public Library.

"23 Feb. 45": "Kraut Diary: 'I Have Had Just About Enough,'" *The Blizzard,* March 15, 1945, p. 2; Whitlock and Bishop, *Soldiers on Skis,* pp. 104–5.

173 *"seemed to be relieved":* Meinke, *Mountain Troops and Medics,* p. 110.

The Allies' absolute control: "Rover Joe Is Really a Bunch of Joes Who Tell the Spitfires Where to Spit," *The Blizzard,* March 7, 1945, p. 6.

Territory won with grenades: "The War Diary of Dan L. Kennerly," Dan L. Kennerly Papers, TMD309, 10th Mountain Division Papers, Denver Public Library; Jack R. Smolenske to parents, March 11, 1945, Jack R. Smolenske Papers, TMD70, 10th Mountain Division Papers, Denver Public Library.

174 *"It was horrible":* Jack R. Smolenske to "folks," March 11, 1945, Jack R. Smolenske Papers, TMD70, 10th Mountain Division Papers, Denver Public Library.

"They are lying everywhere": "The War Diary of Dan L. Kennerly," Dan L. Kennerly Papers, TMD309, 10th Mountain Division Papers, Denver Public Library.

175 *"like grotesque balloons":* Daneman, *Do Well or Die,* pp. 91–92; Whitlock and Bishop, *Soldiers on Skis,* p. 105.

176 *"better to have it happen":* Marty Daneman to Lois, March 9, 1945, Martin L. Daneman Papers, TMD25, 10th Mountain Division Collection, Denver Public Library. Also see Daneman, *Do Well or Die,* p. 88. A month later, in another letter to Lois, he returned to the question of how war had changed his outlook: "It's strange trying to stand off from myself and try to analyze myself — before + after Belvedere. Before I came over, + for a while afterwards — I actually itched for action — glory boy that I was, but it sure changed fast." Marty Daneman to Lois Miller, April 4, 1945, Martin L. Daneman Papers, TMD25, 10th Mountain Division Collection, Denver Public Library.

"What the real story is": Stan Cummings to Jean Cummings, February 29, 1945 [misdated], Stan and Jean Cummings Papers, TMD7, 10th Mountain Division Collection, Denver Public Library. For the discovery of the corpses at Ronchidoso, see Corporal Mel Diamond, "82 Bodies Reveal Nazi Italy Atrocity," *Stars and Stripes,* March 23, 1945. (The official death toll was later set at sixty-eight.) Also see Massimo Turchi, "Ronchidoso, Gaggio Montano, Bologna, 28–30.09.1944," http://www.straginazifasciste.it/?page_id=38&id_strage=5168. Field Marshal Albert Kesselring was convicted of war crimes by a military tribunal in 1947 in connection with the massacre of civilians in Italy and initially sentenced to death. He was spared that fate and was sentenced instead to life imprisonment. In 1952 his sentence was commuted to time served and he was released from prison. Shelford Bidwell, "Field Marshal Albert Kesselring," in *Hitler's Generals,* ed. Correlli Barnett (New York: Grove Weidenfeld, 1989), pp. 286–87.

the most difficult and prolonged: CSI Battlebook, pp. 43–45.

177 *"we stepped over and around":* Jack Leslie's postwar letter describing his experience in the battle is reprinted in Krear, "The Journal of a US Army Mountain Trooper," p. 47.

"Dug in on crest of ridge": "Transcription of War Diary," Robert B. Ellis Papers, TMD58, 10th Mountain Division Collection, Denver Public Library.

178 *still a few months shy:* Jenkins, *The Last Ridge,* p. 194.

He was the only officer: Levitan's personal account of his capture and his experiences as a POW are reprinted in A. B. Feuer, ed., *Packs On! Memoirs of the 10th Mountain Division in World War II* (Mechanicsburg, PA: Stackpole Books, 2004), pp. 62–70.

Daneman's was particularly scathing: For Daneman's appraisal of Colonel Stone, see *Do Well or Die,* pp. 82–83, 120–21. Flint Whitlock, by contrast, notes that some of Stone's soldiers felt he was being scapegoated and treated unfairly. Whitlock and Bishop, *Soldiers on Skis,* p. 103. Also see Woodruff, "History of the 85th Mountain Infantry," p. 14; Burton, *The Ski Troops,* pp. 161–63; Sanders, *The Boys of Winter,* pp. 138–39.

"All nite we sweated out": "Transcription of War Diary," Robert B. Ellis Papers, TMD58, 10th Mountain Division Papers, Denver Public Library. Also see Robert B. Ellis, *See Naples and Die: A World War II Memoir of a United States Army Ski Trooper in the Mountains of Italy* (Jefferson, NC: McFarland, 1996), pp. 141–43.

179 *The twenty-eight-year-old Hay:* Meinke, *Mountain Troops and Medics,* p. 84; Sanders, *The Boys of Winter,* p. 112.

"Hell no": Wellborn, "History of the 86th Mountain Infantry in Italy," p. 16.

At dawn the counterattacks ceased: "How the 86th's 3rd Battalion Took the Peak of Belvedere," *The Blizzard,* March 7, 1945, p. 8; Richard M. Emerson, "A Squad Leader in Company I," in *Remount Blue: The Combat Story of the Third Battalion, 86th Mountain Infantry,* ed. David R. Brower (Berkeley, CA, 1948), pp. 16–18; Brooks, *The War North of Rome,* pp. 355–57; Whitlock and Bishop, *Soldiers on Skis,* pp. 102–3; Sanders, *The Boys of Winter,* pp. 138–39; *CSI Battlebook,* pp. 46–50; Brooks, "10th Mountain Division History," p. 31.

Among the last Americans to die: Sanders, *The Boys of Winter,* pp. 141–43. A 10,225-foot peak in the Idaho Smoky Mountains was later named Bromaghin Peak in his honor.

180 *it took the 10th five days:* Imbrie and Brooks, *10th Mountain Division Campaign in Italy,* p. 7; Whitlock and Bishop, *Soldiers on Skis,* p. 107; Shelton, *Climb to Conquer,* p. 157; Brooks, "10th Mountain Division History," p. 32. Total casualties for the Belvedere-Torraccia attack vary slightly from one account to another.

"THE SECRETARY OF WAR DESIRES ME": Telegram to Mrs. Hallie E. Mur-

phy, 10th Mountain Division Personal Papers, TMD309, 10th Mountain Division Papers, Denver Public Library.

"American troops of the Fifth Army": Milton Bracker, "Americans Regain Italian Mountain," *New York Times*, February 22, 1945.

Reading between the lines: Burton, *The Ski Troops*, p. 157.

181 *"Made up of especially trained fighters"*: Milton Bracker, "Mountain Division with Fifth Army," *New York Times*, February 26, 1945.

"Using tactics old": "Italian Front, Red Spring," *Time*, March 19, 1945, p. 31. Also see Burton, *The Ski Troops*, p. 157; Jenkins, *The Last Ridge*, p. 210.

"your courage, determination": "'I Am Very Proud of You'—the General," *The Blizzard*, February 27, 1945, p. 1.

"well-worn and well-loved glove": Lieutenant General L. K. Truscott Jr., *Command Missions: A Personal Story* (New York: E. P. Dutton, 1954), p. 465; Burton, *The Ski Troops*, pp. 166–67.

Further congratulatory messages: "Five Commanders Congratulate Division on Operations," *The Blizzard*, March 15, 1945, p. 1. While words of praise from General Hays were welcomed by the mountain troopers, some of them regarded those from the other higher-ups with a measure of cynicism. "We received ponderous letters of commendation" following Belvedere, Robert Ellis noted, with each general "exulting over the accomplishment in the hope that his superior up the line would accord him some credit for its success." Ellis, *See Naples and Die*, p. 154.

182 *"To my surprise—in deep snow"*: Albert Kesselring, *The Memoirs of Field-Marshal Kesselring* (London: William Kimber, 1953), p. 220. Captured German intelligence reports described the 10th Mountain Division as consisting of "physically superior soldiers" as well as "sports personalities, and young men from wealthy or politically significant American families." Quoted in Earle, "History of the 87th Mountain Infantry in Italy," p. 46.

And the curved "MOUNTAIN" tabs: "You'll Have that Mountain Patch in a Couple of Weeks," *The Blizzard*, February 25, 1945, p. 1.

"I've been busy as hell lately": Joseph Berry to Mr. and Mrs. William B. Berry, 10th Mountain Division Personal Papers, TMD309, 10th Mountain Division Collection, Denver Public Library.

"Because the division was drawn largely": "The Mountain Troops Who Stormed Belvedere," *Yank*, March 16, 1945, p. 8.

183 *"The publicity they got"*: Corporal Renzo Guy's letter to the editor was pasted into a scrapbook kept by Richard M. Calvert, HQ Company, 2nd Battalion, 86th Regiment. Richard M. Calvert Papers, TMD189, 10th Mountain Division Papers, Denver Public Library. Also see Burton, *The Ski Troops*, p. 167.

"Rear echelon troops": "The War Diary of Dan L. Kennerly," TMD309, 10th Mountain Division Papers, Denver Public Library. Also see Shelton, *Climb to Conquer*, p. 170.

185 *"I was the one"*: Bob Dole, *One Soldier's Story: A Memoir* (New York:

HarperCollins, 2005), p. 11; Imbrie and Evans, *Good Times and Bad Times,* pp. 11, 13; Woodruff, "History of the 85th Mountain Infantry in Italy," p. 4.
Skier Debbie Bankart: "Red Cross's Debby Dishes Out Doughnuts, Skiing Chatter, and Feminine Charm," *The Blizzard,* February 17, 1945, p. 6; "Doughnut Girl Has Become Doughnut Duo," *The Blizzard,* February 27, 1945, p. 6; Whitlock and Bishop, *Soldiers on Skis,* p. 136; Arthur G. Draper, "Doughnuts to Doughnuts with the Mountain Troops," *American Ski Annual* (1945–46): 41. On rest and relaxation before the resumption of the offensive, see Dan L. Kennerly, "'You Have Come a Great Way from Colorado to Die': A 10th Mountain Division Diary of War in Italy," *Colorado Heritage* (Spring 2004): 10–11; Shelton, *Climb to Conquer,* pp. 157–58; Daneman, *Do Well or Die,* pp. 96–97; Woody, "Charlie Red One — Over and Out," p. 143.

189 *five of its seven objectives:* Wellborn, "History of the 86th Mountain Infantry in Italy," pp. 20–23; "CSI Battlebook," pp. 54–55. Iola today is home to the Museo Iola di Montese, which has an extensive exhibit devoted to the 10th Mountain's battles along the Gothic Line. http://www.sulleormedeinostri padri.it/it/.
"the land of olives and signorinas": Fred Wendorf, "Lieutenant, You're One Lucky Son of a Bitch," in Andrea and Giuliano Gandolfi, *Gotica Rosso Sangue* (Modena: Il Trebbo, 2016), pp. 44–45; John Parker Compton to parents, February 23, 1945, John Parker Compton Papers, TMD42, 10th Mountain Division Papers, Denver Public Library. After the war, Compton's family donated funds to help rebuild the church in Iola damaged in the fighting. A plaque in the memory of John Parker Compton is mounted on the outside wall of the church. And in 2005, a memorial bridge was dedicated in his memory at the site of Camp Hale. See Burton, *The Ski Troops,* pp. 164–65.

190 *When the news of his death:* "Foe Kills Tokle, Skiing Champion," *New York Times,* March 17, 1945, p. 5; Whitlock and Bishop, *Soldiers on Skis,* pp. 112–13; Shelton, *Climb to Conquer,* p. 159. Two days after the initial article, the *Times* ran a second piece profiling Tokle, praising his ski achievements and his sacrifice for his adopted country: "Ski Man," *New York Times,* March 19, 1945, p. 18. Research by Charles J. Sanders suggests that the round that killed Tokle and Tokola was friendly fire from an American battery. Sanders, *The Boys of Winter,* p. 148. Lieutenant Stan Cummings wrote to his wife, Jean, after news of Tokle's death appeared in papers in the United States: "So you heard the news of Tokle. It was in the papers here so I thought it would be released in the states too. You spoke of others in the old outfit that you knew who might have got the worst. We are not at liberty to mention names but I can allay your fears a lot. I can't recall anyone besides Tokle who was killed who you knew. Naturally many I knew got it. Several of our mutual friends were wounded but most of them are out of the hospital now and well again." Stan Cummings to Jean Cummings, March 29, 1945, Stan and Jean

Cummings Papers, TMD7, 10th Mountain Division Papers, Denver Public Library.

One other notable casualty: Douglas Martin, "Pete Seibert, Soldier Skier Who Built Vail, Is Dead at 77," *New York Times,* July 28, 2002; Sanders, *The Boys of Winter,* p. 147.

The worst loss: Earle, "History of the 87th Mountain Infantry in Italy," pp. 28–34; Brooks, "10th Mountain Division History," p. 31.

191 *the town of Sassomolare:* Wellborn, "History of the 86th Mountain Infantry in Italy," p. 25; Earle, "History of the 87th Mountain Infantry in Italy," pp. 34–37; Brooks, "10th Mountain Division History," p. 32.

The 87th continued its drive: Earle, "History of the 87th Mountain Infantry in Italy," p. 38.

192 *"this dung heap we've taken":* Kennerly, "'You Have Come a Long Way,'" pp. 19–20; "Nazis Snared by 85's Trapp," *The Blizzard,* March 15, 1945, p. 7; Woodruff, "History of the 85th Mountain Infantry in Italy," pp. 19–21; *CSI Battlebook,* p. 57; Imbrie and Brooks, *10th Mountain Division Campaign in Italy,* p. 12.

"B Co was on a bare knoll": Stan Cummings to Jean Cummings, May 10, 1945, Stan and Jean Cummings Papers, TMD7, 10th Mountain Division Papers, Denver Public Library.

193 *"A three-day offensive":* "Fifth Army Gains 5 Miles in 3 Days," *New York Times,* March 8, 1945. *The Blizzard* published more commendations from leading generals in the theater: "Five Commanders Congratulate Division on Operations," *The Blizzard,* March 15, 1945, p. 1.

"The crossing of the Rhine": Earl E. Clark to "Mother, Nana and all," March 16, 1945, Earl E. Clark Papers, TMD8, 10th Mountain Division Collection, Denver Public Library.

194 *Field Marshal Kesselring admitted:* Kesselring, *The Memoirs of Field-Marshal Kesselring,* p. 220; "Mountaineers Push Surprised Krauts from Ten Peaks," *The Blizzard,* March 7, 1945, p. 1.

The cost to the 10th: Imbrie and Brooks, *10th Mountain Division Campaign in Italy,* p. 12; Brooks, "10th Mountain Division History," p. 32.

"too quiet and spring like": "Birds and Bees Take Over After War Leaves Battlefield," *The Blizzard,* April 8, 1945, p. 4. On civilian refugees, see Earle, "History of the 87th Mountain Infantry in Italy," p. 45.

195 *"The place is littered with bars":* Martin Daneman Lois Miller, March 23, 1945, Martin L. Daneman Papers, TMD25, 10th Mountain Division Collection, Denver Public Library.

Easter Sunday fell on April 1: "Division Celebrates Easter in Spring Setting—For Once," *The Blizzard,* April 8, 1945, p. 1. Kenyon Clarke describes a Catholic Easter service in "C Company in Action," p. 82.

"one of those delightful Spring days": Arthur G. Draper to Lili Draper,

April 2, 1945, Arthur G. Draper Papers, TMD199, 10th Mountain Division Collection, Denver Public Library. For a description of the arrival of spring on the blood-soaked hillsides of Mount della Torraccia, see "Birds and Bees Take Over After War Leaves Battlefield," *The Blizzard,* April 8, 1945, p. 4.

"Except for the routine exchange": Donald Potter to "Mom," April 8, 1945, Potter family collection.

196 *"Tanks, tank destroyers":* Earle, "History of the 87th Mountain Infantry in Italy," p. 44.

"a captured German machine gun": Albert N. Brockman to his mother, March 13, 1945, Albert N. Brockman Papers, TMD84, 10th Mountain Division Papers, Denver Public Library.

"Another day, another $2.88": Marty Daneman to Lois Miller, April 2, April 8, 1945, Martin L. Daneman Papers, TMD25, 10th Mountain Division Collection, Denver Public Library.

"You probably won't hear": Robert B. Ellis to his mother, April 13, 1945, Robert B. Ellis Papers, TMD58, 10th Mountain Division Collection, Denver Public Library.

8. Italy, April 14–May 3, 1945: "All Those Fine Young Men"

200 *"Those dirty bastards":* William Lowell Putnam, *Green Cognac: The Education of a Mountain Fighter* (New York: AAC Press, 1991), pp. 107–10; Charles J. Sanders, *The Boys of Winter: Life and Death in the U.S. Ski Troops During the Second World War* (Boulder: University Press of Colorado, 2005), p. 151.

201 *Putnam's patrol that night delivered:* This account of the March 24 patrol differs in minor respects from the version Putnam offered in his postwar memoir, the differences based on an account in the official regimental history, which was written closer to the events described. But contemporary accounts also need to be scrutinized. Although the regimental history says that Köhler's body was recovered that night, Putnam says otherwise in his postwar account—and I've gone with his version because it seems like a detail Putnam would have remembered. See Putnam, *Green Cognac,* pp. 110–13, 131–32; John B. Woodruff, "History of the 85th Mountain Infantry in Italy, 4 January 1945–31 May 1945" (1945), p. 30. Putnam was promoted to the rank of first lieutenant as a result of the patrol.

"I just hope that we don't": Robert B. Ellis to his mother, March 26, 1945, Robert B. Ellis Papers, TMD58, 10th Mountain Division Papers, Denver Public Library. Ellis elaborated on his feeling that a renewed offensive in Italy was unnecessary in his postwar memoir, Robert B. Ellis, *See Naples and Die: A World War II Memoir of a United States Army Ski Trooper in the Mountains of Italy* (Jefferson, NC: McFarland, 1996), pp. 171–72. The official history of the 87th Regiment noted that in the days leading up to the April offensive, "more

than a few hoped there would be no drive in Italy." George F. Earle, "History of the 87th Mountain Infantry in Italy" (1945), p. 48.

"the needless gallantry of war": Hal Burton, *The Ski Troops* (New York: Simon and Schuster, 1971), p. 168.

peace talks were taking place: R. Harris Smith, *OSS: The Secret History of America's First Central Intelligence Agency* (New York: Delta, 1972), pp. 229–32; Stephen P. Halbrook, "America's OSS, Swiss Intelligence, and the German Surrender 1945," http://www.stephenhalbrook.com/law_review_articles/sunrise.pdf.

202 *Clark could not abide the idea:* Ernest F. Fischer Jr., *The Mediterranean Theater of Operations: Cassino to the Alps* (Washington, DC: US Army Center of Military History, 1977), p. 449.

American military doctrine: Russell F. Weigley, *The American Way of War: A History of United States Military Strategy and Policy* (Bloomington: Indiana University Press, 1977), pp. 143–45, 313, 317.

"still plenty of fight": Drew Middleton, "Nazi Die-Hards Man Their 'National Redoubt,'" *New York Times,* April 8, 1945. Also see Peter Shelton, *Climb to Conquer: The Untold Story of World War II's Tenth Mountain Division Ski Troops* (New York: Scribner, 2003), p. 174.

203 *"the 10th Mountain would carry":* Lieutenant General L. K. Truscott Jr., *Command Missions: A Personal Story* (New York: E. P. Dutton, 1954), p. 487. Also see Fischer, *The Mediterranean Theater of Operations,* pp. 448–53; George F. Howe, *The Battle History of the First Armored Division* (Washington, DC: Combat Forces Press, 1954), pp. 398–99, 402.

204 *The Germans had one big advantage:* James Holland, *Italy's Sorrow: A Year of War, 1944–1945* (New York: St. Martin's Press, 2008), pp. 495–98; Thomas R. Brooks, "10th Mountain Division History," in *Tenth Mountain Division* (Paducah, KY: Turner Publishing, 1998), pp. 32–33; Thomas R. Brooks, *The War North of Rome: June 1944–May 1945* (New York: Da Capo Press, 2003), pp. 361–64; Daniel K. Gibran, *The 92nd Infantry Division and the Italian Campaign in World War II* (Jefferson, NC: McFarland & Co., 2001), p. 50.

the terrain, as always: Brooks, *The War North of Rome,* p. 372; Charles Wellborn, "History of the 86th Mountain Infantry in Italy" (Denver: Bradford-Robinson Printing Co., 1945), p. 32; Earle, "History of the 87th Mountain Infantry in Italy," pp. 44–45; Woodruff, "History of the 85th Mountain Infantry in Italy," p. 36.

205 *On April 9:* Gibran, *The 92nd Infantry Division and the Italian Campaign in World War II,* pp. 78–90; James M. McCaffrey, *Going for Broke: Japanese American Soldiers in the War Against Nazi Germany* (Norman: University of Oklahoma Press, 2013), p. 348; Brooks, *The War North of Rome,* pp. 365–70; Fischer, *The Mediterranean Theater of Operations,* pp. 459–69; Howe, *The Battle History of the First Armored Division,* pp. 401–2.

"Funeral arrangements": "Roosevelt Is Dead," *The Blizzard,* April 13, 1945, p. 1.

"He had become in my mind": Earl Clark to his mother, May 3, 1945, Earl Clark Papers, TMD8, 10th Mountain Division Papers, Denver Public Library.

206 *"In a few minutes"*: Ellis, *See Naples and Die,* p. 177.

"We had never witnessed": Ellis, *See Naples and Die,* p. 177; Milton Bracker, "Allies' Italy Push Captures Vergato," *New York Times,* April 17, 1945.

"Packs on": Brooks, *The War North of Rome,* p. 372; Ellis, *See Naples and Die,* p. 178.

"But we watched the Mountaineers reach": Truscott, *Command Missions,* p. 487.

obscured as much as it revealed: As Sergeant Denis Nunan, C Company of the 87th, wrote to his parents a few weeks before the April offensive, "Thanks to the failure of the press, and to the stupidity of Hollywood, the Home Front has no real conception of war, and only by doggies' true fact letters home can the truth be made known." Denis Nunan to parents, March 23, 1945, quoted in McKay Jenkins, *The Last Ridge: The Epic Story of the US Army's 10th Mountain Division and the Assault on Hitler's Europe* (New York: Random House, 2003), p. 209.

207 *"The Germans were reacting strongly"*: Harris Dusenbery, *The North Apennines and Beyond with the 10th Mountain Division* (Portland, OR: Binford and Mort, 1998), pp. 93–95.

"Oh Christ! What's the use": Murray Mondschein to "Patty," May 13, 1945, TMD309, 10th Mountain Division Personal Papers, 10th Mountain Division Collection, Denver Public Library. Mondschein's buddy was Sergeant Dick Wilson of M Company of the 85th, wounded on Belvedere on February 20.

"the world exploded": Bob Dole, *One Soldier's Story: A Memoir* (New York: HarperCollins, 2005), p. 24.

208 *Dole was awarded a Bronze Star:* Dole, *One Soldier's Story,* pp. 29–34; Brooks, *The War North of Rome,* p. 372. The Comune di Castel d'Aiano erected a bronze plaque in 1995 marking the approximate spot where Dole was wounded fifty years earlier. http://www.uswarmemorials.org/html/site_details.php?SiteID=1016.

Congressional Medal of Honor: "Medal of Honor Recipients," https://history.army.mil/html/moh/wwII-m-s.html; Brooks, *The War North of Rome,* p. 373. Among other honors, the John D. Magrath Gymnasium at Fort Drum in Watertown, New York (home base of the reconstituted 10th Mountain Division), is named for Magrath.

the division's costliest day: Fischer, *The Mediterranean Theater of Operations,* p. 474; Flint Whitlock and Bob Bishop, *Soldiers on Skis: A Pictorial Memoir of the 10th Mountain Division* (Boulder: Paladin Press, 1992), p. 140; Milton Bracker, "Allies' Italy Push Captures Vergato," *New York Times,* April

17, 1945. The figure for killed in action is from David Little, personal communication.

209 *"That they should continue fighting"*: Arthur G. Draper to his parents, April 15, 1945, Arthur G. Draper Papers, TMD199, 10th Mountain Division Papers, Denver Public Library.

210 *By the end of April 16:* John Imbrie and Thomas R. Brooks, *10th Mountain Division Campaign in Italy, 1945* (Forest Hills, NY: National Association of the 10th Mountain Division, 2002), p. 17.

"Wherever the men dropped their packs": Wellborn, "History of the 86th Mountain Infantry in Italy," p. 37.

The 10th's advance: Imbrie and Brooks, *10th Mountain Division Campaign in Italy*, pp. 20, 24.

The term "breakthrough": "At 0910 of the 17th, General HAYS visited the CP [command post] and told Colonel FOWLER that the 'breakthrough' had been accomplished and that the 87th must 'keep pushing and exploit the breakthrough.'" Earle, "History of the 87th Mountain Infantry in Italy," p. 89.

more German than American wounded: Albert H. Meinke, *Mountain Troops and Medics: A Complete WWII Combat History of the U.S. Tenth Mountain Division* (Victoria, BC: Trafford, 2002), pp. 169–77.

211 *"a damn band of Gypsies"*: "The War Diary of Dan L. Kennerly," Dan L. Kennerly Papers, TMD309, 10th Mountain Division Papers, Denver Public Library; Imbrie and Brooks, *10th Mountain Division Campaign in Italy*, p. 26; Shelton, *Climb to Conquer*, p. 188.

212 *"Suddenly the mountains were gone"*: Lunday and Hampton, *The Tramway Builders*, p. 73; "10th Paces Central Offensive," *The Blizzard,* April 19, 1945, p. 1; Woodruff, "History of the 85th Mountain Infantry in Italy," pp. 42–50; Wellborn, "History of the 86th Mountain Infantry in Italy," pp. 34–40; Earle, "History of the 87th Mountain Infantry in Italy," pp. 63–117.

April 17 to April 20: Chester G. Starr, ed., *From Salerno to the Alps: A History of the Fifth Army, 1943–1945* (Washington, DC: Infantry Journal Press, 1948), p. 407; Woodruff, "History of the 85th Mountain Infantry in Italy," p. 50; "Firsts," *The Blizzard,* May 22, 1945, p. 5; Milton Bracker, "Americans Break into Po Valley," *New York Times,* April 21, 1945; Imbrie and Brooks, *10th Mountain Division Campaign in Italy,* p. 21. In a famous piece of 10th lore, General Truscott bet a bottle of whiskey with General Joseph T. McNarney, commander of US forces in the Mediterranean, that the 10th would reach Route 9 by 1 p.m. on April 20. He lost; they didn't reach it until 2:30 p.m. McNarney sportingly refused his prize, saying the bottle should go to the first soldier to have reached the road. Truscott passed the bottle along to Hays, who saw to it that it went, rightfully, to PFC Lesmeister. Truscott, *Command Missions,* p. 490; Brooks, "10th Mountain Division History," p. 35.

213 *"it was Minnie's boys"*: Quoted in Burton, *The Ski Troops,* p. 173.

"German trucks, half-tracks, Volkswagen jeeps": "The War Diary of Dan L. Kennerly," Dan L. Kennerly Papers, TMD309, 10th Mountain Division Papers, Denver Public Library; Imbrie and Brooks, *10th Mountain Division Campaign in Italy*, p. 26.

214 *they rode into the Po Valley:* When the 10th crossed the Po River on April 23–24, the 10th Recon was ordered to leave the horses behind. They fought the remainder of the war dismounted. Jeffrey R. Leich, *Tales of the 10th: The Mountain Troops and American Skiing* (Franconia, NH: New England Ski Museum, 2003), p. 91. According to Flint Whitlock in *Soldiers on Skis,* three veterans of the 10th Recon describe what sounds like a major engagement with German soldiers, ending in a near massacre of the mounted troopers, who had to relearn the lesson of 1914 that mounted troops did not fare well when confronted with automatic weapons. But in another account, a different veteran of the unit described a minor skirmish a few days later, in which neither horses nor troopers were injured. And the official roll of 10th Mountain dead in Italy identifies only a single member of the 10th Recon as having been killed in action. So if there was a "last cavalry charge" in Italy, it was likely a very small-scale action, and not as costly as some remembered. Whitlock and Bishop, *Soldiers on Skis,* pp. 146–47; Donald Hubbard, "The 10th Mountain Cavalry Reconnaissance Troop: The Italian Campaign," in *Packs On! Memoirs of the 10th Mountain Division in World War II*, ed. A. B. Feuer (Mechanicsburg, PA: Stackpole Books, 2004), pp. 139–40. For helping me sort out the tangled accounts of the 10th Recon, I'm grateful to Flint Whitlock and David Little, neither of whom will necessarily agree with my conclusions.

"There were few Bolognese about": Truscott, *Command Missions,* p. 492; Brooks, *The War North of Rome,* p. 383; Tom Behan, *The Italian Resistance: Fascists, Guerrillas and the Allies* (London: Pluto, 2009), p. 96.

215 *Hays had other ideas:* Burton, *The Ski Troops,* pp. 172–73; Brooks, "10th Mountain Division History," pp. 35–36; Sanders, *The Boys of Winter,* pp. 190–91; Shelton, *Climb to Conquer,* pp. 184–85; Fischer, *The Mediterranean Theater of Operations,* p. 453.

While they raced ahead: "Maj. Gen. Robinson Duff, Was Security Chief," *Washington Post,* September 30, 1979. For Duff on the front lines in the April offensive, see Kenyon Cooke, "C Company in Action," in *Good Times and Bad Times: A History of C Company, 85th Mountain Infantry Regiment, 10th Mountain Division, July 1943 to November 1945,* ed. John Imbrie and Hugh Evans (Quechee, VT: Vermont Heritage Press, 1995), p. 91.

Asked where the others came from: Wellborn, "History of the 86th Mountain Infantry in Italy," p. 40; Imbrie and Brooks, *10th Mountain Division Campaign in Italy,* p. 26. David Brower offers an account of a prisoner being shot as a sniper during the advance up the Po. David R. Brower, ed., *Remount Blue:*

The Combat Story of the Third Battalion, 86th Mountain Infantry (Berkeley, CA, 1948), p. 70.

216 *"Thousands of vehicles"*: Jack R. Smolenske diary, Jack R. Smolenske Papers, TMD70, 10th Mountain Division Papers, Denver Public Library. A nine-year-old Luciano Pavarotti was one of the Italians by the roadside in the village of Carpi cheering their liberators from the 85th Regiment. Years later Marty Daneman, a supporter of the opera in Dallas, was invited to a post-performance dinner with Pavarotti. As Daneman recounted his own wartime experiences in Italy, including marching through Carpi, Pavarotti "stopped eating, dropped his knife and fork, stood up, and called me his liberator while giving me the bear hug of my life." Marty Daneman, *Do Well or Die: Memoirs of a WWII Mountain Trooper* (Brule, WI: Cable Publishing, 2012), p. 128.

"like a worried sheep dog": Imbrie and Brooks, *10th Mountain Division Campaign in Italy*, p. 26; Wellborn, "History of the 86th Mountain Infantry in Italy," p. 41; Daneman, *Do Well or Die*, p. 128.

The 10th had advanced: Imbrie and Brooks, *10th Mountain Division Campaign in Italy*, p. 26; Allied Forces, 15th Army Group, *Finito! The Po Valley Campaign, 1945* (Milan: Rizzoli, 1945), pp. 17, 52.

218 *the 10th now had the means*: Imbrie and Brooks, *10th Mountain Division Campaign in Italy*, p. 26; Shelton, *Climb to Conquer*, pp. 188–89.

219 *Soon the entire 87th was across*: Earle, "History of the 87th Mountain Infantry in Italy," pp. 137–38, 141; Imbrie and Brooks, *10th Mountain Division Campaign in Italy*, p. 26; Brooks, *The War North of Rome*, pp. 382–83; Whitlock and Bishop, *Soldiers on Skis*, pp. 159–60; Shelton, *Climb to Conquer*, pp. 189–90; Burton, *The Ski Troops*, p. 178.

While this was going on: On the destruction of Darby's Rangers at Anzio, see Rick Atkinson, *The Day of Battle: The War in Sicily and Italy, 1943–1944* (New York: Henry Holt, 2007), pp. 394–96.

Hays asked rhetorically: Burton, *The Ski Troops*, p. 178. In his memoirs, Truscott wrote that the 10th "had exceeded our wildest hopes" by crossing the Po several days before 5th Army planners expected to get any Americans to the northern bank of the river. Truscott, *Command Missions*, p. 493. On von Senger's swim, see General Frido von Senger und Etterlin, *Neither Fear Nor Hope* (New York: E. P. Dutton, 1964), pp. 300–301; and General George P. Hays, letter of May 14, 1945, reprinted in Imbrie and Evans, *Good Times and Bad Times*, pp. 255–56.

"the Remagen of this campaign": Milton Bracker, "Po Crossing Made Under Heavy Fire," *New York Times*, April 26, 1945.

220 *"That advance across 200 yards"*: "North to the Alps," *New York Times*, April 26, 1945; Imbrie and Brooks, *10th Mountain Division Campaign in Italy*, p. 26; Woodruff, "History of the 85th Mountain Infantry in Italy," pp. 53, 56–

57; Wellborn, "History of the 86th Mountain Infantry in Italy," p. 43; Howe, *The Battle History of the First Armored Division,* pp. 422–23.

"This is the first chance": Robert B. Ellis to his mother, April 25, 1945, Robert B. Ellis Papers, TMD58, 10th Mountain Division Papers, Denver Public Library. Ellis also reported in his letter: "The other day [April 14] I killed a sniper at about 15 feet with my .45 revolver. So I've really been having quite a time." He was awarded a Bronze Star for killing the sniper.

221 *"Tedeschi tutta via":* Meinke, *Mountain Troops and Medics,* pp. 210–11.

pressed on to take Verona: Brooks, *The War North of Rome,* p. 386; Woodruff, "History of the 87th Mountain Infantry in Italy," p. 57; Wellborn, "History of the 86th Mountain Infantry in Italy," p. 43.

For once the 10th: Brower, *Remount Blue,* p. 82.

222 *In the seven days:* Imbrie and Brooks, *10th Mountain Division Campaign in Italy,* p. 27.

223 *The lead headline:* Ellis, *See Naples and Die,* p. 207; "MUSSOLINI IS DEAD," *The Blizzard,* April 30, 1945, p. 1. Two days later the newspaper would report on another dictator's demise: "HITLER DEAD, GERMAN RADIO ASSERTS," *The Blizzard,* May 2, 1945, p. 1. On Mussolini's flight, capture, and execution, see Dennis Mack Smith, *Mussolini* (New York: Vintage Books, 1982), pp. 318–20.

224 *Along Lake Garda the 10th:* Earle, "History of the 87th Mountain Infantry in Italy," p. 163.

There was no fighting: Earle, "History of the 87th Mountain Infantry in Italy," p. 156.

The heady days of racing: Woodruff, "History of the 85th Mountain Infantry in Italy," p. 60.

"After much bickering": Earle, "History of the 87th Mountain Infantry in Italy," p. 158.

226 *The tunnels were used to shelter:* Imbrie and Brooks, *10th Mountain Division Campaign in Italy,* p. 32; Woodruff, "History of the 85th Mountain Infantry, in Italy," p. 60.

"gunny sack of arms and legs": Dusenbery, *The North Apennines and Beyond,* p. 127.

the only casualties: Imbrie and Brooks, *10th Mountain Division Campaign in Italy,* p. 32; Wellborn, "History of the 86th Mountain Infantry in Italy," p. 44; Whitlock and Bishop, *Soldiers on Skis,* p. 172. For an example of a friendly fire incident in the Po Valley, see Brower, *Remount Blue,* p. 75.

227 *"should have been in a nightmare":* Meinke, *Mountain Troops and Medics,* pp. 224–25; Wellborn, "History of the 86th Mountain Infantry in Italy," p. 45. For a detailed account of the battle for Torbole, see Skyler Bailey, "Reconstructing the Battle of Torbole: A Neglected Episode in the History of the Tenth Mountain Division in World War Two," *University of Vermont History Review* 24 (2013–14): 1–16.

The Germans' door: Wellborn, "History of the 86th Mountain Infantry in Italy," p. 45; Meinke, *Mountain Troops and Medics,* pp. 228–29.

"everything moveable and mailable": Connecticut Men, *10th Mountain Division* (September 1945), p. 6.

James Henry Francis: Imbrie and Brooks, *10th Mountain Division Campaign in Italy,* p. 32; Woodruff, "History of the 85th Mountain Infantry in Italy," pp. 60–61, 63. On the fate of Mussolini's hats, see Henry Francis to Eugene Hames, September 12, 1968, 10th Mountain Division Personal Papers, TMD309, 10th Mountain Division Papers, Denver Public Library. On Mussolini's convertible, see Donald F. Todd to his brother, May 5, 1945, 10th Mountain Division Personal Papers, TMD309, 10th Mountain Division Papers, Denver Public Library. General Hays appropriated Mussolini's personal speedboat for his own use, but the Italian driver sheared off the driveshaft on its first trip out, leaving it disabled and useless. Putnam, *Green Cognac,* p. 172. Eugene Hames donated Mussolini villa items, which are on display at the Colorado Snowsports Museum and Hall of Fame in Vail, Colorado; see https://www.vaildaily.com/news/state-snowsports-museum-in-vail-has-fabled-ski-troopers-as-its-cornerstone/#.WyXHeqtGcVs.facebook.

On that last day of April: "The Push," *The Blizzard,* May 22, 1945, p. 4.

228 *Another problem in moving on:* For the 10th's unsuitability for a campaign in the Alps in the spring of 1945, see Brower, *Remount Blue,* pp. 84–85.

"Rumors of peace have been flying": Marty Daneman to Lois, April 30, 1945, Martin L. Daneman Papers, TMD25, 10th Mountain Division Papers, Denver Public Library.

"The news is sensationally good": Robert B. Ellis to his mother, April 30, 1945, Robert B. Ellis Papers, TMD58, 10th Mountain Division Papers, Denver Public Library. Also see Ellis, *See Naples and Die,* pp. 205–7.

229 *But an alert German artillery spotter:* Kenneth S. Templeton Jr., "The Last Days of Col. William O. Darby: An Eye-Witness Account," *Army History* (Spring 1998): 5–6; "Col. Darby Killed; Trained Rangers," *New York Times,* May 2, 1945; H. Paul Jeffers, *Onward We Charge: The Heroic Story of Darby's Rangers in World War II* (New York: NAL Caliber, 2007), pp. 267–69.

The twenty-five men who drowned: Imbrie and Brooks, *10th Mountain Division Campaign in Italy,* p. 33; Jenkins, *The Last Ridge,* p. 242. The sunken DUKW was discovered by Italian amateur historians from the Gruppo Volontari del Garda in December 2012, using sonar and remote-control cameras, lying at a depth of 905 feet off Riva. "Duck Boat Sunk in World War II Found in Italian Lake," *Christian Science Monitor,* December 12, 2012. Also see "Remembering Brave Soldiers from World War II," April 22, 2015, https://www.army.mil/article/146908/remembering_brave_soldiers_from_wwii.

"The news reached us this afternoon": Marty Daneman to Lois, May 2,

1945, Martin L. Daneman Papers, TMD25, 10th Mountain Division Papers, Denver Public Library.

230 *"We have achieved final victory"*: "Final Victory," *The Blizzard,* May 22, 1945, p. 1. This was a special illustrated supplement to the regular issue.

231 *"He told us how good"*: Anthony Mascaro diary entry, May 3, 1945, TMD309, 10th Mountain Division Personal Papers, 10th Mountain Division Papers, Denver Public Library.

"About 9 p.m. we reached": Senger, *Neither Fear Nor Hope,* p. 307.

Total US casualties in Italy: Carlo D'Este, *World War II in the Mediterranean, 1942–1945* (Chapel Hill, NC: Algonquin Books, 1990), p. 196; Atkinson, *The Day of Battle,* p. 581; "Fifth Army Lost 109,163 in Italy," *New York Times,* May 4, 1945; Fischer, *The Mediterranean Theater of Operations,* p. vii; "Army Battle Casualties and Nonbattle Deaths in World War II," http://cgsc.cdm host.com/cdm/compoundobject/collection/p4013coll8/id/130.

"Our stint in combat was short": Putnam, *Green Cognac,* p. 210.

232 *Total casualties for the division:* The original estimate for the number of 10th men killed in Italy was 975, later increased to 983. Email from David Little to author, September 5, 2018.

"It's all over here": Wallace Arnheiter to "folks," May 5, 1945, TMD309, 10th Mountain Division Personal Papers, 10th Mountain Division Papers, Denver Public Library.

Its seventy acres: Photographs of the grave markers for the 326 10th Mountain soldiers buried in the Florence Cemetery can be viewed at http://10thmou ntaindivisiondescendants.org/cemetery/index.html.

"I looked up at the mountains": John Parker Compton to his parents, June 20, 1944, John Parker Compton Papers, TMD43, 10th Mountain Division Papers, Denver Public Library.

233 *One can also imagine Compton's parents:* Compton's wartime letters were reprinted after the war by his parents in a privately published volume, *John Parker Compton, Private First Class,* John Parker Compton Papers, TMD42, 10th Mountain Division Papers, Denver Public Library.

Epilogue: "Among My Souvenirs"

235 *"a beautiful weapon"*: James H. Roberts to his parents, February 24, 1945, TMD309, 10th Mountain Division Personal Papers, 10th Mountain Division Papers, Denver Public Library. For the differences between the Luger and the Walther P38, see Chris Bishop, *The Encyclopedia of Weapons: From World War II to the Present Day* (San Diego: Thunder Bay Press, 2006), pp. 15–17.

The champagne was distributed free: Thomas R. Brooks, "10th Mountain Division History," in *Tenth Mountain Division* (Paducah, KY: Turner Publishing, 1998), p. 38; Flint Whitlock and Bob Bishop, *Soldiers on Skis: A Picto-*

rial Memoir of the 10th Mountain Division (Boulder: Paladin Press, 1992), pp. 178–79.

236 *Clark sent the German generals:* Mark W. Clark, *Calculated Risk* (New York: Harper and Brothers, 1950), p. 441.

In mid-May 1945, General George P. Hays: General George P. Hays to Donald B. Douglas, dated May 14, 1945, reprinted in *Good Times and Bad Times: A History of C Company, 85th Mountain Infantry Regiment, 10th Mountain Division, July 1943 to November 1945,* ed. John Imbrie and Hugh Evans (Quechee, VT: Vermont Heritage Press, 1995), pp. 255–56.

237 *"If you got to go to war":* Quoted in Brooks, "10th Mountain Division History," p. 39. On the disaster on the Rapido, see Rick Atkinson, *The Day of Battle: The War in Sicily and Italy, 1943–1944* (New York: Henry Holt, 2007), pp. 338–49.

In the nature of counterfactuals: The unanswerable but unavoidable question of how the 10th would have fared at Cassino has been raised by several previous historians of the division. See, for example, McKay Jenkins, *The Last Ridge: The Epic Story of the US Army's 10th Mountain Division and the Assault on Hitler's Europe* (New York: Random House, 2003), p. 252.

"a perfect example of men fighting": Minnie Dole, "Birth Pains of the 10th Mountain Division," in *Tenth Mountain Division* (Paducah, KY: Turner Publishing Co., 1998), p. 49.

After Riva Ridge and Mount Belvedere: "Five Commanders Congratulate Division on Operations," *The Blizzard,* March 15, 1945, p. 1; Whitlock and Bishop, *Soldiers on Skis,* p. 126.

238 *"We are plenty hot":* Corporal Arnold Holeywell, "STICK TO THE FIGHT," *Camp Hale Ski-Zette,* March 10, 1944, p. 2. Holeywell was a major figure in the creation of the 10th's veterans group, the National Association of the 10th Mountain Division, following the war, serving as one of its first presidents. Arnold C. Holeywell obituary, *Washington Post,* October 10, 2010, https://www.legacy.com/obituaries/washingtonpost/obituary.aspx?n=arnold-c-holeywell&pid=145869739.

"You can only expect me home": Hugh W. Evans to Mrs. E. C. Evans, April 13, 1945, Hugh W. Evans Papers, TMD4, 10th Mountain Division Papers, Denver Public Library.

239 *During the deployment:* Brooks, "10th Mountain Division History," pp. 38–39.

"To the creaking and groaning": Prager Wins Division's First Alpine Ski Race," *The Blizzard,* June 10, 1945, p. 1.

"a high class Lake Placid": Donald Potter to Carol, July 5, 1945, Potter family papers. Also see Maurice Isserman, *Continental Divide: A History of American Mountaineering* (New York: Norton, 2016), p. 266.

240 *On August 14, Japan surrendered:* Charles Wellborn, "History of the 86th

Mountain Infantry in Italy" (Denver: Bradford-Robinson Printing Co., 1945), p. 52; John B. Woodruff, "History of the 85th Mountain Infantry in Italy, 4 January 1945–31 May 1945" (1945), p. 71; George F. Earle, "History of the 87th Mountain Infantry in Italy" (1945), p. 174; John Imbrie, "Chronology of the 10th Mountain Division in World War II," p. 10, http://10thmtndivassoc.org/chronology.pdf, pp. 27–28.

"Men, released from the army": "A 'Ski-Torial,'" *Camp Hale Ski-Zette,* April 28, 1943, p. 2.

"We were the original ski bums": Bill Pennington, "The Legacy of Soldiers on Skis," *New York Times,* March 10, 2006.

241 *Friedl Pfeifer, A Company:* Friedl Pfeifer, *Nice Goin': My Life on Skis* (Missoula, MT; Pictorial Histories Publishing, 1993), pp. 96–98, 105–7, 111, 120–21; Sally Barlow-Perez, *A History of Aspen* (Aspen, CO: People's Press, 1991), p. 44; Abbott Fay, *A History of Skiing in Colorado* (Ouray, CO: Western Reflections, 2000), pp. 67–71.

Pete Seibert, F Company: Douglas Martin, "Pete Seibert, Soldier Skier Who Built Vail, Is Dead at 77," *New York Times,* July 28, 2002; Larry Olmsted, "Skiing's Signature Runs: Down Vail's Riva Ridge with a Helmet Cam," *USA Today,* March 20, 2018.

Walter Prager, HQ Company: Jeffrey R. Leich, *Tales of the 10th: The Mountain Troops and American Skiing* (Franconia, NH: New England Ski Museum, 2003), p. 117; Whitlock and Bishop, *Soldiers on Skis,* pp. 189–91. Also see the excellent undergraduate thesis by David M. Leach, "The Impact of the Tenth Mountain Division on the Development of a Modern Ski Industry in Colorado and Vermont: 1930–1965" (Middlebury College, 2005).

The veterans made their mark: John Leland, "A Village Voice Reunion and Nobody Got Punched," *New York Times,* September 10, 2017, https://www.nytimes.com/2017/09/10/nyregion/village-voice-reunion.html; Richard Goldstein, "Bill Bowerman, 88, Nike Co-founder, Dies," *New York Times,* December 27, 1999; William H. Honan, "Page Smith, 77, Historian, Dies; Praised as an Appealing Writer," *New York Times,* August 29, 1995; Isserman, *Continental Divide,* pp. 272–74; Celestine Bohlen, "Town Where Dole's Life Changed Backs Candidate as a Friend," *New York Times,* August 13, 1996; Steven Hendrix, "Bob Dole's Final Mission," *Washington Post,* June 18, 2018.

242 *Among them were Marty Daneman:* "Martin Lewis Daneman," *Dallas Morning News,* December 3, 2015.

243 *Another such was Robert B. Ellis:* Robert B. Ellis to his mother, June 25, 1945, Robert B. Ellis Papers, TMD58, 10th Mountain Division Papers, Denver Public Library.

Instead he got a master's degree: In 1996 Ellis probably annoyed Marty Daneman no end by publishing an article questioning what he regarded as exaggerated accounts of Bob Dole's wartime exploits. Robert B. Ellis, "Dole's War Record," *The Nation,* August 12–19, 1996, pp. 11–16.

Harris Dusenbery, the classically minded: Ben Jacklet, "10th Mountain Vet Looks Back on 101 Years of Adventure and Exploration," http://www.shred hood.org/news/mountain-characters/825-10th-mountain-vet-looks-back-on-101-years-of-adventure-and-exploration; "In Memoriam, Harris Dusenbery, '36," *Reed Magazine,* March 2016, http://www.reed.edu/reed-magazine/in-memoriam/obituaries/march2016/harris-dusenbery-1936.html.

244 *"On sleepless nights":* Marty Daneman, *Do Well or Die: Memoirs of a WWII Mountain Trooper* (Brule, WI: Cable Publishing, 2012), p. 167.

Index